A Revolution in Movement

UNIVERSITY PRESS OF FLORIDA

Florida A&M University, Tallahassee
Florida Atlantic University, Boca Raton
Florida Gulf Coast University, Ft. Myers
Florida International University, Miami
Florida State University, Tallahassee
New College of Florida, Sarasota
University of Central Florida, Orlando
University of Florida, Gainesville
University of North Florida, Jacksonville
University of South Florida, Tampa
University of West Florida, Pensacola

A REVOLUTION IN MOVEMENT

DANCERS, PAINTERS, AND THE IMAGE OF MODERN MEXICO

K. MITCHELL SNOW

University Press of Florida
Gainesville · Tallahassee · Tampa · Boca Raton
Pensacola · Orlando · Miami · Jacksonville · Ft. Myers · Sarasota

Publication of this paperback edition made possible by a Sustaining the Humanities through the American Rescue Plan grant from the National Endowment for the Humanities.

First cloth printing, 2020
First paperback printing, 2022

27 26 25 24 23 22   6 5 4 3 2 1

Library of Congress Cataloging-in-Publication Data
Names: Snow, K. Mitchell, author.
Title: A revolution in movement : dancers, painters, and the image of
    modern Mexico / K. Mitchell Snow.
Description: Gainesville : University Press of Florida, 2020. | Includes
    bibliographical references and index.
Identifiers: LCCN 2020015412 (print) | LCCN 2020015413 (ebook) | ISBN
    9780813066554 (hardback) | ISBN 9780813057576 (pdf) | ISBN 9780813080079 (pbk.)
Subjects: LCSH: Modern dance—Mexico—History—20th century. |
    Dance—Mexico—History. | Painting, Mexican—History. |
    Dancers—Mexico—History. | Painters—Mexico—History. |
    Nationalism—Mexico—History.
Classification: LCC GV1627 .S66 2020 (print) | LCC GV1627 (ebook) | DDC
    793.3/1972—dc23
LC record available at https://lccn.loc.gov/2020015412
LC ebook record available at https://lccn.loc.gov/2020015413

The University Press of Florida is the scholarly publishing agency for the State University System of Florida, comprising Florida A&M University, Florida Atlantic University, Florida Gulf Coast University, Florida International University, Florida State University, New College of Florida, University of Central Florida, University of Florida, University of North Florida, University of South Florida, and University of West Florida.

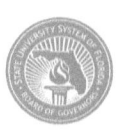
University Press of Florida
2046 NE Waldo Road
Suite 2100
Gainesville, FL 32609
http://upress.ufl.edu

CONTENTS

List of Figures vii

Acknowledgments ix

List of Abbreviations xiii

Introduction 1

1. An Anthropologist Orders a Beer: The Development of Mexican Nationalism 16

2. Mexicanism Russian Style: Roberto Montenegro, Diego Rivera, and the Ballets Russes 36

3. The Precursors of Mexicanism: Anna Pavlova and Tórtola Valencia 55

4. The Philosopher as an Artist Writ Large: José Vasconcelos, Muralism, and Folk Art 78

5. Dancing a Sandunga in English: Carlos Chávez and Diego Rivera in the United States 94

6. A Question of Technique: Carlos Mérida and a Mexican School of Dance 116

7. Competing Modernisms: Anna Sokolow and Waldeen 142

8. Ballets without Ballerinas? José Clemente Orozco and the Ballet de la Ciudad de México 171

9. The Golden Age of Mexican Modern Dance: Miguel Covarrubias and the Academia de la Danza Mexicana 199

10. Dancing beyond the Cactus Curtain: Mexican Theatrical Dance Comes of Age 222

Epilogue: Mexican and Universal 253

Notes 259

Bibliography 301

Index 317

FIGURES

1. José Guadalupe Posada, *La Serpentina* (The Serpentine), 1894   4

2. A performance of Nellie Campobello's *30–30* in the National Stadium, circa 1935   24

3. Ted Shawn's *Xochitl*, with costume and set designs by Francisco Cornejo, circa 1920   29

4. Mauro Rafael Moya, illustration for the Yaqui *danza del venado* (Yaqui deer dance) from *Ritmos indígenas de México* (Indigenous Rhythms of Mexico), 1940   33

5. Roberto Montenegro, illustration of Vaslav Nijinsky in *Schéhérazade,* souvenir program for the Ballets Russes' tour of the United States, 1916   44

6. Anna Pavlova and Mieczyslaw Pianowski in *Fantasía Mexicana* (Mexican Fantasia), with costumes and set designs by Adolfo Best, 1919   61

7. Tórtola Valencia as a "China poblana" in Mexico, 1918   72

8. Roberto Montenegro, *El jarabe tapatío* (Mexican Hat Dance), 1921   80

9. Roberto Montenegro, detail from *El Arbol de la Vida* (The Tree of Life), 1922   91

10. Diego Rivera, *The Man,* from the ballet *H.P.,* 1927   111

11. Nellie Campobello performing in her *30–30,* circa 1935   123

12. Carlos Mérida, cover illustration for the Festival de danzas mexicanas (Festival of Mexican Dances) program, 1934   134

13. Anna Sokolow's *El renacuajo paseador* (The Wandering Tadpole), with costumes and set design by Carlos Mérida, 1940   155

14. Julio Castellanos, set design for Leonide Massine's *Don Domingo de Don Blas*, 1942   175

15. José Clemente Orozco, program design for the Ballet de la Ciudad de México, 1943   184

16. José Clemente Orozco, program design for the Markova Dolin/Ballet de la Ciudad de México, 1946   193

17. José Limón's *Los cuatro soles: Sol del aire* (The Four Suns: The Sun of Wind), with costumes and set design by Miguel Covarrubias, 1951   213

18. Guillermo Arriaga's *Zapata*, with Rocío Sagaón as Tierra (Earth) and Arriaga in the title role, costume designs by Miguel Covarrubias, 1953   226

19. Adriana Siqueiros, Anna Sokolow, and the cast of *Homenaje a David Alfaro Siqueiros* (Homage to Siqueiros) in the theater of the Polyforum, 1984   249

20. Rufino Tamayo, detail from the set designs for Guillermina Bravo's *Constelaciones y Danzantes* with members of the Compañía Nacional de Danza, 1987   256

ACKNOWLEDGMENTS

Through the countless hours choreographer Gloria Contreras shared with me in the studios of her Taller Coreográfico de la UNAM, I gained an appreciation for and background in theatrical dance in Mexico, which provided the foundation for this book. Working with her provided my initial awareness of the role that Mexico's painters played in promoting the nation's theatrical dance. Arguably, I would have never found myself in her presence had my fourth grade teacher, Marian Sutherland, not provided me with my first words of Spanish, daily rhythm exercises to the music of Tchaikovsky, and an appreciation for the "100 Great Masterpieces of the Metropolitan Museum of Art." My friend from university days, Char Harding, insisted on taking me, under protest, to my first ballet performance, so thanks are due also to her.

When I discovered Roberto Montenegro's cover design for a Ballets Russes souvenir program hanging alongside Rodin's powerful sculpture of Nijinsky in *L'Après-midi d'un Faune* in the National Gallery of Art's 2013 exhibition *Diaghilev and the Ballets Russes, 1909–1929: When Art Danced with Music*, I was moved to address in a more formal way the ways Mexico's artists had been influenced by, and in turn, influenced theatrical dance. Diaghilev scholar Lynn Garafola, professor emerita at Columbia University's Barnard College, and specialist on early twentieth-century Latin American modernism Rodrigo Gutiérrez Viñuales of the University of Granada both went well beyond the call of duty as I began this project. They provided me with the detailed guidance and advice on source materials, which made it possible for me to understand the European art and dance world that helped shape artists like Montenegro and Diego Rivera.

Patricia Aulestia's decades of research into Mexican archives, captured in her books *Despertar de la república dancística mexicana* and *Historias Alucinantes de un mundo ecléctico. La danza en México 1910–1939* served as an invaluable resource throughout the writing of this book. Her support and encouragement throughout the process, as well as the provision of images from her extensive collection, were key to its completion. Patricia's colleague at the Centro Nacional de Investigación of Documentación e Información de Danza Margarita Tortajada's nearly encyclopedic overview of twentieth-century Mexican dance, *Danza y poder*, provided much of the information about how midcentury critics responded to the works of Mexico's early choreographers. Claudia Carbajal kindly provided me with a copy of her masters thesis on the beginnings of the Escuela Nacional de Danza, which materially enriched the chapter on Carlos Mérida's efforts on behalf of the dance. Musicologist Christina Taylor Gibson's essays on Carlos Chávez's participation in the dance world deeply influenced my thinking on the role he played in the development of theatrical dance in Mexico. During the course of writing this book, she became a personal friend, and her counsel and insights permeate my text.

A host of additional scholars, dancers, researchers, and arts administrators on both sides of the border helped me research various topics, engaged me in stimulating discussions, and provided advice and encouragement as this project unfolded. In the United States, these people include Juliet Bellow, Danielle Castronovo, Michelle Clayton, Tatiana Flores, Alison Hilton, Jennifer Josten, Rick López, Gregorio Luke, Les McBee, Joellen Meglin, Norton Owen, José Reynoso, Paul Scolieri, Sharon Skeel, and an anonymous reviewer for the University Press of Florida. The International Center for the Arts of the Americas (ICAA) at the Museum of Fine Arts Houston's Digital Archive and Publications Archive provided an invaluable and easily accessible source for a variety of otherwise nearly impossible-to-locate items. The staff of the Library of Congress, particularly its dance curator Libby Smigel and her colleagues in the Music Division, have also been uniformly helpful.

In Mexico, Esperanza Balderas, Carmen Bojórquez, Leticia Gámez, Hector Garay, Roberto Kolb, Lorena Luke, Hayde Lachino, Alfonso Lorança, Rocío Melgoza, Ana María Molina, Alejandra Monroy, Gilberto Ramírez, Olga Rodríguez, and Arturo Vázquez all helped at one stage or another in the development of this project.

For assistance with securing images and permissions, I wish to thank Hayley Blomquist, Antonio Castellanos Basich, Teresa González Borrajo, Jonathan Hernández Otañez, Aarón Lozano Aguilar, María del Refugio Paisano Rodríguez, Maria Elena Rico Covarrubias, Robbi Siegel, and Susie Morgan Taylor.

At the University Press of Florida, I am particularly grateful to Mindy Aloff, whose championing of this project and continued motivation made its publication possible, and to Meredith Babb for her vision of what this book could be. Eleanor Deumens, Mary Puckett, and Jenny Wilsen were efficient and tireless guides through the technical end of producing the book. I also owe a debt of gratitude to Jill Twist for her editing.

Finally, I would be remiss if I did not thank my friend, neighbor, and fellow fan of Mexico, John Coppola, for his years of patiently listening to me describe my research and his willingness to read and comment on multiple drafts as I attempted to grapple with all the material I was uncovering. Another friend, Rebecca Phipps, provided a lay-reader's insights on issues that needed to be clarified.

All of these people have made this book a far better work than it would have been without their assistance. For any errors, and I'm certain that in a work that attempts to deal with multiple fields of study at once there will be far more than I would wish, I take full responsibility.

ABBREVIATIONS

INBA   Instituto Nacional de Bellas Artes (National Institute of Fine Arts)

LEAR   Liga de Escritores y Artistas Revolucionarios (League of Revolutionary Writers and Artists)

PNR   Partido Nacional Revolucionario (National Revolutionary Party)

PRI   Partido Revolucionario Institucional (Institutional Revolutionary Party)

SEP   Secretaría de Educación Pública (Ministry of Public Education)

TGP   Taller de Gráfica Popular (People's Graphic Workshop)

Introduction

The paint on Mexico's first postrevolutionary mural, Roberto Montene-gro's (1885–1968) 1922 *Arbol de la Vida* (Tree of Life), was barely dry when painters David Alfaro Siqueiros (1876–1974) and Jean Charlot (1898–1979) embarked upon a series of harsh critiques of the country's emerging na-tionalist art.[1] Under the pseudonym of Juan Hernández Araujo, they traced the country's overt "Mexicanism," which they abhorred, to its two "spiri-tual precursors": the Spanish-born, early modern dancer Tórtola Valencia (1882–1955) and the Russian ballerina Anna Pavlova (1881–1931).[2]

In fact, theatrical dance helped to shape the artists who created Mexico's postrevolutionary nationalist art. Several leading Mexican painters were residents in Paris during the early years of Serge Diaghilev's (1872–1929) Ballets Russes (1909–1929) and had firsthand experience with the compa-ny's up-to-the-minute ballets and their influence on Western culture. Mex-ico's leading postrevolutionary intellectual, José Vasconcelos (1882–1959), shared this experience with the painters he would commission to paint murals when he was leader of Mexico's Secretaría de Educación Pública (SEP, Ministry of Education). They, in turn, would help shape the form that theatrical dance would take in twentieth-century Mexico as it was born and flourished under state sponsorship. *A Revolution in Movement* traces the story of this interaction over nearly half a century, from the 1920s' urge to embrace Russian ballet to the adoption of US-style modern dance in the early 1940s and the eventual triumph of balleticized folk dance in the 1960s. This book is an initial attempt to illuminate the ways in which the decisions made by visual artists who sought to present Mexico to itself and to others were also made manifest in what and how the country's dancers danced.

The visual artists who promoted the creation of Mexican theatrical dance—all of them involved in one way or another with the rebirth of mu-ralism, Mexico's most widely recognized nationalist expression—may well have been what writer Carlos Monsiváis (1938–2010) described as "instant figures in the popular urban culture."[3] Still, as a group they enjoyed a care-fully established status. Even when Mexico was called New Spain, its gov-ernment sent its most promising visual artists to Europe to complete their studies. As much as some of the beneficiaries of this program, like Diego Rivera (1886–1957), may have wished to present themselves as revolutionar-ies, they were members of a hand-picked elite.

The muralists themselves were all involved in the creation of their own myth, an effort in which they were aided by any number of writers. Charlot would become one of the leading mythographers of Mexico's postrevolu-tionary art for the English-speaking world through his *Mexican Mural Re-naissance*. His selective memoir of the early years of muralism, along with writings by anthropologist Anita Brenner (1905–1974), art entrepreneur Alma Reed (1889–1966), and many others, would help shape the perception of muralism as the wellspring of Mexican modernism and as a reflection of the nation's postrevolutionary politics and policy. Neither perception was accurate; both have, nonetheless, proven resilient. Only in the past few years have historians outside of Mexico begun to look beyond the monolith some of its creators and promoters claimed Mexican muralism to be and discovered the diversity and complexity that thrived as Mexico sought to redefine itself as a unified nation in the wake of its divisive revolution.

The revolution did not bring modernism in the arts to Mexico; it was already present. What is now Mexico had been immersed in international art currents since the beginnings of the sixteenth century. Its visual culture was rife with imagery imported from Europe and from Asia, courtesy of the Manilla Galleon, which transshipped goods through Mexico to Spain. Influences from the Eastern and Western Old World met in Mexico to join with a visual culture that guarded survivals from its pre-Hispanic past, of-ten in the form of its folk art. Some of the most intriguing creations of the professional artists of what was then New Spain were its *casta* paint-ings, which documented the racial mixing, or *mestizaje,* that was taking place there. The audience for these artworks was European and the style the Mexicans used in these works for export was consonant with that of their contemporaries there; its subject mater, however, was unique to the Ameri-cas. Over time, the idea of mestizaje itself would become an integral part of Mexico's self-definition. By the beginnings of the twentieth century, Julio Ruelas (1870–1907) was Mexico's leading painter in the symbolist vein, a style that emerged in Mexico at about the same time it emerged in France.[4] Ruelas had trained in Danzig and spent his last few years living in Paris and contributing images to the *Revista Moderna* (Modernist Magazine) that cultivated what cultural historian Adela Pineda calls Mexico's "cosmopolitan nationalism."[5] At that time, the elite of Mexico City's fondest desire was to have it seen as the American equivalent of Paris.[6] One striking example of this aspiration appeared on the city's stages in the form of imitators of dancer Loïe Fuller (1862–1928).

Just a few years after Fuller, born Marie Louise Fuller on a farm outside of Chicago, created a furor at the Folies Bergère with her *Serpentine Dance* in 1892, Mexico City saw a heated competition between two of the many dancers who sought to capitalize on her success.[7] Both Stella Follet, who appeared with Aldo Martini's vaudeville company at the Nacional and Principal theaters, and Jossie Lindsay, at the flashy new Circo Teatro Orrin, claimed to have originated the dance, though Mexican critics knew they were only seeing pale copies of Fuller's original.[8] Nonetheless, in 1894 publisher Antonio Vanegas Arroyo (1850–1917), whose penny press mined current events to keep its offerings ever fresh on the market, recognized a news story when he saw one.[9] He commissioned printmaker José Guadalupe Posada (1852–1913) to represent a serpentine dancer for his latest collection of songs, *La serpentina: Colección de canciones modernas* (The Serpentine: Collection of Modern Songs). Posada's cover features an alluring woman looking back across her shoulders as she actively manipulates her flowing silk gown into a symmetrical arabesque.[10] She is flanked on either side by a pair of somewhat ungainly assistants who keep the viewer's eye from moving away from the figure at the center of the page. Their boots anchor them to the floor, while the dancer herself floats above the stage in her ballet slippers.

The selection of Fuller's *Serpentine Dance* as the cover for a booklet of "modern" songs was not happenstance. The dance relied on stage effects made possible by the advent of the latest technological marvel, electrical illumination, for its success. Its performance lent a body to the idea of the modern years before the term "modern dance" entered the vocabulary.

When Fuller herself arrived in Mexico City in 1897, she was accorded a welcome that rivaled any offered to a media celebrity today, including a late-night serenade from a military band at her hotel. In his elaborate nineteenth-century prose, poet and art critic José Juan Tablada (1871–1945) enthused that

the public has already seen Joan [*sic*] Lindsay and Stella Follet in our metropolitan theaters, falsified Serpentines who only offered the most minuscule, opaque idea one could possibly provide of the

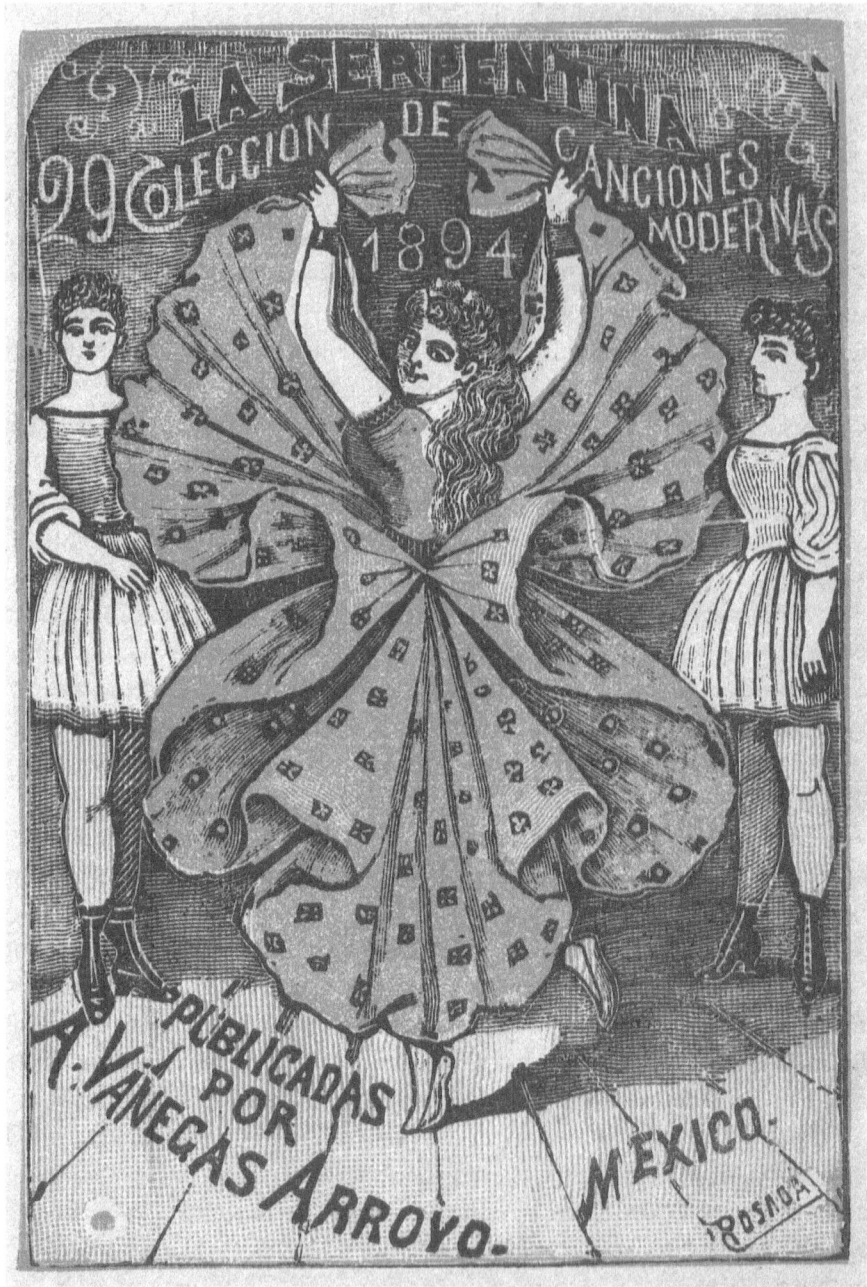

FIGURE 1. José Guadalupe Posada (1852–1913). *La Serpentina* (The Serpentine), likely a representation of Loïe Fuller imitator Jossie Lindsay. 1894. Collection of the author.

original, something comparable to what a projected kinetoscope can give us of a live theatrical performance. . . . Readers, you can admire Loïe Fuller; you can see her appear from the depths on the proscenium in the semi-darkness where the light barely casts a vaporization of opals, a haze of gauze, a luminous dust more tenuous then the first light of a new moon. You will see her, then, confounding her outlines in the dusk like the phantasm of some Ophelia and begin to affirm, bit by bit, her ultra-terrestrial profile until she materializes in a light that now washes her with its watered beams, now bathes her in the halo of the frank, full moon. Finally, you will see her amidst the strains of music flaunting the brave beauty of this Amazon, or languishing with the spasms of an Arabic dancing master rhyming the turgid strophes of her carnal exuberance in the brilliant poem of her wise choreography.[11]

Judging from Tablada's praise, the theatergoing public of Mexico City was prepared to embrace the latest in theatrical dance.

As much as the city's theatergoers may have appreciated Fuller and her performance there, Mexico still held deep seated reservations about theatrical dancers. Although Mexico City's first dancing school opened in 1526, within two years of its re-establishment by the Spanish, not all of the popular dances of the time were deemed suitable for public presentation.[12] Some half century later, Father Diego Duran described the local performers of a "lascivious," African-tinged *zarabanda*, destined to become the Europeanized dance form the sarabande, as "dishonest women and lightweight men."[13] When Mexico City's Nuevo Coliseo (New Colosseum) opened in 1753, ballet formed a regular part of its programming.[14] These ballets were staged by foreign impresarios who brought their lead dancers along with them; dance historian Maya Ramos-Smith proposes that there must have been a group of resident performers capable of serving as the corps de ballet for these guest performers.

Theatrical dancers may have enjoyed a period of popularity during Mexico's viceregal period, but the social status of anyone associated with the professional theater was a different matter. During the twilight years of Spanish rule, Mexico saw a public debate on the fitness of using the honorifics *señor* (mister) or *señora* (madam) for stage performers.[15] By the time Fuller arrived in Mexico City, ballet had lost its place on the city's stages. The social standing of the city's professional female dancers was at its nadir, perilously close, as Ramos-Smith observes, to that of its prostitutes.[16] Little wonder, then, that Fuller's visit did not inspire a wave of young women from the city's upper classes to enter its dance studios as Pavlova's visits would a generation later.

The difference in response by potential dancers to these two critically acclaimed performances likely lies in the Mexican Revolution itself. For historian Enrique Krauze the social upheaval caused by Mexico's civil war was part of the reason for the capital R that the event was always given in Mexico: "During the years of war," he wrote, "hundreds of thousands of people, men and women, old and young, abandoned their plots of land, the haciendas [ranches] they worked on or the 'tiny fatherlands' of their villages, willingly or against their will, and traveled by train through their country on a kind of revolutionary tourism, at once frightening and hallucinatory."

The role of women during the revolution was highly varied. Poor and working-class women followed its armies and sometimes fought alongside their male companions as *soldaderas*; the attitudes of middle- and upper-class women ranged from full support of revolutionary leader Emiliano Zapata, who appointed female officers among his troops, to complete opposition of the revolution's anticlerical stance.[17] For historian Mary Kay Vaughn, the revolution was the "arena through which women moved noticeably into public spaces as performers. . . . [its] soldaderas heralded a more open, mobile, and experimental womanhood. They were the forerunners of the chicas modernas (modern girls) who popped up all over Mexico City in the 1920s."[18] As Anne Rubenstein points out, theatrical dance offered Mexico's women an opportunity to claim "the New Woman as their own, they made a healthy Mexican revolutionary out of her . . . [eliding] art and physical education."[19]

For Monsiváis, the revolution's upending of "conventions and prejudices" liberated the "new woman" and made homosexual men a visible presence in Mexico City, where both groups found refuge in government bureaucracy, particularly in the programs of the SEP.[20] Monsiváis also believed that the revolution ushered in the countervailing "national and nationalist myth, the Mexican Macho to the hilt." Mexican machismo had a prerevolutionary antecedent, the *charro*, the valiant horseman of its haciendas who played heroic roles in its nineteenth-century wars of independence and resistance. Their traditional attire is still readily recognizable in the costumes of mariachi musicians. In resistance to the "new woman," postrevolutionary Mexico would also embrace regional exemplars of femininity as representations of the nation, the *China poblana* (the legendary "Chinese" woman who supposedly once lived in Puebla) and the *Tehuana* (the woman from Tehuantepec) from Oaxaca.

The China poblana was marked by her "black braids, big eyes, flirtatious nature, coquettish but honest, wearing the colors of the . . . nation in a clearly mestizo outfit, a mixture of Spanish clothing and indigenous embroidery with some oriental features."[21] She was, in other words, an embodiment of traditional gender attributes. As historian Rick López points out, "authentic indigenous women were supposed to stand as comforting symbols of the endurance of patriarchal norms and traditional ethnic hierarchy," but the Tehuana was a much more complex exemplar of femininity.[22] In a story published in the general interest monthly *Everybody's Magazine* shortly before the revolution erupted, US travel writer Alexander Powell (1879–1957) described the Tehuana as possessing "more physical attractions than any other woman that I know." Among the comparisons he made as equals to the Tehuanas were dancers Isadora Duncan and Ruth St. Denis.[23] He also characterized their home in Oaxaca as a "Utopia of the suffragette. . . . Woman dominates the city [of Tehuantepec] on the torrid isthmus. Here her rights are recognized and undisputed. The women run the place and do ninety per cent of the business. Not only are the women *the* power in the district, but they are fully aware of it."[24] He did, however, relate a story reputedly passed on to him by President Porfirio Díaz (1830–1915), who claimed he quelled an uprising in Tehuantepec by jailing its women, thus depriving the city of its supply of tortillas, which even there maintained its gendered production role.

If women were still treated as minors subject to their fathers or husbands as a matter of law, postrevolutionary changes in legal status did little to displace the social effects of what Monsiváis called the "patriarchal dictatorship."[25] The daughters of both Siqueiros and Guatemalan-born abstract painter Carlos Mérida (1891–1985) were active participants in Mexico's modern dance scene. Regardless of the daughters' roles as successful working artists in their own rights, their fathers remained their fathers, and the female colleagues of Siqueiros's and Mérida's daughters responded to them as such.

At the beginning of the 1920s as reconstruction from its civil war began, Mexico City did have a small community of professional dancers. For the most part the country's leaders saw them as less-than-reputable entertainers. For example, Eva Pérez, the woman who taught Anna Pavlova how to perform Mexican folk dances, would, years later, be classified by functionaries of Mexico's Secretaría de Relaciones Exteriores (Ministry of Foreign Relations) as a "well-known Mexico City madam," based on apparently no more evidence than that of her career as a professional dancer.[26] Mexican dancers had no leading "artistic" figures in the early 1920s to speak out on their behalf. The nation's painters, acting in concert with its musicians and writers, took on that task. The creation of a Mexican theatrical dance tradition as an art form in and of itself was an issue for these artists, and they made it an issue for the state. In doing so they wielded both formal power as participants in its cultural bureaucracy and informal power stemming from their celebrity status to form Mexico's nationalist dance culture.

As dance historian Margarita Tortajada demonstrates in her multivolume *Danza y poder* (Dance and Power), the existence of theatrical dance in Mexico is due almost exclusively to state support, making it a useful illustration of the operation of politics in the realm of nationalist aesthetics. That theatrical dance emerged concurrently with the rise of Mexico's postrevolutionary nationalism makes it a doubly telling example. Indeed, as dance historian Sophie Bidault de la Calle phrases it, the Mexican state would exercise one of its "preferred rituals" through dance, that of its continual evocation of the "metaphor of a new country."[27]

For political scientist Benedict Anderson (1936–2015), what would become nationalism had its beginnings in the Americas, as its peoples of European stock developed a consciousness of their geographically derived second-class status.[28] He also mentions a second, far less commented upon phenomenon, an awareness among American communities that they shared a similar trajectory with places outside their own.[29] At least in the case of Mexico, an understanding of itself as part of a larger collection of "parallel" communities may lie behind its desire to produce an art that was both "national" and "universal," a goal that permeated its critical writings during much of the twentieth century. This aspiration had nothing to do with shoring up dynastic underpinnings that underlay much of the European practice of nationalism. Its most effective expression required forms of communication that transcended linguistic boundaries. Because, as Anderson noted, nationalism develops in ways that are "out there for all to see" through the news media, the success of theatrical dance troupes such as the Ballets Russes and the Ballets Suédois (1920–1925) was readily evident, even to people in Francophile Mexico who had never seen them perform.[30] The performances of traveling artists, such as Pavlova and Valencia, characterized by cultural historian Michelle Clayton as "portable world's fair[s]," had also shown them in their own theaters how well dance could embody an art that was both "particular" and "universal."[31] Mexico's painters saw theatrical dance, with its multimedia combination of movement, music, and the visual arts as an ideal means of expressing the meaning of their nation to both itself and to the world at large. They wished to establish their country as a distinct presence on the international stage, metaphorically and literally, exactly as their counterparts and colleagues from across the Western world were doing during the period that historian Eric Hobsbawm (1917–2021) calls the apogee of nationalism.[32]

The difficulty in doing this lay in deciding how to define Mexican theatrical dance. Was it classical ballet, one of the many regional dances of Mexico that melded European forms with a range of indigenous and African influences, the ritual dances of its indigenous populations, a combination of them, or something entirely different?

Answering that question proved to be anything but a straightforward task. Anderson described the transplanting of different manifestations of nationalism as a kind of "modular" process, but creating a nationalist theatrical dance tradition without the benefit of a strong foundation required a large investment in both thought and action.[33] Reliant as theatrical dancing is on cadres of trained dancers, choreographers, musicians, and designers, and as reliant as a country's sense of nationalism is on the tastes and temperaments of its political leaders and arts bureaucrats, the definition of Mexican dance remained under constant revision as Mexico sought to deploy it.

Throughout the process, the struggle to find a dance form that was national and universal remained a constant. Dancer Pedro Rubín (1903–1938) introduced the *jarabe tapatío*, better known in English as the Mexican hat dance, to Broadway in Florenz Ziegfeld's (1867–1932) *Rio Rita* (1927). He advised the Mexican press that the nation's folk dance had to be divested of "everything that was local" and subjected to "elegant stylizing" for the "benefit of universal understanding."[34] The socially engaged muralist José Clemente Orozco (1883–1949) actively resisted the use of subjects drawn from Mexico's popular culture—a term that, in its Spanish form, can embrace both folk art as well as works designed to appeal to the urban masses—as representative of his homeland. He would spend his final years promoting classical ballet as the form for Mexican theatrical dance. By way of contrast, Mérida, who had studied with Montenegro and Rivera in Paris, spearheaded a drive to document the nation's indigenous dance as a resource for its socially committed modern dancers.

Three folk dances in particular would come to exemplify the shifting tides of aesthetics and state policy that Vasconcelos initiated through his efforts in the SEP. They appear time and time again in the art and discourse of the period and indeed continue to serve as identifiers of different aspects of *mexicanidad*, or Mexicanness, in our time. Two of them, the jarabe tapatío from the state of Jalisco (although danced in the attire of the China poblana from the state of Puebla) and the *sandunga* of the Tehuanas, represent the nation's mestizo blend of Hispanic and indigenous influences.[35] The third, the *danza del venado*, or deer dance, of the Yaqui people who inhabit Mexico's northern borderlands, would come to represent a survival of its pre-Hispanic past. The mestizo dances provided the initial focus for Vasconcelos's cultural program—the more indigenous danza del venado would emerge as a representation of Mexico largely after his departure from power.

Both the China poblana and the Tehuana competed for primacy as representations of the nation early in the twentieth century. As folk dance scholar Anthony Shay observed in his *Choreographic Politics*, every "nation seems to have a geographic area, with the accompanying dances, music, and/or clothing, that are emblematic of the entire nation state. Generally, there is also a secondary geographic area or dance style that forms a national icon."[36] In Vasconcelos's day, Jalisco—home to artists Dr. Atl (born Gerardo Murillo, 1875–1964), Jorge Enciso (1879–1969), and Montenegro, all of who worked with the educator on his programs—served as the primary national cultural area. Vasconcelos's home state of Oaxaca became its secondary representative. As Mexico's political and cultural situation evolved, painters and dancers would repeatedly cite the "touristized" jarabe tapatío as an example of the "inauthentic" in Mexico's representations of itself, although the dance and its mariachi musicians remain as durable a representation of Mexico in the popular imagination today as they did a century ago.

Despite the "borrowed" decision to use theatrical dancing as an expression of the "parallel" aspect of Mexico's nationalism, concerns about foreign influence were a similar constant. Siqueiros's and Charlot's joint text would be the first of many questioning the role of foreign dancers in creating Mexico's identity. Other advocates of the dance were far less concerned about who did the dancing so long as they were performing on behalf of the nation. In 1927, a writer operating under the pseudonym "Ben Alí" for *El Universal Ilustrado*, the weekly cultural supplement to one of Mexico City's daily newspapers, even went so far as to encourage Texas-born Lettie Carroll (1888–1964) and the dancers from her private school to Mexicanize their classical dancing. Miss Carroll had achieved a notable degree of success with the lavish recitals she staged for her dancers, mostly daughters of wealthy businessmen from Mexico City's English-speaking community. Even if her dancers were mostly blue-eyed blondes, "Ben Ali" found it "necessary that Lottie [sic] Carroll rummage about in our ancient legends, and with the cooperation of Mexican musicians and writers, forge a national ballet."[37]

Because the revolution upended old certainties, even the long consecrated idea that Mexico's preconquest past provided a central point of reference on which to build a national identity was subject to debate. While some saw the revolution as an opportunity to cement the ties between Mexico's indigenous and European cultures, Vasconcelos promoted a culture based on European classicism.

Vasconcelos may be best remembered today as the father of Mexican muralism, though he was not in accord with the political messages that it ultimately promoted. The textbooks distributed during his tenure at the SEP treated the revolution as a social disaster thrust upon the people of Mexico.[38] Nonetheless, he happily accepted the recognition that muralism achieved because other nations, the US in particular, imitated his example.[39] He began what he hoped to be the creation of a uniquely Mexican classical dance culture through incorporating Mexican folk dances with prominent Spanish roots as an integral part of his public school curriculum. As the SEP's charge grew from a limited number of schools in Mexico City and environs to well more than twelve thousand schools in less than two decades, this single decision probably did as much to effectively secure a national identity over time as any other program Vasconcelos initiated, murals included.[40] Children in schools scattered across the country would learn their "national" dances and that an integral part of being Mexican involved dancing, not just as their immediate families had done in local celebrations stretching back for generations, but also in the manner of other Mexican communities hundreds of miles away. Steps in one school were repeated in thousands of others by millions of children in school performances as the years went on. The dances given to them as part of their physical education blended seamlessly into the concepts they were given in their civic education as residents of a unified nation. Even today, nearly a century after Vasconcelos initiated his efforts, the children in several of Mexico City's public schools continue to receive instruction in folkloric dance—specifically the mestizo dances combining Spanish and indigenous characteristics, such as the jarabe tapatío that Vasconcelos promoted as evidence of the national.[41] Outside the urban metropolis, the schools in Mexico's many regions continue to teach their elementary school students the dances that originated in their areas, as continuing testament to the idea that Mexico as a whole is a nation of dancers.

Attempting to link himself to the patronage that begat muralism, composer Carlos Chávez (1899–1978) claimed Vasconcelos as the source of his first attempts at composing ballets, which he hoped to see produced by the Ballets Russes. It would take more than a generation for him to see one of his ballets choreographed and performed by dancers born in Mexico and presented in a Mexican theater. Chávez would work within the SEP arts bureaucracy that Vasconcelos created through most of his career, advocating that the state educate professional dancers and that Mexican painters direct these educational efforts. While the emphasis on dancing styles taught at state institutions would shift over the years, from classical to modern and back again, folk dance remained a central pillar of the SEP's educational efforts and was always a presence at its schools.

As political tides shifted following Vasconcelos's departure from the SEP, the vision of its revolution as a unified uprising led by its people came to the fore and the role of its indigenous communities assumed new political meaning. At the same time, Mexico began to formalize its dance education efforts, largely under the leadership of its male painters. The first to lead what would become its Escuela Nacional de Danza (National School of Dance) was Mérida. Just as he drew from indigenous sources in his abstract painting, he looked to preconquest dance forms to lay the foundations for an equally "universal" theatrical dance. His daughter Ana joined him as a student at the school he led; she followed his lead as an advocate for modern dance.

Mérida was seconded in his position by Nellie Campobello (1900–1986), whose ultranationalist stance permeated multiple sectors of Mexico's cultural scene. She saw herself primarily as a writer—her 1931 novel *Cartucho* (Cartridge) lionized Pancho Villa's role in the revolution, while her 1937 *Las manos de Mamá* (Mother's Hands) made heroes of the women whose ideals molded that historical moment. Nellie claimed she became a dancer only because she was supporting her half sister Gloria's (1917–1968) desire to emulate Pavlova. When Mérida was removed for being insufficiently nationalistic, Nellie took his place as the school's director, adding the word national to its name and ruling what she treated as her personal domain with an iron hand from 1937 to 1984.

The young women who would become leading dancers and choreographers in the field of modern dance included several graduates of the National School of Dance, while many others had been driven from the school by Nellie. They united behind two dancer choreographers from the US who had divergent approaches to technique: Anna Sokolow (1910–2000), who trained under Martha Graham (1894–1991), and Waldeen Falkenstein (1914–1993), who claimed her movement-style derived from Mexican folk dance. The creative differences between these dancers and their followers closely echoed the formalist/nationalist divisions among Mexico's visual artists. Although Sokolow's and Waldeen's Mexican disciples would deny any influence from "foreign schools" in their works during the 1950s, the tacit but shared aspirations of artists from both nations facilitated the role that they played in creating Mexico's postrevolutionary dance.[42]

The Campobellos managed to secure state support for a short-lived ballet company with SEP underwriting during the relatively conservative political era that marked World War II in Mexico, with Gloria's lover Orozco as their spokesman. Mexico's critical community was mostly dismissive of the Campobellos's efforts, which, combined with the continuing controversies associated with Nellie's dominating style, doomed their initiative.

In the post–World War II period when the Mexican state had consolidated its power, Chávez would appoint himself to lead the nation's dance programs before turning the reins over to Miguel Covarrubias (1904–1957). Covarrubias was probably more famous in the United States than he was in Mexico at the time. Covarrubias's modernist caricatures were favorites of editor Frank Crowninshield (1872–1947) at *Vanity Fair*. Crowninshield's dedication to modernism also made the promotion of modern dance one the editor's projects, adding an additional component to the already charged cultural atmosphere of the US, in which Covarrubias was flourishing.[43]

By the time Chávez named him director of the Department of Dance for Mexico's Instituto Nacional de Bellas Artes (National Institute of Fine Arts, or INBA) at the age of forty-six, he had gained prestige as a caricaturist, anthropologist, and writer, though a fascination with dance was a constant in his career.[44] Covarrubias's appointment as head of Mexico's dance program secured the nation's move away from classical ballet and toward modern dance. He labored to bridge the divides between dancers who sought a Mexican dance based on its folkloric heritage and those who took a more internationalist stance and for a short while at least managed to do so. Covarrubias brought José Limón (1908–1972) back to his native land to work as a choreographer. He also contributed heavily to the success of the dance program at Bellas Artes as designer for many of its productions—leading directly to what is widely considered the golden age of nationalist modern dance in Mexico of the 1950s.

The golden age of dance marked the culmination of Mexico's nationalist art. When Siqueiros proclaimed in 1945 that "there is no route but ours," he clearly, if unintentionally, signaled that muralism had entered a sclerotic state. At that time, art historian Robin Greeley argues, Mexico's leaders were not interested in "the content of what the muralists had to say, but . . . wanted to manipulate the personas of the painters to serve the state."[45] The state-supported dance companies played a small supporting role in this effort. So long as they were sufficiently modern they could dance what they pleased. But by the time Mexico's nationalist modern dance began to reach maturity and make its mark internationally, the painters and sculptors of the "ruptura" were already hard at work dismantling what visual artist José Luis Cuevas (1934–2017) famously called the *cortina de nopal*, the cactus curtain, which separated the artists practicing Mexico's nationalist aesthetics from the rest of the world.[46]

What Cuevas wanted for Mexican art in 1951 were "broad highways leading out to the rest of the world, rather than narrow trails connecting one adobe village to another."[47] Although his colleagues in the field of dance were still dedicated to the socially engaged tenets of the muralists, they began performing overseas, and this experience changed their approach to dance. A 1957 trip by members of two Mexican modern dance companies to Moscow for the World Festival of Youth and Students, initially opposed by their government sponsors, brought them face to face with the results of a consistent and sustained national policy on the dance their nation lacked. The great majority of Mexico's dancers were committed leftists, and they rose to the defense of modern dance when Galina Ulanova (1910–1998) of the Bolshoi Ballet dismissed their work as bourgeois.[48] Ulanova epitomized, as dance critic Anna Kisselgoff puts it, "a specifically Soviet esthetic, derived from Socialist Realism, that sought to imbue classical ballet with modern dramatic expressiveness," which was precisely what the Mexican dancers were attempting to do through emulating the approach of their country's muralists.[49] Guillermina Bravo (1920–2013), then gaining visibility as the leading exponent of the modern dance in Mexico, stood to ask Ulanova why, if the Soviet Union was truly renovating its reality, it continued to do so through traditional forms.[50] The Mexican dancers emerged from the experience with their commitment to modern dance even firmer than it had been on their departure but with their dedication to overt nationalism on the wane.

The modern dancers from Mexico had also witnessed firsthand what choreographer Igor Moiseyev (1906–2007) was doing with his classically based reinvention of dance materials drawn from the Soviet Union's varied ethnic groups. At the same time, the Mexican government took note of the popularity of the folk dances its modern dancers also presented in the Soviet Union, China, Romania, and Italy. In short order, modern Mexico would be represented abroad not by its modern dancers but by massive folkloric displays complete with overtones of the Russian ballet, which Vasconcelos longed to see.

After a career dedicated to denouncing "Mexicanism," it seems strange that Siqueiros's massive final mural, 1971 *La marcha de la humanidad* (The March of Humanity) covered a building that contained dedicated spaces for folk art sales and folk dance performances. The building's opening ceremonies featured a performance by the Ballet Folklórico de México.[51] Yet, the elevation of folk forms to classical status may also have been consistent with the painter's pro-Soviet politics. Mexico was not using popular folk forms to achieve the classical culture that Vasconcelos had urged; rather it was using the classical to lionize the folk.

From Siqueiros's earliest works, which were inspired by touring ballet and modern dancers, to his condemnation of the influence wielded by these same dancers in the formation of his nation's postrevolutionary culture, and onward through his daughter's own career as a modern dancer, he was actively engaged in an attempt to shape the direction that theatrical dance would take in his homeland. His passion for dance was shared with his leading colleagues, no matter how much they may have differed over the specifics. This is the story of the period in Mexico's development that dance historian Alberto Dallal describes as "a nation of dancers and artists in full discovery of itself."[52]

1

An Anthropologist Orders a Beer

The Development of Mexican Nationalism

The turmoil associated with the decade-long armed segment of Mexico's revolution provoked widespread concern as to how the country would remake itself into a viable entity once the violence ended. The factional nature of the struggle itself—there weren't two sides to this conflict, but many—ensured that a wide range of voices expressed opinions on the direction that Mexico should take. The issue of establishing a national aesthetic as a means of unification played a significant role in this discussion, which began midconflict. Some of the early manifestations of what might be regarded as Mexican nationalism arose from an appreciation of the land's indigenous heritage when it was still part of Spain. Although the willingness to more fully embrace the indigenous components of its culture was largely a twentieth-century phenomenon, by the late nineteenth century Mexican intellectuals understood the nation to be essentially mestizo, or mixed race. If was from these premises that discussions about Mexico's national art departed.

For Carlos Monsiváis, the nation's postrevolutionary circumstances obliged the government to take action on the cultural front. The struggle had shown its leaders that "Europe was not only too distant, Mexico (its cruelty, its barbarity, its primitivism) was too near."[1] The government's prime motivator was to establish some sense of stability and unity to replace the divisiveness of its civil war. The followers of Pancho Villa (1878–1923) trended socialist; the forces behind Emiliano Zapata (1879–1919) leaned anarchist, while the supporters of Venustiano Carranza (1859–1920), who ended up leading the nation, were mostly classical liberals.[2] In the view of Mexican-born anthropologist Anita Brenner, the revolution was formed by multiple bands, each "like a tribe, a class unto itself, with its chief, its code, its own currency, its songs, its tactics and its war whoop," which—although it failed to account for the substantial number of citizens who opposed the revolutionary movement altogether—vividly captured the complexity of the nation's political situation.[3]

The nation's new leaders saw promotion of selected elements from its popular culture as the most viable response to the challenge of reweaving the raveled threads of its political tapestry into something resembling a coherent whole. As Rick López notes, Mexico's early postrevolutionary government was far too weak and impoverished to take definitive actions to effectively dictate the content of a new nationalist art.[4] Nonetheless, it was during this time that the foundations of much of what came to define postrevolutionary Mexico began to receive state support.[5] Enrique Krauze even classified what he called the postrevolutionary government's "cultural originality" as its greatest claim to legitimacy.[6]

Mexican Nationalism before Mexico

For Benedict Anderson, it was among the Creoles, American-born individuals of European ancestry in Spanish America, that nationalism itself was born. In one of its earliest manifestations, the Jesuit Francisco Javier Clavijero (1731–1787), born in what is now Mexico, wrote his 1780 *Storia antica del Messico* (History of Ancient Mexico) to rebut the arguments of European authors that the preconquest peoples of the New World were mere savages. Clavijero's history treated indigenous Americans as equals to their European conquerors. As historian Enrique Florescano points out, this allowed Clavijero's history to evolve into "a symbol of Creole patriotism and a historical argument to demand the independence of the nation."[7] Arguments of legitimacy based on such historical ties would become one of the bedrocks of later concepts of nationalism across the globe. .

The resurrection of the past as a national symbol became more widely visible, at least in Mexico City, in 1790 when a public works project in the Zócalo, the city's principal plaza, unearthed the Aztec Sunstone and a massive sculpture of the earth goddess Coatlicue. The sunstone, with its orderly, calendarlike arrangement, engaged the sensibilities of Mexico's viceregal leaders, then heavily influenced by Enlightenment thought. It was placed on an exterior wall of the cathedral for all to see. There, as historian Salvador Rueda points out, it began its life as "a work of art" and "became an emblem of a glorious (albeit unknown) millenary history that prefigured Mexican nationalism."[8] The statue of the serpent-headed goddess dressed in the snakeskin skirt secured with a human skull was more challenging to the dominant tastes and sensibilities of the Enlightenment in Mexico and was soon reburied. Benito María Moxó y Francoli (1763–1816), bishop of Michoacán, claimed that "said statue . . . reignited the poorly extinguished passion for idolatry among the Indian converts."[9]

The dark-skinned Virgin of Guadalupe also served as what Hobsbawm called a protonationalist symbol in Mexico.[10] The first flag of the insurgency, which established Mexico's independence from Spain, featured the Virgin of Guadalupe—a Christianized version of the Aztec mother goddess Tonantzin—on one side and a serpent-devouring eagle perched atop a cactus, a symbol of the Aztec foundation of what would become Mexico City, on the other in a conjunction that began in the mid-seventeenth century.[11]

A MESTIZO NATION AND ITS SYMBOLS

As committed as the regime of Porfirio Díaz was to modernizing Mexico through creating infrastructure and adopting mostly French cultural norms, it was equally dedicated to reinforcing its legitimacy as an heir to the Aztecs. Díaz would use this argument both internally and externally. For domestic consumption, his government would erect an impressive monument to the last Aztec ruler, Cuauhtémoc (1497?–1525), honoring his ceaseless resistance to the Spanish conquistadors. For international consumption, he would employ references to Aztec and Mayan architecture to represent Mexico at world's fairs in Paris and the United States.[12] In what Mexican historian Juan Ortega y Medina called "archeological Monroism," the United States also leaned on Mexico's preconquest past to refute European arguments that it lacked the history necessary to be taken seriously as a nation.[13] As Ortega y Medina describes it, Mayan ruins promoted as "American" by adventurer and erstwhile diplomat John Lloyd Stephens (1805–1852) helped the United States assert a native cultural independence that justified its political independence.

Díaz had been a leader of Mexico's resistance to the imposition of French power following its invasion in 1861 during the Second French Empire. Mexico's charros, the accomplished horsemen of its rural haciendas, had played major roles in the resistance movement that expelled the French.[14] Rather ironically, Maximilian I, the ill-fated French "emperor" of Mexico, also chose to present himself as a charro, which temporarily made the horsemen's attire fashionable among Mexico City's upper classes.[15] Following Maximilian's fall, the charro attire became associated with the largely mestizo republican forces that had ousted him. By 1884 Mexico City's first

Orquesta Típica (Typical Orchestra), dedicated to playing popular Mexican music, attired itself in charro outfits.[16] This attire is still in use today by mariachi bands across the globe. Mexico's national symbol of masculinity became firmly entrenched at about the same time that the China poblana and the Tehuana began to emerge regionally as symbols of femininity—their rise to full national status would occur following the revolution. By then, López argues, they had become nothing more than a particular style of dress.[17]

Although the idea that Mexico as an "indivisible nation" made up of "all classes . . . and races" had even been propounded by Maximilian I, the concept of Mexico as a mestizo nation came to the fore during the Díaz administration.[18] The publication of the four-volume *México a través de los siglos* (Mexico across the Centuries), beginning in 1884 under the direction of historian Vicente Riva Palacio (1832–1896), made the idea that the nation was united by its racially mixed people the unofficial policy of the state.[19]

Manuel Gamio and Mexico's Many Nations

With the revolution that ousted Díaz from his stranglehold on the presidency still boiling in Mexico's northern states, anthropologist Manuel Gamio (1883–1960) traveled to the Yucatán as the government's inspector general of archeological monuments. During a break from his professional activities, he sat down to a meal at a restaurant in Mérida and was offered the option of an imported beer. Expecting something from Germany or the United States, Gamio opted for the import. When the waiter returned with a Dos Equis from Orizaba, in the state of Veracruz, Gamio repeated his request for an imported beer. "That's the only foreign beer we have available," the waiter replied. "If you'd like a national beer, I can bring you something from the Yucatán."[20]

Following further protests that the Yucatán was part of Mexico, Gamio yielded to the waiter's argument that Dos Equis beer was a foreign commodity. In his 1916 book *Forjando patria* (Forging a Nation), Gamio enlarged on the waiter's points as he explained why the Yucatán saw itself as a separate entity: Unlike the rest of Mexico, most of its inhabitants could communicate in both Spanish and Mayan; although there were gradations in the quality of clothing, both rich and poor dressed in the same simple white cotton outfits and straw hats; they all used hammocks instead of beds for sleeping. Even the state's music and dance, Gamio concluded, were different from that of the rest of Mexico.[21]

In *Forjando patria*, Gamio recognized that the separate reality of the Yucatán was common throughout his country. Visitors from the capital city to Mayan communities in Chiapas, to the Yaqui lands in Sonora, or to the Huichol peoples in Durango, Nayarit, and Zacatecas, he argued, would find these areas at least as foreign as any European land. As a patriotic Mexican fully immersed in the intellectual world of the revolutionary period, he was deeply concerned about the divisions that these differences represented for his country. These areas exemplified what he called *pequeñas patrias*, tiny countries, each with its own sense of identity, that made up his homeland. Some of Gamio's "tiny countries" were almost exclusively indigenous and had suffered unduly from a lack of governmental attention. Others, like the Yucatán, were mestizo but, according to Gamio, had also been ignored by Mexico City's elites. "When," he asked, "has the Yucatán seen the cream of Mexico's capitalists, its professionals, its artists? Never! We think of it as a rich state, like the goose who laid the golden eggs, without ever offering sympathy, material or intellectual aid, the fraternal love of brothers and compatriots. That explains why the people of Yucatán constitute their own tiny nation, and have claimed for themselves the legitimate concepts of nationality."[22]

Gamio's book provided a number of prescriptions intended to help unite Mexico's diverse peoples. Given his training as an anthropologist at Columbia University under German-born Franz Boas (1858–1942), many of Gamio's recommendations reflected the ideas about this field's emerging science that Boas propagated. *Forjando patria*'s chapters on sociology and statistics, and Gamio's urging of a new constitution based on a sociological analysis of a wide ranging set of demographic and geographic data, are good examples of its author's roots in nineteenth-century positivism.

Gamio's prescriptions demonstrate that he was equally immersed in nineteenth-century thinking about nationalism. Even the meaning of the Spanish word patria, as Gamio used it, had been given to the word in the nineteenth century. The 1726 dictionary of the Royal Spanish Academy defined patria as "the place where one was born"—exactly the kind of perspective that so worried Gamio.[23] It wasn't until the 1884 edition of the dictionary that the concepts of government and nation were intentionally joined together in the definition of patria. The situation in Mexico, with its multiple indigenous ethnicities and associated languages, was particularly complex. Gamio was concerned that the relations between those who were mestizo and those who were purely indigenous had not developed to the extent necessary to truly unite Mexico.

Gamio was most interested in the ongoing encounter between peoples of the New World and the Old World, which he believed produced truly national results. The challenge, he believed, was to more closely align the tastes of Mexico's indigenous peoples for European art and the tastes of the nation's emergent middle class for its indigenous art. He saw little hope in attempting to alter the tastes of the aristocratic class, which, he claimed, saw art as purely European. "When the middle class and the indigenous have the same criteria in art, we will be redeemed culturally," Gamio declared. "There will be national art, which is one of the major bases of nationalism."[24]

To help create this convergence, Gamio called for the creation of a national Department of Fine Arts to help direct Mexico's artists along a nationalist path. This organization was not to create art but to "promote the conditions appropriate to the spontaneous emergence of nationalist art. . . . In our four centuries of Europeanized intellectual life, no Velázquez, no Wagner, no Rodin, no Anatole France has bloomed, and it is unlikely that one will ever bloom so long as we continue to dedicate our efforts exclusively to cultivating foreign modes of art, instead of promoting our own."[25]

Employing literature as his example, he affirmed his belief that

national literature will appear automatically when the population manages to unify itself racially, culturally and linguistically. In that moment, without doubt, the ethical, esthetic and religious ideas, scientific knowledge, the aspirations, the ideals of the distinct groups of the country will not diverge as they do today, instead they will have agglomerated and consolidated. . . . The national spirit will then be receptive to the beauty of this literature whether it be indigenous or Spanish, Pre-Hispanic or colonial in the basis of its episodes or passages which awaken the esthetic emotion. . . . It is necessary to encourage all current manifestations of literature, rather than exalt some and discourage others. It is indeed a fool's errand, to ridicule the broadsides of Vanegas Arroyo, publications such as 'La Guacamaya,' the poignant compositions declaimed by our plaza troubadours, and the stories that come from the lips of nannies and maids, as all that is Mexican literature, however much the self-proclaimed purists preach otherwise.[26]

José Vasconcelos and European Classicism

Though Gamio's book proved influential, he was but one of the lead-ing thinkers who took up the revolution's potential to reshape a Mexico that had been "a nation of the few" into a state that better represented its broader population.[27] It was José Vasconcelos, another young thinker with very different ideas as to what Mexico needed in the aftermath of its revo-lution, who, as minister of education, created a government agency that encompassed promotion of the fine arts.

In what Monsiváis classified as the "first apparent contradiction" of Mexico's postrevolutionary cultural project, Vasconcelos was an avowed proponent of European classicism.[28] In his post as minister of education, he was well placed to see his ideas implemented as government policy, even given the constrained budgetary realities of the time. Though he was just as steeped in nineteenth-century philosophical thought as Gamio, Vascon-celos's approach to the creation of a nationalist art was not to meld indig-enous and European tastes but to make Mexico more European.

Also unlike Gamio, Vasconcelos never provided a summation of his ideas about what constituted nationalist art. But he wrote passionately about the possibilities he perceived in Mexico's racial mixing. In his 1925 *La raza cós-mica* (The Cosmic Race), a quasimystical manifesto on Mexico's destined role on the world stage, he claimed that the racially mixed people of Ibero-America were uniquely destined to lead the planet's inhabitants forward into "the universal era of Humanity."[29] The "universal" result of that blending was to be a race, however, in which the "characteristics of the white pre-dominate."[30] He tempered his argument somewhat by proposing that this "supremacy ought to be the fruit of the free election of taste and not the result of violence or economic pressure." In short, the new race Vasconce-los envisioned was what historian Nancy Stepan calls "a eugenics mestizo race."[31] The trajectory he promoted moved only in one direction; the genu-ine intermixing of race and culture that Gamio had proposed was not part of Vasconcelos's agenda. The same held true for his cultural project. As art historian Esther Acevedo succinctly phrased it, Vasconcelos's vision was to employ the "folk as the basis for achieving the leap to the classical."[32]

Vasconcelos's tenure as the minister of education from 1921 to 1924 was marked by a burst of institutional creation and construction activity un-equaled in the country's history. Stepping into the post from his position as rector of the Universidad Autónoma (Autonomous University), he im-mediately embarked on a massive literacy campaign. Less than 5 percent of Mexico's population at that time could read. This was a problem of the first order that demanded his attention. To help reach the nation's almost completely unserved rural population, he enlisted thousands of "cultural missionaries" to teach basic literacy skills to the residents of isolated communities.[33] Many of these missionaries also gathered information about the folk culture of the regions in which they served. A third of the budget for his SEP was dedicated to building schools wherever he could. He also opened well over five hundred small public libraries throughout the country, which had fewer than forty such institutions, mostly in Mexico City, when he assumed his ministerial position.

Given the similarities between Mexico and the new, postrevolutionary Soviet Union—both had populations that were largely rural, illiterate, and multi-ethnic—Vasconcelos borrowed ideas from Maxim Gorky (1868–1936) and the Soviet People's Commissar of Education Anatolii Lunacharsky (1875–1933) to help create his cultural program. Vasconcelos's SEP underwrote the publication of a series of low-cost books to help fill the bookshelves of his new schools and libraries. Demonstrating his classical bent, the first book to emerge from its presses was Homer's *Iliad*. It was followed by the *Odyssey*, the collected tragedies of both Aeschylus and Euripides, Plato's *Dialogues*, Plutarch's *Lives*, and the *Enneads* by Plotinus, along with the four Christian Gospels, Dante's *Inferno* (1320) and Goethe's *Faust* (1808). The only near contemporary authors among Vasconcelos's selections were Leo Tolstoy (1828–1910) and Rabindranath Tagore (1883–1902).[34] Unlike the series of titles edited under Lunacharsky, which were rich in books by the Russian authors who had inspired him, the titles Vasconcelos added to the libraries and schools didn't include the work of a single Mexican author.

Vasconcelos also looked to the newly established Soviet government for guidance in organizing festivals of folk culture and developing and promoting concepts of national patrimony. He embraced Lunacharsky's ideas about the value of mass performances consisting of "rhythmically moving masses embracing thousands and tens of thousands of people—and not just a crowd, but a strictly regulated, collective, peaceful army sincerely possessed by one definite idea. . . . Small groups of pupils from our rhythm schools will advance and will restore the dance to its rightful place. The popular holiday will adorn itself with all the arts, it will resound with music and choirs and that will express the sensations and ideas of the holiday by spectacles on several stages, by songs, and by poetry reading at different points in the rejoicing crowd: it will unite everything in a common act."[35]

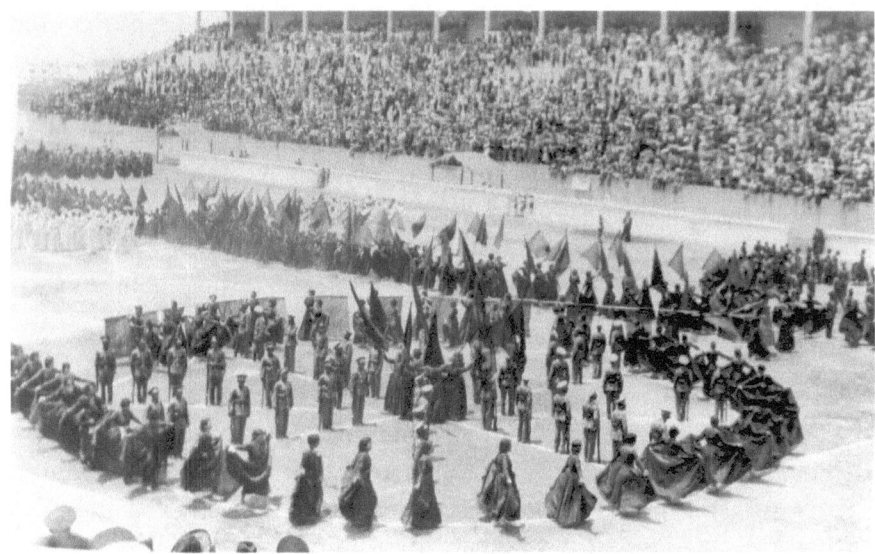

FIGURE 2. A performance of Nellie Campobello's *30–30* in the National Stadium. Circa 1935. Photographer unknown. Fototeca-CENIDI DANZA/INBA. Fondo documental Felipe Segura.

Vasconcelos successfully promoted construction of a national stadium for presenting massive-scale performances of folk songs and dances. There he envisioned creating a synthesis of popular entertainment and the music of his new philharmonic orchestra; "folk and classical united without passing across the bridge of mediocrity," as he put it.[36] Writing several years after he had stepped down from his position, Vasconcelos went on to specify that the classicism he wished to impart to the students of Mexico's schools was that of the contemporary Russian ballet: "In effect, it was easy to derive gymnastics, disciplined by music, toward its natural evolution: the dance. It was the teacher's responsibility to lead athletic groups, particularly the feminine ones, to the more ample spin of the cabriole and the leaps of the dancer. At the same time . . . we did not wish to fall into the conventional figures of the operatic dance with its spinning, crinoline and pointed toe. We aspired to create an art like that of the Russian dancers: perfect in technique, but expressive of our own temperament, illuminated by local color and ethnic peculiarity. One might tolerate the classical dances of Duncan as an exercise, but not as the crowning artistic development that longed to be the expression of a people that, to this day, have been mute to History."[37] As this text indicates, he viewed theatrical dance as a primarily female domain, although not exclusively so.

As part of the broad-scope of his educational plan, which had also been influenced by the Soviet system, and just as Gamio had recommended in his 1916 book, Vasconcelos established a Department of Fine Arts within the SEP.[38] This organization, and its successors, would play the leading role in the nation's development of theatrical dance.

How Indigenous Should a Modern Nationalist Culture Be?

One of the many questions opened by Mexico's revolution was whether, as Monsiváis noted, it "reinitiate[d] what was destroyed" by the Spanish conquest; a related question was what aspects of Mexican culture were "indebted to the Spaniards, the outside world, and modern industry"?[39] Vasconcelos's program was based on the idea that Mexico's Spanish heritage and modernity provided his nation's only viable hope for its present and future. His successors came down firmly on the side of promoting the indigenous side of the equation as the basis for Mexico's nationalist art. For the postrevolutionary Mexican government, as art historian Robin Greeley points out, indigenism was a way of producing history. The result was the "construction of a highly ideological version of Mexico's past under the rubric of mexicanidad."[40]

The most widely recognized of Vasconcelos's initiatives was, and remains, his effort to adorn the walls of his nation's public buildings with murals. Yet, with the possible exception of his first commissions, Vasconcelos never defined what he was looking for from the men he hired to paint the walls of his buildings. Both he and his artists referred to their ongoing project as providing decorations, nothing more.[41] They were first created to establish an atmosphere conducive to learning. Disagreement about what constituted a truly national art for Mexico certainly grew more heated during his tenure at the SEP, yet the socially charged indigenism and didacticism that came to distinguish the Mexican school of painting still lay in the movement's future.[42] It was Vasconcelos's extension of state support to the leading artists of his day, nonetheless, that established the link that explicitly joined the projects of Mexico's visual artists with those of its government.

Many of the Mexican painters Vasconcelos employed had firsthand experience with the explosion of "isms" that marked European modernism early in the twentieth century; all of them avidly followed aesthetic developments beyond their borders. Writing on Mexico's visual arts scene for the *Revista de Revistas* in 1923, Efrain Pérez Mendoza summarized the resulting chaos: "Our artistic environment is the most anarchic and most improvised

of all current art movements, and therefore, the most apt, likely to produce and bear fruit, given that all of the systems and all of the approaches
imported from Europe are in play, opposing the routine that is traditional
in our environment, and contending in the confused but imperious vehe-
mence of renewal which motivates a few of our youngsters."[43]

Some voices called for Mexico to abandon its indigenous past and embrace a vision of a technological present. Poet Manuel Maples (1898–1981)
attempted to rally a movement of *Estridentistas* (Stridentists) who employed no reference whatsoever to Mexico's history. Through his "Strident
Prescription," the only story in his "avant-garde newspaper" *Actual*, which
Maples distributed like an advertising poster around the streets of Mexico
City in 1921, he praised the "subliminal emotions of the roadside, patch-
worked with the wonderful billboards and geometric posters." He went on
to assert that Mexicans could "no longer stick to the traditional chapters
of national art" when news was sent by telegraph from the top of modern
skyscrapers. He sought an art "miraculously illuminated by the vertiginous
light of the present."[44]

While Orozco avoided Maples's self-conscious references to an urban
modernity that would have been alien to the majority of the population of
Mexico, he was just as adamant that Mexico be of its time:

> The art of the New World cannot take root in the old traditions of
> the Old World nor in the aboriginal traditions represented by the
> remains of our Indian peoples. Although the art of all races and of all
> times has a common value—human, universal—each new cycle must
> work for itself, must create, must yield its own prodigies its individual
> share to the common good.
>
> To go solicitously to Europe, bent on poking about its ruins in order
> to import them and servilely to copy them, is no greater error than
> is the looting of the indigenous remains of the New World with the
> object of copying with equal servility its ruins or its present folk-lore.
> However picturesque and interesting these may be, however produc-
> tive and useful ethnology may find them, they cannot furnish a point
> of departure for the New Creation. To lean upon the art of the ab-
> origines, whether it be of antiquity or of the present day, is a sure
> indication of impotence and of cowardice, in fact, of fraud.[45]

While he was still a militant modernist, Siqueiros offered a more nuanced
middle ground, which acknowledged the ongoing presence of the nation's

past. In the manifesto opening his *Vida Americana*—the single-issue publication that was a companion to the numerous "little magazines" fueling
modernism in the United States at the same time—he insisted that the nation's young painters seek inspiration in "the work of the ancient inhabitants of our valleys."[46] Building on the idea of the nation as a mixture of
Indian and Spanish cultures, Siqueiros's essentialist argument asserts that
this strategy would serve artists as a point of departure for their "universal-
ization," allowing their own "natural RACIAL AND LOCAL physiognomy"
to appear in their work. He opposed what he called "lamentable archaeological reconstructions ('Indianism,' 'Primitivism,' 'Americanism')"—subsequently replacing the inclusive "Americanism" with the more specific
"Mexicanism." What he sought instead was an art that reflected "aspects of
our daily lives, the lives of our cities under construction."

Mexico's rural folk culture could be expressed in modernist form just
as readily as an "urban," international approach to asserting a postrevolutionary identity; the debate centered on which was the most "authentic"
representation of the land and its people.

Mexico was not alone in its decision to adopt indigenism as its official
approach to nationalist art, and the issue of authenticity was never far from
the center of the debate wherever indigenist currents surfaced. In his study
of Latin American nationalism, musicologist Thomas Turino points out
that the region uniformly relied on a mix of local culture and modern techniques to achieve its aims.[47] For Turino, the nationalist music produced by
urban elites contained local elements intended to satisfy internal audiences
and modern approaches intended for their external peers. This was, however, not the way that Mexican modernism was perceived in the US.

Perhaps the most intriguing parallels to Mexico's internal debates over
modernist aesthetics were those occurring at the same time north of its
border. Mexico's longstanding discomfort with its neighbor—captured in
the adage attributed to Díaz: "Poor Mexico, so far from God, so close to
the United States"—was at least as intense in the 1920s as it had been in the
era before its revolution. The situations of Mexico and the US at the time
were widely divergent; Mexico sought a way out of the political and economic shambles of its revolution while the US basked in the pride and the
profits from its successful participation in World War I. In another major
difference, the national government of the US was not directly engaged
in the arts. Nonetheless, the artists of both nations were closely aligned
in their desires to identify an aesthetic that distinguished them from their

European colleagues. Prior to World War I, European art held a superior position to that of the Americas in the minds of artists from both sides of the Atlantic; the war permanently altered that perception, as Orozco's pointed reference to the uselessness of "poking about [the] ruins" of Europe demonstrates. While New World artists would continue to embrace the aesthetics of modernism, they would spurn "imported" ideas—a stance that would affect the development of both theatrical dance and the visual arts on both sides of the Rio Grande.

In *The Great American Thing*, art historian Wanda Corn laid out a "three-part drama" of postwar "homecoming, of forging a new alliance with one's own country regardless of its barbarity and philistinism," for artists from the United States.[48] This became the "standard modernist narrative in the 1920s and 1930s. . . . First, early indoctrination . . . in the superiority of European art and the provinciality of one's own culture; second, repeated visits to Europe; and finally, the collapse of Euro-idolatry in the realization (sometimes an epiphany) that one's own culture had unrecognized value and needed its writers and artists at home."

This same narrative is matched, step by step, by Mexican artists such as Montenegro, who wrote about the "new meaning" his country assumed from him on his return from Europe, and Rivera, who reported that he had returned from Paris to study Mexico's folk and preconquest art in order to give "a new and ample sense" to his work.[49]

The divide between artists who looked to their booming urban environments and those who mined the indigenous past as representatives of the national also existed on both sides of the border. Frank Crowninshield, of *Vanity Fair* magazine, declared for an art inspired by the age "of telephones, submarines, airplanes, cabarets, cocktails, taxicabs, divorce courts, wars, tangos, dollar signs . . . that mirrored accurately their time, with all of its complexities, graces, horrors, pleasures, agonies, uncertainties and blessings."[50] Conversely, pioneering modernist Marsden Hartley (1877–1943) argued for the wholesale adoption of what he called a "redman esthetics" by artists in the United States in a 1920 essay for *Art and Archeology* magazine that fits comfortably beside Siqueiros's manifesto.[51] The American Indian, Hartley pointed out, did not need "imposed culture, which is essentially inferior to their own." Significantly Hartley focused his argument on the aesthetics of Indian dancing, a category that would ultimately serve as a rhetorical tool for advocates of both ballet and modern dance in forming Mexico's approach to theatrical dance.

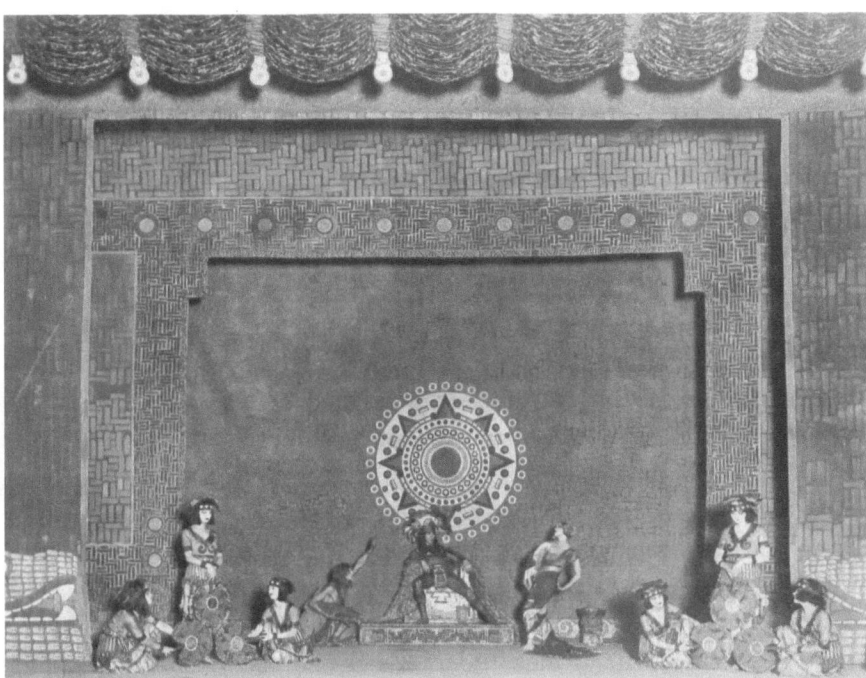

FIGURE 3. Ted Shawn's (1891–1972) *Xochitl* (1920), with costume and set designs by Francisco Cornejo (1892–1963). Photographer unknown. Collection of the author.

Even before the postrevolutionary boom of interest in Mexican culture that captured the attention of artists north of the Rio Grande, evocations of Mexico's pre-Hispanic past provided material for popular dance numbers in vaudeville theaters across the United States. Ted Shawn (1891–1972) would present his *Aztec Dagger Dance* in 1914, a work he followed up with *Xochitl* (1920) and, much later, with the "La Noche Triste de Moctezuma," a segment of *O Libertad!* (1936). Ballet choreographers fed the audience for imagined preconquest dances as well. Diaghilev alumni Theodore Kosloff (1882–1956) gave audiences an *Aztec Spring* (circa 1917) while Mikhail Fokine (1880–1942) and his wife Vera Fokina (1886–1958) staged an "Aztec" ballet they called *The Thunderbird* (1921). Shawn's *Xochitl* would form its lead performer Martha Graham's understanding of what dance historian Elizabeth Kendall called the "link between the visible dance shapes and the dancer's inner passion."[52]

For Shawn, Indian dancing not only represented a still vital manifestation of what he thought to be a doomed culture but the ideal to which all theatrical dancers in the US should aspire:

I have seen Hopi men do the Eagle Dance. There is no living white man today (and that includes all of the greatest of the Russian Ballet, as well as American dancers, including myself) who, after spending a year studying this dance, would be able to reproduce it. . . . The Pueblo Indians have dances whose choreographic form is equal to anything the Russians have ever done, costumed with an understanding of color as great as that of Bakst, and executed with such technique, combining clear-cut execution, variety of movement and extraordinary rapidity and lightness, that the most superlative technician of all the ballet schools would have to admit defeat if he tried to learn these dances under the most favorable circumstances. . . .

There are Indian civilizations whose art product is as high in every way as that of ancient Egypt, and which has never been revealed to the outer world. This, surely, is one great charge laid upon the American dancers—to study, record and translate the dance art of the Indian to present and future generations.[53]

This was a call Shawn's former student Martha Graham would echo in her 1930 essay "Seeking an American Art of Dance," in which she challenged the theatrical dancers of her homeland to use its "primitive sources, dangerous and hard to handle in the arts, but of intense psychic significance—one of which was the Indian," with "his intense integration, his sense of ritualistic tribal drama."[54]

Literary critic Edmund Wilson (1895–1972) would have none of these remnants of nineteenth-century romanticism and what Shawn described as tribes "mystically endowed far beyond the most sensitive and advanced souls of the entire white race."[55] Wilson's essay on the "Indian Corn Dance" barely touched on Indian dancing itself. Instead he described the social misfits among the Anglo-Americans in the audience for his corn dance. One of the first characters he introduced was the wealthy and promiscuous Muna Gibbs, "who ended up going to live in a pueblo, where she tried to look as dumpy as a squaw," a parody of the Taos-based promoter of southwestern folk arts, Mabel Dodge Luhan (1879–1962).[56] Wilson's imaginary audience of would-be Hollywood movie makers, underemployed musicians, hack writers, and tubercular anthropologists mirrored the eclectic group of celebrities and intellectuals Luhan gathered around her in Northern New Mexico in the 1920s. "It is thus that the white race is represented at such of the Indian dances as the public are allowed to see. . . . Some of the dances have always been secret; but people have done their best get into them. It is as if they felt that the Indians were in possession of some sacred key, some integrity, some harmony with nature, which they, the white Americas, lacked. And as they watch, they imagine the dancers experience some profound satisfaction, renewing themselves with some draft of the ecstasy of religion or poetry which they themselves do not know."[57] For Wilson, Indian dancing was not, and could never be, the creative resource that Luhan and her circle wished it to be.

Because the idea of the Indian figured so heavily in Mexico's notions of mestizaje, and because mestizaje was so closely linked to Mexico's conception of the national, the place of Indian dancing within its emerging nationalist iconography proved a far more durable topic in its discourse than it did in the US.

Writing for *Mexican Folkways*, a bilingual publication documenting the nation's popular arts, Jean Charlot implied a careful construction of each step of its indigenous dances when he asserted an aesthetic superiority for them in the 1920s. "The Indians have not yet lost this special sense forgotten among us, which enables them to transpose all emotion to an artistic plane by taking out of it its accidentals and reducing it to a series of plastic proportions which are its essential representation."[58] This ability, he claimed, made their productions far superior to those of the Ballets Russes and Ballets Suédois, which he could have known from his Parisian youth.

"The Indian," Charlot continued,

is guided by a potent taste of discrimination. His art consists in resuming a whole aglomeration [*sic*] of emotional facts in one unique gesture which, executed with convenient slowness and dignity, is very often the only theme of the dance. . . . Such discretion, such modesty in the representation of strong emotion, was always the mark of true civilization.

The very strength of those pantomimes is in the non definition of the natural gesture. They amplify it, beautify it, without crushing it under parasitic gestures with the pretext of art. Such dances employ not only the most impressive sources of beauty, but also the most delicate, as childish innocence. . . .

Considering the complete decadence of our own dances and the barbarous style of some ladies dresses, we could study with great advantage the Indian taste in dress and dance.[59]

A decade later, Mérida, who had seen the Ballets Russes in its heyday, was less doctrinaire than Charlot about the innate superiority of Indian dancing. He was, nonetheless, convinced that its survival was a positive sign for the future of Mexican theatrical dance. In an essay for a Mexico-themed issue of *Theatre Arts Monthly*, he stated his belief that it was "still possible to find expressions [of indigenous dance] completely lacking any touch of foreign mentality."[60] He also posited an underlying unity in the conception of these truly indigenous forms.

> We find in Mexico dozens of different and sometimes closely related forms, variants of, or related, themes or motives from the same fundamental mythology and similar primitive thinking. Undoubtedly we find among them the most original dances, those with the most character and importance.
>
> The richness of Mexico is such that it should surely have first place among the countries possessing a great spiritual energy in the form of folklore.[61]

Mérida concluded his essay by asserting his confidence that "just as it has been possible to create a Mexican painting, it will be possible to create a Mexican theatre, choreography and literature growing out of the same pure consciousness of the dance, our own consciousness."[62]

Building on the work that Mérida had undertaken to document indigenous dances, Nellie and Gloria Campobello would produce their *Ritmos indígenas* in the 1940s. In its pages they laid claim to the "dances of the Mayas, the Yaquis, the Mayos, the Papagos, the Lacandons, the Tarahumaras, the Tehuanos, and the Huaves, [that] have rhythms, within their scant or rich religious expression, which are found in no other dance in the world. . . . This is what we ought to understand and organize to present as a work of art of our own, and to extract from this the elements that enrich our choreographic patrimony inherited from one of the branches which forms our nationality."[63]

Regardless of whether the debate occurred in English or in Spanish, it was all part of the shared concern with identifying what was uniquely "one's own." As Corn points out, European artists who took up residency in the United States during World War I were fascinated by many aspects of its culture they found "exotic" and treated these aspects "as if they were tribal rituals practiced by a strange barbarian race."[64] The hordes of visual artists from the United States who visited Mexico following its revolution often

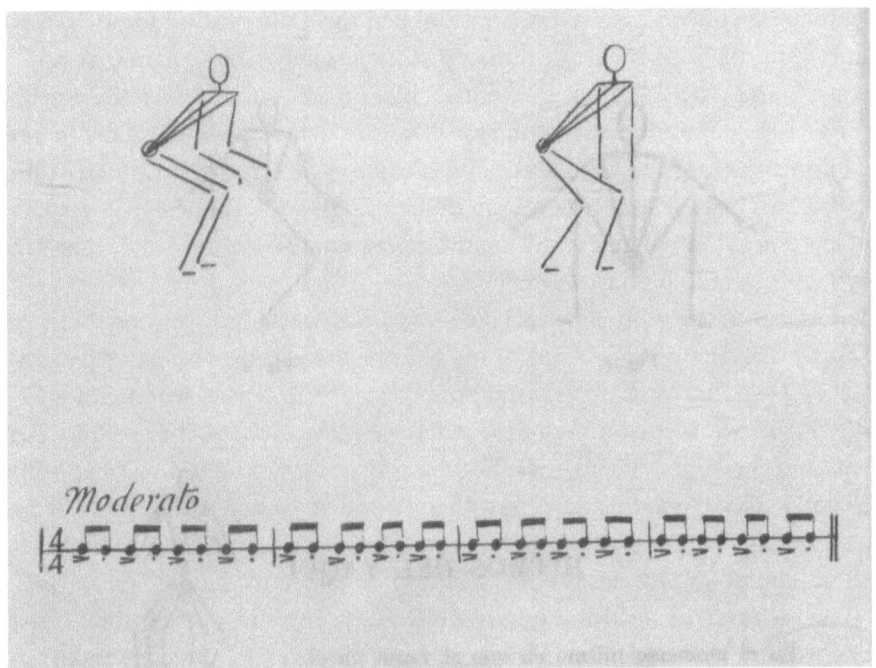

FIGURE 4. Mauro Rafael Moya. Illustration for the Yaqui *danza del venado* (deer dance) from Nellie and Gloria Campobello's *Ritmos indígenas de México* (Indigenous Rhythms of Mexico). 1940. This opening "expression" of the Yaqui deer dance employs the notation system devised by the Campobello sisters and their illustrator, who was Nellie's brother and Gloria's half brother.

imposed a similarly "primitivist" interpretation on the cultural practices of their southern neighbors.

The same thing would happen to Mexico's musicians as their counterparts from the United States began to follow the careers of composers like Silvestre Revueltas (1899–1940) and Carlos Chávez.[65] In an essay for the *New York Times* about Revueltas, composer Aaron Copland (1900–1990) opined that creating a specifically national music was necessarily "easier for Mexicans than for artists in our own country, because Mexico possess a very strong folk art derived from its own Indian civilization, which provides the artist with a rich source of material."[66] Revueltas's music, Copland continued, was "driven from the more usual everyday side of Mexican life. It is often highly spiced, like Mexican food itself. It is full of whims and sudden quirks of fancy and leaves one with a sense of the abundance and vitality of life." He completely missed Revueltas's satiric stylings.

Musicologist Leonora Saavedra has dubbed this kind of thinking the "Tex-Mex" approach to Mexican modernist art.[67] Chávez, for his part, would consciously claim "Indian" elements of his compositions as part of the price for securing attention to his music.[68] Dancer Graham would follow in her compatriot's footsteps by identifying Mexico as an important source of the "primitive," and claimed its Indian dances as inspiration for her own work as she sought to create a movement tradition in the United States that was "art" rather than "entertainment."[69]

Caricaturist Ralph Barton (1891–1931) acknowledged the position of Mexican artists in the minds of his countrymen in his review of his colleague Miguel Covarrubias's first book, *The Prince of Wales and Other Famous Americans* (1925): "At a time when we were on the point of exploding with our own importance . . . he began at once to giggle at us. . . . It has done us good. To be seen through so easily by a boy of twenty, and by a Mexican, a national of a country that we have been patronizing for a century or two, an outlander and a heathen, was a bitter but corrective pill."[70]

As historian of cartooning Bernard Reilly points out, Covarrubias's "use of abstract elements," which "suggest the symbols and characters incorporated into Cubist compositions of Georges Braque and Pablo Picasso," was "likely inspired by geometric motifs found in Mexican Indian crafts and decorative arts."[71] Barton was probably completely unaware of that fact. Covarrubias's subjects at the time of Barton's review were drawn from the celebrity culture of the United States. Consequently, Barton was unable to force Covarrubias into the mold of "exotic" Mexico that was being so freely applied to its other creators, whose work was becoming known north of the border.

Mexican composers and painters employing the tools of international modernism were interpreted as moderns in their homeland but as representations of Mexican "primitives" by their colleagues in the United States, almost without regard to the content of their work. Covarrubias, who used a Mexican Indian–derived "dialect" of the international modern to depict the stars of celebrity culture, was able to dodge this overly facile approach to categorization because his US audience could only see itself in his work.

Regardless of the misperceptions of audiences to Mexico's north, its early postrevolutionary pictorial art was far from the monolithic, ideologically united movement that many of its early chroniclers and critics presented. Mexico's artists may have disagreed about the place of the indigenous peoples in their culture, but the idea that their creations were effectively building a national culture was uniformly strong on both sides of the border.

Less than a decade after the armed portion of Mexico's revolution had drawn to an end, educator Moisés Sáenz (1888–1941) would confidently affirm to an audience in the United States that his nation had "a common ground on which to tread, we have a music, we have a culture, we have a tradition. If words fail to unite, musicians, dancers, and painters will cast their spell and make us one."[72]

2

Mexicanism Russian Style

Roberto Montenegro, Diego Rivera, and the Ballets Russes

Mexico's intelligentsia during the nineteenth century wished to see its indigenous past as a New World analogue to classical Europe; by the dawn of the twentieth century the intelligentsia aspired toward all things Parisian.[1] Mexico would send its most promising art students to Spain for continued studies; both Roberto Montenegro and Diego Rivera ended up in Paris, participants in the controversies surrounding modernist aesthetics in the visual and the performing arts. Both would discover folk art there, through the influence of Serge Diaghilev's Ballets Russes, as a means of expressing national identity. It was a source of inspiration that each of them would pursue in different ways throughout their careers.

When José Vasconcelos set out to create an atmosphere that he thought would be conducive to educating his fellow Mexicans, he turned to painters like Montenegro and Rivera with confidence. They had been trained by Mexico's national academy and by some of the leading artists of Europe. He would trust them as professionals. The education they had received at the Academy of San Carlos, chartered by the viceregal government in 1785, was offered by instructors who had been imported from Europe and who brought its academic traditions with them.

The walls of the Academy of San Carlos were adorned with some of Mexico's finest nineteenth-century art as examples for its student body.[2] Much of it exalted the nation's preconquest past. For art historian Justino Fernández (1904–1972), work's like José Obregón's 1869 *El descubrimiento del pulque* (The Discovery of Pulque), which depicted the "princess" Xóchitl presenting a cup of the cactus-based alcoholic beverage to the "emperor" Tecpancáltzin, provided the nation's past with a European character. "Xóchitl could be a vestal in Greece and the 'emperor' a Hellenistic Apollo, but they are mixed together with fully characterized indigenous types. . . . [The] classicism of the protagonists, combined with the properly indigenous, make this painting a precious document of nineteenth century Mexican art history which fervently wanted to see its indigenous, ancient world as a kind of Olympus."[3]

At the time Montenegro and Rivera studied in San Carlos, the academy's painting program was led by the Catalan Antonio Fabrés (1854–1938), whom Porfirio Díaz selected for the position.[4] Fabrés advocated a realistic, detailed style of painting; the figures in his compositions wore the colorful costumes of musketeers and similar historical characters.

It was in this setting that Montenegro, Rivera, and eight other students gathered at the end of 1904. In a competition that would have been familiar to any student of a traditional European academy, they were to be cloistered for a week to prepare a perfectly rendered painting of a live model—in this case a mason, along with the tools of his trade. The creator of the winning painting would receive a scholarship to study in Europe.

Montenegro was the last to arrive. The remaining seat offered only a view of the model's back. Despite this disadvantage, after the week was up and the students' paintings were reviewed, the academy's panel of judges was unable to decide whether Montenegro or Rivera, Fabrés's favorite student, had produced the superior work.[5]

Because there were funds to support only a single painter, the judges and the students agreed to decide the contest based on the toss of a coin. The loser would receive a subsequent opportunity to travel to Europe. When the peso landed eagle-side up, Montenegro won the trip to Europe, much to Rivera's displeasure. In his memoirs, Montenegro claimed that he thought Rivera's anger at the outcome would last less than an hour because he too was assured of travel funds.[6] Rivera's rancor proved more durable. As José Juan Tablada noted in his diary, when it came time for Montenegro's departure nearly a year later, all of his classmates, "minus the envious Rivera," joined him for a farewell celebration alongside the train that would carry him to Veracruz for his voyage across the Atlantic.[7]

In Spain Montenegro spent his time "memorizing the Prado museum" before moving on to Paris sometime before April 1906.[8] Despite the artistic ferment that permeated the city, the work he exhibited at the Mexican embassy in Paris at the time showed little sign of any incipient avant-garde tendencies.[9] While it is possible he made the acquaintance of Nicaraguan poet Rubén Darío (1867–1916) in Madrid through his poet cousin, Amado Nervo (1870–1919), who was stationed there in Mexico's foreign service, Montenegro cemented a relationship with the symbolist poet when he was in Paris. Darío would dedicate his *Oda a Mitre* (Ode to Mitre) to Montenegro, who, he said, "paints what I write . . . given that I write what he paints."[10]

Correspondence between the academy and its Paris representative documents unfavorable reviews of Montenegro's tendency to become "distracted" by explorations of "insignificant value" and indulge in studies "undertaken by chance."[11] For both good and ill, Montenegro's penchant for exploring a range of approaches to art making—some of them much more successful than others—would mark his entire career. When his scholarship ended, he returned to Mexico in November of 1907.[12]

Rivera made his way to Spain early in 1907, not with the funding promised by the academy but through the support of the progressive governor of Veracruz, Teodoro Dehesa (1848–1936). There he studied under the conservative painting instructor Eduardo Chicarro, who specialized in large-scale *costumbrista* paintings of traditional Spanish characters. Rivera remained in Spain until the spring of 1909, when he returned for a brief stay in Mexico. He traveled back to Europe in the summer of 1909 and went to Bruges, where he painted works inspired by the symbolist painters of that city, before returning to Mexico once again in 1910.[13] The purpose of this trip was two-fold: to secure an extension of his scholarship from Governor Dehesa and to mount a solo show of his work at San Carlos, which was inaugurated by the First Lady of Mexico, Carmelita Romero Rubio (1864–1944). The exhibition was a tremendous success; Rivera sold almost every painting. Although he subsequently claimed to have joined the Zapatista rebels—the revolution began the same day as his exhibition—in truth, after the exhibition closed he packed his bags and the cash he had received from sales of his artwork and went to Paris.[14]

Because Rivera was mounting his solo exhibition, he passed on the opportunity to participate in the academy's student show of 1910, which, in the process of postrevolutionary myth making, was baptized by Jean Charlot and José Clemente Orozco as the spark that ignited the Mexican school of painting.[15]

The exhibition had its impetus in Díaz's plans to celebrate the centennial of the uprising that led to Mexico's independence from Spain. Unlike other Latin American nations that were also celebrating their centennials that year, the fine arts weren't part of Díaz's plans for celebration. Consonant with the "scientific" approach of his administration, he was more interested in marking the electrification of Mexico City's Zócalo and bicycle races.[16]

Díaz did, however, stage an elaborate parade that opened with a contingent representing the conquest, with Moctezuma and the Aztec elite encountering Cortez, the Spanish, and their allies from Tlaxcala.[17] The parade organizers took pains to ensure that the players representing the Aztecs were "'pure' Indians drawn from the communities surrounding Mexico City, serving as a company to the emperor who appeared seated in an elegant palanquin."[18]

Art historian Fausto Ramírez characterized the dictator's attitude toward the arts as one of "infamy. A disdain which he shared with the majority of the dominant group."[19] Noting the lack of an art exhibition in the plans, the community of Spaniards resident in Mexico proposed a presentation of contemporary painting from their nation. Although the event was never part of the official program, it received a stipend from Díaz's minister of education, Justo Sierra (1848–1912), to build a temporary venue for a display.[20]

Unhappy at the news that Mexico's centennial would be marked with an exhibition of Spanish art, the students of the academy, led by Dr. Atl, confronted Sierra and demanded funding for a show of their own.[21] Sierra was sympathetic to the student cause and provided what little he had left in his coffers—less than a tenth of what he had been able to offer the Spanish—to finance a show of Mexican art at the academy. He even offered to purchase three works, an oil painting, a sculpture, and a drawing, selected by the participants, for the nation's collection, though it is unclear if he was able to fulfill his promise.[22]

Joined by his fellow Guadalajarans Montenegro and Jorge Enciso, Dr. Atl organized the immensely popular exhibition. At various points during the exhibition's run, policemen had to be called in to establish order among the crowds seeking access to the art.[23]

Enciso's larger-than-life-sized oil painting of an Aztec priest greeting the rising sun took first prize in a poll conducted by the newspaper *El Heraldo*. For Tablada, writing for the September 16, 1910, edition of *El Imparcial*, Enciso "created a virile figure from old Anáhuac [the valley of Mexico] to symbolize the triumphant peace of modern Mexico"—a peace that would last only a few weeks longer.[24]

While the student exhibition may not have been the "revolutionary moment" referred to by Charlot and Orozco, it did mark a turning point in the spirit of Mexican art. Ramírez described the works on view as demonstrating that the "sumptuous, labored reconstructions of heroic episodes from the ancient past no longer tempted the painters. What young artists like . . . Enciso began to investigate, influenced by Symbolist esthetic, was the construction of evocative, legendary atmospheres in which to pour their rigorously subjective 'modern' sentiments and yearnings."[25]

Given the success of the student show, Sierra offered the students the opportunity to create a mural in the amphitheater of the National Preparatory School, the site where Rivera would eventually paint his first mural.[26] It was to have been an entirely collective enterprise aimed at representing the positivist theme of "one of the manifestations of human evolution," but the onset of the revolution obviated the project.[27]

This group effort was not the only postexhibition project to receive Sierra's blessing. He also commissioned Enciso to paint murals for two schools, the Gertrudis de Armendáriz school for girls and the Vasco de Quiroga school for boys, both located in the Morelos neighborhood of Mexico City.[28] Most of what we know about these murals comes from a mention in Charlot's *Mexican Mural Renaissance*, which provides some of the artist's notes. The images for the girl's school featured mostly domesticated animals, whereas the boy's school mural incorporated more wild animals, including coyotes, lizards, and snakes. While the murals were praised in the pages of the September 1912 edition of *Cosmos* magazine as exemplars of inspiration derived from "the beautiful traditions of the Aztecs," they did not survive the buildings' subsequent remodelings.[29]

One of the disappointments for art lovers attending Mexico's Spanish exhibition was the absence of paintings by Hermen Anglada (1871–1959).[30] Although now largely unrecognized outside of his native Spain, Anglada was one of the more influential painters in Belle Époque Paris. According to Catalan art historian Francesc Fontbona, Anglada's exhibition in the Sala Parés in the spring of 1900 "opened Pablo Picasso's eyes to a radically different way of conceiving painting."[31] Russian critics also found traces of Anglada in the transitional works leading to the groundbreaking abstract paintings of Wassily Kandinsky (1866–1944).[32]

It may have been the opportunity to work with Anglada that lured Montenegro to return to Paris in 1912, when the revolution that toppled Díaz was fully under way.[33] Montenegro had busied himself with renovating the interiors of Guadalajara's Teatro Degollado and creating cartoons lampooning the presidency of Francisco Madero (1873–1913), whose opposition to yet another Díaz re-election gave rise to the revolution, but he wasn't happy back in Mexico.[34] The revolution also meant that his once comfortably situated family faced a precarious future, a situation that would prove to be a constant worry for him during his second European residence.

If Anglada was missing from the Mexican exhibition of Spanish painting, he had been a major participant in the centennial exhibition of international art held in Buenos Aires in 1910. He won the grand prize of the
exhibition's international section with work that specifically evoked "the
ostentatious colors of electric lights, modern theatrical scenery, the decoration of the Ballets Russes."[35]

Anglada was one of the earliest and most avid supporters of the Ballets Russes. His encounter with Diaghilev's designers resulted in an almost
immediate change in his painting style. According to Catalan critic Alexandre Cirici Pellicer (1914–1983), it was the Ballets Russes' "fierce, violent
art, aggressive lines, intense colors . . . interwoven with large swaths of the
folkloric" that drew Anglada's interest.[36] Anglada replaced the pale palette of his early female portraits with a rainbow of brilliant hues inspired
by Léon Bakst (1866–1924), one of the dance company's leading designers; these were colors that Bakst had absorbed from the folk-inspired style
prevalent in Moscow.[37] Bakst was well received by many of the Mexican
artists resident in Paris. When Tablada traveled there in 1912, he wrote of
his desire to see "what I heard so expressively from my friends the painters
of the marvelous scenography of the painter Bakst, who raised the illusion
of the marvelous and a radiant brightness of color to levels of imponderable
wonder."[38]

Anglada's success in Buenos Aires inspired a substantial group of Ar-
gentines to join his atelier in Paris. Upon his return to Paris, Montenegro
shared a residence with several of these painters, including Roberto Ramaugé (1892–1973), Rodolfo Franco (1890–1954), Gregorio López Naguil
(1894–1953), and Alberto Lagos Nocetti (1885–1960). Mexican painter Adolfo Best (1891–1964) and his sister Emma also shared the same abode.[39]
Guatemalan-born Carlos Mérida was a participant in Anglada's academy
(1906–1914) during his Paris stay, and Mexicans Dr. Atl and Jorge Enciso
maintained friendships with Anglada as well.[40]

This group of Latin American painters, known informally as the *grupo
de la Rue Bagneux* after the address of Montenegro's home, was "steeped in
the decorativism of Anglada, the revivalist currents surrounding primitive
and oriental arts then in vogue in Paris, and the aesthetics of the Ballets
Russes," according to art historian Rodrigo Gutiérrez.[41] "They turned Paris
into a spiritual extension of America as they forged the Americanist awakening that would emerge in the twenties."

Anglada almost certainly served as Montenegro's introduction into
the world of the Ballets Russes, although as a great theater aficionado

Montenegro probably would have found his way there on his own. The *Revista Moderna* Montenegro had worked for in Mexico—his first work for the magazine was published when he was only sixteen—was a kind of cousin to Diaghilev's *Mir iskusstva*.[42] Both publications promoted the international symbolist aesthetic, featuring writers such as Edgar Allan Poe and Charles Baudelaire and reproducing works by artists from Europe's early avant-garde movements in their pages. Given such shared tastes, it comes as no surprise that Montenegro's encounter with the Ballets Russes in Paris ignited his imagination.

If the impact of the Ballets Russes had been immediate in stylistic terms for Anglada, it was just as decisive for Montenegro. Rather than transform his style, which was heavily influenced by English illustrator Aubrey Beardsley (1872–1898), it provided him with an expanded subject matter. As art historian Ana María Torres has noted, until that time, Montenegro had been known for his female figures that "do not represent women, but a female state of desire and of dark sexuality."[43] These figures would be joined by drawings of the sexually ambiguous *bailarino* of the Ballets Russes, Vaslav Nijinsky (1890–1950).

Although Montenegro complained in his autobiography that in Paris "the grand spectacles were forbidden to us" and that "tourist dollars created magnificence that was unknown to us," his drawings of Nijinsky show that he was a patron of the Ballets Russes.[44] He had missed a significant portion of Nijinsky's career with the company between 1909 and 1913 but still managed to draw him in *Les Sylphides* (1909), *Carnaval* (1910), *Schéhérazade* (1910), *Le Spectre de la Rose* (1911), *Petrouchka* (1911), *Daphnis et Chloe* (1912), *Le Dieu Bleu* (1912), *L'Après-midi d'un Faune* (1913), *Jeux* (1913), and a work Montenegro called "Dans Orientale," probably from *Les Orientales* (1910).

Pioneering dance historian Cyril Beaumont (1891–1976) described the 1913 visit of a "dark young man who looked like a South American" with "something of the air of a buccaneer" to his bookshop. "Having seen books on dancing in the shop window, he thought I would be interested in some drawings he had done of Nijinsky which he wished to sell. . . . I said I would buy the set provided that I could publish them in a small edition. He agreed and the transaction was completed."[45]

In his introductory essay to the published portfolio *Vaslav Nijinsky: An Artistic Interpretation of His Work in Black, White and Gold* (1913), Beaumont lavished praise on Montenegro's drawings:

To assert that a New Interpretation of Nijinsky's art is possible will come as somewhat of a surprise!

The work of our talented artist, R. Montenegro, is the solution. A glance at his designs will show that Nijinsky is no longer represented as a great dancer, arrayed in the dress, and playing the part of the character he assumes.

No! They reveal a New Thought, a word hitherto unspoken concerning the dancer's art. And with their charming decorative scheme of black, white and gold they are worthy of ranking with any of the fine work which in appearance has preceded them.[46]

Beaumont knew of what he wrote. He had just finished publishing the English version of George Barbier's (1882–1932) *Dessins sur les danses de Vaslav Nijinsky* (1913).

Still, not everyone was enamored of Montenegro's Beardsleyesque style. When Nijinsky reappeared on the London stage in 1914 after his dismissal from the Ballets Russes for having abandoned Diaghilev's bed and married a woman, the Fine Art Society gallery on Bond Street held an exhibition of artworks inspired by the dancer's performances. Its two drawings by Montenegro of Nijinsky's performance in *Jeux* were savaged by the art critic of the *Daily Telegraph*, who found the work "repulsive" and "a blot on the exhibition."[47]

Diaghilev, who met Beardsley in 1897 and had promoted his work in *Mir iskusstva*, didn't concur with this assessment of Montenegro's drawings.[48] The impresario, who managed every detail of his company's operations, including its promotions, approved the use of a slightly modified version of Montenegro's rendition of Nijinsky as the Golden Slave in *Schéhérazade* to illustrate one of the souvenir programs sold during the company's 1916–1917 tour of the United States.[49] How Diaghilev, who provided selected artists with access to his company and typically commissioned works directly from them, became acquainted with Montenegro's published drawings remains unclear.[50] Given Montenegro's sale of the reproduction rights for his Nijinsky drawings to Beaumont three years earlier and the limited circulation of the souvenir program within the United States, he may have never known that his work was consecrated by Diaghilev himself.

Beardsley's influence on Montenegro's style would also earn the artist continued condemnation in Mexico. Siqueiros had blasted the influence of Beardsley's "anemia" on Latin American artists in his 1921 manifesto in

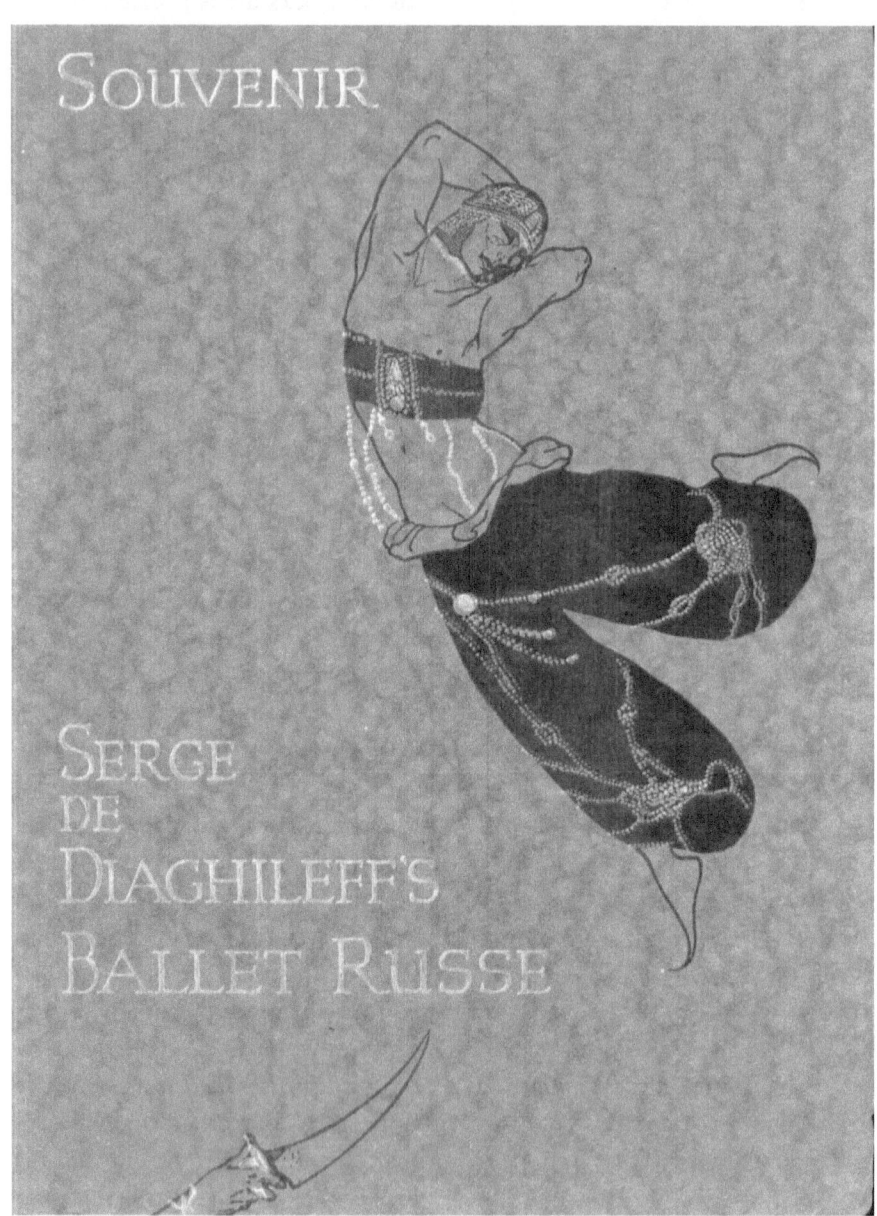

SOUVENIR

SERGE DE DIAGHILEFF'S BALLET RUSSE

FIGURE 5. Roberto Montenegro (1885–1968). Illustration of Vaslav Nijinsky in *Schéhérazade*. Cover of the souvenir program for the Ballets Russes' 1916–1917 tour of the United States. The light beading depicted in the drawing and the type are both printed in gold ink. Collection of the author.

Vida Americana, widely considered a foundational document of the Mexican school of painting.[51] Without doubt, Montenegro was the target of a subsequent article praising Rivera published that same year by *El Universal Ilustrado* in which Siqueiros identified the "fatal error ... of frequently considering a painter who makes use of our typical aspects as truly Mexican, even though he does so through Aubrey Beardsley."[52]

The association of Beardsley, who gained infamy for his illustrations of Oscar Wilde's (1854–1900) *Salome* (1891), like Montenegro's association with Diaghilev's Ballets Russes, which served as a refuge for what one critic euphemistically characterized as "velvet voiced youth," bore sexual connotations.[53] Rivera underlined that point in his address to the academy on his return to Mexico in 1921, telling the assembly, Montenegro among them, that anyone who did not share in his brand of modernism "was not worthy of being called an artist or a man."[54] In the heavily macho rhetoric of postrevolutionary Mexico, this reference should probably be understood as condemning both Montenegro's aesthetics and his homosexuality. As Carlos Monsiváis noted, nationalist machismo would prevent homosexuals from receiving the credit they merited.[55] "Homosexuals with money, talent, ingenuity, audacity, are granted a 'moral dispensation' that without isolating them completely never allows them full integration. . . . And if the law does not prohibit consensual homosexuality among adults, society demands a very high payment for transgression."

Anglada's Ballets Russes–inflected style also came in for specific criticism from Siqueiros in his "Tres Llamamientos." According to Siqueiros, the "fireworks" of Anglada were among the "FLABBY INFLUENCES from Europe which poison our youth, obscuring our PRIMORDIAL VALUES."[56] The ideas of Diego Rivera figure in Siqueiros's manifesto, and Rivera had a more than passing knowledge of the operations of Anglada's studio.[57] Rivera's common-law wife, the Russian painter Angelina Beloff (1879–1969), studied at Anglada's academy along with Montenegro and his Argentine housemates.[58]

For Ramírez, two main elements of Anglada's teaching were reflected in the work of his students from the Americas: a preference for decorative painting and a fascination with folk-derived elements.[59] Given Anglada's insistence that the incorporation of folkloric elements would liberate the artist from the dominance of the French, Ramírez believes that Anglada's circle felt "impelled to extrapolate the lessons of their teacher to their own regional spheres." It was Anglada who inspired his students to use folklore in their art, both through the example of his own paintings and through the productions of his friend Serge Diaghilev.

Diaghilev's friendship with Anglada began in 1901 when the Russian impresario began discussing the painter's work in the pages of *Mir iskusstva*. He continued to present Anglada's works for the remainder of the magazine's life. In 1904, the last year of its publication, Diaghilev included eight works by the painter in the magazine's pages, including one on its cover.[60] Vsevolod Emilyevich Meyerhold created a theater piece inspired by Anglada's *Los enamorados de Jaen* (1910–1913) and set it to the Preludes of Claude Debussy. It was possibly in the company of Meyerhold, who was a visitor to the artist's studio at the time, that Anglada attended Diaghilev's production of the notorious premiere performance of Nijinsky's *Le sacre du printemps* (The Rite of Spring) in 1913.[61]

Fontbona characterized Anglada's incorporation of elements drawn from Spanish folk sources as the link that connected him to the early Russian modernists Diaghilev promoted in *Mir iskusstva*. The Spaniard, Fontbona observed, used "folklore not as picturesque element, but as a means of sparking creativity, based on the purity and contrast of its colors and genuine originality of its forms."[62] This approach to making art had been debated at length in the pages of *Mir iskusstva*; the same debates would be echoed by Mexico's artists as they began to shape postrevolutionary culture in accord with modernist ideals.

Prerevolutionary Russia and Mexico shared similar social problems, and their communities of artists and intellectuals actively questioned the value of late nineteenth-century positivism. In Russia, the issue of what constituted an appropriate representation of the nation was a central concern, and folk art had become one "of the most contested arenas" of its tsarist legacy.[63] In contrast to elite attitudes toward rural crafts in Mexico during the Porfiriato, the tsar promoted Russian folk art, with its anti-industrial implications, as a way of demonstrating the legitimacy of his government's connection to the people.

In an official response to concerns that would be echoed by Gamio's worries about Mexico's pequeñas patrias, Russia chose to revive its *kustar*, or peasant, folk crafts. As art historian Wendy Salmond points out, this was "both a way to maintain a precious status quo in the face of disruptive social change and a tool for promoting apparent concord within an empire of disparate and discontented nationalities."[64] As a result of the official efforts to revive kustar work on a national level, objects originally made for personal use were converted into commodities designed to compete on the international market.[65] Despite his concerns about the commercialization of kustar crafts, critic Georges Lukowsky did equate the importance of the kustar artists to that of the Ballets Russes, as "the only export articles which have propagated the renown of Russian art abroad."[66]

Both of Diaghilev's original underwriters for *Mir iskusstva* sponsored major kustar workshops, Slava Mamontov (1841–1918) at Abramtsevo and Princess Maria Tenisheva (1858–1928) at Talashikno, so he was aware of their positions on the subject.[67] In 1901 painter Viktor Vasnetsov (1848–1926), who was associated with the Mamontov workshop, captured the official view of kustar work when he wrote that "the destruction of our native ways, in the name of blissful aims and by dint of inevitable historical conditions, began from above; and from above we should wait, in the name of aims perhaps even more blissful, for the mighty initiative for their restoration."[68] Vasconcelos represented a similar position from Mexico's postrevolutionary standpoint: "Arts and industries do not spring spontaneously from the people, rather they require the constant intervention of cultured artists to initiate or revive artistic productions. It necessarily follows that the functions of the State must be vested in intelligent and well-trained people, as the artist, left to his own resources, can do nothing and, at the present time, it is the Government alone that, as Maecenas and Director, can systematize both the major and the minor activities."[69]

A faction within *Mir iskusstva*, represented by illustrator Ivan Bilibin (1876–1942), argued against the official folk style but supported the use of folk-inspired motifs by fine artists.[70] Bilibin's arguments were couched in the form of support for art for art's sake. "One should not forget that all old churches, old utensils and old embroideries are art and thus are completely free of any statist tendencies. All this was crafted because it was considered beautiful, no more. . . . Artist-nationalists face a colossally difficult task: using the rich, ancient heritage, they must create something new, serious, logically flowing out of what has survived."[71] Mérida reached the same conclusion: "To make nationalist art, it is necessary to fuse the essentials of our autochthonous art with our current spirit and our current way of feeling, but not in its exterior, which is to say theatrical, form, rather in its essential spirit."[72]

Under the leadership of future Ballets Russes' scenic designer Alexandre Benois (1870–1960), a third faction within the *Mir iskusstva* group appreciated the aesthetic value of peasant handicrafts—Benois himself had a collection of traditional handmade toys—but opposed both the official folk style and the contemporary artists who used folk materials as points of departure.[73] The art of this faction emphasized Russia's ties to western Europe.[74] For Benois, the Europeanization under Peter the Great had accomplished the "zenith of our culture."[75] Although he was far from a proponent of the arts of Mexico's viceregal period, Orozco projected a similar internationalist outlook.

> Painting in its higher forms and painting as a minor folk art differ essentially in this: The former has invariable universal traditions from which no one can separate himself for any reason, in any country, and in any epoch. The latter has purely local traditions that vary according to the life, the changes, agitations, and convulsions of each people, each race, each nationality, each social class, and even each family or tribe.
>
> To confuse the one with the other is a serious error, to apply to the one the laws that govern the other is a regrettable mistake because it denaturalizes it and disorients and confuses the collectivity, causing a delay in its aesthetic development.
>
> That is why one is justified in applying what is understood by "nationalism" to the minor folk arts. But to try to apply it to great painting, to mural decoration for example, is an inexcusable blunder. . . .
>
> True nationalism must not consist in this or that theatrical costume or even in this or that popular song of more than doubtful merit, but in our scientific, industrial, or artistic contribution to human civilization, and the painter who works in the Italian tradition of the fifteenth and sixteenth centuries, for example, is more of a "nationalist" than the one who goes crazy over the nationalistic pots and pans that are very suitable for decorating kitchens but not drawing rooms, and even less libraries or laboratories.
>
> These ideas induced me to abjure, once and for all, the painting of huaraches [sandals] and dirty cotton pants, and naturally I wish with all my heart that those who use them will discard them and become civilized, but I do not glorify them, just as one does not glorify illiteracy, pulque, or the heaps of trash that "adorn" our streets.
>
> All aesthetics, of whatever kind, are a movement forward and not backward.[76]

The Parisian audiences who had formed a major component of the international market for Russian kustar crafts would display a similar taste for aestheticized folklore when Diaghilev introduced his Ballets Russes to the world in 1909. Diaghilev had prepared a salute to the French heritage of Russian ballet, *Le Pavillon d'Armide*, which featured designs by Benois, for his troupe's Paris premiere. The standout of the first Paris Saison Russe was, however, the performance of the *Polovtsian Dances*, which sought to capture the spirit of an encampment of tribal warriors in twelfth-century Russia.[77] Male dancers in the ballet had virtually disappeared from the French stage in the 1830s.[78] Mikhail Fokine's intensely athletic choreography for the company's men came as a complete surprise to the French audience. They were so enthusiastic about the performance of lead dancer Adolph Bolm (1884–1951) that they tore the rail from the orchestra pit in the Théâtre du Châtelet at the ballet's premiere.[79]

The costumes for the *Polovtsian Dances*, designed by painter-archaeologist Nicholas Roerich (1874–1947), startled the Parisian audience. Constructed from brilliantly dyed silk ikat fabrics from Uzbekistan, purchased by Roerich in the street markets of St. Petersburg, they echoed the costumes of the weavers who produced the fabric and were a world away from the traditional ballet tutu.[80] The success of *Polovtsian Dances* may have inspired Nijinsky in his choreography for *Le sacre de printemps*, for which Roerich also designed the costumes based on his research into traditional Russian textiles.[81] Roerich's costumes for *Sacre* would have blended into the indigenous marketplaces in the Mexican states of Oaxaca or Chiapas at the time of the ballet's premiere; this fact was probably not lost on the few Mexicans, including José Vasconcelos, who saw the work in Paris.[82]

Diaghilev's focus on folklore was what interested Vasconcelos in his productions. In an extended discussion of the Ballets Russes that appeared in *Estética* (1936), Vasconcelos praised him for having "created a system of folklore, enriching it through the contributions of all the arts of the theater."[83] He supported this observation with an extensive analysis of both *Schéhérazade* and the *Polovtsian Dances*.

The *Polovtsian Dances* was wildly successful—it became one of the most frequently performed ballets in the company's repertory and it was later taken up by the company's successors. The Ballets Russes de Monte Carlo would bring the *Polovtsian Dances* to Mexico City to help inaugurate the stage of the Palacio de Bellas Artes in 1934.[84]

The reception of the company's 1909 season showed Diaghilev that succeeding in Parisian public meant emphasizing the color and exoticism of his homeland rather than its cultural borrowings from France. As curator Geoffrey Marsh writes, "Diaghilev was shrewd enough to realize that continuing commercial success would depend on playing to their [the Parisian audience's] prejudices, particularly the view that Russia had a bloody history and was a vast country full of exotic tribes, music and dancing."[85]

This realization led Diaghilev to determine he needed "a ballet and a Russian one—the first Russian ballet, since there is no such thing."[86] The result was the ballet widely regarded as his first true *gesamtkunstwerk* creation, *The Firebird* (1910). Following unsuccessful attempts by Diaghilev, Bakst, Benois, and Fokine to identify a suitable story for it, Fokine created a scenario from several different tales, which the group edited and approved. Diaghilev asked the then unknown Igor Stravinsky (1882–1971) to compose the score.[87] Alexander Golovin (1863–1930) designed the original sets and most of the costumes; Bakst designed the Firebird's attire.

When Stravinsky arrived in Paris before the work's premiere, he suffered a moment of panic. "The words 'For Russian Export' seemed to have been stamped everywhere, both on the stage and on the music," he later wrote.[88] Stravinsky need not have worried. As the critic for *Le Figaro* proclaimed, "the management of the Russian ballet has just set the seal on its season by the most complete, the most beautiful, spectacle it has yet afforded us . . . the choreographic story of MM. Fokine and Stravinsky herald an entirely new direction for the art of dancing."[89]

Cultural historian Irina Shevelenko locates these early Diaghilev ballets and their associated scenic designs within the late Tsarist attempts to adopt "folk and medieval traditions as 'national'" that "continued its life in Russian Modernism, inspiring poets, artists, composers to experiment in aesthetic archaization."[90]

The popularity achieved by Ballets Russes' productions with its Parisian public produced an opposing reaction in Russia. Dance historian Hanna Järvinen points out that Diaghilev was "accused of exporting a false image of Russia."[91] The comments of music critic Leonid Sabaneev (1881–1968) were representative: "That Russian art might in fact not be barbaric at all, that it might be just as refined as the French—this is something Diaghilev either does not know or does not wish to know. Russian art must be barbaric—period!"[92]

The excoriation aimed at Diaghilev from Russian critics was echoed by the sentiments about the concept of Mexicanism expressed by Charlot and Siqueiros when they wrote under the pseudonym of Juan Hernández Araujo in 1923. Without acknowledging the Ballets Russes by name, they condemned the "Mexicanists" for their adaptation of "foreign influences (from modern choreography, especially Russian and North American) which seek Mexican characteristics in the PICTURESQUE side of its folk art and its regional particularities (ceramics, retables, etc., etc.)."[93] Unfortunately, they never identified the Russian or the North American choreographers they had in mind.

The two artists went on to accuse the "Mexicanists" of having "especially preferred the so called picturesque, that is to say that which most distinguishes us from the foreign, selecting its eccentric spectacles as its most genuine, which demonstrates their tourist mentality. The beautiful and the eccentric are incompatible; in effect, the eccentric, or the strange, is essentially abnormal or monstrous and the beautiful is essentially normal or general or universal." While they conceded that "the idea of NATIONALISM is good (and, in part, indispensable) in and of itself because it attracts attention to LOCAL BEAUTY AND TRADITION," they also argued that "its results have not corresponded to the transcendence of its fundamental idea."

Writing on José Guadalupe Posada in 1925, Charlot raised the specter of Diaghilev's company yet again. He praised Posada for being "genuinely Mexican" before concluding that "neither the Ballets Russes nor the jarabe Tapatío . . . are the most legitimate manifestations of an Indo-American art."[94]

Charlot's criterion of an "Indo-American art" for Mexico recalled a 1923 article by Rivera that attacked the two best-known painters affiliated with the Ballets Russes. "Our youth pass . . . from the influence of Léon Bakst thinking that they make national art and from the Ballet Russes move on to an enthusiasm for the meritorious work of someone who, with a mixture of misunderstood cubism and classicism 'by the book' is making something that oddly recalls the work of the awful Austrian Klimt."[95] The "meritorious" practitioner of "misunderstood cubism" Rivera denigrates could be none other than Pablo Picasso (1881–1973), who prepared the highly publicized designs for the Ballets Russes' productions of *Parade* (1917), *Le Tricorne* (1919), *Pulcinella* (1920), and *Cuadro Flamenco* (1921).

While Rivera would disparage the influence of the Ballets Russes on Mexican nationalism, he did not escape its example. He was impressed by a Ballets Russes–inspired exhibition of Russian folk art in Paris during the 1913 Salon d'Automne.[96] It included a wide range of objects, from toys to popular prints and icons, much of which came from the personal collections of Russian artists such as future Ballets Russes designer Mikhail Larionov (1881–1964), who believed folk art to be on par with contemporary art.[97]

In the catalogue essay introducing the exhibition, critic Iakov Tugendhol'd (1882–1928) insisted that one of its aims was to "show original folk art, and to contrast it with the pseudo-Russian style" kustar work.[98] Another aim was to demonstrate that "a love of folklore has become a factor in artistic progress." The concepts that gave rise to the endeavor, he concluded, were "the perfectly logical conclusion to that interest in our art that began abroad with the triumphs of Russian music, ballet, and theater design" embodied in the Ballets Russes.[99]

Art historian Ramon Favela observes that Rivera's interest was "either awakened or reinforced" by what he saw in the Russian section of the Salon. "Rivera surely must have recognized that similarity between the Slavic folk art admired by his Russian friends for its artistically pure and plastic properties and such Mexican popular traditional arts as candied bread skulls (Pan de Muertos), retablos (votive icons), weavings, and other crafts that he had seen as a child in Mexico."[100] What may be a component adopted from a Mexican weaving appears in a drawing of a teapot he created after he saw the exhibition. Rivera's 1914 *Despertador* (Alarm Clock) includes elements derived from a serape, while the 1915 *Naturaleza muerta con tazón gris* (Still Life with Gray Bowl) may contain a reference to a *petate*, or straw mat.[101]

His response to the show received its most complete expression in his first masterwork, the 1915 *Paisaje Zapatista* (Zapatista Landscape) with its prominent rendition of a serape. Decades later Rivera would describe the *Zapatista Landscape* as "probably the most faithful expression of the Mexican mood that I have ever achieved."[102]

Rivera told newspaperman Martín Luis Guzmán (1887–1976) that the painting was his "Mexican trophy" shortly after he had completed the work. For art historian James Oles, the painting "marked a momentary and very Mexican triumph on the battlefields of Montparnasse: a public assertion that he [Rivera] had beaten the Cubist leaders at their own game and on their own territory."[103] Oles points out that Rivera "likely . . . invented that the painting had something to do with the rebellious forces unleashed by the Mexican Revolution" years after it was completed and argues it originated as a representation of a nineteenth-century charro who "embodied Mexican bravery and virility" when Rivera departed Mexico for Paris.[104]

The portrait of Guzmán that Rivera started shortly after he had completed the *Zapatista Landscape* featured the same textile. Guzmán complained about sitting in the serape for six days in the summer heat of Rivera's studio.[105] Guzmán would go on to encounter the Ballets Russes during its 1916 tour of the United States, a manifestation of modernist art that he embraced just as fully as he had Rivera's early cubist paintings. He would spend much of the rest of his life advocating for the creation of a Mexican ballet.

Although Montenegro wrote about the effects of the exhibition of Russian folk art on his artwork, these effects didn't work their magic as immediately on him as they had on Rivera. Like Rivera, he began to explore cubism on his return to Paris, working under the influence of his friend Juan Gris (1887–1927), but he ultimately abandoned the style as unsatisfying.[106] When World War I required him to leave Paris, he was unable to return to Mexico because all voyages had been cancelled for fear of German submarines. Instead, he joined many of his Argentine companions from the grupo de la Rue Bagneux, again gathered around Anglada, in Mallorca. Rivera, Enciso, and Best would also take up temporary residence there, along with at least a few members of the white Russian community of Paris, including Ruzhena Khvoshchinskia, a member of Diaghilev's circle.[107] Montenegro later recalled his time in Pollensa as "the most beautiful four years of my life."[108]

The most notable project of his stay was his first mural, which was commissioned in 1919 by the Marquis de Zayas (1896–1970) for what was originally the Círculo Mallorquín and which now serves as the Parliament of the Balearic Islands. "Like a good disciple of Anglada," Ortíz writes of Montenegro's mural, "he represents the Mallorcans in their typical costumes, as fishermen and peasant women immersed in their daily chores, in a plenteous landscape of golden luminosity."[109]

He also worked on Mexican-themed works during his stay in Mallorca. In the 1915 *Escena Mexicana* (Mexican Scene), he painted an Indian woman wrapped in a rebozo nursing her child against a background of maguey cactus. It was not one of his finest works, but, as art historian Esperanza Balderas points out, the image would become an archetypical scene for the Mexican muralists.[110] In 1918, he also held an exhibition of his works in Madrid that he entitled *Motivos Mexicanos*.[111] This was followed in 1919 by a second exhibition in the city's Salón de Arte Moderno. In the opinion of Spanish art critic José Francis, this exhibition's work responded "to the tradition of pre-Columbian art, to the hieroglyphics of the primitive teocali and its cruciform signs and the symbolic figures of the primitive Mexican miniatures."[112]

Yet, when Montenegro did return to Mexico, he found that "everything surprised me. I returned to an alien country; everything attracted my attention, the colonial architecture, the palaces, the churches had a new meaning for me. The indigenous peoples, their handicrafts, their folk art, costumes, dances, customs that I really did not know, for the short time I had studied earlier at San Carlos was not enough for me to comprehend all of this, plus my interest in folklore research had not yet revealed itself to me. At any rate, I was disconcerted by my country."[113]

3

The Precursors of Mexicanism

Anna Pavlova and Tórtola Valencia

If the modernist references to Mexican folklore that arose from the influence of the Ballets Russes disturbed artists like Charlot and Siqueiros, their condemnation of the effects of theatrical dancers on Mexico's nascent image of itself was a strong statement of dance's power. It also emphasized the formative role of foreign dancers in shaping that image and the ongoing tensions over who decided what was "authentically" Mexican.

The fact that neither Tórtola Valencia nor Anna Pavlova was Mexican was central to Charlot's and Siqueiros's condemnation of Mexicanism: "With the help of Jorge Enciso and of Best Maugard, they presented choreographic spectacles to the public with TYPICAL MEXICAN COSTUMES that gave birth to countless pictorial works in which our regional customs were represented through the stylizations of the BALLETS created by said ballerinas. The foreign origins of the birth of MEXICANISM as a collective pictorial orientation are the principal reason for its TOURISTIC aspect."[1]

Siqueiros knew his subject well. He had been a major contributor to the stream of pictorial works inspired by the two dancers. His first formal art exhibition had been dedicated to the "incomparable" Tórtola Valencia.[2] An unnamed reviewer for the daily newspaper *Excélsior* proved prescient in noting that Siqueiros's pastels and drawings of "the notable princess of the Dance who visits us today, have, in addition to vigorous coloring of a supreme elegance, very peculiar characteristics of the young painter, who first of all wanted to mark his personality in them, abdicating any idea that could lead him to be always a bad imitator of the great masters and rejecting, likewise, all that mannerisms that have distinguished the works of our so-called artists, exhibited in the last exhibitions." None of the works from this show appear to have survived but they are evoked in critic Raziel

Cabildo's praise of Siqueiros for abandoning cliché elements in his depictions: "The ballerinas of Alfaro are a whirlwind of limbs and crazed scarves, of panting flesh that traverses an atmosphere of rainbow iridescence, disjointed by unspeakable foreshortenings. And this is only just, for this is what is true. This is the sensation that lingers after a festival of dance."[3]

Siqueiros's depiction of Pavlova was equally notable. He painted her in a rain-drenched pantsuit, one breast visible through its wet fabric, imbuing her with an eroticism not typically associated with the ballerina, whom an admiring Agnes de Mille once described as "almost sexless."[4] The watercolor earned him a full-color reproduction of *La danza de la lluvia* (Dance of the Rain) on the January 24, 1919, cover of the Mexico City newspaper supplement *El Universal Ilustrado* and a fifty-peso gold coin presented by the dancer herself.[5]

Although these early works seem unrelated to the painting style for which he would become famous, Siqueiros's images of Pavlova and Valencia played a role in developing his approach to painting. Art historian Xavier Moyssén classified his watercolor of Pavlova as pure art nouveau, although he thought its "undulating line" only "appeared to obey the dictates of that style," which Siqueiros had "interpreted in a manner that was *sui-generis*."[6] In his *Mexican Mural Renaissance*, Charlot argued that this work, "while still immature in style . . . leans to Ruelas, Bakst, Montenegro . . . but a personal factor intrudes. Siqueiros shows a deeper understanding of form in the round than did the draftsmen he copied."[7] And for writer Guillermo Rousset Banda, the painting of Pavlova presents the first appearance of "the dynamic tendency . . . that would characterize the post-1930s work of Siqueiros."[8]

Although Siqueiros recalled depicting an "almost obese" Valencia in his autobiography, his wife, Angélica Arenal (1909–1989), observed that his omission of most of his early works from his memoirs was due to a "perhaps voluntary" forgetfulness on his part.[9] His condemnation of the Mexicanism he saw among his contemporaries began as a reaction to his own early embrace of "COMMERCIAL ART NOUVEAU . . . which has such a splendid market among us" in his "Tres llamamientos" manifesto in 1921.[10]

Charlot, by contrast, expressed an active dislike of theatrical dance. In the Spanish version of his essay on the aesthetics of indigenous dance, Charlot asserted that "modern 'civilized' dance proceeds from a deviation of the sexual instinct."[11] He went on to declare that, when it came to transposing emotion to its "essential representation. . . . (Russian and Swedish ballets) were simply proofs of how much this instinct is dead in our sophisticated races."[12] Speaking to the animators of Disney Studios in 1938, he compared bad pictorial composition in painting to the "idea of the modern ballet."[13]

Although his essay on indigenous dance cited a number of Mexican folk dances to support its claims, his condemnation of Western theatrical dance was unsupported by references to particular works. Charlot was able to appreciate dance as an art form; he denied that the theatrical dance of his time merited any such consideration.[14]

Probably unwittingly—they were concerned with painting, not dancing—the two artists spotlighted one of the principal roles that Pavlova, Valencia, and their touring colleagues played early in the twentieth century, when dancers served as a kind of "portable world's fair."[15] As historian Michelle Clayton explains, these dancers' dizzying transformations from Asians to Arabs to Andalusians in the space of a single performance "rendered them peculiarly attractive to artists and intellectuals from other countries involved in elaborating new cultural figures for their own nations."[16] The countries that hosted these traveling dancers hoped that they would depart with choreographic souvenirs of their stays, aspiring to see reports of their own dance heritage presented on stages beyond their borders. Valencia in particular was aware of this desire and advised her fans about foreign performances of works inspired in their local culture.

Pavlova and Valencia were not the only dancers to have audiences urge the incorporation of nationalist-themed works into their repertories; Charlot and Siqueiros simply captured the results in an argument embracing other manifestations of the construction of a national culture. The two budding muralists traced the maternity of Mexicanism to Pavlova's resoundingly successful version of the jarabe tapatío and Valencia's far less famous version of the sandunga, both theatricalized folk dances. The female protagonists of both of these dances—the China poblana of the jarabe and the Tehuana of the sandunga—were cementing their roles as iconic embodiments of Mexico's postrevolutionary nationalist spirit at the same time. Art historian Fernando Ibarra characterized the frequent appearance of these two figures in Mexico's illustrated press as a kind of informal competition to determine which of the two would emerge as the national representative—a competition the China poblana eventually won.[17]

DRUNK ON MEXICANISM—ANNA PAVLOVA AND THE JARABE TAPATÍO

Anna Pavlova's presence in Mexico was a matter of presidential importance. She was among the host of fine artists invited in 1917 by Mexico's first postrevolutionary president, Venustiano Carranza (1859–1920), who had banned bullfighting, which he through barbaric, and was seeking edifying entertainment to replace it.[18] Pavlova initially regarded his invitation rather dubiously. After being told by acquaintances in Cuba that travel to Mexico was still inadvisable, Pavlova telegraphed the president asking for a guarantee of personal safety before making her decision.[19] Carranza agreed and in order to avoid what her biographer Valerian Svetloff called "unpleasant contingencies in a country then swept by the winds of revolution" he arranged for troops loyal to him to ride atop the train carrying Pavlova and her company of dancers from Veracruz to Mexico City.[20] Members of her troupe were disturbed by the corpses they saw strung up alongside the railroad tracks, but that was the only direct evidence of the revolution they encountered.[21]

Pavlova was disappointed by her meeting with Carranza; she was apparently expecting someone who looked rather more like Pancho Villa: "We were very surprised . . . when we saw Carranza himself. We had imagined that the president of the Mexican Republic would be a dusky Mexican, with a cruel, tyrannical face, dressed in an exotic uniform covered with gold lace, but instead we saw what looked like a German professor, bald with a long silvery beard and wearing spectacles."[22]

The reception of her January 25, 1919, Mexican debut at the Teatro Arbeu from the nation's small critical community was almost uniformly ecstatic, but Carlos González Peña was not impressed. He was expecting that the Russian dancer would bring "that marvelous revelation of art that is the contemporary ballet" represented by Diaghilev's Ballets Russes.[23] "We don't want Gounod," he complained in the pages of El Universal. "What we want are modern and original works. We want Mussorgsky, Rimsky-Korsakov, Glazunov and Borodin and Tchaikovsky. Moreover, we want scenery by Bakst." Pavlova's company was not as technically adept or as richly attired as Diaghilev's, but González eventually came around after a performance of segments from Sleeping Beauty (1890), which he found sufficiently representative of Diaghilev's production style.[24]

Pavlova's performances inspired a number of the young women from Mexico's moneyed classes to take dance instruction. Actress Dolores del Río (1905–1983), whose performance at a benefit inaugurating Los Angeles's Olympic Auditorium early in her Hollywood career billed her as "the greatest dancer in Mexico," was among their number.[25] Gloria Campobello, who would teach at the national dancing school under the direction of her half sister Nellie, was also inspired to take up dance as a career by Pavlova's return visit to Mexico in 1925.[26]

When it came to Pavlova's *en pointe* version of the jarabe tapatío, Best hadn't simply helped her mount the work, as Charlot and Siqueiros had accused; it had been his idea in the first place.[27] The details of how Best and his friend Jaime Martínez del Río y Viñent (1896–1928) learned that Pavlova wished to commemorate her stay in Mexico with a new work and how they presented their idea of a balleticized jarabe to her remain unrecorded. Ballet promoters understood that incorporating local references into their performances could be a good business decision; Diaghilev's productions of the *Good Humored Ladies* (1917) in England, *Le Tricorne* (1919) in Spain, and *Pulcinella* (1920) in Italy being prime examples.[28]

Pavlova herself had done the same during her visit to Buenos Aires, when she added a minuet lifted from an Argentine historical opera into her performances.[29] According to the souvenir program accompanying Pavlova's 1921 tour of the United States, the intent of Best and Martínez del Río "was deeper than a mere desire to create a new stage offering. It was to send an artistic message from Mexico out to the world—to show that their country possessed more real indigenous art forms and other things more worthy than tangoes [*sic*] and revolutions."[30] That Martínez del Río offered to underwrite the undertaking likely figured in Pavlova's willingness to take their proposal seriously.[31]

A number of classical dancers visiting Mexico shortly after it had achieved its independence from Spain—Celestina Thierry, Giovanna Ciocca, Rosa Espert, and Armella Galletti among them—would close their Mexican tours with renditions of the jarabe.[32] The report in *El Panorama Teatral* of the frenzied reception of Espert's interpretation, where "everyone cheered, everyone applauded, everyone shouted," could have been used to describe the audience's reaction to Pavlova's own rendition in Mexico City's bullring more than half a century later. Porfirio Díaz also saw fit to present a provincial dance troupe performing the jarabe tapatío at a reception honoring US Ambassador Elihu Root in 1907.[33] However, the standing of the jarabe, alongside the reputations of professional stage dancers, had suffered a steep decline during the last half of the nineteenth century. It was not to be seen in the city's finest venues but could be found in its working-class theaters, music halls, and nightclubs. While José Clemente Orozco thought the jarabe was "inevitably associated with the memory of the nauseating 'Teatro Mexicano,'" many of his fellow painters enjoyed forays into working-class theaters, just as modernists elsewhere participated in "slumming in natty dress" as part of their antibourgeois personas.[34] Best was one of the most avid fans of these venues. According to film historian Masha Salazkina, Soviet film director Sergei Eisenstein (1898–1948), who accompanied Best on at least one of these expeditions in the 1920s, thought what he saw in Mexico was "more outrageous and subversively obscene than anything he had seen in Paris or Berlin."[35]

So, what Best and Martínez del Río proposed to Pavlova wasn't necessarily respectable. She knew the repertory of balleticized folk dances in the Russian tradition but had garnered her own experience with popular dance forms, and it was not positive. She made an incognito visit to a dance hall in San Francisco's notorious Barbary Coast neighborhood in 1910 and, partnered by Mikhail Mordkin (1880–1944), improvised a performance to a ragtime piece that cleared the dance floor.[36] In an essay by Pavlova printed in Mexico's *Revista de Revistas* in 1913, years before her first visit, she looked back at the experience with something less than equanimity: "The 'Turkey Trot,' for example, doesn't have much in the way of artistry. I have seen lovely English women dancing the 'Turkey Trot' and 'Cake-Walk.' It's a horrible spectacle! And I know, because I myself have wanted to test the 'Turkey Trot,' so I speak from experience. I openly confess that that kind of dance puts me in an extremely nervous state because of all the anti-esthetic that it embraces, so much so that when I recall my experiments with this order of things, I still cringe in horror."[37]

Somehow, her reaction to the Mexican dance, which she saw in a performance dedicated to her at the working-class Teatro Lírico—one of the preferred theatrical venues of Best and his friends—was different.[38] True to the popular roots of the theatrical revues it offered, the performance in her honor began with a parody of the "ridiculous postures" of Tórtola Valencia—the fact that she was subject to such a lampoon, and that its presenters thought Pavlova would understand their joke, is the best demonstration of just how widely Valencia and her work were recognized—before proceeding on to the Mexican numbers. It ended with the cast presenting Pavlova with wax figurines of the China poblana and her partner the charro.[39]

Best designed the work's set and costumes, Martínez del Río wrote its scenario. The musical director for the Teatro Lírico, Manuel Castro Padilla (1897–1940), arranged its traditional melodies, which would come to be regarded as definitive.[40] Although many dancers would lay claim to teaching Pavlova and her partner Mieczyslaw Pianowski (1890–1967) the jarabe

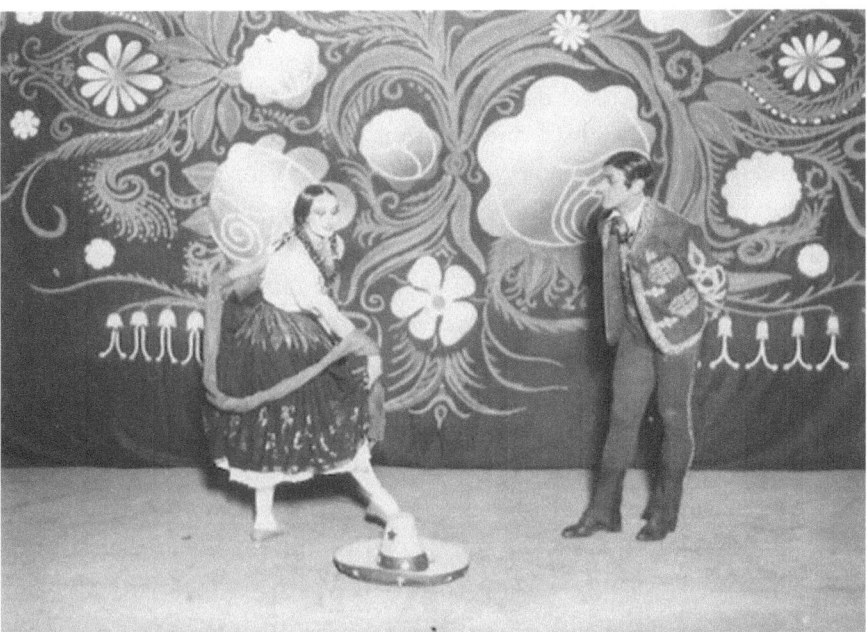

FIGURE 6. Anna Pavlova and Mieczyslaw Pianowski in *Fantasía Mexicana* (Mexican Fantasia), with set and costume designs by Adolfo Best (1891–1964). 1919. Photographer unknown. Collection of Patricia Aulestia, Mexico City.

tapatío, Eva Pérez, one of the lead performers at the Lírico, assumed the responsibility.[41] According to Oleg Kerensky, Pavlova's balleticization of the work consisted of her substituting pointe work for the steps of the jarabe that were traditionally danced on the heel.[42] The *Fantasía Mexicana* (Mexican Fantasia) premiered at the Teatro Arbeu on March 18, 1919.

Martínez del Río's scenario was tissue thin. According to González Peña, the story line consisted of "poppy sellers, partnered by their *charros*, who come to offer a pair of lovers the divine fruits of the eternal spring of the canals. The loving couple dances. The flower vendors and their *charros* dance and that is all. . . . But isn't that enough?"[43] The description of the work in the 1921 souvenir program for Pavlova's US tour, then retitled *Mexican Dances*, propagated both fairly accurate art history on the Asian influence in Mexican art alongside the relatively recent myth of the China poblana: "The first number, 'China Poblana' is named after 'the Chinese Girl of Pueblo' [*sic*], a character of ancient Mexican history, who has become almost a saint in the legends which carry her name from generation to generation. A strong Chinese influence is notable in Mexican textile art works, embroideries, laces, pottery and metal works. Such oriental feeling is apparent in the quaintly beautiful costumes worn in this number. 'Jarabe Tapatio' is a characteristic dance form peculiar to the natives of a certain region in the state of Jalisco and environs of the city of Guadalajara. The third and last number 'Diana Mexicana,' is named for a familiar Mexican folk melody of rapid, fortissimo movement and buoyant rhythm employed by the composer in this typically Mexican dance."[44]

Both the jarabe tapatío and the Diana are traditional jarabes, while the China poblana may have incorporated elements of other folk dances. It was Pavlova's en pointe version of the jarabe tapatío that was the undisputed sensation of the production and drew all its comment, much of which centered on her having elevated this once "lower-class" form to high art. As dance historian José Reynoso points out, Pavlova's performance effectively allowed the Mexican elite "to construct a distinctive mestizo modernity that was Mexican in character but also more universally appealing."[45] In the pages of *El Universal Ilustrado*, critic Luis Rodríguez expressed his pleasure that the freshly "ennobled jarabe, dignified by its new naturalization papers," would be among the folk dances "exported, and that foreign audiences, in applauding them would know that Mexico, a nation of marvelous vitality, has its art."[46]

Pavlova subsequently presented the *Fantasía Mexicana* for a more diverse audience at the city's bullring on March 23.[47] The event garnered a front-page poem by Rafael Lopez (1873–1943) in the newspaper *El Universal* applauding her for her "hat worthy of Emiliano Zapata."[48] Ballerina Margot Fonteyn recreated Pavlova's memories of her bullring performance based on news clippings in her scrapbooks: "It was a wonderful experience, dancing to a very mixed audience, amongst which were a large sprinkling of Indians. Their enthusiasm at the end was unbounded: they chanted their own weird songs and made extraordinary noises before they would let me go. Some of the Mexicans, carried away by the rhythm of the music and the dance, shouted with excitement and threw their sombreros at my feet. When a Mexican gives you his sombrero, it is like an Englishwoman giving you her pearls."[49]

Fantasía Mexicana also represented a premiere of Best's theories as to what constituted genuinely Mexican art. Pavlova approved of the folk-inspired designs Best prepared for her. She told Mexican art writer Otilio Villaseñor that "Russian and Mexican folk art are so similar that they are identical, so much so that if Leningrad had *pulquerias* [bars that specialize in pulque] they would be decorated as they are in Mexico."[50] Another writer found Best's designs for Pavlova's new ballet to be "beautiful, so expressive, so unified and as complete as the famous compositions of the Russian Leon Baskt [*sic*]."[51]

González-Peña described Best's designs for *Fantasía Mexicana* using the language of modernist primitivism:

The scenery for the small work was enchanting in its originality and good taste. Imagine a large black background, which admirably highlights the colorful floral motif drawn from a gourd of Uruapan. That is all! But at the same time that it captivates our eyes, how greatly and how nobly it makes us think about so many lovely things that are contained within the vernacular arts of our country; things that pass before the eyes of the crowd every day, things which can only be seen and only be discovered by artists like Adolfo Best, who seek interpretations of the deep beauty in popular work.

Add to this the elegance of the costumes. Best has stylized that of the china poblana with such a wealth of color, with such whimsical alluring lines, that it suggests a thousand beautiful possibilities about what might lie in its future uses in painting—inspired by that inexhaustible and unexplored reef of our old national costumes—and popular song and dance. Best also renews the charro's suit, returning it to its primitive purity.[52]

Best began to develop his theory around 1910, working as an illustrator for anthropologist Franz Boas. Boas was compiling a study of the ceramic remains of the valley of Mexico, which resulted in his 1912 *Álbum de colecciones arqueológicas* (Album of Archeological Collections). Drawing the thousands of pottery shards required by the project led Best to conclude that certain key elements were central to preconquest art. He refined his thinking in Europe, where he completed drawings of Mexican artifacts held in European museums during the administration of Francisco Madero.[53] Through his friendship with Diego Rivera and his colleague's Russian connections, Best also became acquainted with the folklore-inflected work of Natalia Goncharova (1881–1962).[54]

The Best method centered on seven basic shapes—the spiral, the circle, the half circle, the S form, the wavy line, the zigzag, and the straight line—which, he maintained, could be combined to create anything an artist desired. Art historians Esther Acevedo and Pilar García point out that Best's approach was based on a mixture of both Mexican attitudes about folk arts representing a synthesis of the national spirit and European modernist thought, which embraced "primitive" inspiration.[55]

Best's theories were formally adopted in Mexico City's schools in 1922, and work by students taught under his direction was featured in the 1922 Exhibition of Independent Artists in New York. The *New Republic*'s art critic Thomas Craven found the student work to be "much better both in drawing and design than the canvases of some rather prominent New Yorkers."[56] This kind of positive attention led to an invitation for Best to present his method in the United States the following year.[57] That year, 1923, was also the year his ideas emerged as a textbook, *El metodo de dibujo* (Method for Drawing), illustrated by a teenaged Miguel Covarrubias and published by the SEP. It was reprinted in an English language version in 1926 under the title *A Method for Creative Design*. Art instructors including Rufino Tamayo (1899–1991), Manuel Rodríguez Lozano (1896–1971), Leopoldo Méndez (1902–1969), and Carlos Mérida used Best's text to teach more than two hundred thousand primary and vocational school students how to draw.[58] One of those students was a young woman named Frida Kahlo (1907–1954), whose first paintings bear the distinctive signs of training in Best's method.[59] Covarrubias would teach his future wife, Broadway dancer Rosa Rolanda (born Rosemonde Della Cowan Ruelas, 1898–1970) the basics of Best's system before she began to paint in 1926.[60]

Although his hybrid method met with success among the student population, it received a mixed reception from the nation's professional artists. Diego Rivera considered the Best method to be an "intelligent, subtle, and sagacious qualification of the line elements in Mexican decorative arts" but faulted its use in schools because it did "nothing more than imprison" a child's creativity, albeit using examples that were superior in taste than its predecessors.[61] Charlot and Siqueiros listed Best first among the artists they condemned as Mexicanists but they separated the painter from his method.[62] Under their Hernández Araujo pseudonym, they wrote: "When I speak of 'NATIONALISM,' I'm not referring to the educational system of Adolfo Best, in use in the government schools, which seems to me to be irreplaceable, and I believe that placing our children in healthy contact with our folk art naturally refines their taste which has been perverted by heredity and by the harmful influences which they receive outside of school; I'm referring to mexicanism as an intellectual orientation among professional painters."[63]

As art historian Karen Cordero Reiman observes, Best's system, with its emphasis on the use of abstract elements, provided an alternative to the "rhetorical, didactic and primarily figurative art that was later to be defined as the 'Mexican School.'"[64] This did not sit well with Argentine-born art historian Raquel Tibol (1923–2015), one of the most doctrinaire advocates for the primacy of the Mexican school. Best, she asserted in the *Historia General de Arte de México*, "was not and is not of any major importance."[65] She did, however, grant his book a role in promoting folk art, a source that had proven to be of importance when used by "cultured artists" rather than its intended student audience.

Best's designs for Pavlova's *Fantasía Mexicana* quickly traveled beyond Mexico. According to Charlot, Best's rendition of the costume design for the China poblana and a depiction of a traditional fiesta figured among the works on view in his one-man show at New York City's prestigious Knoedler Galleries in December 1919. The show also included his rendition of a Tehuana and of an Aztec warrior intended as a design for a prospective ballet. "Best," Charlot later concluded in his *Mexican Mural Renaissance*, "was the first to parade a distinctive Mexican art through foreign capitals, and to prove the truth of Martí's pithy saying of fifty years before: 'Mexican painting has a great future—outside Mexico.'"[66] An unknown Mexican photographer allowed an entire suite of his portraits of Pavlova and members of the company in their China poblana and charro costumes to be licensed to a postcard publisher in Spain before Best's New York exhibit.[67]

Pavlova fulfilled Mexican expectations that her version of their jarabe would maintain a place in her repertory. It appeared in her performances in Europe and the United States. Best continued working on developing additional ballets. In August of 1920 he asked his writer friend Katherine Anne Porter (1890–1980) to provide a new scenario for Pavlova's use—or perhaps for Adolph Bolm, who had recently relocated to the United States.[68] The *New York Tribune* announced the premiere of a new Pavlova ballet inspired in her visits to Mexico in its October 17, 1920, edition. *El Heraldo de México* reported on Porter's work with Best to create "Aztec-Mexican pantomimes" for Pavlova's use when the author arrived in the city on November 7, 1920.[69] Porter apparently referred to her scenario as *Xochimilko* (Porter's spelling), a misspelling of the canal-crossed community that continues to produce flowers for Mexico City.[70]

The author was disappointed by what she thought were the results of her efforts. Porter reported that Pavlova had danced her scenario "in many countries but not in New York, because the scenery was done on paper, was inflammable and she was not allowed to use it in New York. I saw photographs, however, and I must say they did not look in the least like anything I had provided in the libretto. It was most unsatisfactory."[71] Perhaps Best had prepared a set on paper, but the ballet Porter wrote was unrealized. The souvenir program for Pavlova's 1921 New York season specified Martínez del Río as the author of its scenario: "The group of three dances, 'China Poblana,' 'Jarabe Tapatío' and 'Diana Mexicana' made a tremendous hit in Mexico City where after the Pavlowa [sic] season tested the capacity of the theater at all performances, these dances were performed in the Bull Ring before twenty-five thousand people, as a climax to the series. The success of this suite of dances in Mexico might be expected, but its receptions in other countries have been truly surprising, particularly in Paris and London, where it achieved great vogue and started a growing interest in Mexican arts."[72]

British audiences added their own inexplicable twists to their understanding of Pavlova's jarabe. The *London Observer* claimed her China poblana outfit was that of a "Mexican cowboy," while the *Daily Telegraph* found a distinct "Dutch flavoring" in the work.[73] Nonetheless, Pavlova's performances helped establish expectations about Mexican dance for non-Mexican audiences and prepared the way for Mexican dancers like Pedro Rubín who performed the jarabe on Broadway. Eva Pérez, Pavlova's instructor in the dance, accompanied by her sisters, also toured the Americas in the mid-1920s with her original jarabe, generating enthusiasm for the dance across two continents.[74]

Dance historian Josefina Lavalle has traced a resurgence of popularity in music hall performances of the jarabe following Pavlova's 1919 visit to Mexico.[75] It wasn't, however, until the SEP began incorporating folk dance as part of the open-air festivals it sponsored and into its public school curriculum that the jarabe exploded in popularity within Mexico.[76] As historian Ricardo Pérez Montfort points out, these festivals "invariably bore the adjective of national."[77]

Pavlova's melding of visibly Mexican content and classical European form likely embodied exactly the kind of culture that Vasconcelos had in mind for his homeland, though he probably never saw her. He was in political exile during her 1919 visit to Mexico and in Europe during her 1925 return. As the leader of the SEP he thought it was his role to provide alternatives to popular entertainments. He had declared that as long "as there is pulque and bulls, there will be no Mexican theatre, no Mexican art, no

Mexican civilization."[78] That was part of his justification for the creation of a huge national stadium where massive folk dance performances featuring the jarabe could be staged, nurturing his dreams of widespread cultural literacy in his homeland. "When I look at the youth in our schools performing popular folk dances whose rhythms melt into the song in the *sones* [melodies], I think a Beethoven of song and dance is about to be born," he wrote. The stadium would serve as a base from which to create events that would express "the beauty and joy of an entire people" by drawing upon "the most luxuriant sprouts of folk art, original *sones*, colorful costumes which will spawn new luxury arts, dance which creates music and generates lines of beauty."

As a consequence of the SEP's promotion of folk dance, some English language authors have claimed that Vasconcelos declared the jarabe tapatio as the national dance of Mexico, something that was beyond his power to do as minister of education.[79] There is no known document by Vasconcelos, or by any Mexican president or congress, that would have the necessary authority, making the jarabe tapatío Mexico's "official" dance. It achieved its place by popular acclaim, not political fiat.

By 1930, elements of the Pavlova version of the jarabe, with some even more recent alterations, had become an entrenched element of Mexican life. In the pages of *Mexican Folkways*, editor Frances Toor (1890–1956) observed that: "No Mexican festival is complete without the Jarabe, the national folk dance. It is danced in the villages and in the cities; in the theatres, out of doors, at rodeos, on all sorts of occasions and never fails to arouse a joyous response. A city audience is never quiet while the Jarabe is being danced. It is received with cheers, whistling, clapping of hands, and there is never lacking someone who will give that high pitched rancher's yell expressing real *gusto*."[80]

Although she repeated a good deal of the dubious "history" surrounding the dance and the character of the China poblana, Toor also recognized the influence of Pavlova in transforming the jarabe, particularly the segment performed on the brim of the charro's hat. She also charted some of the continuing interventions into the dance due to the desires of one of the SEP's political functionaries, Carlos Trejo y Lerdo de Tejada, who wanted to see the jarabe reinterpreted as a rite of courtship. In the revision provided by Nellie and Gloria Campobello, the dancers instructed by the SEP no longer faced each other "in the usual way"; instead the charro began to "flirtatiously" follow the female "throughout the entire dance, apparently courting her until she yields." Toor reported that this significantly revised version "aroused wild enthusiasm" for most of its viewers, but that a "Mexican teacher, who still has in mind the Jarabe of the villages, danced modestly by maidens in long skirts with downcast eyes, was scandalized. 'This is not Mexican,' she said." Toor countered with her own interpretation. This new jarabe, she wrote, "is the Mexican of the cities."[81]

In his 1937 history of the jarabe, Mexican musicologist Gabriel Saldivar (1909–1981) noted that when it came to selecting music for teaching the jarabe in the nation's public school classrooms, the SEP selected the arrangements that Castro Padilla created for Pavlova.[82] Saldivar thought much more authentic and musically suitable sources were available and that the Castro Padilla arrangements had "laid good taste aside."[83] The tunes used in what he called this "official" version, he went on to complain, weren't even from Jalisco. He also objected that the "hat dance" segment of the jarabe was an interpolation of Mexico City's urban theaters, which had nothing to do with the dance from Guadalajara.[84] Saldivar didn't fault Pavlova for her interpretation of the jarabe; he blamed her followers. Her version of the jarabe was "an outrage, not for the wonderful performance of the famous artist, but in the feet of her imitators," who retained the variations Pavlova had introduced.[85]

What was worse in his view was that it was being performed by massed dancers instead of a single couple: "Unfortunately for tradition, every day the cold, rigid form required [by these mass performances] is spreading, danced by couples who have no notion of the intent and feeling that real dancers always invest in their Jarabe; so it is becoming mechanical, when its spirit is one of dynamism and emotional freedom; and thus we see the decline, the bankruptcy of the immeasurable value of this national dance *par excellence*."[86]

It was necessary, he concluded, to "put an end to hearing and seeing the convulsions and leaps of this can-can that they've given to us as a Jarabe."[87] His recommendation did not meet with success.

As the authority of the SEP began to extend beyond the nation's capital city, incorporating existing school systems developed by the states and cities and building new schools where they were needed, the folk dance festival became a major form of what historian Mary Kay Vaughn calls "learning by doing."[88] These festivals also served to produce a shared national culture based on folk dances from different regions of the country. In Vaughn's review of educational policy in the decade of the 1930s, *Cultural Politics in Revolution* she outlined the results of this approach to education in different regions of the country: "The result was a nationalization of popular culture as Nahuatl-speaking children in Tlaxcala learned the Yaqui Deer Dance and Tarahumara children learned the criollo *jarabe* of Jalisco. This notion of national, popular culture rested heavily on the achievements of the Indian past and contemporary Indian aesthetics, which were nationalized as symbols, objects, and artifacts. The SEP appropriated them out of their daily context in order to build a common culture. Never abandoned was the notion that although being a Mexican rested on strong indigenous cultural foundations, being Mexican meant becoming modern: adopting urban, Western behavior and culture."[89]

Despite the jarabe's popular updating by the SEP, some of the more avid supporters of modernism saw it as an artifact maintained for strictly touristic purposes. The September 1926 issue of *Horizonte* (Horizon) magazine, a publication of the state of Veracruz that attempted to blend politics and modernist aesthetics, contained a drawing by Carlos González that drove this point home.[90] In the drawing, a man in Western dress leans against an electric lamp post, its light illuminating the window displays of a handicraft shop occupying a modern building. The central display is filled with mannequins of China poblana and charros dancing around a sombrero for their serape-clad audience, a scene designed to attract tourist dollars. The separation between practice and the contemporary realities of urban life in Mexico could not have been more clearly rendered.

The elevation of the now iconic figures of the China poblana and the charro may have been "more of a process of north americanization than of mexicanization," as Pérez argues, but their appeal to Mexican audiences, and subsequently to both Anglo and Mexican American audiences in the United States, was, and remains, undeniable.[91] Ironically, in moving to replace the intoxicating pulque from its popularity, Vasconcelos created a massive public for Pavlova's theatricalized folklore that a writer for the SEP's 1923 issue of its *Bulletin* described as "nearly drunk on the Mexicanism" of the jarabe tapatío.[92]

Always Talk about Me—Tórtola Valencia and the Sandunga

Tórtola Valencia served as the Spanish-speaking world's equivalent of Isadora Duncan (1877–1927), whom she sometimes claimed as her teacher of what she called "natural dance."[93] Having established herself as an artist of the first rank in Spain, she toured widely throughout Latin America, disseminating her particular approach to interpretive dance and cultivating followers among its bohemian communities.

Like many of her companions on the professional stage, Valencia was a self-created figure, so much so that it is difficult to make any statements beyond the information given in her birth certificate about who she actually was. She was born Carmen Tórtola Valencia in Seville on June 18, 1882, to an Andalusian mother, Georgina Valencia Valenzuela, and a Catalan father, Llorenc Tórtola Ferrer.[94] She reveled in attention from the press and understood better than most that providing fantastical tales about her life and work guaranteed that her name and image would appear in the media and promote ticket sales.

She once urged a Mexican reporter, "always talk about me, good or bad, it doesn't matter, what is important is that you don't stop talking."[95] Perhaps one of the most outrageous comments she ever made to the press came in response to a reporter's question about her favorite virtue: "I never lie (funny, no?)."[96] Even the generally accepted tale of how she ended up alone in England as a child—having been left in the care of aristocrats, or at least wealthy antique collectors, by her parents who subsequently vanished in Mexico—raises far more questions than it answers.[97]

Valencia made her first appearance as a "favorite of the king of Spain" on the London stage in 1908, performing "Spanish" dances in the musical *Havana* and, after a whirlwind tour of Vienna, Berlin, and Paris, reappeared at a different London theater as an Algerian dancer.[98] When she finally did arrive in Spain in 1911, she claimed her mother was a Sevillian gypsy and her father a Castilian nobleman.[99] Valencia would, at times, demand the respect due to nobility and she claimed to have created a public scene in Mexico to emphasize her supposed status.[100] At other times, however, she presented herself as the daughter of a lapsed priest turned Egyptologist.[101] Unsurprisingly, even some of her strongest supporters in Spain doubted her claim to Spanish ancestry.[102] She looked the part but spoke relatively little Spanish, and that with a heavy British accent.[103]

Her initial reception in Spain was less enthusiastic than that which she had received elsewhere in Europe. Premiering in a popular music hall, just as she had done previously, ensured a hostile audience for her self-styled dance of the *maja*, or Spanish working-class beauty. Not unreasonably, her Spanish public expected a performance drawn from Spain's substantial repertory of folk dances that would match Valencia's traditional costume, not an arty, interpretive dance.[104] She was, nonetheless, adopted and actively promoted by the nation's intelligentsia, including the painter Hermen Anglada, who had helped introduce so many Latin American artists to the Ballets Russes.[105] They would elevate her performance venue from the music hall to Madrid's prestigious Ateneo (Athenaeum).[106] From this secure position, she would lay successful claim to her position as a maja, lending her image to a popular brand of soap with the same name.

By the time she arrived in Latin America she was promoting herself as the "dancer of the naked feet," claiming that the leading modernist poet in the Spanish language, Rubén Darío, had been inspired by her performance to write one of his most popular verses, "La bailarina de los pies desnudos." The poem preceded her debut as a dancer by a year; her invented biography is rife with such chronological impossibilities, though many noted poets and painters did, in fact, attempt to capture her essence in their works.[107]

Like her counterparts elsewhere, Valencia had her share of imitators, although it is sometimes difficult to determine who was imitating whom. As Clayton points out, nearly all of the interpretive dancers at that time presented a *Salome*, a funeral march, a number from Grieg's *Peer Gynt* (1876), and their own version of Loïe Fuller's *Serpentine Dance*. Valencia herself had lifted ideas not only from Fuller, but also from Pavlova, Ruth St. Denis (1879–1968), and Maud Allen (1873–1956), or their imitators.[108] The advertisement by the Teatro Arbeu announcing Valencia's Mexico City premiere could have been used by almost any dancer on the international theatrical circuit: "Symbolic dances, biblical, plastic attitudes, mythological interpretations, exquisite art, particular beauty. Music of the great masters Beethoven, Grieg, Chopin, Saint Säens, Leo Delibes and Tchaikovsky."[109]

Valencia's most notorious imitator was the violin-playing faux-Russian Norka Rouskaya, who billed herself the "dancer of the silken feet."[110] Like her competitor Valencia, Rouskaya was fond of press attention. She was revealed to the world as Delia Francesco, or Delia Franciscus depending on the newspaper account, then traveling under an Argentine passport in what appears to be a publicity stunt gone awry.[111] In 1917, her postmidnight performance of Chopin's *Funeral March*, clad only in fleshings and gauze, for a group of bohemians in a cemetery in Lima, Peru, earned her all the news coverage she could have desired, as well as prison time.[112] Rouskaya continued to capitalize on that experience, falsely declaring that she had been forced to leave the country because of the incident.[113] Had it not been for this singular event, traces of her presence on the stage would be scarcer than they already are.

Valencia took a safer route by inventing some of her publicity stunts after the fact. She claimed that the January 1918 premiere of her version of *Salome*, by then a well-worn cliché in the world of theatrical dance, created an uproar in Mexico because the prop head of John the Baptist that she

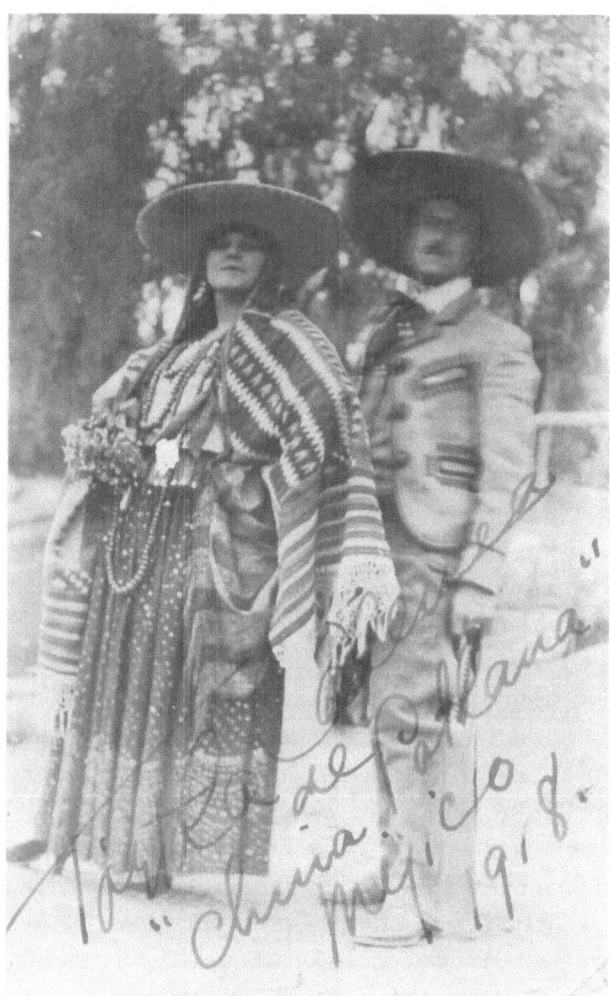

FIGURE 7. Tórtola Valencia as a "China poblana" in Mexico. 1918. Valencia took some liberties with the China poblana's costume by adding the masculine hat and serape, which she used as a kind of rebozo, or shawl. Photographer unknown. Centre de Documentació i Museu de les Arts Escèniques. Institut del Teatre.

used for the performance resembled a recently slain revolutionary leader.[114] Tellingly, none of the dance reviewers in Mexico City made any reference to the supposed controversy, but the story made perfect fodder for writers in other countries eager for exciting tales of her performances in a nation just beginning to emerge from a bloody revolution.[115]

In at least one way, Rouskaya bested Valencia in designing works calculated to please domestic audiences and encourage their aspirations of seeing themselves appear on foreign stages. In Rouskaya's 1919 return to Mexico, she premiered her *Danza Guerrera Azteca* (Dance of the Aztec Amazon). It featured music by Mexican composers Arnulfo Miramontes

(1881–1960) and Alberto Flaccheba (1883–1951), along with sets and costumes by Carlos González.[116]

The pseudonymous Abbot Mendoza, who reviewed Rouskaya's Aztec piece for the *Revista de Revistas*, provided an evocative response to the work for his readers:

> The chant of the war conch echoes and fades away. Hieratic as a figure in a bas-relief, the artist elevates a flash of plumage: heraldic quetzal. Her dark hair sprouts beneath her feathered helm. Mystical offering. The angular music guides and directs the gestures, rhythms rectilinear as an architectural frieze. The Amazon in ambush unfolds like a serpent. Dust, sweat, iron, arise—in the loin of the music—the conqueror. The combat burns. In the leaps, in the steps of march and of attack, the entire beautiful body vibrates, elastic and firm. The race of bronze sinks slowly, vertical, like a crumbling pyramid. The final gesture is of homage: invisible and present, bleeds the new god who came in the caravels amid the turbulent plates of steel, the merciful god on whose forehead the spines interlace like the serpents on a block of trachyte consecrated to Quetzalcóatl.[117]

Other reporters were more attracted to her costume, which apparently made ample use of leopard skin. González explained his design choices in the pages of the newspaper *El Universal*: "It isn't possible to make an exact reconstruction of the attire, nor the music, much less the eurithymic [*sic*] figures of the Aztec dances; the dancer must feel the civilization of the Pre-cortesian epoch from its 'prodigiously barbarous and admirably beautiful' vestiges which remain to us. . . . What's more, the outfits faithfully copied from the codexes and bas-reliefs needed something more visual; one must keep in mind that we weren't attempting an archeological reconstruction to delight ancient, shiny-pated scholars in gold rimmed spectacles, but something theatrical that lent color and brilliance to the show."[118]

In his review, the "abbot" went on to report that this performance, based on a poem by the Yucatecan poet Antonio Mediz Bolio (1884–1957), had "galvanized" the public of Paris—a bit of information apparently gathered from the performer herself. He went on to provide a description of the nationalist hopes that these touring dancers embodied for their publics, unaware that Ted Shawn had already tapped Xochitl for a successful theatrical dance, declaring that Rouskaya's Aztec Amazon was "the first attempt to show the world an aspect of the endless beauty of Mexico. It has nothing to do with presenting Mexican dances to the world, but introducing something much grander to theatrical dance, cosmopolitan dance, the Mexican nuance. An entire theater, an entire school of dance, an entire approach to design esthetics could result from this happy attempt by Norka Rouskaya. What Fokine did in 'Petrouchka' or Nijinsky in 'Noces' can be done with the legend of the 'queen' Xochitl or the maidens sacrificed in the sacred cenote of the Itza, the myth of the 'pustulant' Nahuatl who became the Sun, and a thousand beautiful matters more. Some Mexican 'ballets' using the formula initiated by Norka could do for Mexico what the 'Ballets Suédois' did for Sweden and the 'Ballets Russes' for Russia."[119]

In a 1925 interview in Madrid with Diógenes Ferrand of *El Universal Ilustrado*, Rouskaya claimed to have danced a "Mayan lyric poem" when she appeared in Mérida in 1919. This work was also based on a scenario she claimed was written especially for her by Mediz Bolio, with music drawn from one "Señor Cárdenas." Given a lack of press reports of any actual performance outside the Yucatán, her assertion that the Mayan work was "the number that with the greatest pleasure and the greatest success I have interpreted since that time" is likely as probable as her claims for a standing ovation from a Parisian audience responding to her Aztec dance.[120]

Valencia's biographer Odelot Solrac, the pen name of Cuban Carlos Toledo, claims that although Valencia considered creating works on both Aztec and Mayan themes, they were never produced.[121] Writing of her first visit to Mexico in 1918, Solrac noted that "she began to visualize a solemn pre-Columbian dance. Yet, she could not make it a solo number. She could not explain why but this tentative Mexican creation was seen 'in her mind' as a group of dancers. Yet she was an individualist and could not reconcile her artistic convictions with her choregraphic [*sic*] intuitions. Therefore, her 'Mexican' number never materialized."[122]

On Valencia's return to Mexico in 1923, archaeologist Sylvanus G. Morley (1883–1948) was excavating the Mayan ruins of Chichén Itzá, an event that, Solrac reported: "quickened Tortola's imagination and kept her busy with dance projects on that lost world. There was so much material to work on that it would have taken months to put all that research together and outline a theatrical dance pattern out of it. But she had no time to spend on such projects."[123]

In 1925 Valencia did create a pre-Columbian dance in Peru, which shades of Norka Rouskaya, she called her *Danza Incaica Guerrera* (Dance of the Incan Amazon). Solrac claims that this work was "her favorite number for the rest of her career." He also writes that, following the work's premiere, the president of Peru decorated her for her contribution to Peruvian art. "The decoration consisted of a golden brooch of rubies and diamonds combined as to resemble the Peruvian flag."[124]

When she was back in Spain, Valencia boasted that a museum in Lima had given her the signal honor of extracting an "authentic Incan war costume" from its collections and presenting it to her for use during the work's premiere. The facts were far more prosaic. Just as she had done many times before, Valencia designed her own costume for the work. Judging by a photograph of her attired for performance, the outfit she created owed a substantial debt to Natacha Rambova's (born Winifred Kimball Shaughnessy in Salt Lake City, Utah, 1897–1966) designs for opera star Geraldine Farrar (1882–1967) in Cecil B. DeMille's (1881–1959) Aztec epic *The Woman God Forgot* (1917). According to Solrac, Valencia had visited Hollywood in 1917, where she could well have seen the film or encountered its publicity images.[125]

The Spanish decadent author Antonio de Hoyos y Vinet's (1884–1940) musings about Valencia's Danza Incaica Guerrera illustrate how readily foreign audiences could create a confused Pan-American past from such performances. He claimed her Incan dance evoked images of the Mexican pyramids of Tenochtitlán and that the Aztec court of Moctezuma

led by the hand of the Inca Garcilaso, landscapes, architecture, jewelry, dress and customs were displayed before me in an extraordinary evocation, in a wonderful, blinding flash of colour.

In this concentrated vision, I saw Tenochtitlán, the Venice of the Americas, the city built on a lagoon, with its pyramidal temples made of basalt, its vast palaces with room for entire squadrons of soldiers, and its square-columned glorietas reflected in the still waters: the capital of the Aztec Empire on the solemn day of a religious festival in honour of Huitzicopuli [*sic*]. Under a cobalt-coloured sky, reddened by the sun, I saw the holy cortège of Moctezuma, the High Priest, Tehuatecotl, followed by their retinue, clad in linen tunics embroidered in rare colours and bearing wonderfully-shaped jewels of gold evoking the fauna and flora. And in front of them, weightless, noble and as harmonious as a sculpture, vibrant and ondulating [*sic*] like a serpent, the exalted figure of the wonderful dancer.

. Then, in a cloud of mother-of-pearl, I made out, in front of the holy figure of the Inca, the Son of the Sun, in an extraordinary mise-en-scène, the magnificence of the buildings made in enormous blocks of stone, soldiers clad in gold against the backdrop of the eternal snows of the Andes, and on the horizon the purest blue of the sky where the condors fly, the prodigious scenario of the palace of the Virgins of the Sun, and among the exotic bushes and flowers, jewels of gold and silver that recall Aladdin's royal garden, I make out the holy virgin covered in the richest wools dyed in flaming colours—red, green, blue—and weighed down by golden necklaces. And the face of the virgin always presented the purest Oriental profile, the colour of translucent alabaster, and the emerald, almond-shaped eyes of Tór-tola Valencia.[126]

It was a far less successful work by Valencia that earned her a place in Siqueiros's and Charlot's estimation as a precursor of Mexicanism. During the same 1923 trip to Mexico that had inspired her to consider the possibilities of creating a Mayan work, she offered her version of the sandunga, a traditional dance long associated with strikingly costumed Tehuanas from a Zapotec-dominated region of southwestern Oaxaca. When Vasconcelos was unsatisfied by Rivera's work on his first mural commission, the 1922 *Creación* (Creation), the minister of education sent the painter to the home of the Tehuanas in an attempt to encourage the artist's adoption of a more overtly Mexican subject matter.[127] The trip had its intended effect. Rivera claimed it was then that his "brushes were mexicanized."[128] As Charlot described it, Rivera was smitten by the Tehuanas, "beauteous in their theatrical costume—embroidered blouse as short as a breastplate, stiff conical lace-fringed skirt, incredible headdress of starched linen, huge as a cartwheel."[129] They would become signature figures in his work. According to Charlot, when Tehuanas began multiplying in Rivera's subsequent murals for the patio of the SEP, the comedians at the Teatro Lírico staged a "skit entitled 'The Frescoes of Diegov Rivera.' In its final tableau a very male chorus in Tehuana skirts and cotton braids hopped in a cloppety-hop dance with platters of vegetables stuck to their wigs."[130] Probably at Rivera's request, his wife Frida Kahlo would subsequently adopt more flattering versions of Tehuana attire as her own.[131]

Rather than the melody traditionally associated with the sandunga, Francisco Domingo's *La Tehuana* provided Valencia's score. And contrary to Siqueiros's and Charlot's ascription of the work's designs to José Enciso—who was among the artists that Valencia had gathered around her in Mexico—Carlos González, the same artist who has created Rouskaya's Aztec costume, created Valencia's Tehuana attire.[132] She danced her version of the sandunga in her own "peculiar manner of glossing and animating artistically . . . a Mexican 'air.'"[133]

Truthfully or not, Valencia reported to her fans in Mexico that this piece appeared in Barcelona the following month. In a letter to critic Armando de María y Campos, she transformed it into a work specifically designed to showcase Mexico to a European public, which "was surprised by the costume and not a few asked me 'But does Mexico have the artists to create such a costume?' 'Mexico, my friends,' I replied, 'is a paradise' and when some of my friends, cultured people, of course, have paged through my scrapbooks of news clippings, chronicles, etcetera, they have been surprised and declared that they didn't believe Mexico had such cultured people. Doesn't it seem to you, my friends, that I'm not at all ungrateful, when I show here what you are worth?"[134]

Although Valencia recognized that her version of the sandunga hadn't created a sensation in Mexico, its premiere, occurring just months before Siqueiros and Charlot penned their condemnation of Mexicanism, was fresh on these painters' minds as they sat down to write on the state of the nation's art.

4

The Philosopher as an Artist Writ Large

José Vasconcelos, Muralism, and Folk Art

One of the more enduring myths about Mexican muralism is that it was politically engaged from its very conception. It began, instead, as a manifestation of José Vasconcelos's commitment to an educational theory derived from the Greek classics that equated beautiful environments with more effective learning. He understood the "revival" of muralism as decoration pure and simple and hired his artists for that purpose. What his artists created was to be Mexican—this was a given; how it was to be Mexican went largely unspecified.

Vasconcelos, then rector of Mexico's National University, announced his first mural commission in one of the opening events of Mexico's celebration of the centennial of its independence from Spain on September 8, 1921. He provided a tour of an active construction site that Jean Charlot described as "a forest of scaffolding" permeated by plaster dust raised by the masons.[1] In his haste to convert the chapel of the former Jesuit Escuela Maximo de San Pedro y San Pablo (High School of Saint Peter and Saint Paul), then a disused military barracks, into a centrally located hall for free public lectures, Vasconcelos got a bit ahead of himself. With the assistance of Minister of War Enrique Estrada (1890–1942), he secured control of the barracks and began to convert it into an educational annex for the National Preparatory School. The Ministry of Health attempted to put a halt to his plans. As Vasconcelos noted, the soldiers stationed there used the chapel's apse as their latrine, and the Ministry of Health wrote him to advise that he needed their permission to remove these facilities. "I replied that I lamented their complaint, and that in opening the envelope that contained it I had expected to find congratulations for having removed a focus of infection in the city's center."[2]

Shortly after he commandeered the deconsecrated church, he ordered his first decorative addition to its former choir, a stained glass version of the escutcheon he had created for the National University, designed by Jorge Enciso and realized by Enrique Villaseñor.[3] Borne aloft over the volcanoes and cactus of the Valley of Mexico by a Mexican eagle and an Andean condor, the shield depicts the Americas from the Rio Grande south to Patagonia. It encapsulated Vasconcelos's hopes for the creation of an Ibero-America united against what he saw as the spiritually arid money grubbing of Mexico's powerful neighbor to its north.

Vasconcelos's centennial event culminated with the unveiling of additional stained glass panels, a pair of windows he had commissioned from Roberto Montenegro to decorate the dome that crowned the crossing of the nave. One of them, inspired by a visit Vasconcelos and Montenegro made to Manzanillo, depicted a woman selling birds in a marketplace.[4] The other was a China poblana with her charro and their accompanying musicians, who were performing the jarabe tapatío, a dance from the artist's home state of Guadalajara. The composition's background of a "colonial church and a village street, was redolent of the poetry of our provinces," as critic Julio Torri wrote.[5] Charlot, in his version of the inauguration, reminded his readers that the jarabe was "a tap dance with trimmings, which for certain city folk combines the leg art of a floor show with the uplift of the national anthem."[6]

Vasconcelos had a point to make that extended beyond the content of the window's images. He compared his commission to the twenty-seven-ton Tiffany glass curtain for the city's Palacio de Bellas Artes that the Porfirian government ordered from New York before the revolution began. The work carried out under his direction, he explained, was designed by a Mexican artist and produced by a Mexican artisan, once again Villaseñor. It had cost only 3,500 pesos.[7] No matter that the expensive Tiffany Favrile glass depiction of the volcanoes, which form the backdrop for Mexico City, designed by Harry Stoner (1880–1960), was orders of magnitude larger than the future lecture hall's stained glass lunettes. The fact that the Tiffany curtain also provided fire protection for the theater through its cement and bronze frame was also absent from Vasconcelos's comparison.[8] What was important was that it was an entirely Mexican product from start to finish.

The stained glass windows were not the end of his plans for San Pedro y San Pablo. He was going to have the walls of the church decorated—that was the term that he and the artists he commissioned used to describe their

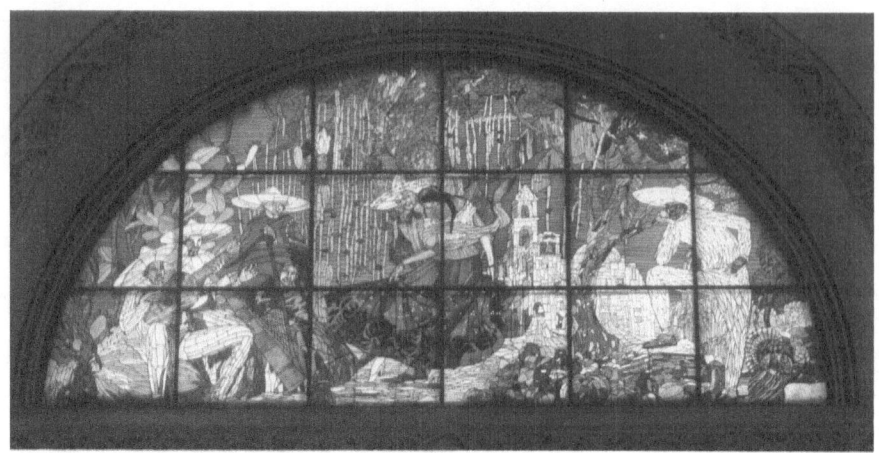

FIGURE 8. Roberto Montenegro. *El jarabe tapatío* (Mexican Hat Dance). 1921. Design executed by Enrique Villaseñor in stained glass. Photograph by the author.

work—with murals.[9] Vasconcelos cited Iamblichus's (245–325) summary of the teachings of Pythagoras (570–495 BCE) in his extended essay on the philosopher, with his claim that people were more impressionable when they contemplated "beautiful forms and figures."[10] His own conclusion was that "what really happens is that in viewing a beautiful object, a new activity is born within the self, a manner of sensing to which one is unaccustomed in the daily tasks or struggles of living."[11] He wished to promote such "new activity" in the temples of learning that he was creating.

The decoration he envisioned was to replace the missing retable at the altar end of the nave, which he also entrusted to Enciso and Montenegro.[12] At the time however, the two artists, along with their friend Dr. Atl, were too busy with another centennial project to take up their new commission. Just as they had worked as a team to create the exhibition of Mexican paintings for the centennial celebrations of 1910, they were then engaged in mounting their Exposición de Arte Popular Mexicano (Exhibition of Mexican Folk Art), which opened a week later.

THE EXPOSICIÓN DE ARTE POPULAR MEXICANO

President Obregón wanted a populist approach to differentiate the centennial celebration under his "revolutionary" administration from the mostly elite events associated with the 1910 event. Rural popular culture was a prevalent theme for those who sought to fill a slot left open by a cancelled industrial fair, which figured prominently in the original plans.[13] Manuel

Gamio, for instance, recommended an exhibition of "aboriginal art."[14] It was the proposal by the three artists from the state of Guadalajara, however, that won the approval of Alberto Pani (1878–1955), minister of foreign relations, who was the driving force behind state sponsorship of the 1921 celebration.[15]

What helped set their proposal apart was its intent of displaying what historian Rick López characterizes as "a common aesthetic foundation that, once revealed, might serve as the basis for national cohesion."[16] This was a concept that the team of artists borrowed from the Russian folk art exhibit at the 1913 Salon d'Automne in Paris, an event that owed its existence to the success of the Ballets Russes on the international stage. As Montenegro phrased it in his autobiography, that exhibition showed him that "the decorations of their chests, their embroideries, their pottery, shared a certain similarity that revealed itself through the artistic intuitions of a people."[17] The trio's secondary aim was to position folk creations as an equal to any other art, which was also an idea behind the Paris exhibition. The catalogue that accompanied that show insisted that "in selecting materials, the organizers were guided solely by the artistic level of each object, independent of its historical or ethnographical meaning."[18]

With only three months to plan and execute the exhibition, the trio, operating as the Comisión de la Exposición de Arte Popular, had to surmount logistical difficulties and educate Mexico's political leadership. The team began writing the governors of each Mexican state requesting samples of the finest Indian handicrafts their people produced, including such items as the toys they had seen in Paris. Their language confused the letters' recipients, who were unaccustomed to seeing the word art associated with locally handcrafted objects. Many replied that their Indians produced no artwork. In response, Enciso sent out a second communication, instructing the governors that the objects made by people "following the traditions of their ancestors and guided by their own artistic sensibility" were "works of art, esteemed by the national and international public."[19]

As they arranged the submissions that arrived, along with items from their own collecting expeditions and loans from the storage rooms of various wealthy families, the team deliberately sought to evoke the outdoor markets where many of these items could be found.[20] The intent, as López explains, was to make it clear that the trio was not simply presenting individual items but evoking an entire way of life in a way that illustrated the possibilities of national unity.[21]

When the exhibit opened, with President Obregón, all his ministers, and the diplomatic community in attendance, its spaces were packed with an appreciative audience.[22] Unlike the limited numbers of attendees necessarily associated with the brief dedication ceremony for Vasconcelos's lecture hall, the longer-term folk art exhibition drew large groups of people from different classes of Mexican society, as well as a number of foreigners. The brief catalogue that Dr. Atl had assembled to document the work quickly sold out, and demand was such that it was re-issued in an updated and expanded two-volume format the following year.

Because the exhibition resembled an overstuffed rural market, it is difficult to determine what was on view through the photographs of this event. The expanded version of the catalogue, however, suggests that the event may have borrowed two of the most revolutionary aspects of the Salon d'Automne exhibition of Russian folk art—its inclusion of religious icons and the urban, and often politically subversive, *lubki* wood-block prints. *Retablos*, folk paintings offered in recognition of the intercession of the saints and the Virgin Mary, took the place of icons. The productions of José Guadalupe Posada and his publisher colleagues at penny presses, such as Antonio Vanegas Arroyo, replaced the lubki.

Retablos shared some of the functions, if not the form, of Russian icons. In his catalogue entry on the subject, Atl claimed that these manifestations of popular faith had all but disappeared by 1910, but the turmoil occasioned by the revolution had revived them. He added that retablos were particularly prized trophies of war by the revolutionary armies: "The revolutionary who fought against the clergy, against the church . . . continued to be profoundly religious and profoundly Catholic. After having sacked a church, they carried these tiny images to the barracks or to their homes so they could light a candle before them, or offer them a tridiuum or charge them with the protection of their families."[23] He noted that after a particularly ferocious attack by government forces, Zapatista troops on the outskirts of Mexico City abandoned a church they occupied as a stronghold, escaping only with their wounded and the entire collection of retablos that once adorned its walls. For all the aesthetic faults he found in them—their color schemes, their perspective, their renderings of the human figure—Atl concluded by citing Diego Rivera's praise from an article that had appeared in the magazine *Azulejos*: "In reality, these are entirely what is called a complete work of art, and they are natural, their purity, their faith in the reality of the marvelous, their love, and their disinterest, reveal everything, including submission to an entirely abstract expression, the 'pure painting' of the moderns."[24]

In everything from subject matter to the ways their central figures dominate their surrounding compositions and the manners in which illustrations interact with their texts, lubki are quite similar to popular Mexican prints. It was these aspects of the lubki that captured the interest of Russian modernists like Mikhail Larionov and earned their inclusion in the Paris exhibition.[25] By incorporating an urban, dissident tradition into his definition of folk art, Larionov was essentially upending the tsarist-era presentation of national identity. In one of their declarations of aesthetic revolt, what would soon be repeated by the leaders of the Mexican muralist movement in almost identical terms, he and his partner Natalia Goncharova wrote: "Long live Nationality! We march hand in hand with our ordinary housepainters."[26] The muralists' consecration of Posada as their precursor would lead to art historian John Scott's declaration in the 1960s that the popular prints in Atl's exhibition catalogue were "the sole part of its content that we can consider to be high art."[27]

As caricaturist Rafael Barajas points out in his study of Posada's political cartoons, what Charlot, Rivera, and others would later say about the popular printmaker was based more on "their own visions and artistic and ideological necessities than on serious historical investigation."[28] Charlot, for example, took credit for rediscovering Posada in an essay on his work for the *Revista de Revistas*. Not only did the essay repeat Atl's misspelling of Posada's name from his catalogue essay on popular prints, it failed to mention that the magazine's editor, Nicolás Rangel (1864–1935), told the publication's readership in 1917 that when it came to Posada "no one can match his perception of the caricaturesque of the lower classes of the capital."[29] Shortly after his arrival in Mexico in 1921, Charlot planned on executing a series of prints of "Mexican types" with his studio-mate Fernando Leal (1896–1964), but press reports on the project concluded that the idea was hardly original, as the prints published by Vanegas Arroyo already met that description.[30] Charlot didn't rediscover Posada; he had never been lost.

Regardless, Posada's work was immensely important in forming what was to come. According to Barajas: "The idea that folk art in the plastic tradition which ought to inspire young Mexican artists was latent in the post-revolutionary intellectual circles, but in placing this artisan, a proletarian artist through and through, as a direct antecedent of post-revolutionary art, a model for young painters to follow at that time, changes many things: it creates an autochthonous genealogy, rooted in the folk, which permits Mexican creators—Diego among them—to encounter their roots far from European art, unyoke themselves from the cultural tutoring of the old world and establish an original national current, distinct from the academy and the vanguards."[31]

Whether Posada's prints were on view or only included in its expanded catalogue, the Exposición de Arte Popular Mexicano proved to be an effective tool for elevating folk art to a position of primary importance in defining Mexico's national character. Shortly after the exhibition closed, a writer for *Azulejos* urged Vasconcelos to ratify its concepts by creating a museum dedicated to folk art: "The Folk Art Exhibition formed the little that was presented of true national work during the fair-dance-fireworks crazy official month. . . . Mr. Minister, let us make a Museum of Folk Art, it will always be something of interest to present to foreign eyes and will surely serve as a stimulus for these beautiful, characteristic things to endure."[32] Although Vasconcelos demurred, the exhibition continues to serve as a template for Mexico's ongoing effort to present the nation's folk artists to both national and international publics.[33]

In his expanded catalogue Dr. Atl took credit for the results produced by the exhibition he and his colleagues had assembled: "Today people of good taste arrange in their homes a living room, a library, a smoking room, 'in the style of the exhibition.' Those who can't afford the luxury of decorating an entire room make do with adorning a divan with a sarape from Oaxaca or arrange their flowers in a vase from Guadalajara, but the desire to manifest the enjoyment of the things of the country is today quite generalized in all of its social classes."[34]

With his characteristic humor, poet Salvador Novo (1904–1974) confirmed Atl's boast of the exhibition's effect on the tastes of his circle of homosexual friends:

> We were enraptured by our visit to the exhibition of folk art installed in the Regis. A painter, Montenegro, recently returned from Europe, had decorated the hall with friezes of stylized cactus and prickly pears cut from green and red flannel. The gourds made into hanging lamps kicked the Porfirian candelabras right out of fashion; the sarapes from Oaxaca, Saltillo, Tlaxcala, were treated like the Gobelins and Persian rugs of yesteryear.
>
> I devoted myself to this style with enthusiasm, scissors, needle, hammer, in decorating our "studio." We placed a big-assed idol, which we called Saint Polencho, at the head of the couch or "stone of sacrifice" to preside over our scenes. And an extreme nationalism led

me to use a small painted gourd as the most fashionable container for the Vaseline necessary for our rites.[35]

Although Dr. Atl claimed he covered every manifestation of popular arts in his catalogue with the exception of cooking—he thought cooking merited its own volume, not of recipes but of philosophy—he barely mentioned Mexican folk dance.[36] Its value as a national symbol was celebrated in another venue during the centennial celebrations of 1921, the Noche Mexicana in Mexico City's Chapultepec Park, which took place under the direction of Adolfo Best on September 26.

The Noche Mexicana

Best conceived the immense party in the park as what twenty-first-century event planners might call an immersive experience. It was an opportunity for his audience to experience the ideas he expounded in his *Metodo de dibujo* with all their senses. He supervised the creation of regional costumes donned by the upper-class women whom he recruited to serve popular snacks from booths he decorated with appropriate handicrafts. They served this food and drink from the kind of ceramics and decorated gourds that were on view at the Exposición de Artes Populares. As the event participants wandered through the park's newly paved roadways, illuminated by equally recent electric street lamps, they encountered small platforms decorated with backdrops featuring designs similar to those Best produced for Pavlova's *Fantasía Mexicana*. These stages hosted dancers and musicians from the far corners of Mexico, such as the states of Sonora and Yucatán, as well as from the more familiar Jalisco.[37] Other pavilions featured recreations of archeological sites like Mitla in the state of Oaxaca and evocations of important events in the nation's history. As art historian María de las Nieves Rodríguez notes, the attendees were able to take "a historical-artistic tour of the entire country in one night."[38]

All of this was prelude to the evening's featured performance, staged on an island within the park's artificial lake. Announced by an extensive fireworks display, Best's theater piece provided the setting for music from the 350-piece Orquesta Típica del Centenario (Centennial Folk Orchestra) under the baton of composer Miguel Lerdo de Tejada (1861–1949). It provided the accompaniment for the sandunga, its strikingly attired Tehuanas dancing before Best's lush evocation of the nation's southern tropics.

Writing under the pseudonym of Jerónimo Coignard for the newspaper *El Universal Ilustrado*, Francisco Zamora described Best's setting for this dance performance in language that suggests a work somehow better fitted for Isadora Duncan: "Sumptuousness of forests, towering and majestic as vegetable cathedrals. . . . Above this scene, women take on a hieratic aspect, a dreamy sensuality. Polychromes arise amid this madness of flowers and foliage, and the elastic profiles of Greek figures. . . . In the distance, the Tehuanas evoke simple and elegant canephori [a female figure bearing a basket on her head] attitudes. They have the instinct of grace, balanced, harmonic sensuality."[39]

This was, consciously or otherwise, an attempt to link Best's appropriation of Mexican handicraft to the much larger trend in post–World War I European modernism, which focused its discourse around the ordered elements of the classical world.

The applause for the sandunga exploding from the audience cued the rise of an image of one of the city's landmark volcanoes, Popocatépetl, from the park's lake. It erupted in another convulsion of fireworks, crowned by an overflight of small planes trailing flares in the red, green, and white of the Mexican flag. The finale was yet to come. This was a version of the *Fantasía Mexicana* Anna Pavlova danced at Best's suggestion just a few years earlier but expanded to match the event's massive audience. María Cristina Pereda, who performed just a few days earlier in a more intimate event for the diplomatic community, joined her brother Armando to lead a thundering rendition of the jarabe tapatío. Armando assumed the task of creating the gigantic sandunga and resizing the *Fantasía Mexicana* to fit its outdoor setting, incorporating at least two dozen couples into its rendition and setting a trend in performance of the work that would last to the present day. It was this scene that inspired "shouts of joy and deafening ovations."[40]

According to the official program for the event, the finale was intended to emphasize the underlying unity of Mexico's regional cultures. It was "intended to be a synthesis of our autochthonous art, the figures fade into darkness; there will be a simplification of costumes; superficial aspects of the china poblana and the tehuana will be softened to come together in the quintessential Mexican woman, full of grace and discrete harmony."[41]

Estimates of the total crowd at the original event reached nearly two hundred thousand spectators, about 20 percent of the entire population of Mexico City at the time.[42] The presentation proved so popular that it was subsequently restaged in a slightly altered form—presumably without the fireworks—at the upscale Teatro Arbeu, where Pavlova premiered her balleticized jarabe. Even given the likelihood of an exaggeratedly optimistic attendance report, Best's Noche Mexicana reached a far larger swath of the city's tastemakers than the Exhibition of Popular Arts could hope to host within its precincts. Some of the success in promoting folk art as a representation of the nation's essence that Atl claimed as his own was likely due to Best's efforts and those of his assistant in all things artistic for the Noche Mexicana, a preternaturally talented sixteen-year-old named Miguel Covarrubias, who gained his first experience as a set designer through this project.[43]

López divides the approaches taken to promoting folk art as part of the national identity by the Exhibition of Popular Arts and the Noche Mexicana into two distinct categories. He emphasizes Dr. Atl's notion that folk art existed as an inviolate category unto itself and Alt's dictum that for an outsider to touch it was to destroy its nature: "Mexico's handicrafts were expressions of an entire collective history, or a race, and of a nation. Popular arts production could not be rationalized, and their aesthetics could not be improved on. . . . Dr. Atl's artisans did not learn, study, practice, refine their art, or make difficult economic and political decisions. Instead, they possess innate skills as a result of being racially indigenous and culturally pristine."[44]

For López, the Noche Mexicana, by contrast, represents Best's attempt to show how trained artists could take the elements of folk art and, through the adoption of modernist principles, repurpose them to create a new definition of the national.

The difference between these two approaches is not always so easily demonstrated. Montenegro was as enthusiastic a supporter of conserving the qualities of the nation's folk art as was his partner Atl. Yet he was just as involved as Best in adopting elements derived from folk art in the realization of his own work—most visibly in the first mural commissioned by the postrevolutionary government. Even before Montenegro's first Mexican mural, his fellow painter Carlos Mérida credited him with employing this strategy to achieve the essence of the national: "It is necessary, in the making of nationalist art, to fuse the essential part of our autochthonous art with our current spirit and our current sensibility, not in its exterior, or, so to speak, theatrical form, but in its essential, spiritual form. . . . Up until now, no one, with the exception of Roberto Montenegro, has used these elements to give us a nationalist note."[45]

While everyone agreed that nationalist art ought to express some identifiably Mexican spirit, not everyone agreed that folk art properly represented the nation. The use of the folkloric, whether through direct presentation or indirect appropriation, was a far-from-accepted mode of identifying the national in 1921 and remained controversial despite its demonstrated success in the centennial celebrations. An editorial writer for the relatively conservative daily newspaper *Excélsior* complained about the "so-called artists who under the pretext of originality present the rudimentary and primitive forms of the pre-Cortesian peoples to the multitudes as models of art and beauty. Undoubtedly, there is art in them and there is beauty; but this does not lie in its imperfection, resulting from a lack of technical knowledge; and its merits, cannot, and ought not be imitated by a modern man who pretends to call himself an artist. If the painter of popular pots and platters draws imperfectly, all well and good! But that the Nation spends its money on a crowd of poseurs who, unable to produce, entertain themselves in copying badly what the Indian potters and platter creators do well, is beyond our ability to comprehend."[46]

The more liberal Charlot/Siqueiros collaboration criticizing Mexico's emerging nationalist art under the pseudonym of Juan Hernández Araujo was similarly dismissive of what they described as "Mexicanist" art:

They have primarily taken the study (more or less complete) of the folk ceramic decoration as the departure point for the decoration of walls or the painting of pictures, forgetting the immutable law, established by logic, that to learn and properly execute something one should direct oneself to Works that were developed in such media, and used for the same purposes, that is to say: If one wants to learn how to paint walls one should take recourse in the mural tradition and not attempt to discover the secrets of this highly particular specialty in a nationalist jar.

The decoration of a jar, more than any other architecture or material volume, is solely complementary; to rip it from its generative medium is to mutilate the whole, and to transport it to a wall, or any other different surface is an enormous plastic folly.[47]

As Charlot related in *The Mexican Mural Renaissance*, he and Siqueiros had not consulted with Rivera on his views about the subject before publishing their essays. Rivera, who was just beginning work on his murals for the SEP, with their ample representation of topics drawn from Mexican popular culture, was not happy with "Hernandez."[48]

THE FIRST POSTREVOLUTIONARY MURAL

The Hernández alias of Charlot and Siqueiros emerged almost immediately after the dedication of Montenegro's *Arbol de la Vida* (Tree of Life) mural in Vasconcelos's *Sala de Conferencias Libres*. It was this series of essays that took Montenegro to task for employing "foreign influences (from modern choreography, especially Russian and North American)."[49]

Although the Ballets Russes toured in the Americas, it never stopped in Mexico. Diaghilev agreed to present his company in the United States and Argentina only because the circumstances surrounding World War I and the Russian Revolution made touring in Europe nearly impossible.[50] He certainly wasn't going to risk staging his work in another wartime situation; even if Mexico had been at peace, its theaters would not have been able to meet the stringent space and technical demands for staging his productions. Still, Diaghilev's company and its designers left a mark on the Mexican artists working in Paris at the time of the revolution.

El arbol de la vida displays affinities with the early designs Léon Bakst created for the Ballets Russes, just as Rivera pointed out in one of his essays on nationalist art in *Azulejos*.[51] Montenegro's line of flattened female figures also evokes the "primitive" choreography Nijinsky created for his *L'Après-midi d'un Faune*. But it is unfair to suggest that the works of Bakst and Nijinsky were direct inspirations for the mural. Montenegro was exploring similar forms even before his encounter with the Ballets Russes. Still, it was the idea that appreciation of folk art was central to artistic progress that aligned Montenegro with the ideas of Vasconcelos, who admired Diaghilev and wanted to construct a new classicism on the foundation of Mexico's folk art.[52]

Montenegro's mural probably comes closest to expressing the aesthetic that Vasconcelos had in mind. Much to the displeasure of Montenegro's fellow artists, he received the vast majority of the mural commissions that Vasconcelos made. He was, for all intents and purposes, Vasconcelos's de facto official artist.[53]

Although Vasconcelos was much lauded by other artists for his refusal to provide thematic direction on the subject matter for the murals he commissioned, his "hands off" attitude seems to have been something he learned from his first experiences with both Montenegro and Rivera.[54] Vasconcelos confessed his doubts about Montenegro's *Tree of Life* in the first person. The work, he wrote, "suffered from a certain poverty. We couldn't decide what to represent and I gave the painter a bit of Goethian nonsense as a theme:

'Action overcomes destiny: Conquer!'"[55] This motto, which is not, in fact from Goethe, is prominently displayed on a placard adorning the branches of the tree that the mural depicts.[56]

For his *Tree of Life* mural, Montenegro combined elements that he had seen in the ceramics from Tonalá, near his hometown of Guadalajara, and the lacquered *bateas*, or platters, from the neighboring state of Michoacán. In the mural, the tree's branches are alive with a profusion of flowers, birds, and even wildcats, all elements derived from folk art and reinterpreted in an art nouveau sensibility and palette. At the base of the tree stand a dozen women, all but one in "classical" attire; the exception has dark skin and is clad in a dress with designs drawn from the repertory of pre-Columbian textile traditions. In the work's center, an incongruous knight in black armor stands before the tree's trunk. The knight was a last minute addition to the work. Photographs of the original painting depict a nearly nude man, gaze averted and body curved sinuously against the tree. He is held captive by the women who hold the length of fabric that covers his loins.[57]

In her detailed study of Montenegro's murals, Julieta Ortiz Gaitán proposes that the addition of the knight to the mural was made "at the insistence of Vasconcelos, who could not have appreciated the image of a nearly naked man tied to a tree and serving as an archery target for a group of women."[58] By contrast, she finds the figure of the knight "consistent with the aspirations of greatness and the cult of the hero worship in Vasconcelos's thought."[59] Given that several preparatory studies for the mural exist and that Vasconcelos printed photographs of the nearly completed work in his *Boletín de la Secretaría de Educación Pública* with the nearly nude male and the bare-breasted females plainly visible, he likely didn't instigate its censorship.[60] Other sources suggest that it was President Obregón who declined to inaugurate the mural "unless the bodies in their birthday suits were covered."[61]

The mural itself is located above a frieze of *azulejos*, blue and white tiles widely used in postconquest architecture, with insets designed by Gabriel Fernández Ledesma (1900–1983). These include depictions of a caravel in full sail in honor of ex–President Benito Juárez (1806–1872) and a monumental gateway in viceregal style dedicated to Porfirian-era Education Minister Justo Sierra. The four corners of the crossing are flanked by larger-than-life-sized carved stone sculptures of Aztec warriors in elaborate loincloths rendered in an early art deco style. These are most likely by Manuel Centurión (1883–1952), who honed his style in the California studios of Francisco Cornejo (1892–1963) after the fall of President Francisco Madero

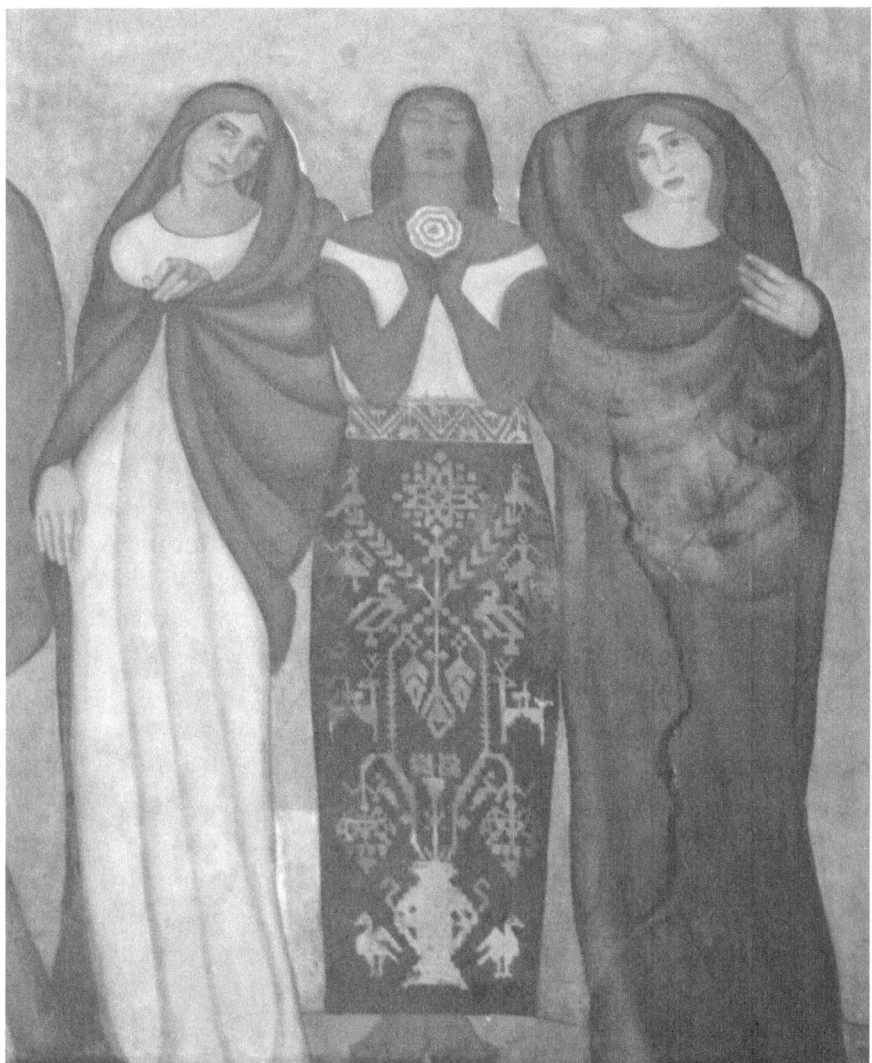

FIGURE 9. Roberto Montenegro. Detail from *El Arbol de la Vida* (The Tree of Life). 1922.
Photograph by the author.

in 1913.[62] Each of the warriors is carrying a stylized platter, which served as
planters for the mural's dedication ceremony and were later refitted as light
fixtures, on his head.[63] The carvings on the platters, in turn, reflect the decorations painted by Xavier Guerrero (1896–1974) and Herminio Jiménez
that extend beyond the mural to cover the arches, vaults, and the surrounds
of the doors leading out of the crossing in jewel-like tones of blue, gold,
pink, and green.[64] According to Charlot, Enciso donated an antique platter

to provide the inspiration for these details, his only notable contribution to the project.[65] The whole, particularly when combined with the stained glass lunettes and the shield of the National University in stained glass at the opposite end of the apse, served to create what Vasconcelos envisioned, an educational space that was also a total work of art.

Even without the nude figure, Montenegro's reinterpretation of the motifs used in decorating traditional Mexican ceramics from Guadalajara and the lacquer ware from neighboring Michoacán provoked controversy. An arts writer for the *Revista de Revistas* declared: "Bluff is the word written on the studio door of each one of those fashionable artists who climb the steps of a certain infatuated Minister. . . . The official backing that artists of the caliber of Roberto Montenegro and Adolfo Best receive can foster only ridicule."[66]

The mural was even less popular with the artists who envied the stream of commissions that Vasconcelos granted Montenegro—including murals for the minister's personal office and other important spaces within the SEP's new building and the National Preparatory School. Charlot raised the influence of the Ballets Russes yet again in the pages of *The Mexican Mural Renaissance*, where he claimed that the finished work, with its "lineal beauty of lacquer and pottery patterns, with their balance of flat areas, was not unlike that of Persian miniatures, then the fashion in a Paris all agog over Poiret turbans and Bakst costume designs. Because of the similarity, the works of Best and Montenegro were enthusiastically received by people of informed tastes."[67] Mexico's fashion-conscious community was well aware of what was in vogue in France and would have known that Poiret's Asian fashions faded from view in Paris nearly a decade before Montenegro completed his mural.[68]

Although he did not cast aspersions on Montenegro's homosexuality as Rivera and Siqueiros did, Charlot made his personal antipathy to the artist and his earliest mural evident in his history of muralism. He reprinted Rivera's insult to *The Tree of Life*, claiming that it was nothing more than an empty attempt to "'pot the walls of San Pedro and San Pablo."[69] He also repeated his pseudonymous condemnation of Montenegro, "hoping to discover the secrets of this very specialized trade in a national jug," as if it were the opinion of an independent authority rather than, as he admitted nearly one hundred pages later, his own words.[70] Charlot failed to explain how this idea squared with his earlier assertion that "in Mexico . . . the utensils of daily use . . . are of as solid a beauty as those of any of the most classic civilizations," which had their own extensive history as subjects for artists from the Renaissance forward.[71] Nor did he explain how Rivera, who was one of the artists Orozco characterized as "tickled silly at the sight of our Mexican pots and pans," was somehow immune from this dictum.[72]

By 1927 Vasconcelos's presidential aspirations earned him the opposition of Mexico's leftists. Siqueiros denounced him for his "strange metamorphosis" from a "mystical Buddhist" to a "reactionary of the extreme right" in an article published in the June 1927 issue of *El Machete*.[73] Vasconcelos's candidacy provided Rivera, who clashed with Vasconcelos, a pretext for including him in a mural, *Los sabios* (The Sages), likely completed the following year, in the *Patio de las Fiestas* of the SEP. He depicted Vasconcelos perched on a tiny elephant, his back turned on the spectator. The entwined hands of Russian-born Berta Singerman (1907–1998), a professional poetry performer whom Vasconcelos reportedly seduced in the ruins of Teotihuacán, shelter his head.[74] Rabindranath Tagore, one of the few contemporary authors Vasconcelos promoted through his publications program, sits in the work's visual center, crowned with a funnel converted into a dunce's cap. Though not visible in Rivera's *Los sabios*, Montenegro is also a presence within its conceptual framework. As its name suggests, *Los sabios* is Rivera's response to the murals Montenegro created for Vasconcelos's office within the SEP in 1922 and 1923, *La sabiduría* (Wisdom) and *Personajes de la historia* (Figures from History). The left side of the first is dominated by a gigantic elephant bearing Buddhist figures, while the right side of the second depicts Singerman.

Whatever good will Vasconcelos may have derived from his early commissions to the members of what would become the Mexican school of painting evaporated, along with his ideas about creating beautiful images to decorate uplifting educational spaces meant to unify the nation. The political posturing that marked what would become known as the Mexican school was entering full bloom. The aesthetic proposed by Montenegro and embraced by Vasconcelos was effectively sidelined by the other muralists whose work was more obviously aligned to the prevailing politics of the time. "The currents of the moment . . . fitted poorly with the artist's elegant decorative sense," Justino Fernández writes in summarizing Montenegro's place within muralism.[75] "It has nothing to do with an inability to resolve compositions or organize forms, but of a spirit distinct from that which drove the works by Orozco, Rivera and Siqueiros."

5

Dancing a Sandunga in English

Carlos Chávez and Diego Rivera in the United States

The single most important individual in determining the role that Mexico's visual artists exerted on the creation of its nationalist theatrical dance was not a painter but a musician—Carlos Chávez. Although *New York Times* dance critic John Martin thought Chávez's score for his first produced ballet, *H.P.* (1932), lacked "a choreographic sixth sense," the composer was determined to make a name for himself through his dance compositions.[1] Just as Serge Diaghilev fulfilled Parisian perceptions of Russia as a colorful, exotic country to ensure the success of his early Ballets Russes productions, Chávez traded on the Indian conception of Mexico that permeated his audience in the US. He parlayed the international attention his music received into a series of highly influential posts within Mexico's cultural bureaucracy, which gave him, at first indirect influence, then eventually full creative control over its state-sponsored theatrical dance.[2]

Chávez's involvement in theatrical dance was unlike that of Stravinsky, who built his composing career on his multiple successes with Diaghilev's Ballet Russes and had a particular interest in dance itself. Although theatrical entertainment, including dance, survived and even thrived during the revolution in Mexico City, in all likelihood, Chávez had never seen a full-fledged ballet, much less a Ballets Russes–style production. He appears to have taken up ballet composition because of the substantial notoriety and financial success that followed, if not accompanied, a commission from Diaghilev.[3] In both word and action throughout his career, Chávez demonstrated that he had little confidence in dancers. His interactions with choreographers ranged from dismissive—with the young Catherine Littlefield (1905–1951), who choreographed *H.P.*—to fraught—with the more established Martha Graham, who arranged the commission for what became

Dark Meadow (1946). He did, however, believe Mexico's visual artists had the talents needed to determine the direction of its dancers.

Writing in 1954, Chávez attempted to claim the same genealogy for his career that Mexico's celebrated muralists enjoyed when he asserted that he was commissioned by José Vasconcelos to compose his first ballet score, the 1921 *Toxiumolpia: El fuego nuevo* (The Binding of the Years: The New Fire).[4] Chávez's version of the commission story begins with minister of public education inviting former Ballets Russes dancer Adolph Bolm to visit Mexico in 1921. The composer claimed that he and Dominican-born writer Pedro Henríquez, who worked alongside Vasconcelos in the *Ateneo de la Juventud Mexicana* (Athenaeum of Mexican Youth) in the opening years of the twentieth century, met frequently with Bolm during his stay.[5] He also asserted that it was the three of them who came up with the idea of producing Mexican ballets, an idea that Henríquez successfully presented to Vasconcelos, "who immediately commissioned [Chávez] to do them, facilitating some economic means." Roberto García Morrillo's biography of Chávez adds that Bolm attempted to conduct rehearsals with a group of dancers he managed to assemble during his short stay in Mexico, but nothing came of the effort due to lack of support from Mexico's musical bureaucracy.[6] As the SEP was not a week old when Bolm arrived back in the US from his visit to Mexico and Vasconcelos had not yet been named as its minister, there are serious chronological problems with Chávez's account of the commissioning of his first ballet score.[7]

It isn't clear why Bolm had been invited to Mexico by its Centennial Committee, of which Vasconcelos was not a member.[8] A likely candidate for having instigated the invitation was the committee's secretary, Martín Luis Guzmán, who had written admiringly about the Ballets Russes for the *Revista Universal* in 1916. Bolm did hold discussions with artists and musicians other than Chávez about the possibility of establishing a Mexican ballet company during his visit. Bolm impressed upon Manuel Castro Padilla, who arranged the jarabes Pavlova used for her *Fantasía Mexicana*, and Adolfo Best, who created her costumes and sets for the work, the importance of Mexico forming its own ballet company.[9] He also imparted his opinion of the certain success of such a company due to the colorful nature of the nation's dances. He had certainly been part of the audience for Best's Noche Mexicana and experienced firsthand the excitement generated by its performances of the jarabe tapatío and the sandunga.

Chávez stated that Bolm was long gone from Mexico before he decided that the New Fire ceremony of the Aztecs provided suitable material for the creation of his first ballet.[10] Both García and musicologist Robert Parker classify Chávez's *El fuego nuevo* as the initial manifestation of the composer's Mexicanism.[11] García went on to stress the purported influence that Mexico's indigenous music had on influencing the composer's decision. In reality, as musicologist Leonora Saavedra points out, in 1921 "Chávez's main ambitions were to become a modern composer and to master the European classical forms."[12] Had the composer used truly indigenous music as his point of departure, Vasconcelos, who supposedly commissioned the ballet, would not have been pleased. Musically, Vasconcelos thought Ludwig van Beethoven (1770–1827) ought to be the source of inspiration for his people.[13]

Vasconcelos was interested in creating a Mexican dance tradition but one that was based on its European inheritance. He recognized that Serge Diaghilev based his success not only on a "system of folklore" but on the specific way that he presented his "system" through modernized classical dance. He saw how Diaghilev combined these elements in a way that allowed Russia to become what art historian Sjeng Scheijen called the "victor in the glittering tournament of European culture."[14] This was one of the aspirations that lay behind Vasconcelos's efforts: a place for his nation in the firmament of "universal" culture—a culture whose "universality" he saw largely in terms of the Western canon.

Looking back on his career as minster of education several years after his departure and embittered by the changes that his successors implemented to his programs, Vasconcelos decided that his aspirations to "create an art like that of the Russian dancers" was misplaced: "The problem was complicated because we counted on musicians and choirs with the most perfect intonation and sweetest timbre for the ensemble exhibitions. And our lucid festivals acclaimed by the full concurrence to a stadium of more than sixty thousand people, did not pass, artistically speaking, the category of the parade and the company of singers and dancers, in their creole costume or Spanish outfits, were completely lacking in any meaning of social and artistic synthesis."[15]

His description focused on the presence of dances from the Creole or Spanish cultures, without any reference to Mexico's preconquest civilizations. As Saavedra points out, Vasconcelos's early festivals included only three pieces with ties to Mexico's indigenous peoples.[16] The first, *Los Inditos* (Little Indians), was indigenous in name only, and with the use of the diminutive in its title it was certainly not intended to exalt Indian culture. The second, Yucatecan composer Cornelio Cárdenas Samada's (b. 1888) *Danza*

Maya, which depicted the last resident of Chichén Itzá bidding farewell to the city, was apparently set to the "Mayan lyric poem" originally composed for Norka Rouskaya during her 1919 visit to the Yucatan.[17] Only the *Baile regional Yaqui*, performed by the Yaqui contingent of the nation's Presidential Guard, which included a version of the Yaqui deer dance that subsequently joined the canon of Mexican folk dances, could be regarded as an indigenous work. Even then, the SEP's Dirección de Cultura Estética worked with the performers of this "strange and suggestive" indigenous dance to stylize it for its urban audience.[18]

In her review of Mexican nationalist music of the twentieth century, Saavedra concludes that Chávez's account of the commissioning of *El fuego nuevo* posed additional problems. "There is little to suggest that Vasconcelos would have had any particular interest in evoking or recreating the ceremony of the New Fire or any other Aztec myth. . . . The conception of *El Fuego Nuevo* was mostly Chávez's."[19] She added that there was "no evidence to suggest that Vasconcelos commissioned any work of Mexican art music: the muralist painters do not find their parallel among the Mexican nationalist composers."

Chávez's treatment of the Aztec ritual in the scenario he created for his ballet also reveals his discomfort with Aztec culture, which he frames, as Saavedra put it, "as an Other from the past."[20] His libretto completely drained the ritual it pretended to represent of its central elements, denaturing its content and vitiating its theatrical potential.

The drama inherent in the Aztec New Fire ceremony was enormous. The close of every fifty-two-year period in the Aztec calendar was a time when its much larger, epochal cycles of "suns" might end in calamity. The daily rounds of life in the Aztec world came to a halt in anticipation of this potentially deadly event. As the sun rose on a possibly "final" day, the people destroyed their woven reed beds, their kitchen hearths and cookware, and began a day of fasting. As night fell, their priests, each clad in the attributes of an Aztec god, assembled for a slow, silent march to the Hill of the Star in Itzpapalapa, roughly 15 kilometers (more than nine miles) from the center of ancient Tenochtitlán. Women and children disguised themselves behind masks made from the wide leaves of the maguey cactus. Everyone extinguished their fires. As midnight neared and the Pleiades reached their apex, the chief priest of the neighborhood of Copilco took a captured warrior, stretched him across the stone of sacrifice atop the Hill of the Star, and cut out his heart. With the assistance of the full pantheon of the costumed priests, he kindled a new fire in the chest of the sacrificial victim. If he failed in his fire-making task, the Aztecs believed the night would never end and beings known as the *tzitzimime* would descend to devour the world and its inhabitants. When the fire was finally kindled, the priests heaved the sacrificial body onto a giant pyre and ignited pitch pine torches from the burning body for runners to carry to all the communities throughout the valley. The priests cut their ear lobes to draw blood, adding their own blood sacrifice to that which was wafting to the heavens from the blazing pyre. The runners, on reaching the surrounding communities, relit the ceremonial braziers in each temple, then continued on to ignite community bonfires. Each householder, in turn, carried a portion of this new fire back to their homes to light their kitchen fires once again and don new attire in this celebration of the continuation of human life.[21] One can only imagine what Diaghilev and his associates might have done with such material.

Chávez's libretto for the ballet contained none of this drama. Its opening segment, the "Danza de temor" (Dance of Fear) was intended to depict the terrors induced by the night dwellers who could destroy humankind.[22] Chávez called for the dancers dressed as priests to enter the stage slowly, their whole bodies contorted by apprehension, and throw themselves face first to the floor. There they were to remain for most of the ballet. They were to be followed by a group of female dancers in what the composer called the "Danza sagrada" (Holy Dance). The female dancers were to use "hieratic movements, simple and contained, that have the plastic values of a frieze in motion. . . . This frieze has no depth, the space within which it develops allows only displacements—always slow and reduced—from right to left and vice versa, and no movement from front to back." The ensuing "Danza de los guerreros" (Dance of the Warriors) called for movements that were "rigid . . . energetic . . . frenetic and savage, although always orderly," employing the basic forms of Aztec circle and line dances described in postconquest sources. A single call from a conch shell trumpet brought the dancers dressed as priests to their knees to mime the creation of fire by rubbing two sticks together, with the entire company of dancers turned away from the audience to monitor their efforts. Once the new fire was kindled, Chávez called for a final "Danza de alegría" (Dance of Joy). This section of the ballet finally allowed all the dancers to make use of the entire performance space with movements that were, alternately, "uniform" and "indefinitely variable" but that still allowed them to carry torches before departing the stage one by one while the curtain slowly descended to bring the performance to its close.

The composer's reference to movement derived from "the plastic values of a frieze" suggests he was aware of Diaghilev's ballet version of *L'Après-midi d'un Faune*'s origins as "a moving bas relief."[23] In doing so, he furthered the idea that the static art of the Aztecs was a source for ideas about dance movement, a proposition that was already accepted by modernist dance makers in the Americas. The publicity team for Cecil B. DeMille's *The Woman God Forgot* produced an interview with the film's costar, former Ballets Russes dancer Theodore Kosloff, in which, as he related, he asserted a "deep study of Aztec paintings and drawings to portray the dance correctly in my present interpretations. . . . The poses used by the Aztecs in dancing were, many of them, quite reminiscent of the ancient Egyptians, and it is not hard for one familiar with the latter to recreate the Aztec dance motifs."[24] A few years later Ted Shawn professed a similar inspiration for developing the movement in his *Xochitl*, which made Martha Graham a star. Shawn's reading of William H. Prescott's (1796–1859) *History of the Conquest of Mexico* (1843) and Lew Wallace's (1827–1905) *The Fair God* (1873) inspired "a constant searching of the libraries of the country, as I one-night-standed [*sic*] month after month, each season. . . . I was fortunate also in spending some days in the library of the University of Texas, just after it had received the shipment of a private library purchased in Mexico City, a collection of over a million pieces, books, codices, pamphlets and prints dealing exclusively with the prehistoric civilizations of Mexico."[25]

Chávez employed the pentatonic scale to create "ancient" Aztec sounds for his score to *El fuego nuevo*, a tool that composers in the Western tradition regularly used for representing non-Western cultures. It was a tool that, as Saavedra notes, Chávez used to "encode . . . Otherness."[26] Despite this, Chávez claimed to have created *El fuego nuevo* based on his memories of the indigenous music from the state of Tlaxcala that he heard as a child.[27] *El fuego nuevo* was Chávez's first attempt to recreate an Aztec sound. He did cite known indigenous themes in later works but usually invented his "ancient" sounds for the pre-Columbian percussion instruments he specified in his scores, just as he did for his first ballet.[28] His ambitious scoring called for thirteen percussionists who used indigenous percussion instruments and whistles, as well as string instruments and a female chorus. Chávez went on to describe the unusual instruments he called for in his score, adding instructions as to how to play them and suggestions for more readily accessible substitutions if the instruments he designated weren't available.

The Mexico City–born composer later claimed that he wrote his works inspired by indigenous music "because this was the first music that I heard in my life, which has nourished my taste and musical consciousness in a fundamental way."[29] Because he also began piano studies at a very early age under the instruction of his older brother, the composer's oft-repeated assertion that the first music he ever heard was indigenous cannot be taken at face value.[30] His claim most likely developed as a response to the political tenor of his times. In their study of Mexican musical nationalism, historians Marco Velázquez and Mary Kay Vaughn called Chávez "a polyphonic opportunist, adopting styles to play to the moment. An experimentalist in the 1920s, he became *indigenista* . . . in the 1930s."[31]

At least as early as 1924, Chávez began to write his acquaintances in New York and Paris for news of Diaghilev and advice as to how he might present his *El fuego nuevo* to him. In 1925 Miguel Covarrubias introduced his and Chávez's mutual friend, Octavio Barreda (1897–1964), then serving in Mexico's consular office in New York, to Matisse's son, who promised to translate one of Chávez's ballet librettos into French and present it to Diaghilev.[32] That same year, Chávez's painter friend Augustín Lazo (1896–1971), who voluntarily prepared stage and costume designs for the mounting of *El fuego nuevo*, reported back from his studies in Europe that he had met Max Jacob (1876–1944), a member of Diaghilev's inner circle.[33] Jacob thought that an Aztec-themed ballet would be a tremendous hit in Paris. Jacob arranged a meeting between Lazo and another poet associated with Diaghilev, Jean Cocteau (1889–1963), who provided the Ballets Russes with the librettos for *Le Dieu Bleu* (1912), *Parade* (1917), and *Le Train Bleu* (1924). According to Lazo, Cocteau presented the idea of an Aztec ballet to Diaghilev, who found it intriguing, but declined to produce it because he lacked funding.[34] Ironically, it was the successes of such theatrical events as the Covarrubias-designed *Revue Nègre* (1925) that placed a strain on Diaghilev's finances at that time.[35] For his part, Covarrubias told Chávez that he found the Ballets Russes programming, with the exception of *Mercure* (1924/1927) and the 1927 *Le Pas d'Acier* (Step of Steel), "unspeakably dull" and that Diaghilev was "interested solely in pleasing wealthy old ladies." He further opined that it was "absolutely useless" for the composer to pursue a Ballets Russes production.[36]

By 1925, Chávez completed the score for another ballet, *Los cuatro soles* (The Four Suns), revisiting the Aztec world through another libretto he prepared himself, this time to music he claimed to have borrowed from the Mazahua people.[37] While acknowledging the work's antecedents, US music critic Paul Rosenfeld (1890–1946) characterized Chávez's score for his second ballet as a departure from Stravinsky's primitivism. Its music was, he wrote, "Amerindian, full of shrill and piping tones, at once ferocious and reserved. Indeed, it has an almost fresco-like quality, as if it, too, were inscribed on a temple wall in Chitchen-Itza [*sic*]. . . . While the score might not have found its present shape had not the ballet-movements of *Petrushka* [*sic*] and *Le Sacre* proceeded it, the mixed rudeness and shyness and austerity distinguish it entirely from Russian works."[38]

Chávez's original score for *Los cuatro soles* called for fewer percussionists than his first ballet, but his ideas for staging it were more ambitious than his plans for *El fuego nuevo*.[39] *El fuego nuevo* simply called for representing the apex of an Aztec pyramid; *Los cuatro soles* required representing distinct stages of creation, the "suns" of water, wind, fire, and earth.

According to Parker, Chávez developed the work's libretto by consulting paintings from the *Codex Vaticanus*, which depicted four scenes of creation and the agents of destruction of the first three suns.[40] Like his future collaborator Diego Rivera, Chávez seemed to prefer the Europeanized images of these postconquest Aztec documents.[41] *Los cuatro soles* demonstrated just as much unease with Aztec thought as *El fuego nuevo*. The codex that provided his text describes Aztec practices in Christian terms as a kind of satanic counterfeit of the Bible.[42] According to the program notes Chávez wrote for a symphonic performance of *Los cuatro soles*, the Aztec's sequential creations described a Judeo-Christian cosmos: "Divine grace had saved a pair, male and female, to whom we owe the continuation of the species. The tradition of the Four Suns repeats, in each catastrophe the very miracle of Noah, saved in his ark."[43] Though beginning with the flood made his libretto somewhat more congruent with the Bible, the disasters he depicted in his ballet are out of the sequence with the more typical Aztec creation story involving five suns that was recorded in the famed Aztec Sunstone and different versions of the myth from other sources.[44] For the Aztecs, the fifth "sun," or sun of movement, represented their own era. Ironically, for a dance composition, the sun of movement wasn't mentioned in Chávez's scenario.

During a multiyear visit to New York beginning in 1927, which he embarked upon with painter Rufino Tamayo (1899–1991), Chávez worked to convince producer Irene Lewisohn (1886–1944) to present his *Los cuatro soles* as part of her performance schedule at the Neighborhood Playhouse. Failing at that, he turned to Rivera's agent, Frances Flynn Paine (1895?–1964?), for help in securing a production of either *El fuego nuevo* or *Los cuatro soles*. It was then that the composer began to present himself as "a Mexican of mixed ethnic background" to help him market his ballets.[45]

One of the ironies associated with the macho rhetoric adopted by members of the Mexican school of painters is that these painters were largely reliant on female promoters to secure their financial success with collectors in the US. Paine and her sister promoters of Mexican art, including Alma Reed (1889–1966), Anita Brenner, and Frances Toor, were largely responsible for creating "the enormous vogue of things Mexican" in the US during the 1920s and 1930s.[46] Chávez could hardly have made a better choice for a champion than Paine. Born in Laredo, Texas, she accompanied her father, who reportedly served for a time as "superintendent of railways" for Mexico, for many of her formative years south of the US border, during which she perfected her Spanish and developed her interest in the nation's folk arts.[47] Somehow her efforts to promote Mexican art and artisans garnered the attention of Abby Aldrich Rockefeller (1874–1948), who supported Paine's efforts for more than a decade. The Rockefeller fortune bankrolled Paine's traveling exhibition of Mexican folk art in 1928, helped her found the Mexican Art Association to promote "cultural contact" and create an art market between the two countries in 1930, and underwrote the Rivera exhibition at the Museum of Modern Art in 1931. Paine also led Nelson Rockefeller on his first folk art collecting expedition to Mexico in 1933.[48] And it was Paine who arranged for Rivera to paint his infamous mural at Rockefeller Center, which the family removed from the building's walls in 1934.[49] José Clemente Orozco recognized Paine as a "very smart businesswoman" but despised her for what he regarded as her use of contemporary paintings from Mexico to advertise her folk art business and for her promotion of Rivera.[50] In a February 1928 letter to fellow artist Jean Charlot, Orozco, then living in New York, excoriated Paine's promotion of "Diegoff Riveritch Romanoff . . . the idea that we are all his disciples is very well entrenched here. To talk about 'Indians,' 'revolution,' 'Mexican renaissance,' 'folk arts,' 'retablos,' etc., etc., is to talk about Rivera. . . . All those words are synonyms of Diegoff, and what we must do is combat by any means necessary that 'Mexicanist' con man whose Prophets are now Mrs. Paine and Anita [Brenner]."[51]

Paine connected Chávez with theater owner Samuel Lyon "Roxy" Rothafel (1882–1936), who was preparing to open his lavish new Roxy Theater in Times Square. Roxy, who was known for the full-scale orchestra that accompanied his silent film offerings, also employed a resident ballet company, with Léonide Massine (1896–1979) as his choreographer. With a signed agreement to present *El fuego nuevo* in hand, the composer rescored the work for a symphony orchestra, complete with woodwinds and bass. He wrote to his wife in Mexico requesting clay flutes from Oaxaca and gourds to provide some of the percussion instruments. He also arranged for a lumber company in New Jersey to provide logs for the distinctive Aztec *teponaxtle* slit drums.[52]

The New York premiere of *El fuego nuevo* was, however, not to be. On further consideration, Rothafel decided against the Chávez ballet. He told the composer in the plainest terms possible that he had no intention of paying to mount *El fuego nuevo*; his provision of the enormously popular venue was enough. Since the original agreement did not specify payments, Paine's lawyer advised her against suing Rothafel for damages. Because Paine signed tie-in marketing agreements for the ballet with a women's wear firm and a ceramic tile company to produce works based on Lazo's designs for the ballet, she arranged a trust fund with $500 to benefit herself, Chávez, Lazo, and Tamayo, who must have somehow been involved in re-alizing the project.[53] That fund ended up covering their legal fees. Chávez ended up with half the flutes and $16.57.

Chávez was still attempting to secure a production of *El fuego nuevo* in 1928. In a letter to Chicago's Pavley-Oukrainsky Ballet Company (1922–1931), he offered his score and the Lazo designs as well as "replicas of Aztec codices and photographs of sculptures, thinking these would be of help in creating the choreography."[54] Possibly in relation to this proposal, he also elaborated on the theme in his suggestions for the choreography of *Los cuatro soles*: "The choreographer ought to carry out . . . a highly detailed and profound study of the indigenous Mexican codexes, in which he will find a study of the attitudes of the human body in the different activities of daily life and the ritual cult. At the same time, because the painting of the Mexican codexes is *por excelencia*, dynamic, the choreographer will be able to obtain invaluable concrete suggestions as to the choreographic composi-tion from them. There are cases in which the succession of figures on the pages of the Aztec codexes truly make us think of the suggestion of film cinematography."[55] Unfortunately, Chávez neither specified the codexes he believed contained a protocinematic quality nor the films he thought evoked the immediately recognizable Aztec style.

Chávez also made the more realistic recommendation that, as "mate-rial for a truly useful study, the choreographer counts with the possibility of witnessing the traditional dances of contemporary indigenous peoples, rich in their unique and original choreographic value." The use of existing

indigenous material, certainly a more practical expedient for studying approaches to movement, also came to form part of the accepted thematic
approach to the creation of a uniquely Mexican form of dance.

When Chávez assumed directorship of the Orquesta Sinfónica de
México (Mexican Symphony Orchestra) on his return from New York in
1928, he placed the expanded version of *El fuego nuevo* that he prepared
for the Roxy Theatre onto its performance schedule, where it stayed for
the next two seasons. Although Parker thought the composition was both
prophetic of Chávez's future career as a composer and held brilliant promise as a ballet, he nonetheless classified it as a youthful work, something
that Chávez also recognized.[56] Parker surmised this was why the composer
never attempted to remount the ballet in subsequent years.[57]

Such was not the case for *Los cuatro soles,* which also joined the Orquesta
Sinfónica's performance schedule. In his program notes for a concert presentation in 1930, Chávez indicated that Covarrubias had already produced
set designs based on the paintings in the Vatican codex.[58] When Massine
arrived in Mexico City in 1934 with Coronel de Basil's Ballets Russes to
help inaugurate the newly completed Palacio de Bellas Artes, Chávez was
on hand to urge a production of this ballet, and Massine expressed some
interest. Chávez once again engaged the services of Paine to bring the production together, this time with Rivera as the designer.

This iteration of *Los cuatro soles* was not Rivera's first attempt at creating
designs for theatrical dance. The Armenian dancer Armen Ohanian (1887–
1976), born Sophia Pirboudaghian in Shamakha in what is now Azerbaijan,
relocated to Mexico in 1921. She held the first Mexican performance of her
own combination of Duncanesque "free dance" and Asian "belly dance"
in the auditorium of the National Preparatory School, which was the site
of Rivera's recently completed first mural, in 1923. As part of that initial
performance, Rivera lectured on Persian art. Shortly thereafter, Ohanian
danced in the Festival of Oriental Art at the Teatro Iris, which featured
design work by Rivera. The young males in the audience created such an
uproar when one of them accompanied her movements with a loud kissing
noise that management called the police to restore order in the theater.[59]

Working in tandem, Rivera and Chávez came up with a production plan
for *Los cuatro soles* that called for six sets, twenty-four costume designs, and
a full recording of the score. They left the realization of the scenic design's
$6,700 price tag for Paine to address. Negotiations continued for some time
with both the de Basil company and Lincoln Kirstein's (1907–1996) fledgling American Ballet for rights to the event, but both companies demanded

a recording of the score before finalizing an agreement, and neither had independent funds to back the production. In 1938, Paine advised Chávez that his hopes for finding financing for his ballet without the promise of substantial box-office returns for the investors were simply unrealistic. Given an entree to Walt Disney (1901–1966) through his friendship with conductor Leopold Stokowski (1882–1977), the composer later attempted to repackage his ballet into an animated film along the lines of the ground-breaking *Fantasia* (1940), which was then under production at Disney's studio. This effort, too, came to naught.[60] Chávez, who rose to the peak of Mexico's cultural bureaucracy in 1947 as director general of the INBA and could finally realize the works he wanted to produce, mounted *Los cuatro soles* in a lavish production in Mexico City in 1951.

Chávez's 1920s trip to New York wasn't a complete failure. He was able to secure a concert performance of the fourth movement of his latest ballet composition, *Caballos de vapor* (*Horsepower*, better known as *H.P.*) (1926–1932). The International Composers' Guild, founded by French-born composer Edgard Varèse (1883–1965) to produce new music, performed the movement under the title "The Danse of Men and Machines" in November of 1926.[61] This score earned Chávez a fully realized production of his ballet.

In the program notes accompanying the guild's performance, Chávez described *H.P.* as a ballet that he was in the process of finishing. Despite its title, he claimed that

[the] intention of this work is neither to describe mechanical processes nor to relate the spirit of the work to the aesthetics of machines.

Horse Power certainly makes one think of machines, but I do not consider them objectively except for the sake of the vitality they possess.[62]

He went on to explain that the ballet he envisioned would be "made up of three tableaux which suggest objectively the life of all America. Yet both the visual work (setting and costumes) by Diego Rivera, as well as the music have their own proper and autonomous life."

Chávez also laid claim to indigenous roots for himself—he was of almost entirely Spanish ancestry—in the same program notes and asserted that "Indian tunes (*sones mariaches*) will be found in my music, not as a constructive base, but because all the conditions of their composition—form, sonority, etc.,—by nature coincide with those in my own mind, inasmuch as both are products of the same origin." Given that for audiences in the US at the time, Mexicanness evoked the concept of the Indian, Chávez was emphasizing his bona fides as an "authentic" American primitive. It certainly reinforced ideas about the nation's music that were being formed through Mexico's traveling Orquestas Típicas, mariachi groups, and works like the Covarrubias-designed "Rancho Mexicano" segment of Broadway's *Garrick Gaieties* (1925).[63]

Paine was able to generate some interest in this work based on its libretto by Rivera.[64] Chávez shared Rivera's libretto with his other collaborators early on in the process, who were generally supportive of the idea. Barreda thought the libretto "superb, full of possibilities and original."[65] He did note that the proposed scenario gave little consideration to the practical elements of performance and concluded that Chávez would "have to find a great company and an incredibly agreeable impresario" if the work were ever to be staged.

Lazo advised the composer that the proposed work bore notable similarities to Sergei Prokofiev's (1891–1953) score for the Ballets Russes' production of *Le Pas d'Acier*: "The ending [of the ballet] in the factory is perfectly achieved in both the music and the choreography and I wanted to let you know of this ballet because it seems to have come from an idea very similar to yours for HP."[66] He added, incorrectly, that he thought the company was headed for New York, where Chávez could judge Prokofiev's "modernist" ballet for himself.[67]

Paine advised Chávez in the fall of 1930 that she had organized a trip to Mexico through her Mexican Art Association and invited Stokowski, who was interested in conducting one of Chávez's ballets. Stokowski told the Philadelphia press that he was going to remote areas of Mexico to listen to Aztec music: "I've heard native American Indian music of different types. How far this Mexican Indian music has developed from the primitive Indian I cannot tell. Some of it may be worthwhile from a musical standpoint. I can't tell until I hear it."[68] He actually spent most of his time far from "Aztec" Mexico in the Yucatán, instead visiting the Mayan archeological sites of Chichén Itzá and Uxmal. Some of the music he heard was under his own baton, conducting Chávez's Orquesta Sinfónica in a performance of the third version of Beethoven's *Lenore Overture* (1806) in Mexico City's Chapultepec Park. Chávez also conducted his *Los cuatro soles* at the same concert, evidently in the hopes that Stokowski would select that work for production.[69] According to Chávez, Stokowski joined him in his studio to review his scores, including *H.P.*, which the composer performed on the piano as "a pretext for dances . . . [a] contrast between North and South," and his guest immediately agreed to present the work.[70]

Documents associated with the performance suggest that their agreement on which of Chávez's works would be presented was still pending. A US production of *El fuego nuevo* still appears to have been a possibility at that time.[71]

Stokowski conferred with Paine on his options, and in a May 1, 1931, letter Paine ultimately advised Chávez that the two of them decided on producing *H.P.* "We think H.P. best because it has an international character and the whole thing will be such an agreeable surprise to the public. I am very anxious to show as many sides of the Mexican culture as possible and the theme, music, and décor of H.P. is perfect."[72]

The problem was that the score for *H.P.* was nowhere near completion. Chávez sent fragments of his composition to Philadelphia bit by bit as he completed it but never on schedule—a practice that he repeated in his dealings with Martha Graham.[73] When he presented the work at a December 1931 concert of the Orquesta Sinfónica de México under his own direction, its second movement was still missing.[74] By early January of 1932, Paine was beginning to panic because the production's collaborators lacked a completed score. Without the necessary music, she suggested that the production would have to be dropped from the performance schedule.[75] By the end of February, Stokowski was beginning to express unease for the same reason.[76]

Despite its still incomplete score, Chávez, Paine, and Stokowski went all out in creating publicity surrounding the event. The success of Rivera's 1931 one-man show at the Museum of Modern Art and his well-publicized mural works in San Francisco made him one of the best-known contemporary artists in the US, which helped Paine gain attention for the ballet in the visual arts community. Paine sought the same level of celebrity for her client Chávez and succeeded to a large degree. By the time of *H.P.*'s sole presentation as a ballet, Chávez, if not necessarily his music, was one of the best-known contemporary composers of the Americas.

Despite her letter to the composer advising him that she was eager to show the multiple sides of Mexico through *H.P.*, Paine focused on the nation's Indian heritage, which was central to her marketing strategies in the late 1920s. Paine's approach was seconded by Stokowski, who also saw the value of stressing the supposed affinities of American Indian creators and the modernist "primitives."[77]

Stokowski traveled to Mexico in January 1932 for a two-week journey purportedly to immerse himself in "primitive" Mexican culture prior to the production of *H.P.*, a visit that Chávez ensured was amply covered in the Mexican press. In a 1976 interview with Stokowski's biographer Oliver Daniel, Chávez laid out an ambitious travel schedule, even by twenty-first century standards. Chávez reported that they visited the colonial cities of Uruapan and Morelia in Michoacán, the lake resort of Chapala in Jalisco, and Toluca, the capital city of the state of Mexico. The duo also took the train from the port of Veracruz to Salina Cruz on the Isthmus of Tehuantepec, home to the sandunga, a central element of the score for *H.P.* He added that during their visit they "saw the festivities, which in those days were very colorful."[78] What "festivities" they may have actually seen is open to question. The sandunga is traditionally performed in late May, and given Stokowski's February 8 arrival date, they also missed the January 19 Festival of San Sebastian in Tehuantepec, where they might have seen it performed.[79] None of the other communities they visited, much less the lake resort in Chapala, have traditional celebrations that take place during the timeframe of Stokowski's visit.

While he was in Mexico, Stokowski told the local press how deeply he was impressed by the diversity of the country's music, claiming that the Mexicans were the only people in the world that did not have a "standardized" music.[80] On his return to the US, however, Stokowski converted his trip into a wilderness adventure worthy of a novelist's pen. *Time* magazine was seduced by Stokowski's romantic inventions: "From one Mexican village to another this winter a white man traveled, asking for and intently listening to music. A swart Mexican accompanied him, explained to Aztecs and Tarascans that it was their own native music the stranger wanted to hear, not the imported hodge podge played in Mexican cities. The stranger was interested in the rude, primitive sounds made by the *chirimia* (clay pipe) [the chirimía is a variety of shawm, a precursor to the oboe, introduced to the Americas by the Spanish], the *marimba* made of gourds, the *teponaztle*, which is the Mexican Indians' drum, the noisy basis for all their music. Indians took to calling the white man Chokopul which means 'one of wandering wits.'"[81]

As the date for *H.P.*'s premiere approached, Stokowski continued to embellish his tales of "primitive" Mexico. He told writer Harry Hewes of the Pan American Union that he traveled south of the border specifically to "observe the ritualistic and symbolic dances of the Indians, the roots of which are lost in dim and unrecorded centuries."[82] A similar story by a writer from the *Philadelphia Record* claimed that "Stokowski actually reenacted the libretto of the ballet. . . . The conductor turned his back on the 'steel edges' of Western Civilization to lose his artificial Northern culture in the languorous sun of Central America. During the fortnight Stokowski lived as the Indians whom he describes as lithe-limbed and athletic people. Night and morning he went swimming in the sea, reclined for hours in the warmth of the sun and slept in the thatched house of their chiefs and elders."[83] As musicologist Christina Taylor Gibson points out in her study of *H.P.*, "The implied suggestion that Stokowski became a musical Gauguin within the space of two weeks is nearly as ridiculous as the popular idea that exposure to Mexican culture could offer a return to primitive, natural simplicity."[84]

As Gibson also highlights in her analysis, despite his mostly Spanish ancestry, the physical descriptions of Chávez offered in the US press emphasized his supposedly Indian appearance.[85] According to one report, he was "half-Indian, half-Spanish," while another report fixed on his "typical Indian locks." One writer even went so far as to opine that the "swarthy" Chávez "looked the true exponent of 'natural music.'"[86]

When Chávez arrived in Philadelphia in March of 1932 to finalize the production, Stokowski went in to conference with him and Littlefield in an attempt to imbue the nascent ballet with what the Philadelphia *Public Ledger* called "the timbre and tempo of Northern modernity and Southern primitive life, [which had] not yet occurred."[87] Chávez and Rivera also met separately with Littlefield to teach her how to dance the sandunga, which was a central part of the ballet. Although press reports at the time indicated Littlefield traveled to Mexico to study its dance culture, these reports do not appear to have been true.[88] According to Chávez, "Diego made her drawings to illustrate the plastique of the dances and [Littlefield], who is very intelligent, did her best to make do."[89]

The notes for *H.P.* that emerged in the performance program were ultimately written by Philip Leidy (1897–1964), legal counsel for the Philadelphia Opera Company Association and son of one of its leading patrons, as well as Littlefield's future husband.[90] Instead of Chávez's original three "tableaux," *H.P.* now had four loosely related scenes—the "Dance of the Man H.P.," a cargo ship at sea symbolizing inter-American commerce, a ship in the tropics, and the "City of Industry"—though still no plot: "The Ballet H. P. symbolizes the relations of the Northern Regions with those of the Tropics, and shows their interrelationship. The Tropics produce things in their primitive state—there are Pineapples, Cocoanuts, Bananas, and Fish. The North produces the machinery with which to manufacture from the products of the Tropics, the necessary material things of life. The Ballet depicts the fact that the North needs the Tropics, just as the Tropics need the machinery of the North, and attempts to harmonize the result."[91]

The explanatory texts by Chávez and Rivera in the program were equally opaque. Chávez wrote: "*H. P.* is a symphony of music that is in the very air and atmosphere of our continent. Music that is heard on all sides, a sort of review of the epoch in which we live. It contains expressions that are natural to our daily life, without attempting to select the 'artistic.' Latin American and Anglo-American culture are giving this continent its own personality and savor. Groups of people of diverse characters and regions. North and South, mingle constantly in the grand ferment of this, our American Continent. That which the present moment has of strife and creativeness, that which in reality lives in the very air which we breathe, is what is contained in *H. P.*"[92]

Other than disowning any explicit leftist agenda for the work, accusations of which haunted his murals in the US, Rivera's comments were also vague: "There is undoubtedly a common destiny for all the men of America. The time will come when they will be held by a common bond in the achievements of art, beauty, and the mind. *H. P.* is not an exposition of ideas of propaganda for or against this or that point of view, but the unfolding of plastic and musical incidents whose theme is in accord with the rhythm of our aspirations, interests, and the necessities of our social existence. In this manner, the production has been created and developed around its central theme with entire abandon. The need for unity makes it necessary that the dance, painting, and form of the scenery definitely express the music of *H. P.* in plastic form."[93]

Art historian Jeffrey Belnap has proposed an unnecessarily "hidden" revolutionary program for Rivera's scenic designs for the work.[94] Those who attended could have hardly failed to recognize the leftist implications of its closing scene, where the character H.P. frees the dancing fruit and leads the workers in a revolt against the material values, represented by the stock ticker. Linton Martin of the *Philadelphia Inquirer* thought the production was about "as revolutionary as your grandmother's ruffles."[95] Dance historian Lynn Garafola describes the dance's closing evocation of the workers' paradise with its happily dancing fruit as pure "comic-book Marxism."[96]

The most intriguing element of Belnap's interpretation of *H.P.* as a subversive work is his identification of the formal similarities between what he called the "posthuman technoid" of the man H.P. and the performers of the

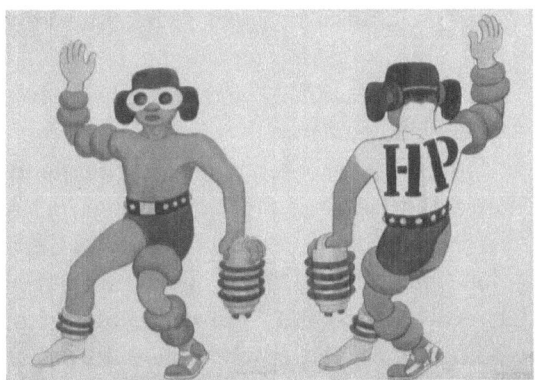

FIGURE 10. Diego Rivera (1886–1957). *The Man*. Costume design for the ballet *H.P.* (Horsepower). 1927. Ink, watercolor, and pencil on paper, 20 ⅞ × 29 ⅜"(53 × 74.6 cm.). The Museum of Modern Art. Gift of Abby Aldrich Rockefeller. Digital image © The Museum of Modern Art/Licensed by SCALA ART/Art Resource, NY. © 2019 Banco de México Diego Rivera Frida Kahlo Museums Trust, Mexico, DF/Artists Rights Society (ARS), New York.

Yaqui deer dance in Rivera's murals for the SEP (1923–1928). Belnap proposes that H.P. should not be understood as a "Euro-American man [who] exploits an empty American landscape through the natural superiority of this technology; the dance is placed . . . within the Native American tradition of ritual exchange with the natural environment, a tradition of which the Yaqui Dance of the Deer is exemplary. . . . Although to some people H.P.'s costume may resemble the pistons and transformers of modernity, its underlying design principles are indigenous. Rather than a domination of American nature by Euro-U.S. technology, the man-machine H.P. represents the assimilation of foreign technology to Native America's indigenous history."[97] In his evaluation, Belnap presents the character of H.P. as an embodiment Rivera's notion that the indigenous elements of America's past would inevitably mold the expression of the hemisphere's technological future.

Technological or not, Chávez certainly had his eye fixed on continuing to promote the indigenous perceptions associated with his music. On his return to Mexico City, *Excélsior* reported on its front page that the composer spoke about the importance of his ballet score "in the renewal of esthetic values . . . in this hour of social concerns, in which the capitalist world is on the margin of catastrophe."[98] Art, Chávez declared to the newspaper, would no longer be a luxury, but a primordial element of life. He went on to specify that this art should be rooted "in the intimacy of each people, always seeking a universal expression and content. In passing along this concept, he alluded to the real dancers of Mexico, who are in the distant regions; dancers like the Yaquis or the Huichols who know their craft, and who spend the best moments of their existence in it."

Out of this amalgam of ideas, Littlefield succeeded in creating moments of successful choreography. She recruited Alexis Dolinoff, under whom Littlefield studied in Paris, to perform the role described in the program as "the man H.P."[99] Martin of the *Times* allowed that, "in the solo dance by 'H.P.' himself [Littlefield] has evolved a composition which has form, in spite of the fact that it is made up almost exclusively of nervous bits at the dictates of the music."[100] Noting that it was Dolinoff's American debut, Martin later added that playing the character of H.P. was "no role to show him at anything like his best. He has practically no opportunity to dance." Nonetheless, Mary Watkins (d. 1974), the pioneering dance critic for the *New York Herald Tribune*, credited Dolinoff, "in whom was observable immediately the trained and seasoned veteran"—he had danced with the companies of Anna Pavlova and Ida Rubinstein (1883–1960)—with the work's "one outstanding performance."[101]

Though she generally thought Littlefield's choreography "totally inoffensive but equally undistinguished," Watkins did praise her for the scene in which the choreographer's sister Dorothie danced as a guitar-playing mermaid, a figure that also has roots in Mexico's indigenous folklore. "The dance of the Sirens who invade the ship in Scene 2, is probably the most perfect realization of [Rivera's] claim to have 'dance, painting and form of scenery definitely express the music of H. P. in plastic form,' and its perfections can be traced to Catherine Littlefield," Watkins wrote.[102] Martin also opined that Littlefield's "theme for the sirens, though not developed," was, nonetheless, "exactly right."[103]

The dancing fruits, rendered in papier-mâché from Rivera's designs, received more mixed reviews. Rivera was likely aware of his onetime enemy Picasso's notorious "cubist" costumes for the Ballets Russes production of *Parade* (1917) and was just as unconcerned with their potential effects on the ability of the dancers to move.[104] Nonetheless, Watkins of the *Tribune* loved what Rivera achieved: "What color and humor and emphasis there is in the work is largely due to him. His fishes, mermaids, cocoanuts, sugar cane, bananas, cigars and gasoline pumps provide something quite new and actually distinctive in ballet investiture and retain the qualities of sunlight and intense simplicity which always has been the secret of his success."[105]

By contrast, Martin of the *Times* appreciated just how difficult a challenge Rivera's costumes posed for the choreographer: "When some of the characters are bunches of bananas, pineapples, coconuts and huge fish in papier-mâché casings, there is not much opportunity to be lyrical without a struggle."[106] In his lengthier review of the premiere for the Sunday edition of the *Times*, he added that "[a] more experienced choreographer than Miss Littlefield might have done a little better, but not much. One such choreographer remarked pointedly that he did not know what he would do if was handed a scenario and read in it as a stage direction: 'Enter three pineapples.'"[107]

In his review for *Modern Music*, which previewed some of Rivera's designs in its pages as part of *H.P.*'s publicity campaign, composer Marc Blitzstein (1905–1964) summarized the choreographic results of Rivera's outsized costumes: "They took up so much room that the logical choreographic plan should have been modeled on the simple *défilé*; instead of which, everybody was made to dance, the Big Fish got in the way of the Grand Pineapple, and the stage was invariably messy and ugly to look at."[108]

For the Mexicans in the audience, the work's biggest failure was the way in which Littlefield represented their dances. Rivera's then wife Frida Kahlo (1907–1954) wrote a friend in the US decrying the choreographer's efforts on the sandunga that her husband attempted to teach her though his drawings. Her condemnation of the work is probably the best recognized of the many criticisms that emerged from *H.P.*'s sole performance: "It turned out to be a *porquería* [disgusting mess] with a *P*. . . . not because of the music or the decorations, but because of the choreography since there was a crowd of insipid blonds pretending they were Indians from Tehuantepec and when they had to dance the Zandunga they looked as if they had lead instead of blood. To sum up, a pure and total *cochinada* [piggery]."[109]

In the pages of Mexico City's *Social*, reporter Herminio Portell Villa, who traveled to Philadelphia to see the premiere, was no less disappointed by what he saw than Kahlo, though his comments were less caustic: "As the music gathers and reproduces a typical air, one notes that the interpretation of the dancers is too academic, they've been unable to achieve the typical dance and they've allowed themselves to improvise gestures and steps embroidered over the elements of the same that they have been able to assimilate: in sum, they danced a *Zandunga* in English."[110]

Chávez, Paine, and Stokowski performed their publicity duties for *H.P.* perhaps a bit too well for an audience that was, in Blitzstein's estimation, "dizzy with advance ballyhoo."[111] *H.P.* was simply too weak a work to sustain the publicity buildup that preceded it. The evident rush to complete the composition made Rosenfeld, one of Chávez's champions, declare the score of *H.P.* premature, and caused him to worry that, by presenting this piece before it was properly completed, it damaged Chávez's career: "While a ballet of Chávez's was the inevitable choice for the theatrical performance, 'H.P.' does not appear to have been the wisest selection. . . . The hitch in the ballet appears the consequence of a want of plan. The 'action,' for example, is very badly worked out. . . . Indeed, for all its beauties, the ballet in several respects gives evidence of a process of composition hesitantly protracted over a period of six or seven years. And it would seem the part of a critical intelligence not to have let as gifted and creative a composer as Chávez make his first appearance before the musical public with this particular work in its present state, and to have postponed its production until it was finished once and for all, and perfectly finished."[112] Blitzstein also thought the work's score failed in what it set out to achieve. Chávez, he wrote, "seems not quite to have realized the Stravinskian equation between an advanced method and a primitivism of effect. . . . It seems to have that idiomatic, strange unreferable [*sic*] finality like the sort found in all 'local-color' art."[113]

On that front, the reviewer from *Time* magazine did note that Chávez was attempting to "develop an authentic Mexican music from purely native sources. . . . But most of H.P.'s music was too obtrusively harsh and loud for listeners on first hearing to detect the Indian tunes which he claims to be part & parcel of his work."[114]

As Robert Reiss of the *Philadelphia Record* summed it up in his ironically "populist" review, Chávez's ballet "was more of a sensation before it began than after it was over."[115]

For all of its failings, *H.P.* did provide a fleeting glance of the possibilities that might be achieved through theatrical dance by Mexican artists on the international stage. In an article on muralism not directly related to the premiere of *H.P.*, art critic Edward Allen Jewell of the *New York Times* raved about Rivera's design work for the production: "In their richness of dance, their color, their employment of 'folk' traditions, the costumes—especially these—proved to be authentic indices, referring straight back to the striking Rivera frescoes in Mexico and seeming, as it were, magically to bring painted figures to three-dimensional life. That choreographically these elements were not made use of, were not composed, not permitted to become integral parts of a picture such as Rivera himself would construct—this was not his fault. It lay outside Rivera's allocated province."[116]

If the unfairly scapegoated choreographer Littlefield was unable to make Rivera's murals dance, *H.P.*'s single night on the boards proved that the vision of a lavish spectacle combining Mexican dance, Mexican music, and Mexican scenic design was no pipe dream. It simply remained a goal that was yet to be realized. Mexican choreographers took up this challenge in the coming years. And, initially, at least, they too heard applause for the sets and costumes produced by their fellow artists but not always for their choreography.

6

A Question of Technique

Carlos Mérida and a Mexican School of Dance

The lack of a dance infrastructure that frustrated Carlos Chávez's attempts to mount his first ballet compositions in Mexico was also evident to the leadership of the SEP. As Mexico's new political leadership shifted the focus of Vasconcelos's educational program from its European heritage to that of its working rural and urban peoples, the SEP's educators sought to employ a still ill-defined Mexican dance as one of its tools to educate the public.

Vasconcelos stepped aside as minister of education in 1924 to run for governor of Oaxaca in opposition to the policies of then presidential candidate Plutarco Elías Calles (1877–1945). Although Vasconcelos won this state-level race, Calles won the presidency and refused to recognize his election.[1] Pascual Ortiz Rubio (1877–1963), the candidate of Calles's newly formed Partido Nacional Revolucionario (PNR), which evolved into Mexico's long-ruling Partido Revolucionario Institutional (PRI), subsequently defeated Vasconcelos in the 1929 presidential elections. That election ushered in a period in the nation's history known as the *Maximato*, which lasted until 1934. Ortiz may have been elected president—Vasconcelos contested the election due to evidence of widespread fraud—but Mexico's political leader was still Calles, its *jefe máximo*, or supreme chief.[2] As founder and head of the PNR, and, concurrently, minister of war, Calles turned the leadership of his political party into a force more powerful than the presidency he once held.[3]

In the PNR's Declaration of Principles, Calles's new party pronounced "the working and *campesino* [agricultural laborer] classes the most important elements of Mexican society," setting the stage for institutionalizing indigenous and mestizo popular culture as official markers of national art.[4] Responding to this change, the SEP began recreating its history texts, transforming its once bleak assessment of the effects of its civil war to recast the working class as what historian Mary Kay Vaughan calls the heroic "makers and heirs of the Revolution."[5] Calles repositioned the leaders of opposing revolutionary forces—Francisco Madero, Venustiano Carranza, Álvaro Obregón, Pancho Villa, and Emiliano Zapata, all conveniently deceased—into what he called the "revolutionary family." It was with the formation of the PNR that the host of warring factions was transformed from an internecine conflict into the Mexican Revolution, with its consecrated heroes and unifying goals. Ironically, Calles enshrined the competing "revolutionary" interests as political pillars of his populist party at the same time he was becoming more conservative.[6] The public rhetoric of Mexico's leaders, and its officially sanctioned manifestation in the arts, was populist; the policies of the government moved in the opposite direction. Rivera's murals for the SEP's headquarters became increasingly political and leftist in their orientation. Something similar began to happen in the embryonic world of nationalist theatrical dance, which became a formal bureaucratic appendage of the SEP.

The Escuela de Plástica Dinámica—In Search of a Classical Aztec Ballet

Ortiz resigned from his brief presidency in 1932, having the misfortune of governing during the worst years of the Great Depression (1929–1930s) and running afoul of Calles, but not before his SEP opened its Escuela de Plástica Dinámica (School of Dynamic Plastique).

As part of its expanding physical education programs, the SEP began hiring dance teachers for its public schools as early as 1930; establishing a specialized dance school moved that effort to a new level. Ortiz's explanation of the school's role in his report to the chamber of deputies echoed the populist line of the PNR. It was to "initiate all kinds of dances, especially Mexican, forming a group that can interpret the works of our artists seeking to educate the people. . . . It has intensified the work in support of our national folklore, in order to promote it and make it a genuine reality," as if the nation's folk culture had no "reality" of its own prior to its formal adoption by the government.[7]

The school's dance program fell to Hypolite Zybin (1891–1965), a thirty-nine-year-old white Russian stranded in Mexico when the Ópera Privé de Paris disbanded there.[8] Zybin trained in St. Petersburg before the Russian Revolution and kept up with developments in ballet as an exile, training under Ballets Russes dancer Elena Poliakova (1884–1972) in Belgrade,

Serbia. Along with traditional ballets from the nineteenth century, such as a version of *Swan Lake*, the Ópera Privé kept works by Mikhail Fokine in its repertory, including the "Polovtsian Dances" from *Prince Igor*, both of which they presented in Mexico City before disbanding. In a nod to Anna Pavlova, its performers took their final bows with a rendition of the *Fantasía Mexicana*, relying on the assistance of Eva Pérez for instruction just as Pavlova did before them.[9]

Before the curtain fell on the company's farewell performance in April of 1930, Zybin wrote to the director of the SEP's Dirección de Educación Física (Department of Physical Education), Franklin Westrup (1901?–1976), seeking employment as a dance teacher. His letter proposed that he could resurrect "Aztec dance" through the application of theoretical principles based on classical forms.[10] Zybin eventually received permission to offer free classes at the Centro Escolar Benito Juárez, one of José Vasconcelos's earliest school-construction projects. His successful mounting of simple ballets with its elementary school students earned him a position as assistant to the SEP's Department of Physical Education in October of that year.

The SEP's dance instructors received help in learning the nation's folk dances from representatives of various indigenous communities who came to Mexico City on government business. In 1931, several of them learned a basic form of the Yaqui deer dance from one such group. Participants in the *misiones culturales* (cultural missions) that Vasconcelos originated also helped train the instructors in the regional folk dances that they learned during their educational service to the nation.[11] The misiones culturales would play an increasingly important role in providing source material for government-sponsored dance programs.

Vasconcelos launched the misiones culturales program in 1923. His earliest push to create a corps of teachers to reach the largely illiterate populations of the nation's rural heartland was not highly selective. The minimum qualification was a third-grade education or a proven ability to read and write in Spanish.[12] For the "apostles" who served as his cultural missionaries, Vasconcelos aimed higher. He called on "young poets, artists, men of letters, and talent from around the country" for help, "like one who offers military service in support of culture."[13]

Although the missions' primary objectives were to provide basic instruction in the economically vital areas of literacy, agriculture, and hygiene, cultural issues were never far from the teaching agenda. The instructors regularly employed short dramas and puppet shows to reinforce their lessons. They were also charged with gathering information about the folk traditions and artistic creations in the communities they served. The first of the cultural missions took place in Zacualtipán, Hidalgo, in October of 1923, providing the community with practical information about agriculture, food preservation, and, in a demonstration of the hygienic component of its charge, soap making.[14]

These short-term missions quickly developed a standard format, including a teach-the-teacher component designed to encourage more locally driven educational efforts. Although there were differences among the missions, each had a chief, a music and chorus teacher, a physical education teacher, an instructor in home economics, a teacher trainer, and a doctor to provide instruction in hygiene and undertake vaccination campaigns.[15] The physical education teachers were in charge of the dance programs and all of them received training in "rhythm and esthetics" prior to their departure for the field. Regardless of their particular assignment, each missionary also received training in instrumental and choral music.[16]

Several different cultural missionaries undertook the task of recording, through whatever means available, the dances in the communities they served.[17] A few of them had motion-picture cameras, though most relied on words and still images. This recording work was under way when Rudolph von Laban (1879–1958) first published his dance notation system in German in 1928; decades would pass before Mexican dancers and choreographers were first trained in its use. Consequently, each missionary developed a personal system to transmit the elements of the dances they were attempting to document, much to the frustration of later dance historians.[18] Person-to-person transmission continued to provide the most effective means of communicating the essence of these dances, just as it did in their communities of origin.

As the SEP evolved from a government agency charged with higher education in the Mexico City area into a truly national institution, it added 12,561 rural primary schools to its portfolio in the two decades following Vasconcelos's ascension to the role of minister of education. This caused the programs of the cultural missions to evolve as well.[19] In 1932, the SEP's Dirección de Misiones Culturales (Directorate of Cultural Missions) began publishing *El Maestro Rural* (The Rural Teacher), a magazine providing ongoing training for its teachers, some of whom began as students of its cultural missionaries. Teachers contributed articles about the folk cultures of their communities, helping to spur a truly national sense of Mexico's folkloric riches among its regions.[20] That same year, the cultural missionaries gathered at the end of their term for a festival in the village of San Juan de

Teotihuacán, just beyond the famed archaeological site, for a presentation of the songs and dances they had learned. It was becoming clearer to the administrators of the SEP that the archives of folkloric material gathered through the missions and its rural teachers were a significant resource for its nation-building efforts. In its six-year plan published in 1934, SEP leadership explicitly cited using its growing store of information on Mexico's "indigenous culture as a source for our general culture, thus invigorating the feeling of our nationality" among its priorities.[21]

The SEP's first attempt at forming a national dancing school took place with this as background. The ministry's inability to articulate how its archive of materials drawn from rural popular culture might be combined with its interest in theatrical dance as a propaganda tool for its Mexico City audience resulted in failure. The SEP wanted "Mexican dance" but it still couldn't define what that might look like. In a sense, this was the same problem that Vasconcelos faced with his first mural commissions but in a different art form.

In the steps leading up to the creation of the Escuela de Plástica y Dinámica, Francisco Pruneda, then director of fine arts for the SEP, advised Zybin that he would be part of the team charged with creating the ministry's new dance section. The group of instructors was to give form to "dance instruction in the schools of the Secretariat" and was also charged with "organizing Mexican dance which could be presented in the diverse festivals of the SEP."[22] Pruneda tapped Carlos E. González, painter and artistic director for the SEP's theater programs to lead the new school. González consulted with Chávez, then director of the Conservatoria Nacional de Música (National Music Conservatory), before charging Zybin with ensuring that the team also produced a unified approach to dance instruction.[23] This resulted in the teaching of Russian classical techniques when what the leadership of the SEP apparently wanted was a dance company capable of immediately performing something identifiably Mexican in its public events.[24]

As dance historian Claudia Carbajal points out in her study of the school, the combination of Russian ballet and nationalist impulses favoring indigenous dance was not a happy one. The aesthetic of classical ballet was "a far cry from the indigenous and mestizo dances that were practiced in Mexico," but Zybin seemed to believe that Aztec aristocracy knew some form of the dance in which he was trained.[25]

When the school opened its doors in a room within the ministry's headquarters on April 29, 1931, Zybin was its technical director. Sisters Adela and Linda Costa, who arrived in Mexico in 1904 as part of Aldo Barili's Italian Gran Compañía de Baile y Pantomima (Grand Company of Dance and Pantomime) provided instruction in classical ballet. Half sisters Nellie and Gloria Campobello were in charge of Mexican folk dance. Enrique Zapata led rhythmic gymnastics.[26] In one indicator of the SEP's intended direction for the school, each of the instructors was asked a series of questions about fulfilling Calles's populist rhetoric. The SEP wanted to know their opinions on which rhythms in Mexican music might be best suited to nationalist dance, whether the country's archeological remains might provide its foundations, and which Mexican works they had already created. Unfortunately, their answers to its questionnaire weren't maintained.[27]

The school enrolled about one hundred students, mostly of primary-school age. All but three were female.[28] According to Carbajal, the absence of male students in this school and its successors was largely due to traditional gender expectations. A career as a dance performer was not seen as a "serious" option for a man expected to support a family.[29] Under Zybin's plan of studies, students were to be admitted definitively to the school only after a two-month observation period. Particularly talented students were able to study at no cost, but even then the tuition was only three pesos a year, allowing for a much broader range of students than those who could afford the tuition at the city's private dancing schools.[30] Mexico City housed a handful of professional dance instructors, just as it had since the days of Hernán Cortéz (1485–1547).[31] At the government-operated Academia Nacional de Música, Armen Ohanian provided instruction in interpretive dancing. Amalia Lepri provided training at the Escuela Libre de Música y Declamación. Carol Adamchevsky specialized in dance training for the female participants in Mexico's variety theaters. Vlasta Maslova, who stayed in Mexico after performing with Pavlova, had her Academia de Bailes Imperiales, while Mol Potapovich opened the Academia de Bailes Clásicos. The Costa sisters also offered private instruction. And Texas-born Lettie Carroll provided all-purpose social and theatrical dance instruction for the young women of Mexico City's high society.[32]

Zybin and his colleagues immediately set to work creating dance theater pieces for SEP events. He understood that his task was to use his art as "a powerful medium of propaganda for the social ideas" of his political leadership.[33] One of the first of his dances, and apparently the most popular, was something he called the *Ballet del árbol* (Dance of the Tree), circa 1931. Its scenario was exceedingly simple: Sunrise in the forest. The trees and flowers welcome the dawn. Suddenly the spirit of evil invades the forest, inducing the woodsmen to cut down the trees. The spirits of good arrive to defend the flowers and the trees, and having gained the victory, all creatures dance in rejoicing.[34]

As superficial as it was, this didactic work fitted perfectly into the broader approach that the SEP was implementing in other venues to simultaneously entertain and educate its citizenry. Media historian Joy Hayes points out that the SEP's educational radio broadcasts were consciously designed as part of its larger program to establish "relations between the whole of the Mexican family and the educational leaders in whom the government of the country has placed the standard of national culture."[35]

Carbajal notes that, for all its didactic intent, Zybin's *Ballet del árbol*, with its fairies and spirits of good and evil, was firmly rooted in the narrative traditions of the nineteenth-century romantic ballet.[36] Zybin, usually in collaboration with his stage-designer supervisor González, created similar works for his students in this format, including a memorial commemorating the death of Anna Pavlova, her soul borne into immortality on a cloud of butterflies. He also devised more overtly nationalist works, including his own version of the *Fantasía Mexicana* set to music by Fernando Villalpando (1844–1902) and a fragment of a larger Aztec ballet, *Fiesta del Fuego* (Fire Fiesta) by Antonio Gómezanda (1894–1961).[37]

It was while Zybin was preparing his Aztec ballet that Nellie Campobello created the single most successful work that emerged from the Escuela de Plástica Dinámica, a piece for massed dancers she called *30–30*. Named after the Winchester rifle in common use by the foot soldiers of the revolution, it was created to commemorate the revolution's twenty-first anniversary. Both Zybin's Aztec ballet and Campobello's homage to the revolution appeared on the same program in the Álvaro Obregón Theater, set within one of the patios of the SEP's headquarters. If the performance had been structured as a competition, Campobello's work would have won.

Assembled in a little over two weeks to an arrangement by composer Francisco Domínguez (1897–1975?) of Genero Codina's *Marcha de Zacatecas* and José Ríos's *Himno a la Industria*, the work was "inspired in the words of the now historic speech of General Calles," according to the Mexico City newspaper *Excélsior*'s announcement of its premiere.[38] Presumably, the reference was to Calles's September 1, 1928, speech to Congress following the assassination of President-elect Álvaro Obregón, who was set to reassume the presidency. At that time, Calles called for abandoning what

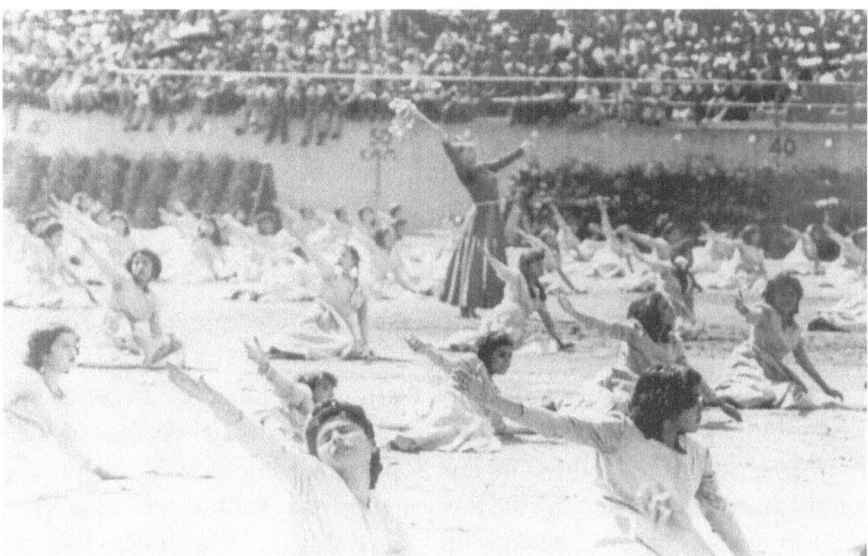

FIGURE 11. Nellie Campobello carries the torch of liberty in a performance of her *30–30*. Circa 1935. Photographer unknown. Fototeca-CENIDI DANZA/INBA. Fondo documental Felipe Segura.

he called the nation's tradition of "government by caudillos," or chieftains, and replacing it with a tradition of governing by institutions, such as the political party he was in the process of assembling.

To achieve the huge cast that she envisioned, Campobello drew on the students of the Escuela de Plástica Dinámica and from schools named in honor of Gabriela Mistral and Ignacio M. Altamirano, as well as the student bodies of the schools of Enseñanza Doméstica (Home Economics), the Industrial de la Beneficencia Pública (Industrial School for the Public Benefit), and the Casa del Estudiante Indígena (House of the Indigenous Student). Given the large cast and the short time provided for ballet's creation, *30–30* must have been a brief and simple work, but it hit home with its intended audience, which included much of the leadership of the SEP.[39]

30–30 consisted of three sections, "Revolución" (Revolution), "Siembra" (Sowing), and "Liberación" (Liberation). Campobello danced the opening section as the torch-wielding virgin who awakens the red-clad women of the countryside to the necessity of revolt. Having succeeded in liberating the land, the women join their men in replanting the earth that now belongs to them. Their need for a secure supply of food having been met,

Campobello returned with her torch to bring the entire cast together—men, women, rural laborer, factory worker, and soldier—in a newly unified country.

The same newspaper that announced *30–30*'s presentation also provided a review following the premiere; its unnamed author designated Campobello's work the "pinnacle number of the fiesta without a doubt . . . the one that most shook the aesthetic restlessness of the audience . . . for its well-balanced dance, its originality, and its authentic beauty."[40] The reviewer placed the work within the aesthetic that Diego Rivera was beginning to formalize during the Calles regime: "In this number, of an exciting plasticity, of a seductive reality, as in the ballet the revolutionary peasants appeared, giving life and animation to a corner of Mexico, where they preside over the living forces of the work and hope for a better Mexico, the humble rural school, embellished by the flowering greenery of the corn cobs from the harvest. In this allegorical group, one could clearly see the undoubted influence of Diego Rivera, whose types and motifs in mural painting have been used to give newness to the dance."

Campobello's success with *30–30* displayed her sense of what the SEP's political leaders sought but were unable to articulate. Her ability to navigate the ever changing shoals of postrevolutionary politics served her well through a long career in Mexico's dance bureaucracy. She may not have realized it, but *30–30* placed her on a trajectory that allowed her to become the de facto "caudillo" within the nation's institutionalized dance structure. It was a role that she enthusiastically embraced. Although she insisted on being addressed as *Señorita* (Miss), she also adopted a truculent management style that could match her most aggressively macho counterparts in the almost exclusively male world of government bureaucracy.[41]

If Zybin noticed the acclaim that Campobello's paean to the revolution received, it was not reflected in his approach to his job. He continued down the classical path he set. Consistent with the policy of the PNR to depict Mexico's rural peoples as revolutionary heroes, Zybin joined some of his colleagues at the school on excursions to rural festivals, such as the famous procession of the Black Christ of the Sanctuary of Chalma, to seek out possible materials for use in the SEP's public presentations. His report on that event used language that would be repeated frequently over the next few years as the state wrestled to define the elements necessary to establish a dancing school that produced appropriately Mexican ballets. His described his task at Chalma as discovering what remained of "pure" indigenous dancing, the purer works being, perforce, the most Mexican.[42] But he did not leave his assessment there, which proved problematic.

He concluded that what he saw in Chalma did not reflect authentic Aztec forms, which he assumed looked something more like classical ballet:

> Some Aztec dance teachers, renegades from the ancient cult, added some of the external forms of Aztec paganism to those of the Christian, the aforementioned teachers introduced these dances to the people as a form of serving Christ. The instructors among the people imperceptibly mixed this ritual dance with those of their villages, and subjecting themselves to the influence of some of the conquistadors, inserted European steps, stereotyped and simplified, into their rites.
>
> As a general rule, in their current aspect the dances that I saw in Chalma are from a community of an almost entirely savage character and one sees no shadow whatever of the refined culture which was unique to the ancient aristocratic priests of the Aztec religion.[43]

By attributing Aztec dance to its "aristocratic" priesthood, which he seems to have equated with practitioners of some sort of classical dancing, and denying the ideologically popular idea that Mexico's rural indigenous communities were the faithful guardians of its pre-Hispanic past, Zybin raised questions with the SEP's political leadership as to how well a Russian could understand and interpret the nation's past, let alone its present.[44] Because they believed his nationality alone rendered him unfit for his position, the Campobello sisters were reportedly his most strident critics on the school's faculty.[45]

His reports to his supervisors also contained criticisms of his colleagues, describing them as better fit for preparing school programs than for teaching ballet. However accurate that may have been, this likely did little to help solidify his position within the SEP's new organization.[46] The internal battles at the school got so vicious that at one point Zybin was given four months in which to leave the country.[47] He appears to have been saved from expulsion by a letter signed by the parents of his students.

Zybin managed to outlast the Ortiz presidency, but not in a leadership position. Before Ortiz stepped down in 1932, he announced the creation of the Consejo de Bellas Artes (Council of Fine Arts) to help guide the SEP in its efforts. The full council consisted of poets José Gorostiza (1901–1973) and Manuel Maples, pianist Salvador Ordoñez Ochoa (1894–1967), playwright Xavier Villaurrutia (1903–1950), and painter Rufino Tamayo.[48] At the same time that Ortiz established the council, he noted that the budget cuts necessitated by the economy reduced the Department of Fine Arts budget by 90 percent, leaving only the funding for arts education intact.[49] Still, at the recommendation of the new council, the Escuela de Plástica Dinámica met its demise, to be replaced by the new Escuela de Danza (School of Dance). Zybin was quietly moved aside, although he continued to teach classical dance at the SEP's new school for a few years. He left the SEP entirely in 1935 to dedicate his attentions to his own Academia de Ballet Clásico y Plástica Dinámica.[50]

THE MODERNISTS TAKE CHARGE

As dance historian Patricia Aulestia points out, the new Council of Fine Arts ignored the detailed curriculum for the Escuela de Plástica y Dinámica that Zybin created, though it did note that, alone among his colleagues, he consistently taught his classes.[51] This choice to ignore Zybin's classical ballet focus could have been the resulting council's modernist orientation. Most of its members were actively associated with what they called the "group without a group," known as the Contemporáneos (Contemporaries), which flourished in the late 1920s and early 1930s. The artists who were counted among the Contemporáneos were largely resistant to the idea that the nation's art ought to be nationalistic or explicitly political and thought that, as its name suggested, artists should fully embrace "universal" modernist ideas. This orientation did not necessarily reject what Tamayo called "a still unresolved Mexicanism," rather it sought something other than interpretations of the folkloric or archeological themes of the nationalists, preferring a more profound, formal probing in order to capture "the essence of true Mexicanism."[52]

Not surprisingly, Rivera detested the Contemporáneos. Even as the group's influence waned, he attacked its insistence on a formalist approach to art using an even more directly macho dismissal of its members' efforts than he aimed at Montenegro's work. "Art for art's sake, that is, abstract art is the spoiled child of the capitalist bourgeoisie in power," he wrote. "Therefore, in Mexico, there are the beginnings of a group of pseudo-artists and bourgeois scribblers who call themselves pure poets but are actually nothing more than pure faggots."[53] It was not the first time that accusations of homosexuality were used in an attempt to discredit the group, that, although largely composed of homosexual men, was hardly exclusively so.[54] The group was united far more by its openness to a range of aesthetic positions than by its members' sexuality. Maples shared Rivera's distaste for the Contemporáneos. His memoirs indicated a profound homophobia as well as his sympathy with efforts in the 1930s to oust homosexuals from government jobs because such individuals were, per se, reactionary and an insult to the honor of heterosexual artists.[55] He was not an active participant in the council's discussions on dance.

The council reviewed only two proposals for the academic program of the new school, though there may have been others.[56] One was from modernist and fellow Contemporáneo Chávez, then director of the SEP's National Music Conservatory. The other was from the considerably more nationalist Campobello sisters, underlining the success that Nellie achieved with the SEP's leadership through 30–30.

The council's reaction to Chávez's proposal suggests that his understanding of the challenges associated with choreographing a work for the stage had not been substantially augmented by his experience with mounting *H.P.* The council's summary of the composer's idea for creating the new school—neither of the proposals they considered seem to have been preserved—laid out a plan to

> use the budget assigned to the School of Dance to appoint, exclusively, indigenous people from each region of the Republic who will perform dancing that will serve as recreation in schools, parks and theaters.
>
> There should be no teaching activities in matters of dance so long as Mexican dance does not exist; it will be created as a synthesis of the indigenous and mestizo dances of the entire country.[57]

The council was underwhelmed by Chávez's proposal. It pointed out that the proposal did nothing to address the interests of a substantial number of students in learning to dance, and that brining indigenous people from throughout the country to dance for the public's entertainment did not address that situation. The council also observed that, while many of the indigenous people were excellent dancers, they were usually not the best of teachers. They knew how to dance but were unable to analyze and explain how they danced. Although there was not a dancer among their number, the council also understood that the formal issue of technique was a basic one to be addressed if the proposed school were to meet its aims:

> Mr. Chávez Ramírez confuses technique with art itself. In negating the possibility of transmitting this technical knowledge he negates

the very essence of education. The educator can transmit a hundred and one manners of managing esthetic materials. He cannot transmit creative genius, but he can facilitate, he can provoke a reaction, by explaining the diverse techniques of the expression of creative genius.

Mr. Chávez Ramírez points out that Mexican dance is dispersed among the different Indian tribes and mestizo centers of the country, being in each case a particular expression of that tribe or center. "We should," he adds, "create a reunion of all of these experiences to achieve a total expression."

It would be interesting to apply this reasoning to the creation of Mexican song or food. It would be the system of the stewpot or the olla podrida. In order to create Mexican food it would be necessary to toss mole poblano, pozole, huevos rancheros, etc., into the pot. The result would be Mexican food.

The creation of a Mexican dance is not a voluntary act (in the case that it proves possible). There is no doubt that the Spanish people know how to dance. There is no doubt that Spanish dance exists. But it does not exist as the sum of the jota, the sardana, the fado and the zorcico, but in the particular expressions, and at the same time universal humanity, of each of those dances.[58]

The council's brief summary, and much longer rebuttal, of Chávez's proposal did not address another key aspect of the composer's thinking about the new dance school, an opinion that he laid out in a supporting letter to the minister of education. Chávez believed that the indigenous dancers who would be gathered to perform in Mexico City as part of his proposal ought to be subject to a kind of artistic director, "an individual who is not a dancer, but who has the aesthetic capacity and the general orientations in the matter of art, necessary to concretize the choreographic expressions of the Indians and to subject them to a process of constant self improvement without imposing any external influence. A guide or channeler of this nature, I think, can be chosen from among any of the young Mexican painters, since they have demonstrated their plastic sensitivity and their ability to understand artistic problems in their work as painters."[59]

More succinctly stated, Chávez argued that painters knew better than dancers how they should dance. Even stranger, he thought a painter could redirect the dancers "without imposing any external influence." The council rejected this argument as well. Dance, the council members countered, was a form sufficient unto itself and should not be subject to the influence of other arts.[60]

The proposal from the Campobello sisters fared no better with the council. They also suggested that the budget destined for the school should be used for performances, specifically their own. According to the council, the Campobello proposal recommended that "the budget of the School should be used to form a group of professional dancers, among them the Mmes. Campobello, as well as other professors and distinguished alumni, that would be dedicated to creating a Mexican School of Ballet, taking advantage of the combined choreographic elements from the different regional dances of the country."[61]

The Campobello proposal also relied on creating Mexican dance through a fusion of elements from various regional dances, again just as Chávez recommended, but in this instance the council rejected the concept on formal grounds. It evoked the specter of Adolfo Best's *Metodo de Dibujo*, a text that one of the council members, Tamayo, once used to instruct students: "In our concept, the dance, considered as a National School in the nature of the Russian School or the French School, is the result of a tradition that is not possible to improvise in a laboratory without risk of falling into an artifice similar to that which we experienced in the decorative arts in the application of a conventional method that wished to constitute itself in a synthesis of the elements of the old Mexican indigenous decoration."[62]

Judging by the council's additional criticism of the Campobello proposal, the sisters wanted to send the dancers of their company to tour the nation's rural communities in search of materials. They found this idea both duplicative—the cultural missionaries were already doing this work, even if they weren't trained dancers—and impractical. The dancers, the council opined, ought to be spending their time in the rehearsal studios and presenting works on stage instead of traveling about the countryside. More specifically, the council declared that "there aren't ten professionals in Mexico who are sufficiently capable of coinciding in a work with some degree [of] unanimity, as is necessary for all creative work."[63]

The council concluded its review of the Campobello proposal by noting that its objections to the sisters' ideas could likely be resolved in short order, if the nation did, in fact, have a dancing school with a corps of professionally trained students. The lack of a school was also the central failing of the Chávez proposal. Going without a school, the council reemphasized, would "leave unsatisfied the legitimate aspirations of many people who, through this activity, wish to provide themselves not with some unnecessary personal adornment, but with the substance itself."

The council devised its own program for the dance school it thought would meet the needs of the SEP, although ideas from the Chávez and Campobello proposals were reflected in its recommendations. It developed a three-year program of studies intended to produce a corps of professional dancers. The first two years included studies in classical ballet, to be instructed by Zybin, and in Mexico's regional dances, under the leadership of Nellie Campobello. Art courses, including set, costume, and makeup design, were also a requirement of the first two years of work. Students were also required to select two "specialty" areas that could consist of "Greek" dance, which it specifically defined as "Duncanism;" "foreign popular dance," including Spanish dancing; and modern theatrical dance, which embraced everything from tap to acrobatics.[64] During the third year, each student would be required to create and mount a work as the "crowning achievement" of her education. The council envisioned the task as a kind of Mexicanized version of Diaghilev's gesamtkunstwerk approach to dance making, specifying that it involved "reconstructing or recreating our dances using the material provided by the Cultural Missions, duly classified and organized by the Academies of Investigation, seeking, at the same time, an effective collaboration by painters, scenographers, musicians and writers."

The council did, however, accept Chávez's notion that a painter should head the new dance school, but for different reasons than the composer offered. In what reads like an circuitous reaffirmation of male dominance, the council determined that "the Director of the School should preferably be a painter, both because professional dancers lack administrative and technical organization abilities, and because they would try to impose their particular professional methods." It successfully recommended that the Guatemalan-born Carlos Mérida be offered the position. The council also named Nellie Campobello as his assistant to deal with the issues of dance technique.

CARLOS MÉRIDA AND THE DANCE: CREATING A MODERN PRESENT FROM AN INDIGENOUS PAST

Historian Aurelio de los Reyes notes that, given the rhetorically pro-indigenous stance of the times, the council's recommendation of Mérida for the post was hardly surprising. From his first exhibitions in Mexico,

Mérida demonstrated that his artworks "assimilated indigenous motifs and concepts and techniques of the European vanguard."[65] Mérida described himself as a mestizo and claimed his indigenous heritage as his primary influence: "Mixture that I am of Maya-Quiché Indian and Spaniard, the brilliant sumptuary spectacle of our aborigines, of their dances filled with fervor and ritual, of the marvelous landscapes one can contemplate in Guatemala, of the millenarial plastic expressions bequeathed to us by our grandfathers—the builders of Palenque and Quiriguá—would make me feel a profound conflict if I were not faithful to my tradition and my race, if I ignored the tenacious appeals of their distant interior voices."[66]

During his years studying painting in Paris, Mérida was among the substantial contingent of students from Argentina and Mexico at the academy run by Hermen Anglada Camarasa, whose work was deeply influenced by the Ballets Russes aesthetic.[67] As did his fellow students at Anglada's academy, Mérida attended performances by Diaghilev's company, and continued to follow the company through its varied reincarnations after the impresario's death.[68] Mérida took to heart Anglada's insistence that national folklore provided painters a route away from Parisian modernism toward a style that was more appropriate for them as individuals. His adoption of this advice dealt with the spirit of the form rather than the external inspiration itself. In a 1920 essay for the newspaper *El Universal Ilustrado* on the recently deceased painter Saturnino Herrán (1887–1918), Mérida insisted that "indigenous art ought to serve as nothing more than a point of departure, it should only serve to orient us, and it is necessary to allow it to evolve, we need to keep in mind that we are no longer in their epoch, neither is our spirit the same as that of the Indians, nor are the elements of our work the same; to make nationalist art it is necessary to blend the essential part of our autochthonous art with today's reality and our current way of feeling, not in its external, shall we say theatrical, form, but in its essential, spiritual form; the mere spectacle of our nature offers us a wide field for creating nationalist painting, but founding ourselves in the spirit of our nature, not expressing its more or less exterior form."[69]

He may not have been Mexican born, but Mérida understood the political necessity of a pro-indigenous stance and developed a personal manner of navigating between European modernity and American identity that avoided the direct imitation of folk art forms. Both critics and politicians understood that Mérida's color palette descended from indigenous embroidery but that the forms he gave them were "modern." In the 1930s he characterized himself as "the representative of Mexican abstract painting."[70]

The Guatemalan artist had additional experience that qualified him for the position. He began his artistic career with aspirations to becoming a professional pianist, a goal that was sidelined by a congenital hearing problem.[71] Nonetheless, given his musical interests he accompanied composer Jesús Castillo (1877–1946) during his studies of the indigenous music of the Maya-Quiché peoples of his homeland. In Mexico, Mérida participated in Manuel Gamio's ambitious ethnographic project registering the life of the community near the ruins of Teotihuacán. He also collaborated as an author and illustrator on Frances Toor's bilingual magazine *Mexican Folkways*. He was more than prepared to put the materials developed by the nation's cultural missionaries to use in the creation of a national dance. As art historian Armando Torres observes, despite the importance of dance to his career, the number of Mérida's paintings that relate directly to dance is relatively small. "Nonetheless, the rhythm of many of his paintings and prints obeys, equally, the dynamism of the dance and the constants of music. One finds this hybrid origin constantly throughout his production."[72]

During his tenure as director of the school from 1932–1935, Mérida oversaw the documentation of some seventy dances that were still performed in various regions of the country. Working in collaboration with Domínguez, who then led the school's music program and had served as a cultural missionary in Michoacán, Mérida set up what he called the Laboratorio de Ritmos Plásticos (Laboratory of Plastic Rhythm) as an informal organization to create a mixture of indigenous forms and contemporary expressions.[73]

Domínguez was uniquely qualified on this front. He served as one of the principal investigators in a parallel project led by Chávez as part of the Academia de Investigación de la Música Popular in conjunction with the SEP's Conservatorio Nacional de Música.[74] By 1935, the Academia de Investigación had transcribed 1,788 tunes gathered from remote corners of Mexico that Chávez and his companions believed were most likely to hold musical evidence documenting the nation's indigenous roots.

At the time it was difficult for urban audiences to witness the nation's indigenous dances in performance. As Mérida noted, "they are performed in an infinity of villages, but on special occasions, and on determined dates. This makes it necessary to go to these villages on their festal days. And as Mexico is large, and the occasion does not present itself often, even we who are passionately attached to these dances do not know many of the manifestations in their original form. They are still outside the purely commercial field, and for that reason are not easy to know. The foreigner knows exactly that which lacks deep significance—our touristized Jarabe Tapatío, for example."[75]

He set out to do something about that issue. In a document directed to the chief of the SEP's Department of Fine Arts, Mérida outlined the school's ongoing research plan shortly after completing his first year as director. The plan sought to capture the most "characteristic" of the dances performed within the nation's borders. It divided these dances into two categories: dances that were ritual in nature, and by definition indigenous, and regional dances that reflected the country's mestizo population. He further subdivided these categories by region, three for the indigenous dances, four for the dances that displayed European influence. His study plan focused on the indigenous; it included sixty-eight of these "ritual" dances, while Mérida deemed only thirty-five "regional" dances as holding sufficient interest to merit the school's attention. Each of these dances was to receive a multilayered investigation to determine, among other things, how "pure" it was in terms of movement, music, and costuming. Unfortunately, Mérida did not specify the criteria he and his investigators would apply in making such determinations. In later writings he affirmed that

> it is still possible to find expressions completely lacking any touch of foreign mentality. We believe that these primitive forms are the most interesting.
>
> Nevertheless, the mixture of races has given greater complexity to many of the aboriginal creations. And the effect of the confluence of the two currents is very curious. The religious sprit of the native mixes his pagan conceptions with the superimposed Christian conception. A goodly number of the mestizo dances make us feel the presence of idols, the flavor of the ancient theogonies.[76]

Studying the dances as they were performed during the appropriate festival celebrations in their sites of origin, he opined, offered the full atmosphere of pure folklore but did not allow for analyzing them in the necessary depth. He proposed instead studying them outside that context, either on nonfestival days or by bringing the dance groups to Mexico City. His research plan added that he planned on bringing three groups of dancers from the nearby state of Puebla to Mexico City as a kind of test case for his proposal. He also expressed a wish that the school be provided with sufficient resources to film each of the named dance performances. His wish list concluded with a request for a trained scenic designer to properly record the costumes and

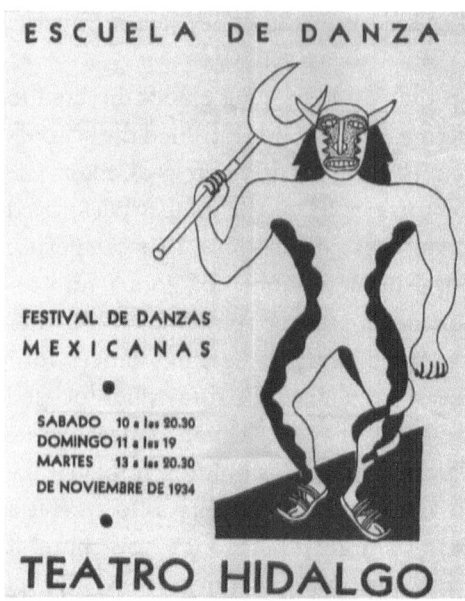

FIGURE 12. Carlos Mérida (1891–1985). Cover illustration for the Festival de danzas mexicanas (Festival of Mexican Dances) program. 1934. Mérida's daughter Ana was among the festival's performers. Collection of Patricia Aulestia, Mexico City. © 2019 Artists Rights Society (ARS), New York/SOMAAP, Mexico City.

props, a musician to annotate the melodies employed during the dance, and a trained ethnographer to provide overall guidance for the effort.

This ambitious research plan was well beyond the school's budget, which barely funded studio instruction, but Mérida was still able to use resources from the cultural missions, Chávez's Academia de Investigación, and elsewhere to carry out some of his agenda.[77]

In 1937, a few years after Mérida departed as the school's director, the SEP arranged a group of performances in the Palacio de Bellas Artes that featured dancers and musicians drawn from across the nation. As he described them, the "presentations were offered in the purest and simplest form possible. Nothing was done to theatricalize the spectacle, to modify the costumes with richer or showier fabrics, or to adapt the music. Care was taken not to alter even the outline of a decoration. A simple, neutral curtain was the background on the stage of the Palace of Fine Arts for the indigenous groups."[78] Mérida thought the event was an "outstanding success." The fact that the dances were decontextualized be removing them from the church atriums or village plazas that were their customary venues and presented on a proscenium stage did not bother him.

In his notes for an autobiography, he recalled selecting four dances, each with a different character, for immediate attention at his school: the *Danza ritual de los concheros*, which was (and is) still performed in Mexico City; dances from Tehuantepec; the *Danza de los malinches* from San Dionosio del Mar in Oaxaca; and what he called a dance drama of the Otomi peoples known as *La virgen y las fieras* (The Virgin and the Beasts). Each of these, in turn, served to provide the materials for one of the dances performed in the school's Festival de Danzas Mexicanas in 1934. Despite budgetary limitations, Mérida ensured that each work on this program had original choreography, music, and scenic designs. Domínguez provided the scores while the school's instructor of stagecraft, Carlos Orozco Romero (1896–1984), provided the artwork.

The program for this performance provides a telling detail about the depth of Mérida's commitment to his new school.[79] One of the performers in the *La virgen y las fieras* was his daughter Ana. She became one of the nation's most noted dancers and choreographers.

Apart from his daughter's appearance in the cast, Mérida held a particular fondness for the 1934 production of *La virgen y las fieras*. He highlighted this work in an essay titled "Pre-Hispanic Dance and Theatre" for the August 1938 issue of *Theatre Arts Monthly*, which focused on Mexico.

La Virgen y las Fieras, based on a legend of the same name, has a very simple pagan story. It contains no Christian flavor, at least in its original form. It is danced (it is given, let us say, since it is a primitive theatrical form) in various Otomí villages in the state of Hidalgo.

The virgin comes out of her hut and enters the forest, enticed by the trills of the birds and the enchantment of the flowers. When she is deep in the woods, she realizes that she has lost her way. Her situation becomes dangerous when she is attacked by unfriendly presences. She asks for help from the animals who love her. At her call, there appear lions, tigers, wolves, bulls, deer and all kinds of animals who shield her, beat off the malign spirits and save her. In the representation of these hostile spirits there has come to be, in many places, something of popular Christian mythology.[80]

Like many of the dances that Mérida singled out as indigenous rituals, *La virgen y las fieras* owed more than "something" of its drama to its Christian elements. Since written legends are of postconquest origin, it is difficult to determine what the "original" version of the story might have been.[81] *La virgen y las fieras* held multiple elements that link it to a Christian worldview. The original program notes by Francisco Domínguez indicate that the story's evil spirits were lifted directly from Christian sources.[82] The virgin that tames wild animals has Christian roots as well, perhaps most memorably expressed in European legends of a virgin capable of capturing the elusive unicorn. According to Domínguez's notes, the only indigenous element actually employed in the performance came from two elements of the work's original melodies.

Nonetheless, if the massive presentations of the Spanish-influenced jarabe tapatío and the sandunga that marked the 1921 centennial celebration helped to sacralize folk dance as central element of postrevolutionary identity, the continuing efforts of the SEP's cultural missionaries and presentations by the SEP's new dancing school began to expand the repertory to include works that were seen as purely indigenous.

NOTABLE VISITORS

During Mérida's tenure at the helm of Mexico's new School of Dance, Mexico City received two visitors whose appearance represented distinct approaches to the dance that were being debated in the corridors of the SEP as it sought to define its approach to the art. The first, Martha Graham, arrived for a little more than a month in the summer of 1932, her visit financed by the John Simon Guggenheim Foundation. She traveled to Mexico as part of the foundation's Latin American Exchange Fellows program, which was intended to foster a "commerce of things of the mind, of spiritual values" among the US and its neighbors.[83] The second was the Ballet Russes de Monte Carlo, then under the direction of Wassily de Basil (1888–1951), which arrived for a two-week engagement in 1934. Graham represented what eventually became the nation's officially embraced aesthetic; de Basil represented the approach Vasconcelos championed.

The Ballets Russes arrived in Mexico as part of the festivities inaugurating the Palacio de Bellas Artes, which had been under construction, although not always actively, since the administration of Porfirio Díaz. The company performed Stravinsky's *Firebird* as part of the building's Opening Gala on October 1, 1934, and mostly presented other works that dated from the era of Diaghilev in its subsequent appearances.[84] Mexican audiences could finally see the impresario's vision of modernized Russian folklore in works such as the "Polovtsian Dances" from *Prince Igor* and *Petrouchka* alongside Picasso's cubist designs for the 1919 *El sombrero de tres picos* (The Three-Cornered Hat). While these ballets had achieved the status of modern classics, their costumes and scenery were ragged with use, a fact that was not lost on the Mexican critics. The reception of the ballets themselves was also mixed; *Les Sylphides* (1909), *Le Beau Danube* (1924), and the brand new *Union Pacific* (1934) failed to please the Bellas Artes audience, while *Petrouchka*, the "Polovtsian Dances," and *El sombrero de tres picos,* by contrast, were resounding successes.[85] Nonetheless, one of Vasconcelos's associates, Antonio Castro Leal (1896–1981), then director of the SEP's fine arts program, received the public praise of his superiors for having secured the company for the building's opening dance performances.[86]

Not everyone was happy with the inaugural events. *Frente a Frente*, the magazine of the pro-Soviet Liga de Escritores y Artistas Revolucionarios (LEAR, League of Revolutionary Artists and Writers), mocked it. The magazine's cover featured a Posada-inspired print by Leopoldo Méndez depicting a theater full of skeletons. In an essay attacking the opening on its inside pages, the magazine noted that Chávez may have conducted the premiere of his *Llamadas: Sinfonía proletaria* (Calls: Proletarian Symphony) as part of the event, but with ticket prices that began at eight pesos when the minimum wage was one and a half pesos an hour it was certain that no member of the proletariat was in the audience to hear it.[87]

Keenly sensitive to the need for placing a populist gloss on the theatre's opening, the SEP declared that part of its mission was to "to place the highest and most beautiful spectacles before the eyes and ears of those who cannot enjoy them when they are presented by private companies" and announced that the Ballets Russes de Montecarlo would make an appearance in the city's bullring.[88] There "the entire Mexican public" could see a performance of the company "without the need to pay a high price." By offering a performance in the same venue that Pavlova used years earlier, "the laborers, and the most modest government or private employees" could afford tickets at prices "below that customarily paid for a bull fight, a boxing match or a baseball game." The company's October 12 performance there drew a crowd of twenty-five thousand spectators, equaling that garnered by Pavlova.[89]

The students at the School of Dance, which was not yet two years old, thought that they and not the Ballets Russes ought to have danced at the opening gala. Mérida harbored no illusions as to his student's capacities, describing their prior public performances as consisting of a few "choreographic exercises of a purely pedagogical nature."[90] The students saw things differently. In a letter to Minister of Education Narciso Bassols (1897–1959), they asked that their school be assigned the task of preparing them for the opening ceremonies: "If the invitation of the ballet of Monte Carlo is an inevitable fact, we want to work in the programs of the inauguration, to prove that Mexico has its own Classical Ballet group which is capable of being presented alongside expensive foreign professional companies. . . . We ask of you, Mister Secretary, that you take under consideration our just and common desire and that you commission Mister Hipolyt [sic] Zybin, giving him the chance and the time necessary to carry out this undertaking with all the success and brilliance possible."[91]

Bassols did not accept their petition for a space on the opening ceremony's program, but he did grant the school a new home within the palacio, allowing it to move from its improvised home within the headquarters of the SEP into a space built to meet the needs of performing artists. Within a few weeks of the opening ceremonies, the students of the School of Dance were enjoying the amenities of their new home.

If the invitation of the Ballets Russes de Monte Carlo to inaugurate the new Palacio de Bellas Artes struck some as somewhat tone deaf on the part of the SEP, the Calles administration's dedication to emphasizing its public support for indigenous and popular causes was on full display in the building's art galleries. Before the theater's Tiffany glass curtain rose on the inaugural gala, the audience could appreciate what was billed as a "new museum" of folk art, assembled by Roberto Montenegro in the building's exhibition halls.[92] In its way, this exhibition was also an inheritance from Diaghilev. Montenegro acquired his taste for folk art through the Ballet Russes' Russian designers and transplanted it to Mexico. The exhibition of masterworks by the nation's rural artisans that greeted the heirs of Diaghilev at the opening of the new theatre completed the circle that began in Paris with the 1913 exhibition of the Russian folk art that inspired both Montenegro and Rivera.

Ostensibly, an interest in Mexican folk culture was what drew Martha Graham to visit Mexico in 1932. Her grant from the Guggenheim Foundation was for "studies of native dances of Mexico and Yucatan," an activity she did not pursue during her visit.[93] Then working in what later critics described as her "primitive" period, Graham's art was likened by more than one contemporary writer to the works of Rivera and Orozco, both of whom were working on mural projects in the US when she visited Mexico. Stark Young (1881–1963), theater critic for the left-leaning New Republic, thought

Graham's dancing was "as solid in drawing and in composition as Diego Rivera at his best."[94] According to Graham's biographer Don McDonagh, she was asked by an unnamed interviewer if *Primitive Mysteries* (1931), her first acknowledged masterwork, which premiered two weeks after Orozco unveiled his controversial cycle of murals at the New School for Social Research, had been influenced by the fresco.[95] Since Graham completed her choreography for the work before her music director and lover Louis Horst (1884–1964) began composition of its score, the possibility of any influence from Orozco's mural was highly unlikely.[96] Still, "with her characteristic flair, she allowed that she had been influenced by the painter José Clemente Orozco but that she had not used him as a model to be copied or even approximated." Comparisons of her work at that time to that of the Mexican muralists, as McDonagh went on to point out, were superficial at best, but reflected the immense interest in Mexican art, as well as its public perception as "primitive," in the US during the 1930s.[97]

Mérida subsequently claimed that he invited Graham to serve as a guest teacher at the new school during her brief stay in Mexico; his deputy, Nellie Campobello, asserted that Graham visited the school specifically to solicit her guidance.[98] The July 18, 1932, meeting among Mérida, Campobello, Graham, and Horst was most likely arranged through Chávez, whom they met at a July 3 tea party.[99] Horst's journal is the only contemporaneous source of information about Graham's visit. Its typically terse entry for the day only mentions meeting with Mérida and Nellie Campobello, nothing more. On her return to the US, Graham told a reporter that what Mexico had done in forming the school was "a good example" for her own homeland, but she did not mention any teaching opportunities then or in her much later interview about her travel to Mexico with Alberto Dallal.[100]

Graham was just beginning to gain attention beyond New York City as a dancer/choreographer with her own technique. Although Graham contacted Chávez about the possibility of securing a dance score as early as August of 1931, the composer hadn't yet collaborated with her.[101] He could well have known about her critically acclaimed performance as the Chosen One in the first complete mounting of Stravinsky's *Le sacre du printemps* in the US through his conductor friend Leopold Stokowski, who wielded the baton for the Stravinsky ballet and Chávez's *H.P.*

Mexican designer Francisco Cornejo, who designed the sets and costumes for *Xochitl*, the Ted Shawn work that secured Graham's fame as a dancer, was also a guest at the July 3 tea party. A native of La Paz, Baja, California, Cornejo moved to Los Angeles in 1911, where he was counted, along with Ramon Novarro (1899–1968), Lupe Velez (1906–1944), and Dolores del Río among the "authentic Mexicans" who were refashioning the image of the country in Hollywood.[102] Cornejo subsequently opened his Aztec Studio in San Francisco, where, with assistance from sculptor Manuel Centurion, he promoted his belief "that the works of these ancient people would be an inspiration for the development of a pure American Art."[103] When Cornejo returned to Mexico in 1930, he opened a graphic design and advertising firm in partnership with painter Jorge González Camarena (1908–1980).[104] By then, he was no longer promoting a pre-Columbian aesthetic. Using property he inherited from his mother, Cornejo expressed his nostalgia for Mexico's rural-village culture by developing what he called his Rancho del Artista. From its foundation in 1937, the rancho gradually grew to reproduce an old Mexican hacienda, with artist's studios—the Costa Rican–born sculptor Francisco Zuñiga (1912–1998) did some of his work there—as well as exhibition galleries, and a restaurant occupying the spaces behind the facades of the rancho's traditional architectural settings.[105] On Sundays, strolling musicians and dancers performed works drawn from communities across the nation in the rancho's streets and plazas. Either Cornejo or Chávez could have alerted Mérida to Graham's presence in México.

Whether or not Graham was a guest instructor at the SEP's new dancing school, Mérida was impressed by his encounter with her. His continuing interest in what she was achieving through her work had long-term effects on the direction of dance in Mexico. Mérida's tenure as head of the SEP's dance school was short—according to dance historian Margarita Tortajada, he was relieved of his position early in 1935 by the leader of the SEP's Departamento de Bellas Artes, José Muñoz Cota—for refusing to limit the school's work to what was dictated by the explicit nationalism promoted during the presidential administration of Lázaro Cárdenas (1895–1970).[106] He was replaced by his deputy, Nellie Campobello.

Mérida's successful international painting career, however, frequently took him beyond Mexico's borders, where he followed dance almost as assiduously as he did painting. As Mérida was far better known as an artist in the US at the time than he was in Mexico, with more than double the exhibitions north of the border, he had the opportunity for frequent reencounters with Graham's work.[107]

Mérida firmly believed that "only through a basis in technique [would] it be possible to make the true choreographic theater" that Mexico needed.[108] He also believed this was possible, just as it had "been possible to create a

Mexican painting." It would prove, as Mérida related, "possible to create a Mexican theatre, choreography and literature growing out of the same pure consciousness of the dance, our own consciousness. This is what I have always aimed at in my activities in connection with the dance, and in prolonged efforts in pictorial work."[109] Through Mérida's impetus, Mexican dancers would subsequently adopt a technique arising from Graham's search for an "American gesture" to express their own realities.[110]

7

Competing Modernisms

Anna Sokolow and Waldeen

Because of Carlos Mérida's advocacy on behalf of the Graham technique, the SEP invited US dancer-choreographer Anna Sokolow to perform and teach in Mexico City. At about the same time it also invited Waldeen Falkenstein, better known by her first name only, to perform. This created a seemingly unintentional competition between their opposing styles of socially engaged choreography. Sokolow's approach was closely aligned to the ideas of her mentor Martha Graham; Waldeen claimed to have found her inspiration in specifically "Mexican" ways of moving. Their antagonistic approach mirrored ongoing divisions in the visual arts community over international orientation versus local inspiration, though the disciples of both dancers rejected any suggestion of foreign elements in their work.

The concerns raised by the SEP's Consejo de Bellas Artes about individual dancers attempting to "impose their particular professional methods" when it formed Mexico's dance school were well founded. The same concerns could have been expressed about the leaders of the SEP, who used their positions to support dancers with competing agendas. Although the activities of the Campobello sisters at the Escuela Nacional de Danza provided the background against which the initial clash of dance ideologies played out, it was the two choreographers invited from the US who provided much of the drama.

Sokolow and Waldeen shared active engagement in labor issues and a commitment to exploring social themes in their work. Their political temperament was appropriately aligned with the leftist orthodoxy that marked the Lázaro Cárdenas administration. Cárdenas was one of the few postrevolutionary presidents of Mexico whose populist rhetoric was not routinely belied by his actions. His administration incorporated dance into its centralized propaganda efforts, making funding available for massive performances of Nellie Campobello's *30–30*.[1]

Cárdenas declared that "culture without a concrete sense of solidarity with the pain of the people is not fecund, it is a limited culture, a mere adornment of parasites who hinder the collective program. Thought is elevated when it is animated by the tragedy of humanity in its search for fecundity, in its battle against nature."[2] The bureaucrats under President Cárdenas who supported the work of Sokolow and Waldeen could do so with confidence that the results would be ideologically congruent with those of their leader.

The choreographers were invited to perform in Mexico in 1939 by Celestino Gorostiza, chief of the SEP's Department of Bellas Artes. Nellie Campobello's fierce defense of what she considered the rights that pertained to her as director of the National Dancing School brought her into frequent conflict with her students, their parents, and the SEP staff, Gorostiza in particular.[3] He, in turn, used his position to promote modern dance performances on the stage of the Palacio de Bellas Artes. As Mexican dance historian Margarita Tortajada puts it: "Perhaps he not only saw in modern dance the language which expressed the new dance, he also saw it as an instrument to apply pressure on the Campobellos in order to strengthen his authority over them."[4] Gorostiza's superior, Minister of Education Gonzalo Vasquez Vela (1893–1963), asked Sokolow to stay on and form a modern dance company after her initial performances in Mexico. It was Gorostiza who provided the backing for Waldeen. For some reason he promoted the 1940 performances of both Sokolow's and Waldeen's different companies under the same name, the Ballet de Bellas Artes.

The disciples formed by Sokolow and Waldeen assembled antagonistic groups that actively resisted each other's work. Followers of Sokolow became known as Sokolovas, while Waldeen's adherents were dubbed Waldeenas. Dancers from one camp refused to perform alongside dancers from the other.[5] With the exception of Carlos Mérida's daughter Ana, who worked with both early on, the opposing groups were estranged from each other for most of the decade. As choreographer Guillermina Bravo, one of the Waldeenas, puts it, "we couldn't abide one another."[6]

It was not simply technique that divided them. It was the nature and content of Mexican theatrical dance. Sokolow sought to express her political vision through implementing her personal version of Martha Graham's technique. Waldeen wanted something more specifically Mexican.

Although Gorostiza did not appear to have been consciously creating a contest between the two choreographers, the juxtaposition of their performances gave critics and the public a chance to compare their contrasting approaches to creating Mexican modern dance. Music critic José Barros Sierra summarized the situation in the November 1940 issue of *Romance*:

> The dance has begun to travel the same path that our music has so quickly traversed. Here, too, we face the same initial question: what should we understand as Mexican dance; whether we use our traditional indigenous wealth that has been preserved in almost the entire country, or whether we should apply an imported technique in the treatment of choreographic matters of a Mexican character. Two schools of dance—one of which has already offered its first fruits in recent seasons and the other which is preparing to present itself to the public shortly—represent these two points of view. A third, first in time and first also in importance because of its permanent character, began from the outset the task of synthesizing in a proper modality the two tendencies first pointed out. We refer to the National School of Dance, dependent of the SEP, that is under the direction of Nellie Campobello. Anna Sokolow has educated a group of students in her own technique imported from New York, that may well be considered as one of the infinite variants that have arisen from the teachings of Martha Graham. Working completely outside the question of taking advantage of the traditional choreographic elements of Mexico, Anna Sokolow believes, so far, that when her disciples have perfectly assimilated her teachings, they will be able to apply the acquired technique to the creation of Mexican dance. The other group, led by Waldeen, starts from an opposing point of view. Waldeen believes, in accord with the opinion of her teacher, the Japanese Michio Ito, that the rich tradition of Mexican popular dance should be used in the creation of a national dance. This purpose has inspired her teachings, based on the observations she has made in the country during her long stay here. She hopes soon to show the public the results she has achieved in his task.[7]

Sokolow and "Imported" Technique

Sokolow's invitation to Mexico came through Carlos Mérida. He followed the works of several dancer choreographers from outside Mexico, some of whom visited Mexico in the 1920s and 1930s, as he traveled to show his artwork. In his notes for an autobiography, Mérida charted his experiences: "The ballet fascinated me and in my wanderings through the United States and Europe I got to know up close the new directions that it was taking; though the best experiences I had were in the United States, where they were making the most modern attempts. I was a regular at Martha Graham's studio; in Chicago I made the acquaintance of Katherine Dunham, who was beginning her rehearsals in Caribbean folklore, which crystalized in shows that made a triumphal tour around the world. . . . In California, I became friends with the great Adolph Bolm, who, along with Massine and Dolin labored to keep the Russian ballet alive. When I was in Denton, Texas, I saw Charles Weidman in works along the same line as Graham. Another form of dance which I was able to see there was that of the extremely talented Agnes de Mille."[8]

Mérida's familiarity with what was occurring in the dance world beyond Mexico's borders placed him in a strong position to advocate for the art form when the LEAR convened its January 1937 Congreso de Escritores, Artistas, Hombres de Ciencia e Intelectuales (Congress of Writers, Artists, Men of Science and Intellectuals). Although many of the delegates participated in one way or another in shaping Mexico's nascent dance community, only one individual invited to participate in the congress, Armen Ohanian, was a dancer.[9]

Allied with the efforts of the Popular Front, the LEAR was organized in 1933 and served as a major cultural force in Mexico through much of the decade. It presented itself as an organization in opposition to "bourgeois arts and sciences" laboring "in the service of the working class against the current capitalist regime and its dire consequences of crisis and degeneration, and its consequences fascism, Imperialism and war." For its members, the Soviet Union was "the only country where culture performs its integral functions with beneficial purposes for laboring humanity, it is the Torch which points the way forward for the proletariat of the other countries of the earth."[10] Consequently, it took more than a modicum of fortitude for Mérida to rise before the congress and advocate that Mexico adopt the Graham technique as the basis for its efforts to use dance as an expression of the nation.

After providing the congress with a statement of his intent to propose "the technique of modern dance, and also the study of popular Mexican choreography, in the observation of the life of a community that works, lives and suffers, to give the authentic forms necessary to lay the foundation for a living and useful expression," he went on to provide a brief history of theatrical dance.[11] He directed most of his attention to classical ballet, which had secured its position within the Soviet system.[12] For Mérida, Diaghilev's "Russian ballet constituted the perfect use of elements from the imperial ballet to the point of encountering new attitudes . . . but these were only new attitudes," which were not relevant to Mexico's situation.[13]

The rhetoric of classical dance, which still lingers anachronistically in more than one dance school, even in our own Palace of Fine Arts, established rigorous laws to develop part of the human body to achieve certain attitudes that were undoubtedly the image of its time. . . .

But time does not stop. . . . The new expression needed new rules, which logically turned towards a return to the human sense of dance. Not in the Greek way of delighting the eyes, but to the deepening of its character, the dramatizing its form, the socializing of its content.

It is in the United States where this new form of dance is being most strongly affirmed. This is undoubtedly due to the special conditions of present-day life in the United States. To the extraordinary Martha Graham, without a doubt the greatest exponent of contemporary choreography, we owe its greatest teachings, its most sensitive discoveries, its most notable collective achievements. . . . The movement gestated by Martha tends to spread, to grow, taking on increasing vitality as it is taken up by new groups, and with them, new intentions and new efforts. . . .

It uses the human body—and this is central—in all its beautiful and radiant capacity of tension and muscular distention, dignifying it, not as the classic dancers did by creating a kind of *star* but in collective form, of the group, of union, of the relationship between man and his fellows.

My intent . . . aims to find ways to inject a new life into Mexican dance, to make it a vitally expressive element that, while maintaining its special character, is a latent expression of our time. And for this I believe that there is no more secure way than that which the powerful North American choreographic expression marks out for us.[14]

Mérida's proposal was the subject of lively debate. Many of the participants in the congress, including its president, writer José Mancisador (1894–1992), readily admitted that they knew little about dance. Another official of the event, Stridentist poet and former Zapatista rebel Germán List Arzubide (1898–1998), waded into the battle regardless, and was attacked for his lack of knowledge. Fernando Ramírez de Aguilar (1887–1953), who served as the theatre critic for *El Universal* under the pen name of Jacobo Dalevuelta and had reviewed a bit of theatrical dance, spoke with a bit more reserve. Several of those involved, such as painter Santos Balmori (1899–1922) and composer Luis Sandi (1905–1996), went on to work in the dance program of the future INBA. Interestingly, ballet fanatic Martín Luis Guzmán, who helped lead the congress, does not seem to have participated in the discussion. The newspaper *Excélsior* provided a brief overview of the exchange on the topic among the delegates:

The delegate Balmori believes that the North American technique should not be taken as a prototype and asks the commission that has made the ideas of Mérida its own to explain the reasoning for its support. The delegate of the commission, Sandi when answering Balmori, states that none of the members of the commission knows about dances, hence the ideas of the painter Mérida seemed right to them.

The delegate Avila begins saying "now that it is fashionable for painters to meddle in dances," he thinks it appropriate to say that schools like the one proposed by Mérida are but means to mystify and pulverize the already almost extinct choreographic tradition of Mexico.

Mancisador clarifies that he, like the rest of the assembly, does not know anything about dance, but that he believes "that we must use the social meaning of dance with a more just and more human sense."

Mr. Jacobo Dalevuelta expresses that there is a profound ignorance in this matter, expressing that the dances he knows, when imported to Mexico, are commercialized, a very unpleasant thing.

The official Germán List Arzubide says the teaching methods of the United States are the best to learn to dance. Balmori attacks Germán

List Arzubide as ignorant, since he speaks without knowing the choreographic traditions of Europe.[15]

Nonetheless, when the measure went to vote it passed, "in the sense that
the government will be asked to create an experimental dance school with
modern technology."[16] The congress did not, however, specifically name
Graham as the creator of the "current choreographic currents relating to
techniques" it recommended for adoption. At the same time, it insisted
that for painters, sculptors, and printmakers, "a truly important new Art
can only be created through the process of its integration to the service of
the interests of the great masses of workers, as an art that lives on the favor
of the bourgeois can only serve that class and every individual approach
within such partial values is condemned to failure."

With a clearly stated social purpose to guide the future of nationalist
art and an endorsement for using the latest in technique, Mérida eventually went forward with an invitation to one of Graham's dancers, the socially engaged Anna Sokolow, to work in Mexico.[17] Sokolow recalled her
first meeting with the painter after a performance of her Dance Unit at the
New School for Social Research in 1939. Mexican painter Emilio Amero
(1901–1976), her neighbor at that time, invited his colleague Mérida to accompany him to that event. Following the performance, Amero introduced
his fellow artist to Sokolow. She remembered Mérida telling her how much
he enjoyed her program and saying that she ought to come and work in
Mexico. "I replied, 'Yes, of course,' I didn't know who he was and I thought
he was joking. Later I received an official letter from the Department of
Bellas Artes inviting 'Anna Sokolow and her dance group' to Mexico. That
was my introduction to Mexico."[18]

This encounter between Sokolow and Mérida, however, does not appear
to be the result of a sudden, chance discovery as she presented it from her
perspective. Mérida was aware of Sokolow and her works well before their
meeting and must have been following her career. His presentation to the
LEAR cited a number of specific choreographic works to support his proposal for Mexico to adopt Graham's technique as a means of nationalist expression. The majority of the works he named as examples were Sokolow's
creations—*Histrionics* (1933), *Speaker* (1935), *Inquisition* (1936), and *Suite
of Soviet Songs* (1936).[19] In fact, none of the works Mérida listed were by
Graham, although what he called *Gesture* may have been a reference to one
of Graham's handful of political pieces, *Imperial Gesture* (1935).[20]

Sokolow, who trained under Graham and Louis Horst at the Henry Street Settlement and Neighborhood Playhouse in the late 1920s, was one of Graham's leading performers in the 1930s. She earned a name for herself in New York City as a member of Graham's company, which lent her a degree of credibility.[21] She also won plaudits from the leftist press for her role in creating the Workers Dance League and for treating "proletarian" themes through the works she presented with her own company, the Dance Unit, that she formed in 1932.[22] In that sense, her dance was different from that of her mentor Graham. She was interested in treating social issues, not psychological ones. Her journey to the Soviet Union—she followed her lover, composer Alex North, there in 1934—was not entirely successful; her style of dance was too different from that which was acceptable there.[23] Sokolow later reported that the Soviet "idea of Revolutionary Dance was to wave a red flag at the audience as they balanced in their toe shoes. It didn't interest me at all."[24] Through her dedication to a more "revolutionary" application of Graham's style, which she described as arising from the point of view of the working class, she effectively opened a chapter in Mexican theatrical dance.[25]

Sokolow's Popular Front credentials fitted well within the ambit of the political positions laid out by the LEAR. When Mérida approached Sokolow, he had the approval of the LEAR for establishing modern dance instruction and an ally in Gorostiza, who issued the formal invitation to Sokolow's Dance Unit to perform at the Palacio de Bellas Artes.

According to Larry Warren's biography of Sokolow, the invitation from Gorostiza only covered the costs of the Dance Unit's travels within Mexico. The costs of getting the company, along with North, to the Mexican border were covered by Rita Morgenthau (1881–1964), who had supported Sokolow's work since her days at the Neighborhood Playhouse. Upon arrival they discovered, as Warren noted, that "jumping turned out to be easier in Mexico City; breathing was not."[26]

The company soon adjusted to the city's altitude and attacked a vigorous performing schedule that was heavy on Sokolow's political works. They opened in the Palacio de Bellas Artes in April of 1939 with a program that included *Case History No.—*(1937), depicting the deprived life that leads to juvenile delinquency, and *Strange American Funeral* (1935), which portrayed the death of an immigrant steelworker who falls into a vat of molten ore.[27] The tenor of her work held an immediate appeal for the nation's visual artists.

Dance Unit member Rebecca Kramer told Warren that the members of Mexico City's Taller de Gráfica Popular (TGP, People's Graphic Workshop) "were particularly drawn to us, partially, I think, because they were social realists and recognized that we were too."[28] Warren added that the artists of the TGP "always seemed to be there after performances, waiting with gifts of flowers and drawings and invitations to lunch." The TGP was founded in 1937 as a printers' collective dedicated to the promotion of radical social causes, partially in response to the collapse of the LEAR. According to TGP member Antonio Rodríguez, the group not only employed "social realism"; the idea of creating more easily affordable and accessible graphics themselves was part of the group's motivation. "The print became, through its spirit, a version of a mural in another 'language;' that is to say in its capacity of movement, a more active mural."[29]

As cultural critic Humberto Musacchio points out in his study of the TGP, despite the decidedly pro-Soviet sympathies of its artists, which included Leopoldo Méndez, Alfredo Zalce (1908–2003), and José Chávez Morado (1909–2003), their prints were highly popular with audiences in the US but not in the Soviet Union. A 1940 exhibition by the artists in Moscow was attacked because its subjects were not beautiful.[30] "The artists of the TGP," Musacchio writes, "were largely of popular extraction, they knew the reality of their own experience and repeatedly declared their realist vocation, but they evidently knew that their human beings were made of imperfect clay and that they performed poorly in their service to the public by giving them costumes. For these reasons, more than once they would show themselves distant, and even contrary to, the norms of the official art of the USSR." Just as Sokolow has been uninterested in waving red flags en pointe, they were uninterested in sanitizing the particulars of their nation's reality.

Years later, Sokolow recalled the impact that her encounter with Mexico's artists exercised on her vision of life.

I was totally disarmed by my encounter with Mexico's artists and my learning about them during my first visit to Mexico. I had never had the experience of seeing how important art was to people, as it is here. I still feel it. Confronting the murals of Orozco, Diego Rivera, Siqueiros and Tamayo was overwhelming and, simultaneously, I met a group of artists called Taller de la Gráfica Popular, who were artists dedicated to the issues of the life of the people. That was a very deep experience for me and very close because that [focus on the lives of the people] was what I had done all my life; the themes that inspired me to do things in dance, were the subjects of the working class. I had an intimate sense of identification both in my encounter with the Taller de la Gráfica Popular and seeing the murals of those great artists where they represented, in their profoundly noble work (the themes) that would be a great lesson for the people. I was deeply moved by my origins and felt deeply the themes of life, of the people. I think that for this reason Mexican artists responded (to my work) and I also responded, not only to painting but also to literature and music, to the atmosphere of art in Mexico. I still think it's one of the greatest in the world. And there is something else that touched me very deeply; the great respect for the artists you have here. I remember—and I will never forget—that once I was in Bellas Artes, in the corridor where you have the murals, a simple native entered, saw the mural, took off his hat and stood there as if he were in the church. It was very beautiful.[31]

During her first visit to Mexico, Sokolow ended her relationship with North, taking up, instead, with Ignacio Aguirre (1900–1990), a veteran of the revolutionary-era army under Venustiano Carranza and a founding member of the LEAR and the TGP. She maintained a relationship with him for a number of years, over frequent and prolonged absences in the US.

Sokolow's relationship with Aguirre received a boost when Vasquez Vela offered her the opportunity to stay with an eight-month contract to develop a Mexican modern dance company at the Casa del Artista. This was shortly before Vasquez Vela's employee, Gorostiza, made a similar proposal to Waldeen. As a consequence, Arturo Perucho, in his pioneering history of the nation's modern dance movement, designated Sokolow as, "strictly speaking, the initiator of modern dance in Mexico."[32]

According to Warren, Sokolow told a Mexico City newspaper that she would "not attempt to impose a particular, predetermined foreign style on our dancers, but rather will try to develop a means by which they can, themselves, creatively solve the problems of evolving an indigenous Mexican dance form. From this, it is hoped, a style will develop that will take full advantage of the folkloric fountains, which are of incomparable richness and value."[33] Whatever she may have said, this was not her intent, and she consistently militated against the use of folkloric elements in Mexican modern dance.

Almost all of the fifteen teenaged dancers Sokolow selected to work with her graduated from the National School of Dance under Nellie Campobello's direction. Sokolow's appearance in Mexico proved most timely for them. As Claudia Carbajal points out in her study of the nation's dancing school, the institution was producing its first graduates, and performing opportunities for them barely existed.[34] Sokolow offered them the opportunity for continued professional growth. At first, communication with her company of dancers proved difficult. Rosa Reyna (1924–2006), one of the original Sokolovas, later observed that all she knew of dance before Sokolow's arrival was classical European technique.[35] Warren cites conversations with members of that first company who claimed that "at first we could only understand a few words. We followed what she did—watched her body and gestures. Then a few more words. Finally, we understood. She spoke of 'light' and 'force.' . . . These concepts were novel for us. We were a little frightened but we had strong personalities and were dying to be dancers. It was the most important thing in our lives at that time. Anna found a group that was well prepared for her and one with fire inside."[36]

Just as they were regulars at the performances of her Dance Unit in Mexico, the members of the TGP began to haunt the rehearsal sessions of the Mexican dance company under Sokolow's direction. The members of the TGP also invited their friends from the broader artistic community to join them as witnesses to the creation of a new art form. It was through friendships with the artists of the TGP that composer Rodolfo Halffter (1900–1987) and avant-garde dramatist José Bergamín (1895–1983), two of the thousands of émigrés from the Spanish Republic whom President Cárdenas welcomed to Mexico, began to attend the dancers' rehearsals. This encounter led to the creation of Sokolow's first major success there, *Don Lindo de Almería.*

Bergamín began the scenario for his proposed ballet following the multiple successes of Manuel de Falla (1876–1946)–Pablo Picasso collaborations with Serge Diaghilev's Ballets Russes when World War I brought the company to Spain for an extended stay.[37] The dramatist sought de Falla's collaboration in producing the score; de Falla, in turn, recommended Halffter, who began composing it around 1930. The resulting work received its orchestral premiere in Paris in 1936, followed by performances in Barcelona and Madrid. It logged a repeat performance in Paris during the 1937

Exposition Internationale des Arts et Techniques dans la Vie Moderne—as part of the same program in which the Spanish Republic unveiled Picasso's *Guernica*—but not in its intended form as a ballet. Having carried the score and scenario with them to Mexico, Bergamín and Halffter wanted to see it performed as originally envisioned.

Halffter created his score with the intention of abstracting and commenting on the true nature of popular culture.[38] He believed that Sokolow's abstract approach to the dance provided the appropriate visual counterpart to his score. Furthermore, both the writer and the composer viewed Sokolow's lack of specific knowledge of the Spanish folkloric elements they incorporated into their work as a distinct benefit.[39] They wished their allusions to remain precisely that—with no specific evidence of Spanish stereotypes in the ballet's presentation.

Through the cooperation of Antonio Palacio, a Spanish actor and producer of *zarzuelas*, Spanish-language operettas, then presenting *La del manojo de rosas* in Mexico City's Teatro Fábregas, Halffter and Bergamín secured a performance opportunity for their work with Sokolow's choreography after one of the zarzuela's performances. Mexican painter Antonio "El Corzo" Ruiz (1892–1964), onetime designer for Universal Studios, provided the sets and costume designs. This single performance by the group then known as the Grupo Mexicano de Danzas Clásicas y Modernas (Mexican Group of Classic and Modern Dance) came just as Sokolow's teaching contract was reaching its end.[40]

As music historian Consuelo Carredano observes, the contrast between the traditional operetta and the modern dance work, with its avant-garde scenario, could hardly have been more stark, but against all odds, the performance was a triumph for all involved.[41] To add to the victory, the major Mexican composers of the era—Carlos Chávez, Blas Galindo (1910–1993), and Silvestre Revueltas—were all in attendance. The music critic for *El Universal*, Jesús Bal y Gay, thought the work, with only "abstract references to Spanish folklore," hit the mark. "That its realization is in accord with its designs is the greatest praise that one can offer a work of art, and the music of Don Lindo earns it."[42] As was often the case then, far less was written about the dance. Perucho quoted the declaration of one unnamed newspaper critic that "with this stupendous seed we can achieve magnificent fruit; but we must plant and cultivate it with careful attention."[43]

Don Lindo appeared on the program again when the group made its formal premiere in March of 1940 in the Palacio de Bellas Artes, this time under the name of the Ballet de Bellas Artes. It was preceded by two additional new works, *Los pies de pluma* (Feet of Feathers), a suite of dances set to early music, which reflected Sokolow's early studies of choreography under Martha Graham's music director and lover Louis Horst, and *Entre sombras anda el fuego* (Fire Walks among the Shadows), a new work by composer Galindo. Like Halffter, Galindo hoped to evoke Mexico in his score without reference to its folk heritage. Again, Sokolow proved to be the apt choreographer for the composer's approach. The program notes claimed that she "used this music, fresh and young, without any specific argument as a frame in which to present her group's use of the modern dance technique."[44] Art critic and dancer Raúl Flores Guerrero (1930–1960) later described the works Sokolow created during her first stay in Mexico as "Mexican from 'within'—without the need for resorting to folkloric topics."[45]

With the success of this program, Halffter and Bergamín began seeking sponsorship for Sokolow. They dubbed the support group they formed *La Paloma Azul* (The Blue Dove)—after the name of a popular Mexican song adopted by the bar that they frequented along with the members of the TGP. With the financial support of architect Carlos Obregón Santacilia (1896–1961) and his wife Adela, the group brought Sokolow back to Mexico in the summer of 1940 to work on a number of pieces. First among them was a new Bergamín/Halffter collaboration, *La madrugada del panadero* (The Baker's Dawn), with designs by Manuel Rodríguez Lozano. She also worked with the group on *Lluvia de toros* (Rain of Bulls), a surrealist work based on Francisco Goya's (1746–1828) etchings from his *Disparates* (Follies) series capturing the social collapse that followed Napoleon's invasion of Spain, with music by Antonio Soler (1729–1783). Sokolow soloed to Chávez's *Sinfonia de Antígona* (Antigone Symphony), with the scenic designs provided by her current sponsor, Obregón Santacilia. She also created a work to a popular children's story, *El renacuajo paseador* (The Wandering Tadpole), by Colombian author Rafael Pombo, about the ill-fated wanderings of a tadpole who disobeys parental instructions to stay close to home. For the critic from *El Nacional*, Sokolow "perfectly dramatized" the children's story, making it one of the finest achievements of La Paloma Azul.[46] *El renacuajo paseador* featured sets and costumes by Sokolow's original promoter Mérida and a score by Silvestre Revueltas, whose compositions were often classified as nationalist works, particularly by critics from the US.

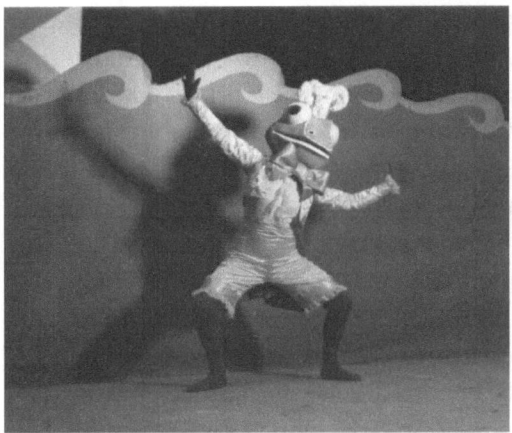

FIGURE 13. Anna Sokolow's *El renacuajo paseador* (The Wandering Tadpole), with Alba Estela Garfias as the title character. Set and costume designs by Carlos Mérida. 1940. Photographer unknown. Larry Warren Collection. Music Division. Library of Congress. © 2019 Artists Rights Society (ARS), New York/SOMAAP, Mexico City.

Due to the circumstances of its premiere, Revueltas's score for *El renacuajo paseador* developed its own legend. In an ironic twist of fate, the composer was unable to attend the performance of his first dance work, which he originally composed for puppet theater several years earlier and reworked for Sokolow's company.[47] The forty-year-old was breathing his last when the curtain was raised. According to one music critic, as Sokolow's choreography unfolded, Revueltas cried out for his coat so he could be properly dressed for an appearance in the orchestra pit. He wished to ensure that a particularly difficult segment of his composition was properly conducted.[48] Revueltas died of pneumonia early the following day, leaving a second, much larger dance work only partially completed.

Revueltas was born in Santiago Papasquiaro, Durango, to a notably artistic family. His younger brother Fermín (1901–1935) was a member of the *Estridentistas*, his sister Conseulo (1907?–1999?) was also a painter, while another sister, Rosaura (1909–1996), was an actress, and his youngest brother José (1914–1976) was a writer on left-wing issues. He studied music at Mexico's National Conservatory and in the US, where he supported himself by providing musical accompaniment to silent films. In addition to his composing career, he also served for a time as Chávez's assistant conductor for the National Symphony of Mexico. Temperamentally, Revueltas was a good match for Sokolow and her approach to choreography. He saw his ideas as arising from "the people, the workers, the oppressed, and the exploited, the makers of the future. . . . I myself, a teacher, an intellectual worker, as exploited, as oppressed as the rest of the workers under the actual conditions of the Capitalistic countries, have to consider my duty—my human and manly duty—to fight at the sides of my comrades for a new and better life."[49] Revueltas scholar Roberto Kolb questions the nationalist label that has been so often applied to the composer's creations, particularly by US critics. Kolb sees the composer's early compositions as critiques of "essentialist expressions of cultural identity in music," which reflects Revueltas's perceptions of Mexico's hybrid culture, while the social focus of his mature work became "not the picturesque Mexican Indian, but the poor and forsaken street wanderer in need of social empowerment."[50]

Despite achieving a notable degree of artistic success in what was to be its only season, La Paloma Azul suffered a public collapse in the fall of 1940. Obregón Santacilia and his wife raided the studio of Rodríguez Lozano, carrying off a group of paintings that they sold to underwrite some of the company's production costs. This resulted in a media battle between the politically connected architect—both his great-grandfather and his great-uncle had been presidents of Mexico—and their collaborating artist.[51] Sokolow herself evidently experienced a less public run-in with Santacilia's wife over the content of a solo that was to represent the life of a prostitute, something Adela Formoso found completely inappropriate for any company under her sponsorship.[52]

To complicate issues, the impression that Paloma Azul and its predecessors were more Spanish than they were Mexican did nothing to generate sympathy for the endeavor. As one anonymous critic complained: "If La Paloma Azul wants to do something worthwhile, it must Mexicanize itself. This same effort supported by a national sap would yield infinitely superior fruits, for the dancers would dance not only with their feet but with their souls and with the rivers of blood that run through their veins; by incorporating this they would supply virtuosity that they lack; they would not suffer angry comparisons, since theirs, being their own, would be incomparable, and their work would grow as trees grow with roots well secured in their earth, insensibly, naturally, inexorably.[53]

On top of all of this, Barros Sierra found Sokolow's version of modern dance was not "the one that best suits nor the one that best adapts to the physical characteristics or the sensitivity and temperament of the Mexican girls, whose femininity seems at odds with the athletic, abrupt and angular movements of this rude calisthenics."[54] He was not alone in his assessment.[55] Of course, such judgments on modern dance were not limited to Mexican critics. Late in life, Martha Graham told the *New York Times*, "If you're not stark and simple the way I was at the beginning, you're not modern. One time [drama critic] Stark Young was asked to go and see a concert of mine. He said, 'Oh, must I go? I'm so afraid she's going to give birth to a cube on the stage.'"[56]

The failure of Santacilia's sponsorship and a change in administration meant that funds to cover Sokolow's continued residence in Mexico were not available. At that point, Sokolow and Aguirre, who understood his partner's creative career was her priority, jointly decided it was time for her to return to New York City. They maintained a long-distance relationship, and Aguirre even joined her in New York City for part of 1944. He found her northern home less welcoming than Anna had Mexico City.[57] When Chávez asked Sokolow to stay and become a full-time instructor at the newly created Academia de la Danza Mexicana following her 1947 visit there, she declined his offer.[58] In a reply to a press inquiry in 1980 about her reasons for not remaining in Mexico, she replied: "Should I have stayed? I had to live where I was born, whether I liked it or not. If I had stayed I would not have done works like *Sueños*, *Rooms* and others, that in Mexico would not have been possible. I had to return to the United States."[59]

But Sokolow did create important work during later visits to Mexico, such as her *Lyric Suite* (1953). She recalled her mentor Horst visiting her backstage in New York City following the work's first performance there, where he told her, "Now you are a choreographer."[60] She also created works with Mexican subject matter, such as her *Cantata a Hidalgo* (1960) in honor of the leader of Mexico's nineteenth-century independence movement.[61]

Regardless of the critical opinion on their "rude calisthenics," dancing for Sokolow was a transformative experience for her first troupe of Mexican dancers, which, in addition to Reyna, included Mérida's daughter Ana and Martha Bracho, who played major roles in developing Mexican modern dance.

Reyna recalled the impact of that single season and the Sokolovas's determination to continue on the path the choreographer set:

Even though Anna knew very little of Mexico at that time, we, because of our youth, knew even less. Nonetheless, the close contact that she had with people like the painter Nacho Aguirre, and with so many other artists who had a clear sense of national identity, helped her. The collaboration with the Santacilias,' Bergamín and Halffter, and the contact with the composers Carlos Chávez, Blas Galindo, Silvestre Revueltas, and with Rodríguez Lozano, Fernández Ledesma, Antonio Ruiz and Carlos Mérida who created the scenery and the costumes was marvelous for us. All of them were people with immense reputations, but they still worked with us and we were just a bunch of girls. This enriched us. They helped us a great deal in forming our own point of view about the dance. . . .

For me it was a novelty to feel that at last we could do something Mexican in the dance. . . .

After the sponsorship fell apart, we had to pay for our own costumes, and even the rehearsal halls at times. We worked that way year after year for the first ten years, without subsidy or sponsorship. Anna came every year, two or three months, sometimes more. She came paying her own travel, housing and food and the dancers paid for everything else. When she wasn't here, we trained ourselves where ever we could. Zybine [sic] wasn't happy with us, so we took classes from [ballet teacher] Madame [Nelsy] Dambré and others. We danced whenever we could. At times we gave five, six or seven programs every six months, more or less, never more. . . . All of us lived as daughters in our families, and I was married. We had housing, food, clothing and enough to pay our dance expenses. We were very young and we didn't live independently. . . . It wasn't until 1948–49 when Gorostiza brought her to create the dances for the Temporada Internacional de Opera [International Opera Season] that we could earn something dancing for Anna. They began to pay us; 80 pesos a month, which was very little in those days. But we did extraordinary work there, very serious and formal. After working in the opera the "Sokolovas" began to study and dance in the Academia de la Danza Mexicana, which was formed originally by the group of Waldeen and we had no contact with them when it was founded.[62]

Reyna's positive assessment of the value added by the participation of older Mexican artists in the development of their approach to modern dance would be echoed by other dancers of her generation.

WALDEEN

Because Waldeen's major successes as a dancer and choreographer took place in Mexico, she is much less known in her homeland than Sokolow. While Sokolow may have been the initiator of modern dance technique in Mexico, Perucho chose his "strictly speaking" qualifier for a reason. It was Waldeen who created the watershed work that defined Mexican modern dance.

Waldeen was born in Dallas, Texas, to a father whose family emigrated from Europe, fleeing the conservative policies of Otto von Bismarck (1815–1898). Upon arriving in the US her father discovered the transcendentalist authors, and it was his feminization of Henry David Thoreau's (1817–1862) *Walden* (1854) that provided his daughter with her name.[63] Her mother hailed from Georgia and evidently harbored artistic aspirations, which she bestowed on her daughter. Unusually for the time, Waldeen began to study dance at the age of five and began full-time ballet training at the age of seven.[64] When her family moved to Los Angeles a few years later, her parents enrolled her in the studio of the Ballet Russes alumnus Theodore Kosloff.

Kosloff noted Waldeen's talent early on. By the time she was thirteen, she made her first appearance with his company in a performance of the Los Angeles Opera.[65] Two years later, she voluntarily retired from the ballet stage, after eight years of study with Kosloff.[66] Her mother had given her Isadora Duncan's autobiography, and inspired both by her reading and her encounter with a painting by El Greco at the Art Institute of Chicago while on tour with Kosloff's company, she insisted on holding her hands in the painter's style during performance. Kosloff was outraged. Both she and Kosloff found it artistically necessary for her to depart his company.[67]

She continued to pursue her interest in modern dance, mostly on her own. In 1936 she told dance writer Dorathi Pierre that her most important teachers during that period were Leonardo da Vinci (1452–1519), William Blake (1757–1827), and Ludwig von Beethoven.[68] Later, she also claimed to have undertaken studies with two German modern dancers, Mary Wigman (1886–1973), who completed three tours of the US from 1931 to 1932, and Wigman's student Harald Kreutzberg (1902–1968), who made significant tours of the US during the 1920s.[69]

Waldeen returned to the stage with the group of dancers associated with Michio Ito (1892–1961), whom she accompanied to Japan in 1932.[70] In 1934

Ito's company toured Mexico, where she garnered enthusiastic reviews. The critic for *La Prensa* praised "Miss Waldeen—as full of grace as an Ave Maria—an artist who gives herself entirely to her public from start to finish, who captivates them with her eurhythmics, with her temperament, with her force of expression, who dances with her entire body and her entire spirit."[71] The critic for *El Nacional* wrote that she was the most prominent dancer on stage during the group's performance: "her rich emotional qualities, her exquisite grace, her youth and beauty and her notable technique, make of her an incommensurate artist."[72]

Given the warmth of her reception, the twenty-one-year-old Waldeen decided to stay in Mexico when Ito's company departed.[73] As she put it: "Everything was opening up for Mexican artists and they just carried me with them. They were my teachers—they introduced me to Mexico. They took me all over the country. We didn't have cars, so we took buses, trains, rode on horseback. We went to marvelous fiestas out in the countryside. I danced barefoot in the dirt. I was simply saturated with Mexico. I didn't want to go back to the United States. . . . I remember walking down the street and trying to see how people walked so I could incorporate that into my dance. I remember that everything I saw went into the dance I was creating."[74]

Before she left Mexico for the US, she gave a farewell performance that included her *Impresiones mexicanas* (Mexican Impressions). Theater critic Roberto Núñez y Domínguez described it as divided in two parts, "Romanticismo" and "Revolución." In both dances, he wrote, Waldeen managed, through "her delicate temperament as a priestess of rhythms," to capture "the tone of soft melancholy and the dramatic impulses of the themes suggested by the landscape of these latitudes."[75] So Waldeen and her approach to the dance were known to the audiences of Mexico when she returned there in 1939.

According to Pierre, in 1936 Waldeen thought "every young artist should make a pilgrimage to Mexico. To work in Mexico is a vital experience for one senses that art is essential to the people and not only an entertainment. Art and life there are one. . . . She says it is a mistake to think of Spanish dancing in connection with Mexico, for the really great thing they have to give us is Indian ritual and ceremony. She feels that we have a great deal to learn from the Mexicans, especially in their attitude toward art."[76]

In the interim between her first and second trips to Mexico, Waldeen moved to Hollywood, where she found work in the film industry. She later

claimed film work for MGM and RKO studios and appearances with performers such as Fred Astaire, Ginger Rogers, and the Marx Brothers.[77] Her
experience in Hollywood ignited her passion for labor organization. She
discovered that dancers were represented by a variety of unions depending
on their place of employment. The Screen Actors Guild covered those who
worked in motion pictures, the American Guild of Musical Artists covered
opera and concert performers, and Actors' Equity covered those who performed in vaudeville and nightclubs. All of them were under the umbrella
of the Associated Actors and Artistes of America, which was under the
authority of the AFL-CIO. None of the unions counted dancers in their
leadership, and dancers who worked in multiple venues faced overlapping
membership dues. Waldeen helped create the Dancers Federation with her
colleagues in Los Angeles to address those issues.[78]

She made her first visit to New York City as a solo performer to help
promote the concept of the Dancers Federation on the East Coast. She also
taught at the Neighborhood Playhouse and the Roerich Museum.[79] John
Martin of the *New York Times* devoted a considerable article to Waldeen's
efforts at labor organization and a much shorter one to her premiere as
a solo performer. He found her "technique, though free in style . . . entirely objective, so that it serves her best when she is dealing with maters of
decorative import and design. It is a highly serviceable and well-mastered
technique within this field, for all that it leaves something to be desired
when the dancer turns to emotional and expressive matters. . . . The method
she has evolved for herself still contains strong markings of both the ballet
style and that of the Japanese dancer. The former has given her a certain
brilliance that serves her well and the latter a sharpness of attack that is
inclined to be a trifle overworked at times."[80]

Jerome D. Bohm of the *New York Herald Tribune* echoed Martin's response to Waldeen's work. Although he praised her efforts to acquire a
"thorough grounding in the principles of her calling," he also found that
"only here and there . . . was there a suggestion in an occasional gesture or
movement of a more modern art. . . . At no time could her efforts be closely
associated with the newer trends in her art."[81]

The arrangements behind Waldeen's solo performances in the Palacio
de Bellas Artes in February 1939, shortly before the performances by Sokolow's Dance Unit, aren't as well documented. Waldeen's reappearance
on the stage of Mexico in 1939 confirmed her position there as a "non-
conformist artist" because of her rejection of ballet style.[82] According to

the *New York Times*, which provided an update on Waldeen's activities in Mexico in August of that year, she also offered classes in technique at multiple venues and began participating in a group that called itself *Nuestro Teatro* (Our Theater).

Evidently, what the *Times* called *Nuestro Teatro* was a project led by another recent resident of Mexico, the Japanese theater director Seki Sano (1905–1966). Gorostiza and Rufino Tamayo arranged for Sano, who was banned from his native Japan because of his activities in support of communism, to receive political asylum in Mexico in April of that year.[83] Sano founded what he called the Teatro de las Artes within the Sindicato Mexicano de Electricistas (Mexican Electrician's Union) in August. The group's foundational documents characterize it as "a theater of the people and for the people" aimed at creating a program with a national spirit and an international reach.[84] It also aspired to produce works that were "free from the absurd mix of 'folklore' and *pochismo* [a Mexican term for slang composed of English elements] that is seen in certain manifestations of contemporary Mexican theatrical art." Sano named Waldeen as head of the theater's dance section. The Teatro de las Artes also included visual artists Miguel Covarrubias, Germán Cueto (1893–1975), Gabriel Fernández Ledesma, and Xavier Guerrero in various posts. Both of the company's composers, Revueltas and Halffter, were also actively engaged with Sokolow's efforts.

According to Josefina Lavalle, who worked with Waldeen's first Mexican company, the painter Fernández Ledesma was the choreographer's closest collaborator. He was well qualified to serve as her artistic advisor on things Mexican. Employing a convention used by many of his colleagues, Ledesma told Carlos Mérida that he received his first artistic training by watching the potters from his home state of Aguascalientes at work decorating their wares.[85] He served as editor of the SEP's art magazine *Forma* 1926–1928 and authored well-received books on Mexican toys and sandals. Lavalle described his role as similar to that which the TGP played for Sokolow. For Waldeen he was "guide and teacher in the art of knowing our country deeply: Muralism, architecture and above all popular creation. It was he who, with possibly the greatest eagerness, showed Waldeen popular art and culture, and he was the first to take her through hills and mountains to live the traditional festivals, to know and value indigenous dance, and to immerse herself in 'deep Mexico.' Ledesma had lived in the depths of this; his knowledge and passion were evident in his work. The dancers absorbed his love of Mexico and learned to perceive and to value the other esthetic, that of popular culture."[86]

Concurrently with Sano naming Waldeen to his project, Gorostiza invited her to create the Ballet de Bellas Artes—the name he also applied to Sokolow's presentations in the spring of 1940 at the same venue. In effect, Waldeen's version of the Ballet de Bellas Artes was an extension of the Teatro de las Artes. The only member of the Consejo Artístico del Ballet de Bellas Artes (Artistic Council of the Ballet de Bellas Artes) under Waldeen who wasn't a member of the Teatro de las Artes was its president, Gorostiza.[87]

In contrast to the invitation from the minister of education earlier in 1939, which allowed Sokolow to stay and develop a modern dance company, Gorostiza's work with Waldeen appears to have had a secondary agenda—punishing Nellie Campobello. Several of the actions Gorostiza took in regard to furthering his invitation to Waldeen seem to be aimed directly at circumscribing Campobello's domain.

While Sokolow mostly drew her dancers from graduates of the National Dancing School, Gorostiza sent a telegraph inviting a number of the students studying with Estrella Morales to audition for the company. Morales, and many of her students, left the National Dancing School due to disputes with Nellie Campobello.[88] Gorostiza and Waldeen also went exploring for dancers in Hypolite Zybin's school whose departure from Campobello's domain was similarly unhappy.[89] Gorostiza offered the company's postulants their diplomas as dance professors from the SEP if they were accepted into the new company—a proposal that Campobello resisted. She and the instructors who remained with her refused to participate in the auditions for the new company and also refused to provide the records of the postulants' studies within her school. Waldeen made no secret of her opinion that the SEP's school was a "doleful mediocrity."[90] The combination of all of these events is likely what led to Nellie's infamous use of a pistol in her warning to Waldeen to stay away from "her" territory—a threat that lends additional credibility to the many complaints about Campobello's behavior both before and after this particular confrontation.[91]

While Sokolow engaged fifteen dancers, Waldeen found room for twenty in her newly minted company—though they received the same pay that Sokolow's dancers enjoyed, free training in a new approach to theatrical dance. Just as with Sokolow, the dancers Gorostiza and Waldeen selected for the company developed intense attachments to their new leader. Guillermina Bravo, who became the leading modern dance choreographer in Mexico, recalled her first encounter with Waldeen: "I saw her in the studio as in a dream, like a fairy, like an apparition, surrounded by professionalism, seriousness and charm. She was very beautiful! At that moment I caught the love for Waldeen and it did not leave me during the next ten years. That was a discovery in my life."[92] Amalia Hernández was another early member of Waldeen's dance group, but once her mother discovered Waldeen intended to make a professional dancer out of her daughter, she withdrew Amalia from its rehearsals.[93]

The major difference between Sokolow and Waldeen was that of style. Because Waldeen's style was personally driven, documenting it proved difficult. For Lavalle, what Waldeen offered was "a formative technique, she transmitted a style of movement, which she found for herself, and always with the warning that each creator had to construct her own. Because of this insistence, she did not have the luck—as was the case with Martha Graham—that her students would take pains to codify her style."[94]

Lavalle observed that Waldeen's approach to dancing shared much with that of Isadora Duncan. "She said that the source of all movement was located in the impulse that originates the action, which is potentially embedded in the innermost core of our body's center. . . . In general Waldeen preferred to give way to the force of gravity instead of working against it, although she liked to combine small, light, rapid movements in the manner of an *allegro*."[95] And, unsurprisingly for someone who gave up classical dance so she could hold her hands in imitation of a painting by El Greco, "another of the fundamental characteristics of her movement was the use of accent in the hands."

Theater director and critic for the weekly news magazine *Todo* Víctor Moya found Waldeen's style

> fortunately much more harmonious and flexible than that of the well-known Graham school.
>
> Waldeen's particular technique does not have the angular rigidity which dominates nearly all of the modern dancers and lends her movements a lightness that is pleasing to the eye and alleviates some of the painful impression of having watched a weightlifting contest generally produced by a dance group of the Modern School.[96]

Sokolow was always critical of the "Welcome-to-sunny-Mexico" style she ascribed to Waldeen, and Waldeen was equally critical of the "imported" style that Sokolow brought with her.[97] Waldeen recalled: "[I] did not bring my dance to Mexico as did Anna Sokolow. . . . She [Sokolow] saw the importance of bringing a new technique to Mexico, I also wished to train, but I wanted to create a Mexican technique, different from that of the United States. I think that there is a kind of sensuality that ought to be expressed through technique, and I don't see that in the technique of Martha Graham."[98]

More specifically, Waldeen claimed that her work "created a movement in accord with the physiognomy, philosophy and psychology of the Mexican. For me, the Mexican man, the Mexican woman, are unique. Mestizaje has produced something very special: their temperament, their emotive capacity." Although she asserted free use of movement derived from Mexican folk dances, Waldeen also assured her audience that her use of this material was "free of false folklorisms, as well as imported forms and ideas imposed on the public which haven't the least root in our country."[99] For her 1945 work *En la boda* (In the Wedding), Waldeen asserted that "Everyone who saw it thought it was an authentic dance. I'd found a movement that approximated the traditional steps but that was modern. Of course, folklore can be used, but one has to keep the contemporary context in mind. . . . Otherwise it is artificial."[100]

If Waldeen's stylistic approach to dance was different, the emphasis on collaborative work she shared with Sokolow proved to be one of her strongest assets. Both dancers could have been quoting from the *Manifiesto del sindicato do obreros técnicos, pintores y escultores* (Manifesto of the Union of Technical Workers, Painters and Sculptors) penned by David Alfaro Siqueiros in 1932, which declared collective work to be the basis of Mexican creativity. It was through the contributions of the members of the Teatro de las Artes group that Waldeen created and mounted her masterwork, *La Coronela* (The Woman Coronel), loosely based on the female officers of the revolution. Revueltas and Blas Galindo provided the score, with an orchestration by Candelario Huízar (1882–1970).[101] Efraín Huerta (1914–1982) provided the texts for its spoken chorus. Ledesma provided the sets and costumes, and one-time Stridentist Germán Cueto provided its masks. *La Coronela* forever altered the trajectory of Mexican theatrical dance when it appeared on the stage of the Palacio de Bellas Artes in November of 1940.

La Coronela was preceded by three other Waldeen creations in its debut, only one of which—*Seis danzas clásicas* (Six Classic Dances), set to Bach's *Goldberg Variations*—was not overtly Mexican.[102] *Procesional*, a dance using pavanes and sarabandes to contrast the wealthy of Mexico's viceregal era with its indigenous poor, featured music by Eduardo Hernández Moncada (1899–1995). Its scenic designs were produced by Roberto

Montenegro's former assistant Julio Castellanos (1905–1947). The other work on the program brought the dancers into the revolutionary era with *Danza de las fuerzas nuevas* (Dance of the New Forces), set to music by Blas Galindo, with designs by Fernández. For Perucho, this work demonstrated the strength and renewed vigor of a nation in charge of its own destiny, but it was *La Coronela* that won the critical praise.[103]

La Coronela consisted of four parts. The first segment, "Damitas de aquellos tiempos" (Young Ladies of Olden Times) depicted the uncaring elite of Porfirian Mexico, the stock villains of the era's revolutionary rhetoric. The second, "Los desheredados" (The Dispossessed), showed the negative results of Porfirian policies. According to the work's program notes, this segment represented "the pain, the impotence and the submission of the disinherited, whose suffering, at last, arouses in them impulses of rebellion against those who have plunged them into atrocious servitude for centuries."[104] The third section, "La Pesadilla de Don Ferruco" (The Nightmare of Don Ferruco [Mr. Bourgeoisie]), introduced the Coronela herself, who symbolized the revolution. She bore witnesses to the discomfort of the bourgeoisie at the "healthy pursuits" of the nation's liberated underclass. The final section was the "Juicio Final" (Last Judgment), which resolved the conflicts laid out in the earlier segments. It was introduced by a short interlude danced by a "toy grim reaper with a violin"—likely the suggestion of Fernández, who wrote a book on the topic of traditional Mexican toys. The cast, some converted into José Guadalupe Posada–style skeletons, erupted into a can-can while the devil sorted them out—the Coronela and her band of revolutionary rurals were the only ones to escape the gaping mouth of hell.[105]

As Lavalle points out, *La Coronela* wasn't inspired in a musical composition or by literature. Instead, its elements were generated by the visual arts. Much of the work's success, as the commentators observed, was due to its use of the visual ideas generated by Posada. The artistic team didn't attempt to recreate specific scenes from his prints, rather they used them to demonstrate social inequality and to draw upon imagery associated with the popular celebration of the Day of the Dead.

Ironically, it was Sokolow, with her close ties to the TGP, who should have hit upon the prints of Posada as the inspiration for a dance. He was the "patron saint" of that organization. When the TGP founded its own publishing arm in 1942, its first product was a portfolio of thirty works by Posada, printed from his original plates.[106]

The muralists created a fictional biography for Posada, defining, and publicly promoting him, as the precursor of their art. Rivera and Orozco both invented stories about youthful encounters with Posada so they could claim him directly as the forerunner of their work.[107] As caricaturist Rafael Barajas points out in his study of Posada, the muralists adopted him because "a substantial portion of his work refers to the daily life of the poor, with its pain and its wants; many of his prints protest against the abuses of the bosses, police and authority of every stripe; a few of them speak to the revolutionary events and leaders. . . . Through these images a sector of the artists and intellectuals who 'rediscover' Posada conclude that the popular printmaker sympathizes with the Revolution of 1910."[108]

Waldeen claimed credit for the idea of using Posada's work, asserting that she saw the entirety of one segment of *La Coronela* appear before her mind's eye in the New York subway system in 1939.[109] Tortajada reports that it was Sano's idea to use Posada's work as the element that united the composition's segments.[110] Both Waldeen and Sano, who directed theatrical projects in New York before arriving in Mexico, would have known of the US vanguard's use of tabloid news headlines to help set their stages.[111] Using Posada's often lurid images for the same purposes in Mexico took only the smallest leap of imagination.

According to Lavalle, who danced in the work's premiere, all of the participants in *La Coronela* were "profoundly convinced that a true work of art ought to serve the construction of a national consciousness, using historical and political messages as its medium of transmission, just as the Mexican School of Painting had done."[112] *La Coronela*, thus, became a synthesis in movement of the two-dimensional explorations made by the muralists and their followers since the 1920s. Despite the antipathy of Nellie Campobello toward Waldeen, Campobello partisan Orozco cited *La Coronela* as one of the "first steps toward a new school of Mexican dance."[113] Although he thought its technique was not yet fully realized, Siqueiros also granted Waldeen and the company's creation the same pioneering status.[114]

By instructing that the work's scenic changes be undertaken in full view of the audience, Sano added a dash of Dadaist irony to the production. The audience was in on the modernist universe of *La Coronela* from the first stagehand's lumbering into view with the oversized fishing poles that the stage crew used to reel the sets and props into place.[115] The audience apparently loved Sano's immense theatrical joke.

All in *La Coronela* was not irony and satire, however. The emotional effect produced by the women in rebozos among the "desheredados" in *La Coronela*'s second section proved the most durable element of Waldeen's production. This too was a visual convention borrowed from the canon of images established by the muralists as what Jean Charlot called "accepted ciphers of a Mexican mural alphabet."[116] For the often acidic theater critic Víctor Moya, the dance of the desheredados was a triumph. He though it "perfectly realized from the first pantomime, full of movement and action, the music and the dance combine harmoniously to leave us a profound impression of tragedy. This drama-filled scene is the finest movement of the evening, and the paralyzing desperation of our people is admirably expressed by attitudes and choruses of severe greatness. This scene alone is so intense and well realized that it justifies the entire evening and I highly doubt that one can ask for more in the way of theatrical dance."[117]

He added that the costuming for this segment of the work, which "highlighted the great plastic value the rebozos and skirts of the women of our people," overshadowed that of the rest of the production.

One additional element set the desheredados apart from the rest of the work. This segment was performed to a spoken chorus—a device to which Waldeen later returned. Dancing to the rhythm of the spoken word was completely new to Mexico, though Waldeen was likely aware of the practice through her association with Mary Wigman, whose *Totenmal* (1930) used a similar device that allowed dead soldiers and their wives and mothers to speak, both literally and figuratively through their performance.[118]

Lavalle summed up "los desheredados" as "a renovating vision, fresh in its moment," but the popularity of its dance images rapidly turned it into a cliché, as it was adopted wholesale by other choreographers.[119] As Miguel Covarrubias put it, "the 'Danza de los Desheredados,' danced by a group of women wrapped in somber rebozos, became a landmark in the annals of Mexican dance as it has been copied past the point of satiety and been converted into a formula, 'rebozism,' used by any dancer who wants to express the pain and suffering of the women of the people."[120]

For dance historian Margarita Tortajada, *La Coronela* achieved the status of a watershed work precisely because it placed "woman at the center of history, as a fundamental social actor in the armed struggle and as a vehicle for transformation through her expression of herself."[121] Tortajada situates Waldeen's decision to create a work with strong female characters as something other than an expedient generated by the composition of her dance company. Instead, she believes Waldeen saw her lead as "the incarnation of the revolutionary struggle and its triumph over exploitation: the Coronela, with her beauty and power, her bandoliers across her chest and her firm step as she crossed the stage." In Tortajada's view, the work itself allowed Waldeen and her followers to not only "propose a new aesthetic and social proposal for dance, but to confront the problems and rejection occasioned by their work. . . . They took the risk and won. They sought their own language, the means of communicating their social message; this went beyond technical resources, it meant the creation of something totally new for our country."[122]

Even before the work was consecrated by the critics, *La Coronela* was effectively co-opted by the outgoing Cárdenas administration as representative of the art that the revolution gave the Mexican people. The final performance of the work was dedicated to an audience of ambassadors who came to Mexico for the inauguration of Cárdenas's handpicked successor, Manuel Ávila Camacho—who would lead Mexico in a different direction.[123]

Like Sokolow, Waldeen's source of sponsorship disappeared with the change in presidential administrations, but she was able to fall back on work with the Teatro de las Artes, which also provided her and her dancers with performance space. In contrast to Sokolow's return to New York, with sporadic visits to Mexico following for years, Waldeen reversed the equation. She spent large blocks of time in Mexico with sporadic visits to the US. According to Waldeen, she also invited Sokolow to participate in the progressive Teatro de las Artes, an offer that Sokolow refused because she believed that they could not work within the same organization.[124] In 1942, Waldeen announced the opening of the Escuela de Danza del Teatro de las Artes under her direction, with Bravo, Lourdes Campos, and Dina Torregrosa as her teaching assistants. It was, she advertised, the sole authorized source in Mexico for instruction in her technique.[125] That same year, Waldeen also took her Mexican dancers, accompanied by some of their mothers, with her on a performing tour of various universities in the US.[126]

Waldeen's support from the SEP was renewed by Jaime Mario Torres Bodet (1902–1974) in 1945, when she received a commission to create the large-scale dance production *Siembra* (Sowing) as part of Bodet's effort to promote literacy throughout the nation. She mounted this work, which counted a cast of thousands, using actual folk dances of the state of Michoacán. She relied on former cultural missionaries Luis Felipe Obregón and Amado López, who gathered the material, to help her with this task.[127] Sets and costumes came from an artist associated with the TGP member José Chávez Morado and from scenic designer Julio Prieto Posadas (1912–1977).

Waldeen did return to New York City for an extended period in 1946, teaching at the New School and Hunter College in New York City.[128] In this same period she began her translation of sections from Pablo Neruda's (1904–1973) *Canto General* into English. She met the poet while he was serving as the Chilean Consul in Mexico (1940–1943), where they frequented the same artistic circles. Press notice of her continuing choreographic work in the US was limited to a handful of performance announcements; through these we learn that she presented dance versions of her *Two Poems by Neruda* at the Hunter College Playhouse in the spring of 1948.[129] Even her occasional visits to the US came to an end in 1952, when the McCarran-Walter Act blocked her from returning because of her affiliation with the Communist Party, which she joined in 1945. She remained in Mexico ever after, where she and her Waldeenas were the dominant force well into the 1950s.

8

Ballets without Ballerinas?

José Clemente Orozco and the Ballet de la Ciudad de México

The socially conscious dance associated with the Lázaro Cárdenas administration suffered a decline when his successor pointed Mexico in a more conservative direction in economic and cultural policy. Ballet temporarily re-emerged as the favored form. Foreign ballet companies figured prominently in the programming decisions of the government's Palacio de Bellas Artes, and the Ballet Theatre's production of a Mexican-themed ballet, Léonide Massine's *Don Domingo de Don Blas*, revived Mexican aspirations for increased international exposure through ballet. On a bet, the government even extended its support to the creation of the Ballet de la Ciudad de México, led by Nellie and Gloria Campobello. While initially well received, the company soon fell into disfavor; the critics could applaud the scenery, created by the company's spokesman José Clemente Orozco and his colleagues, but not the dance it was designed for.

It is difficult to square the positions the Campobello sisters staked out in their *Ritmos indígenas* with an abiding passion for properly executed pirouettes.[1] Yet they had few other options for pursuing theatrical dance productions. The fervent populism of the Cárdenas years was rapidly fading in 1940, and the Campobellos had ceded leadership in the modern field to Anna Sokolow and Waldeen. They would reclaim the ballet, a decision that helped ensure the primacy of modern dance in Mexico during the ensuing years.

BALLETS: RUSSIAN AND MEXICAN

The repertory that de Basil's incarnation of the Ballets Russes brought to Mexico in the 1940s was more conservative than what the audience in the Palacio de Bellas Artes saw when the theater was dedicated almost a decade earlier. The company offered up *Swan Lake* alongside works by Fokine, with long records of box-office success.[2] In a nod to politics, its opening-night performance in Bellas Artes was dedicated to the new President Ávila Camacho; unable to attend, he sent Miguel Alemán (1900–1983), the man who would be his successor, to represent him.

During the company's 1941 season at Bellas Artes, de Basil raised the possibility of creating a Mexican ballet with the press, exciting the same level of anticipation that accompanied Anna Pavlova's *Fantasía Mexicana*. *El Universal Gráfico* reported the story with the observation that "everyone in Mexico understands that if the genius of these Russian artists is applied to the creation of a ballet with the music of Revueltas or some other composer of our own, the result would be the best propaganda that our country could possible hope for."[3] Ultimately, de Basil did not produce a Mexican ballet; his former business partner and current competitor Léonide Massine did so under the aegis of the Ballet Theatre in 1942.

The new works that Ballet Theatre created while the company was in Mexico during its four-month stay in 1942 engaged the attention of the press: an abridged version of *Coppelia*, with designs by Roberto Montenegro; the premiere of Massine's *Aleko*, with designs by Marc Chagall (1887–1985); and Massine's new "Mexican" ballet *Don Domingo de Don Blas*, with designs by Julio Castellanos. In the first two instances, it was the sets and costuming of these productions that captured the critic's interest. In the latter, it was Massine's use of Mexican folk dance.

Adolfo Salazar of *Hoy* found Montenegro's designs for *Coppelia* to be the production's only point of interest.[4] Nellie Campobello, writing in *El Universal Gráfico*, offered a more generous assessment of the work and its performers but she too highlighted Montenegro's accomplishments in set design for its "grace and great imaginative force, for its drawing and its color."[5]

Chagall traveled to Mexico to paint his sets for *Aleko* in order to escape the restrictions of US stage painters unions, which would have obviated his direct participation in the project. According to Tina Sutton's biography of Alicia Markova, Chagall purchased samples of indigenous textiles from one of Mexico City's markets as part of his costume design process, and Markova created the "gypsy" jewelry she wore as Zemphira, the lead female role of the ballet, from gold coins purchased in this same market.[6] Chagall and his sets and costuming were the unquestioned stars of the Mexico season. Enthusiasm for the ballet itself was more muted.

Massine reportedly expressed interest in working with Revueltas on a Mexican ballet as early as 1932 but never actively pursued a commission during the composer's lifetime. His extended stay in Mexico gave him time to take up that endeavor. He worked with his music director Antal Doráti (1906–1988) to assemble bits and pieces of the composer's existing compositions, including *La Coronela,* which he seems to have acquired from Waldeen, to serve as the score for his intended Mexican ballet.

Massine's use of Revueltas's music assured his ballet attention from local audiences. It was his use of folk dance elements, however, that drew most of the critic's attention. According to the souvenir program for the "Coast-to-Coast" tour of the US that followed the Ballet Theatre's 1942 stay in Mexico, *Don Domingo*

takes place in Mexico during the early 18th Century and concerns the efforts of the wealthy and respected Don Domingo and his poor young adventurer rival, Don Juan, to win the love of the beautiful Eleanor, daughter of Don Remiro, a rich old man and personal enemy of the Viceroy. The story deals with the rivalry of the two lovers and the illfated [*sic*] conspiracy against the Viceroy uncovered by Don Juan who, in the end, wins Eleanor.

The gifts presented Eleanor by the two suitors and dramatised [*sic*] by old Indian dances, material for which was provided by the Mexican Ministry of Education. These are the Dance of Fertility, Dance of the Flyers, Tiger Dance and the Dance of the Virgin Devil.

Massine claimed to have been inspired to create the ballet based on his observation of "the odd blend of Spanish and Mexican movements" he saw in the cafes of Mexico City, which he perceived as a "rollicking vulgarization of the flamenco."[7] According to Massine biographer Leslie Norris, the choreographer's intent was to blend Spanish dancing with Mexican popular dance and indigenous dance, but he found Indian dancing "stubbornly resistant to such fusions."[8] The Russian choreographer appreciated the Yaqui deer dance, but the work was too strong for his purposes: "The only really powerful Mexican folk-dance," Massine later wrote, "is the *jaki* [*sic*], in which the dancer imitates animals, but because of this rough peasant quality this dance would have been out of place in *Don Domingo*, and I was unable to use it."[9] Consequently, Massine "relied heavily upon straight classical ballet or a balletization of Spanish folk dances. But this resulted in such garbled cultural references that they pushed credulity to the limit."[10]

The weekly newsmagazine *Hoy* ran two separate reviews of *Don Domingo*, discussing its *mexicanidad*. Both of these reviews touched on the struggle over Mexico's folk dance, which was the issue that divided the nation's modern dance community. Agustín Souchy asserted that Massine was comfortable working with folk material given its prominent use in Russia's nineteenth-century ballets and contended that he used only elements derived from Mexican dance in his choreography.[11] Adolfo Salazar wanted the work to be something more than he found it to be. He opened his September 26, 1942, review by opining that previous uses of folkloric material by other artists had done a disservice to the genre. "Even when the magnificent resources of color and movement of our popular Mexican dances have been repeatedly used by attempts of various sorts, such essays were too close to the 'natural,' to the direct document taken from the community, without having been submitted, up until now, to the elaboration of high art."[12] With the creation of Massine's ballet version, Salazar found that

the elements of the Mexican style pass beyond the locally picturesque to an international category. . . . The dances, still somewhat crude, are flooded in the whirlwind of the action. It is this whirlwind, and the strong jumble of color that predominates in each moment of the ballet, that raise it to the first category, dominating with the powerful action of its presence and relegate the argument and the folk document to a secondary plane. . . . The end result is still not perfect; it is a first attempt and, in this quality, should not be disdained. The action is incomprehensible, because it is complex, and in a ballet it is hardly possible to follow any other action than the one entrusted to the only three "eternal" characters of the theater: the woman, the husband and the lover, around whom the rest is but the chorus. The grafting of our typical dances is still somewhat forced, and the desire to leave nothing in the museum carries the excess of the aforementioned materials. It is a step toward the "Mexican ballet." An important step.

Critics in the US were far less generous to *Don Domingo* than their Mexican counterparts. Hints of the work's reception outside of Mexico emerged in rehearsals. Jerome Robbins, then a beginning dancer with the company, was chided about his evident lack of interest in Massine's choreography, to which he replied that "if he ever made a ballet this bad, he'd deserve whatever he got."[13] Massine's attempt at incorporating folk dance fell completely flat in New York, and members of the opening-night audience reputedly

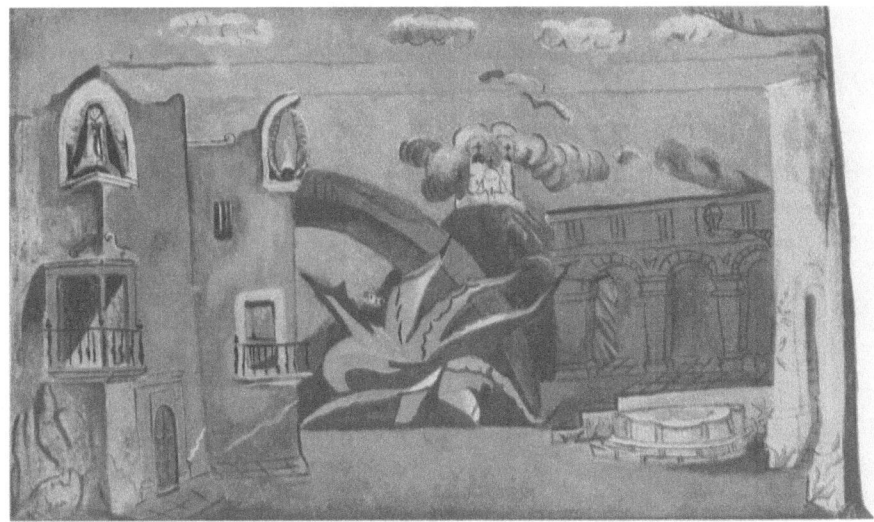

FIGURE 14. Julio Castellanos (1905–1947). Set design for Leonide Massine's *Don Domingo de Don Blas.* 1942. Courtesy of Antonio Castellanos Basich and the American Ballet Theatre. Used by permission.

booed and hissed its performance.[14] "Localisms, no matter how authentic, do not contribute to the success of a ballet," Robert Lawrence of the *New York Herald Tribune* declared.[15] While Lawrence reported that the opening-night audience was unimpressed by the work, he added that he personally enjoyed its "blazing color" and Julio Castellanos's "dazzling scenery and costumes," which "reward and enrich the eye."

Composer Paul Bowles (1910–1999) was appalled at what the production did to Revueltas's music:

Massine put Revueltas at a disadvantage in *Don Domingo*, the ballet he pieced together for the Ballet Theater out of old scores by that Mexican composer. . . . The inclusion of a dismemberment of Revueltas's last work, itself a ballet, I consider a shameless procedure. If at some distant time in the future someone wants to compile a posthumous Stravinsky ballet, it might be considered legitimate if parts of the *Symphony for Wind Instruments*, the *Capriccio*, the *Dumbarton Oaks Concerto*, and a magnified version of the *Octet* were strung together to provide a score (although the result would be esthetically worthless). But if the complier added one page of *Petrouchka*, his action would be, as far as I am concerned, unethical and lousy. *La Coronela* is a very good ballet in its own right. Why should anyone break it up in order to make an inferior one?[16]

John Martin of the *New York Times* was even more pointed in his dismissal: "Some wisely anonymous arranger has put together six piano pieces by the late Sylvestre [*sic*] Revueltas and made of them one of the most consistently annoying ballet scores on record."[17] While Martin found the music "undanceable" and "utterly unrelated to the style of the movement," he objected to the imposition of a "narrative and movement almost entirely in the folk vein" on top of it. Like his counterpart at the *Herald Tribune*, Martin also liked the Julio Castellanos designs and he thought it unfortunate that so much money had been invested in the production because it was unlikely that *Don Domingo* "would be with us for long."

Far from realizing the "best propaganda" Mexico could hope for, *Don Domingo* rapidly departed the Ballet Theatre repertory, while *Aleko* had continuing repercussions for the creation of Mexican dance. Nonetheless, the presence of both ballet companies in Mexico provided models, complete with proven repertory, for the nation's first state-sponsored ballet company.

THE CAMPOBELLO SISTERS, OROZCO, AND THE BALLET DE LA CIUDAD DE MÉXICO

Without much need for adaptation to the small screen, a dramatization of the documented lives of the Campobello sisters would make for a scintillating telenovela.

Nellie was a self-created character, heavily involved, as were the muralists, in the creation of her own myth. Dance historian Patricia Aulestia recalls how, during a 1972 interview, she struggled to maintain her focus on Nellie's professional achievements. Nellie simply claimed that she was "born knowing" how to dance, and, like the seasoned cultural politician that she was, nearly invariably replied to a question with another question. This tactic would lead the discussion off on tangents that allowed her to hold forth on the Egyptians, the Aztecs, and even astrology—at which she claimed to be an expert—rather than onto the almost always fraught subject of what became, under her leadership, Mexico's Escuela Nacional de Danza.[18]

Nellie Campobello was born María Francesca Moya Luna in Villa Ocampo, Durango, in 1900. According to the mythology she created for herself, her father was killed fighting in the army of Francisco "Pancho" Villa, although recent research located him in California, with a new family, after the revolution.[19] She claimed that her birthplace and ancestry imbued her with her notoriously strong character. "I owe all of my verve to my Comanche blood, and I'm from the Sierra de Durango home of the most ferocious fighters."[20] At the beginnings of her career as a writer, she penned a poem she called "Yo" (I), in which she proudly laid claim to her difficult personality. It opened with these lines: "They say I am brusque, / That I don't know what I say / Because I came from out there."[21] This poem provided the title of her first book, published with the assistance of Dr. Atl, in 1929 under the single name of Francesca.[22] As historian of literature Patricia Rosas points out, at that time her real name served as a kind of pseudonym, as she was already presenting herself as Nellie Campobello.[23]

In 1923 Nellie moved from the northern borderlands to Mexico City with her half sister Gloria. Nellie's version of this event says they followed her mother and stepfather—a doctor she identified as Joseph Campbell, either Bostonian or British, depending on her interviewer. The duo then Hispanicized his surname. Although no one then could define what Mexican theatrical dance was supposed to be, it must have appeared rather probable that credit for its creation would not be assigned to a twosome known as the Campbell sisters.

Dance historian Sophie Bidault believes this story, too, was likely an invention, intended to shield the identity of whoever it was who actually provided the sisters with their entry to Mexico City's upper-class Anglophone immigrant community and underwrote their first dance lessons.[24] When Pavlova returned to Mexico in 1923, Nellie's much younger half sister Gloria saw her perform there and declared her intentions to study ballet; Nellie accompanied her to dancing class. The duo moved rapidly through a number of the city's instructors, the Costa sisters, Carme Galé, Mol Potapovich, and Carol Adamchevsky, none of whom proved satisfactory.[25] By 1927 they were studying and performing with Lettie Carroll, whose student body was, according to an unnamed commentator for the entertainment magazine *Ovations*, "composed for the most part of the exquisite young ladies of high society."[26]

After scoring a number of successes performing with the "Ballet Carol" in its elaborately mounted productions, the sisters departed Mexico for

Cuba, where they danced professionally and rubbed shoulders with literary luminaries. Among Nellie's acquaintances there was Langston Hughes (1902–1967), who translated some of her poems into English for the 1942 *Anthology of Contemporary Latin American Poetry*.[27]

On their return to Mexico in 1930, Carlos Trejo y Lerdo de Tejada of the SEP hired them to teach dancing in the public schools, including the new Casa de Estudiante Indígena.[28] According to Frances Toor, it was Trejo y Lerdo de Tejada who asked the Campobellos to alter the jarabe tapatío and convert it into a dance of courtship, a presentation that became the new standard.[29] It was from there that they began their rise through the nation's educational bureaucracy.

Nellie continued to write while her career as a dancer/choreographer began to flourish. As dance scholar José Reynoso points out, her creation of *30–30* occurred at the same time as she published her second book, *Cartucho* (1931), which presented the Mexican Revolution from a pro-Villa perspective.[30] According to dance historian Sophie Bidault, the book's child's-eye view of the revolution, filled with gruesome scenes of death and bodily decay, "was just as corrosive as that of Orozco," which stands in contrast to the celebratory tone she adopted for her *30–30*.[31]

Nellie pursued the themes of *30–30* jointly with her half sister Gloria in two additional "revolutionary" ballets they prepared for the students of the SEP's dance school in 1935, *Barricada* and *Clarín*. The program notes for *Clarín*'s premiere indicate it was intended to represent the "painful moments of our armed struggle, not only the tragedy of the men who marched, playing with death, but also the painful tragedy of the men and women who lived on the margin of the Revolution." It centered on the dance of "Valentina, a strong woman who loves soldiers," and the "tragic" dance of the "Chinita, free from the fear of death and also free from love," while also incorporating incidents from the "tumultuous life" of the guerrillas who fought under no particular flag "in the grotesque dance of the brave."[32]

Rather more generally, the notes for *Barricada* described it as "created with the freedom of a poet who only pretends to speak his own truth, the truth of his class. This is how the 'ballet' Barricada was built, which is, in its interpretation, in its technique, in its development, simply an essay of what may be, one day, dance at the service of the best social cause."[33]

For Bidault, these mass ballets were the descendants of Mexican muralism, directly concerned with capturing "their own time, and their own place."[34] The cast for these gigantic works was augmented by recruits from the Escuela Nocturna de Artes para Trabajadores (Night School for Laborers), Escuela Nacional de Maestros (National Teacher's School), and the Escuela de Educación Física (Physical Education School). Their equally huge musical scores, provided by Russian émigré Iàkov (Jacobo) Kostakovsky (1883–1953), required not only the participation of the National Symphony but the student orchestra of the National Conservatory and members of its chorus. Mérida described *Barricada* from a structural standpoint, focusing on its "forms very similar to those of the choreographic-theatrical spectacles of Soviet Russia. In *Barricada* the role of the soloists, so to speak, is founded in the large groups that move across the stage, furthermore, it uses human voices, and generally follows a mechanical rhythm congruent with the thesis which animates the dance work."[35]

The press, mostly made up of music critics along with a few theater reviewers, was less dispassionate in its assessments. The sisters promoted these works as something "new, distinctive and even 'audacious.'"[36] The critics begged to differ, although most were willing to attribute the failures they saw as evidence of initial efforts. In the pages of *Todo*, Baltasar Dromundo opined that "Nellie Campobello needs more effort and an ample development of action in her work to occupy the place which she deserves. . . . The very defects in execution and in the architecture specific to the work presented demonstrate not only their quality but the necessity of insisting on this direction."[37]

Music critic José Barros Sierra had been paying attention to the dance performances he witnessed over the preceding months on the stage of the Palacio de Bellas Artes and, based on this context, offered an extended assessment of *Barricada* and *Clarín* in the August 28, 1935, issue of *El Universal*. He focused on the lack of a strong technical base in both the choreography and its execution, an issue that was repeatedly raised by critics of the Campobellos over the coming decade:

On repeated occasions of late we have spoken of the creation of a Mexican ballet that would have characteristics similar to those of the famous Ballets Russes which has amazed the world since 1909. This theme has given rise to various commentaries, which, for the most part, consider it perfectly possible that a completely national theatrical dance, capable of achieving international value, will emerge just as occurred with the Slavic ballets. This trend in efforts toward an authentic Mexican ballet is worthy of applause, as well as deserving of censure for those who are attempting to resurrect it on the same dated, sterile, worm-eaten foundations. . . .

We say that we do not have a firm foundation . . . to create a ballet, because, with exception granted for the orchestra, and that only relatively, we do not yet have, nor has anyone worried about creating, the permanent bodies that will permit these intents so well begun to crystalize. . . . We have no orchestra, no chorus, no dance company, no dance school to prepare the material from which our creators can benefit. It will be noted that some of these entities already exist; but to date their existence is embryonic, which—excepting the orchestras—makes them practically useless for theatrical ends. . . .

Neither have any figures emerged to lead a movement with such lofty aspirations—nor will it be easy for them to do so under present conditions.

It is certain that in our student festivals of greater or lesser importance we have achieved images that reaffirm our confidence in the future existence of a Mexican ballet; but such performances, no matter how plausible or successful, are not yet ballet.[38]

Barros Sierra then went on to enumerate what he perceived as poorly assimilated borrowings from Massine's *Les Presages* (1933) and the failed *Union Pacific* (1934) and even Sergei Eisenstein's *Battleship Potemkin* (1925) in the choreography.[39] He concluded that Nellie's work on *Barricada* "ought to serve as a definitive, albeit costly, experience, so that we do not once again make the same errors we have attempted to point out in these lines."[40]

One of the Campobellos's companions in this endeavor was painter José Chávez Morado, who was then serving as the chief of the Division of Fine Arts of the SEP. In another theme that would be repeated for ballets the Campobellos's staged in the future, the critical response to his design work was uniformly positive. As Dromundo put it, Chávez Morado's designs showed him to be "a scenic designer of the first order. Motifs, color, order and structure of the scenery were an indisputable success. A sense of modernity and an agile comprehension of our revolutionary contemporaneity well understood in the materials of the plastic arts, produced an effective rendering of the artist's talents as a scenographer."[41]

It was the Campobello sisters' long-time friend and Nellie's fellow writer on revolutionary themes Guzmán who provided them with the opportunity to create the Ballet de la Ciudad de México. As Diego Rivera's striking cubist portrait of him testifies, Guzmán was present in Paris during the heyday of Diaghilev's Ballets Russes but he made his acquaintance with the company during its 1916 tour of the US.[42] He was deeply impressed by what he witnessed and became a confirmed balletomane. According to an article about his activities promoting the Ballet de la Ciudad de Mexico in *Tiempo*: "In successive journeys in countries of the two continents, he attended as many performances of the ballet as he could find. He realized, thus, the great expressive possibilities that were contained in the mimed language of the ballet. . . . Upon his return, he untiringly propagated his ideas about this art and the necessity of providing Mexico with a ballet company worthy of its secular choreographic tradition and the innate miming talent of its people."[43]

In an essay written before the Ballets Russes' visit to Spain in 1916, Guzmán posed a challenge to that nation, which sums up the efforts that he took upon himself in creating the Ballet de la Ciudad de México: "Spain has everything it needs to create a ballet of grand proportions: it has an inexhaustible mine of themes, it has the artists of the dance; it has the painters; and it has, albeit on a smaller scale than other countries, the musicians. They simply seem to lack the bold imagination to sit down together with these materials, and the technical ability to occupy them with success. Will there be anyone who can, and will, decide to do so?"[44]

Guzmán secured funding for the first performance of what became the Ballet de la Ciudad de México through a high-stakes wager. If the group failed in its first performance, he promised to refund the five-thousand-peso production cost provided by Benito Coquet of the Dirección General de Educación Estética (General Directorate of Esthetic Education), the parent organization of the Departamento de Bellas Artes within the SEP.[45] The group of dancers Guzmán and the Campobello sisters assembled traveled to Xalapa, Veracruz, in December of 1942 to present a program made up of works lifted from the Ballets Russes: Gloria Campobello's interpretation of *Les Sylphides* and Nellie Campobello's versions of *L'Après-midi d'une faune* (1912) and *Le Spectre de la rose* (1911), likely with an all-female cast.[46] All of these works had recently graced the stage of the Palacio de Bellas Artes in performances by de Basil's company.

Guzmán won his bet on the regional stage. Leveraging that success, he secured additional funding from various governmental entities and established the company in June of 1942 with himself as president, Nellie Campobello as treasurer, Gloria Campobello as secretary, and José Clemente

Orozco as its spokesman.[47] It was a role that Orozco eloquently adopted, dropping his typically acid wit when speaking about the company and its efforts.

"Many painters other than myself have been interested in the creation of a Mexican school of Ballet," he affirmed in a promotional interview in the August 7, 1943, issue of *Hoy*.[48] "The Ballet is just as important as mural painting. Our painting was and represents a Mexican effort, achieved within the tradition of the universal in the arts. The movement in favor of our own 'ballet,' with Mexican essence and characteristics, can be developed just as was done with mural painting."

It is with the Ballet de la Ciudad de México that a picture of Gloria finally begins to emerge from the shadow cast by Nellie. According to Gloria's biographer Felipe Segura, who danced with her as a member of the company, Gloria was happy to let her sister take the publicity limelight. Nellie, Segura asserts, created the company around Gloria; her choreography was designed to make her sister shine—though it was Gloria who provided Nellie's choreography with a degree of technical polish.[49] And it was Gloria who drew the company's famous advocate, Orozco, into its orbit.

Given Orozco's stated aversion to painting "*huaraches* and dirty cotton pants" and to the use of the "ridiculous 'charro'" and "vapid 'china poblana'" to represent Mexico, it is probable that the image of Nellie as the charro to Gloria's China poblana in their version of the jarabe tapatío during their folk dancing years was not what stimulated his interest in their work.[50] Orozco apparently harbored a weakness for classical dancers. According to art and dance critic Raquel Tibol, he was in the company of a pair of dancers from the Ballets Russes de Colonel de Basil in a nightclub when he was approached by journalist Oliver Toro about the project that led to the creation of his *Autobiography*.[51] Tibol asserted Orozco's judgment on the ballet company was "clouded by his deep affection for Gloria."[52]

The few surviving love letters from Orozco to Gloria display both his passion for her and, through her, for her art:

Gloria, my love, I have never sent you a letter like this that you are about to read, it is a love letter, read it with your soul, listen, and see what I am going to say with your heart, in a letter filled with love and confidence in you, because I am absolutely certain you will understand it, beloved Gloria. Look: the only thing I now desire, my only ambition, the only thing I hope for and claim, and ask and long for is your love, your heart, your thought. And loving you means for me that I desire your well-being and your happiness, for which I am ready to make *the sacrifice* that may be necessary, whatever it may be: dancing is what makes you happy, I want you to dance; and everything, absolutely everything I can do, I will do it with the greatest joy to help you do what you like, to do what you have always wanted, so that your soul expresses all its beauty.[53]

As Segura notes, despite Orozco's professed willingness to make "the sacrifice," Gloria knew he was highly unlikely to leave his wife and family for her.[54] Nellie, however, was unwilling for Gloria to do anything that might endanger Orozco's support for the company and took whatever steps she could to maintain this relationship.[55]

According to Orozco's gallerist, Alma Reed, with whom he also may have maintained a romantic relationship, the artist met Nellie and Gloria at a 1937 reception in her apartment on Calle Reforma.[56] The sisters came as guests of the Yucatecan poet Luis Rosado Vega, author of the popular song "Peregrina" (1922), which was inspired by and dedicated to Reed. Their encounter, Reed observed, fulfilled Orozco's "long thwarted desire to create in the sphere of the dance, which he regarded as the most complete of all art forms."

Anita Brenner, an early promoter of the artist who he grew to mistrust, summarized his work in her 1932 tourist guidebook *Your Mexican Holiday* in a single blunt sentence: "At his best, sublime; at his worst, bitter."[57] In her study of Orozco's designs for the ballet, Mexican art historian Laura González Matute paints a more nuanced picture. For her, Orozco's work "evoked a world marked by disenchantment, hopelessness and pain," but it could also present "a promising vision of humanity in which one can appreciate a certain hope and the revindication of the human being."[58] When he was working on set designs for the ballet, Orozco's art became "audacious and festive and filled with movement, in contrast to the dramatic forms and critical content that had characterized his earlier work."

This change was not limited to Orozco's subject matter. According to González, "the majority of the works created during this period were realized with great vivacity, with an exuberant chromatic range which contrasts with the half tones, the ochers, grays and blacks which predominate in his prior productions."[59] Part of this stemmed from the necessities imposed by working as part of the team assembling a work of dance for the stage, a

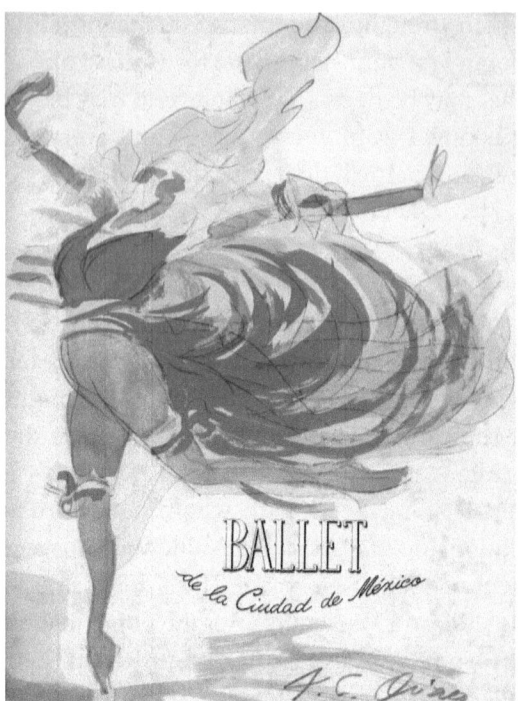

FIGURE 15. José Clemente Orozco (1883–1949). Program design for the Ballet de la Ciudad de México. 1943. Archivo Vertical-CENIDI DANZA/INBA. Fondo documental Patricia Aulestia. © 2019 Artists Rights Society (ARS), New York/SOMAAP, Mexico City.

different task than painting a mural. As Orozco noted in an interview with Ulises Monferrer in the August 7, 1943, issue of *Hoy*, what was "important here is that the two arts, painting and the dance unite. I almost prefer a mural in movement, with life, to a mural with static figures, and that is what 'our ballet' ought to be."[60] Nonetheless, with Gloria Campobello as his muse, the sublime in his art was in the ascendant.

Orozco's exposure to the world of the ballet had something to do with this change. He was impressed by watching Chagall at work in the Palacio de Bellas Artes as the Russian created, with the assistance of Roberto Montenegro, the backdrops for the ballet *Aleko*.[61] Orozco even drew a comparison between Chagall's approach to the designs for the ballet and his own first effort as a stage designer. In the March 5, 1943, issue of *Tiempo* he stated he had "personally painted the backdrop, finding myself in my element despite the fact that this is the first time I have done decoration. I think that scenography is very similar to mural work in its conception, proportions, and technique. The scenographic work of a painter necessarily reflects his personality as an artist. The delicious stage designs that Chagall did for *Aleko* resembled an exhibition of his paintings. I imagine that mine will give the impression of one of my murals."[62]

The designs to which he referred represented his first work for Gloria, the 1943 ballet *Umbral* (Threshold). He created its scenery and costume designs and collaborated in crafting its scenario. Tibol's synopsis of *Umbral*'s storyline shows just how central the figure of Gloria was to the work: "The title of Umbral corresponded to the threshold of life, through which a young woman discovers love, laughter, games, her own desires to know everything, including love. Egoism, hypocrisy, hatred, vanity and pain stand in the way of her journey. Life, with all of its temptations and its monstrosities, begins when one crosses the threshold of infancy."[63] González suggests that Orozco proposed some of the evils that confronted the lead dancer, as they referenced topics and figures he used in the murals for the Hospicio Cabañas in Guadalajara (1936–1939).[64]

The satirical "explanation" Orozco offered for the six-panel portable mural *Dive Bomber and Tank* (1940) that he painted for the Museum of Modern Art also bears some relationship to the concepts he used in creating the scenery for *Umbral*. He asserted that each of the work's panels was fully interchangeable with any other panel, though he did offer a series of "preferred" arrangements using anything from three to all six of the panels. "A painting is a Poem and nothing else," he wrote.[65] "The forms in a poem are necessarily organized in such a way that the whole acts as an automatic machine, more or less efficient but apt to function in a certain way, to move in a certain direction. . . . Each part of a machine may be by itself a machine to function independently from the whole. The order of the inter-relationships between its parts may be altered, but those relationships may stay the same in any order, and unexpected or expected possibilities may appear."

As González explains, three years later Orozco was able to employ lighting and the elements of the proscenium stage such as its hoist system and wings to experiment with theatrical design space in a somewhat similar way.[66] In commenting upon his set for *Umbral*, Orozco noted that "the scenography of a ballet cannot be, in any way, the fixed one used in other [theatrical] spectacles, given that, in the ballet, everything is movement."[67]

Gloria was also inspired by her collaboration with the muralist. Her ballet, set to the Eighth Symphony of Franz Schubert (1797–1828), was anything but Romantic. According to critic Jaime Luna, *Umbral*'s choreography was "a violent blow of modernity; a philosophical ballet par excellence; without pointe work, gauze or pas de quatre."[68] Dance historian Margarita Torta-jada suggests that Gloria's direct interaction with the "monumental" figures of Orozco's murals may have helped her conceive this new approach to her art.[69]

The June 27, 1943, premiere of both *Umbral* and the company itself on the Palacio de Bellas Artes stage was a major social event attended by President Ávila Camacho as well as his guest, President of Paraguay Higinio Morinigo (1887–1983), and a substantial segment of Mexico's diplomatic community. The initial reception of the ballet, the other premieres on the opening program, and of the company that preformed them was highly positive.[70] Although Orozco's designs overshadowed the other contributors to the evening, Roberto Montenegro's set for *Fuensanta* was also singled out for critical praise. Choreographed by Gloria from a libretto provided by Guzmán, it related the story of a young poet whose fiancée, Fuensanta, has died but who haunts the church where the poet used to pray. He encounters her there, accompanied by a woman in black gloves who keeps them apart. Resolved to die in order to join his love, the poet's body is discovered and returned to the church, where Fuensanta and the woman in black gloves await.[71]

Gloria's *Alameda 1900*, which sought to evoke the Porfirian era with a sense of nostalgia through designs by Julio Castellanos, was set to a pastiche of music from various Mexican composers and based on another Guzmán libretto. According to the unnamed reviewer for the newspaper *Excélsior*, the work was set "one Sunday in the Alameda. Heterogeneous strollers congregate around the central fountain. All the frivolities of the time are represented. The betrothed in Sunday's clothes looking for her fiancé, the governess, the old man, the children, the dandy, the presumptuous girls, the snow cone vendor, the seller of sweets. The ballet looked like an old print."[72]

Orozco provided new stage designs for the November 20, 1943, premiere of Nellie's *Obertura Mexicana*. It was yet another incarnation of Nellie's *30–30*, so the set he created echoed the flaming torch and red banner Nellie once carried in the lead role, along with a sea of ochre rifles and an enormous maguey cactus.[73] The ballet was set to Carlos Chávez's 1935 composition of the same name, though expanded by Chávez with the addition of two additional segments to convert it into a ballet-length piece.[74] Like *30–30*, *Obertura Mexicana* was praised by *Tiempo* as "an authentic

'Viva Mexico' which would bring honor to Mexico on any international stage."[75]

When the Ballet de la Ciudad de México returned to the Palacio de Bellas Artes for its second season in 1945, its critical reception was far less favorable. The critics—at least those associated with publications beyond Guzmán's reach—expected concrete improvements, perhaps a less than realistic expectation for a company whose dancers' pay amounted to little more than fifty pesos per performance.[76]

Once again, the season opened with premieres of new works by the Campobello sisters and designs by an array of the nation's best-known artists: Orozco, for Gloria's *Pausa* (Pause); Carlos Mérida, for Gloria's *Circo Orrin* (The Orrin Circus) and Nellie's *Ixtepec*, named after the city near Tehuantepec; Antonio "El Corzo" Ruiz for Nellie's *Vespertina* (Evening News); and Montenegro for Enrique Vela Quintero's version of *El sombrero de tres picos* (The Three-Cornered Hat). *Obertura Republicana* also returned to the stage. The critics were mostly pleased by the scenic designers, but not by the contributions of its choreographers.

Víctor Reyes, the music critic for *Hoy*, represented the majority opinion when he observed: "Ballets of this sort require creation by eminent choreographers who can resolve every kind of problem based on ideal preparation and vigorous talent and preparation. We are not in agreement with the subjective expression in *Obertura Republicana*, much less in its movement and plasticity. In sum: we ought to underline principally the invaluable contribution of the painters Orozco, Castellanos, Mérida and Montenegro, who indisputably provided vigorous talent, imagination and sensitivity."[77]

In the February 1945 issue of *Siempre!* magazine, theater critic Victor Mora assailed *Pausa*. "Pausa, contrary to what you might believe, lasts three quarters of an hour in a program that lasted altogether three and a half hours; a true dance of the hours. In Pausa, the music is too long for its scenario and to accommodate this they have filled it out with minor incidents; first three young ladies, whose age fluctuates between eleven and fifty years old, perform a dance that lasts a quarter of an hour; the curtain rises and another one appears that the entire world looks upon with ecstasy, and finally the scenario, 'really' appears." Mora never specified what this scenario was, but concluded that its choreography was "completely disappointing."[78]

The critic for *Excélsior* asserted that the "choreographic conception" for Nellie's *Ixtepec* "did not exceed the most basic evolutions of any run-of the-mill revue, though it was clearly opulent due to the showiness of its costumes," which were designed by Mérida.[79]

The bullfighting magazine *El Redondel* even weighed in with a report that the company was so poorly prepared for *El sombrero de tres picos* that Carlos Chávez stepped down from the conductor's podium during the dress rehearsal and attempted to correct the dancers.[80] The results were evidently no more successful than those he and Diego Rivera achieved with their attempt at conveying the sandunga in Philadelphia. In an open letter to Guzmán, "S. H." of *El Redondel* posed the provocative question: "Can we have ballets without ballerinas, without maestros, without choreographers, and based solely on painters and fashion designers?"[81]

In the face of this criticism, Orozco penned an impassioned defense of his beloved Gloria and the company he helped found:

This ballet is not an improvisation, but the result of more than ten years of continuous, intense, intelligent, daily work by the Campobello sisters. . . . They have given life to the only formal organization of classical ballet that exists in the entire nation. They have been, and continue to be, the most fecund choreographers and scenario writers, and if that brilliant effort weren't enough, one of them, the prima ballerina, is a performer whose possibilities and personal skills could take her to the leading stages of the world. . . .

For now we have our ballet, their work, in full bloom; not a simple promise, not a project, not an experiment, but a reality, an accomplished fact, something that cannot be destroyed or overlooked, as the envious would wish, and that might have all the defects that anyone might wish, as does all human work, because it already contains in itself the divine spark of creative power, the vital principle that guarantees permanent and definitive life. . . .

The Ballet de la Ciudad de México emerges to the salvation of the art of the dance, thriving in its youthfulness, enthusiasm, disinterestedness, generosity, ingenuity and efficiency.

Those who would have us believe that the Ballet de la Ciudad de México is inferior and incapable because it is a Mexican organization, arrive too late with their stupid argument; those times have already passed or were made to pass by the force of the contemporary painters of this country. We will always be willing to take the lessons of universal art, wherever they come from and whoever can offer them to us, but that is absolutely different from considering ourselves inferior to the rest of the world and incapable of creating and living our own art. . . .

Our ballet, just in its second season, has shown enormous progress and we will see in the near future the strength of its force of renewal. It will have the opportunity to rectify paths, to correct errors of detail, to perfect this or that work, to carry forward, far ahead, the invention, the surprise, the magic of the passionate art that it cultivates. The ballet only looks to the past as a good disciple who views its old masters, but it directs its ambitions towards the future, in a world shaken to its foundations by an irrepressible desire for renewal, and, at the same time, the most furiously revolutionary.[82]

Orozco was apparently unaware that Chagall's designs for *Aleko*, which inspired him in the creation of his sets and costumes for the dance, received much the same response in New York. Martin of the *New York Times* thought Chagall's designs were magnificent, so much so that they entirely overpowered Massine's ballet: "It is Chagall who emerges as the hero of the occasion. He has designed and painted with his own hand four superb backdrops, which are not actually good stage settings at all, but are wonderful works of art. Their sequence is independently dramatic and builds to a stunning climax. So exciting are they in their own right that more than once one wishes that all those people would quit getting in front of them."[83] When the Ballet Theatre commissioned sets from Chagall yet again, this time for a new production of Mikhail Fokine's *Firebird*, Martin reached a similar conclusion: "Ballet Theatre apparently did not learn from its first experience with Chagall in 'Aleko' that no ballet can stand up against his designs. They are overwhelming, and in front of them the conventional human being looks insignificant and the traditional danse d'école faintly foolish."[84] It seems that the choreography by the less experienced Campobello sisters suffered at least as much in the presence of work by the painter who was their advocate.

As Gloria, Nellie, and the supporters of their company assessed their future options, an upcoming change in the nation's presidency signaled a potential new trajectory. As an early part of his campaign for the presidency, Ávila Camacho's Interior Minister Miguel Alemán announced that he intended to create the INBA to explicitly extend state power over the arts. He appointed Chávez as a member of his campaign team to study the idea.[85] When Alemán won the seat, a foregone conclusion given the pervasive operations of the political party whose predecessor was formed by Calles, he appointed Chávez to head his new institute. To celebrate Alemán's inauguration, the company offered what Nellie called *Alelyua,* a version of Johann Strauss II's (1825–1899) *Emperor Waltz* (1889), its male dancers outfitted as nationalist charros.[86]

For Chávez the instituto, which, temporarily at least, brought the Ballet de la Ciudad de México under its wings, signified:

1. The strengthening of character and national personality, which automatically brings a general movement of national allegiance.
2. The aggrandizement of the universal cultural heritage through contributions made by the talent and the genius of Mexicans, highlighting the position of our country within a universal culture.
3. The development of the artistic activities with universal appeal in Mexico, which would be attractive to international audiences.[87]

Less than a month after taking office, Alemán signed a decree moving the Escuela Nacional de Danza out of the Palacio de Bellas Artes and granting it, and the Campobellos's company, a new home.[88] Per the president, both were to be located in the "former building of the Club Hípico Alemán [German Riding Club], surrounded by gardens, with the swimming pool and other appurtenances."[89] It is not clear how the Campobellos saw this change in circumstances. The move itself provided them with a spacious facility in an upscale neighborhood of the city. At the same time, it took them away from the center of power in the Palacio de Bellas Artes, something that was likely viewed as a blessing by the facility's professional staff, with whom Nellie often clashed.

Not long after the company's change of home, Gloria departed for New York with the company's lead male dancer, Fernando Schaffenburg, to undertake studies with ballet master Vincenzo Celli (1900–1988). According to her biographer Segura, the company members, apparently unaware of Orozco's more intimate interest in Gloria, thought that she and Fernando were nurturing a relationship.[90] It was presumably sometime during that period that Gloria informed Orozco that their affair was over.

Orozco had been in New York seeking a new gallery to represent him since September of 1945. He found a one-bedroom apartment on the top floor of a house at 6 East Sixty-Ninth Street to serve as his base in the city. He was joined by his wife Margarita in February of 1946. She brought artwork to consign to the Knoedler Gallery for a one-man show that never materialized. They returned to Mexico City in March.[91]

Segura's biography of Gloria closes with excerpts from two letters dated 1988 he received from another former company member, Mariano Tapia, offering a highly readable account of what supposedly happened between Gloria and Orozco at that time. Tapia's story transformed Orozco's walk-up one-bedroom rental apartment into "the penthouse that Orozco kept in New York," an elaboration that may have come directly from Gloria, with whom he worked recording indigenous dances in a later incarnation of the misiones culturales.[92] Tapia supposed that they went to New York "to work out their differences. Gloria returned and within a few days she told us that she was pregnant with Melchor Peredo's child."[93] Peredo (b. 1927) was Orozco's student. Segura explains that Peredo was assigned by Orozco to improve his artwork by drawing from the company's dancers but "ended up concentrating on Gloria."[94]

According to Tapia, Peredo and Campobello married and "lived happily together for a short time. . . . They began to drink and I believe this arrived at the ears of Miss Nellie. . . . They carried Miss Gloria away under the pretext of drying her out, as, according to Miss Nellie, she was going crazy. Yes, they dried her out, but they also saw to it that she lost the child that she so wanted."[95] This was, Tapia opined, because "Miss Nellie did not want to lose the official support and money that José Clemente Orozco contributed to the Ballet de la Ciudad de México."

Tapia closed one of his letters with a post script that was nearly as dramatic as the story he related: "There is a Madonna seated on a bench, crowned with little angels, bearing the living face of Miss Gloria. This was painted by José Clemente Orozco. Gloria is the Madonna and the little angels are the children they would not allow Gloria to have. His adored muse Gloria Campobello appears in all of the paintings by the master in the Palacio de Bellas Artes, with her beautiful face and her tempting body, delight of the artist, the great artist, J.C.O. God forgive me for telling what I saw, and you, Felipe, pardon me for telling you what I ought not."[96]

Striking as this claim is, it is, at least in part, unlikely. Orozco completed his only work in the Palacio de Bellas Artes, *Katharsis* (Catharsis) in 1934, with its voluptuous, leering blond prostitute dominating the foreground, before he met Gloria in 1937. She was only a teenager when he painted it.

In Reed's interpretation of the mural, "It is the alert, aggressive harlot that Orozco . . . portrays as both cause and symbol of the terrible configuration that reduced civilization to rubble," which can hardly be considered a sign of the painter's romantic devotion to his purported muse.[97]

Tapia's timeline has other problems as well. The incidents he reported with Peredo seem to have taken place in 1948, more than a year after Gloria returned from her studies in New York. That said, Tapia probably witnessed some of what he described. According to a 1949 report in *Hoy*, Nellie used her "official influences" to have him arrested "under accusations that she could not then prove," apparently in an attempt to keep him quiet.[98]

Whatever may, or may not, have happened between Gloria and Orozco in New York during the first few months of 1946, her studies with Celli in New York improved her dancing. As Segura remembers it, she returned "dancing very well, quite slim, there was something that had been transformed in her, she was better than ever . . . her face, her smile, her blue eyes, everything shined."[99] The trip to study in New York also resulted in contacts that allowed the Ballet de la Ciudad de México a path forward in its effort to refute its critics.

Early in 1947, Nellie announced that the Ballet de la Ciudad de México would appear on the Palacio de Bellas Artes stage in joint performances with the Markova-Dolin Ballet. Anton Dolin (born Sydney Francis Patrick Chippendall Healey-Kay, 1904–1983) and Alicia Markova (born Lilian Alice Marks, 1910–2004) formed their partnership in the 1930s when they danced together as part of the Vic-Wells Ballet, precursor to London's Royal Ballet. They formed their own company in 1935 and were active in other companies at the same time. Both Markova and Dolin performed with the American Ballet Theatre as well, including its 1941 and 1942 seasons in Mexico City, so they were familiar with the Palacio de Bellas Artes and its dance audience. Dolin arrived in June of 1947 for a few weeks to begin mounting his version of *Giselle*, one of Markova's best-known leading roles, that had already proven successful there.

A month before their August 25 opening, Dolin returned with the rest of the company so they could familiarize themselves with the ballets of the Campobello sisters that they would also dance: Nellie's *Ixtepec* and *Feria*, along with Gloria's *Alameda 1900* and even her version of *Les Sylphides*. Working alongside an entire company of better-trained performers, who were, nonetheless, suffering from Mexico City's altitude, helped the

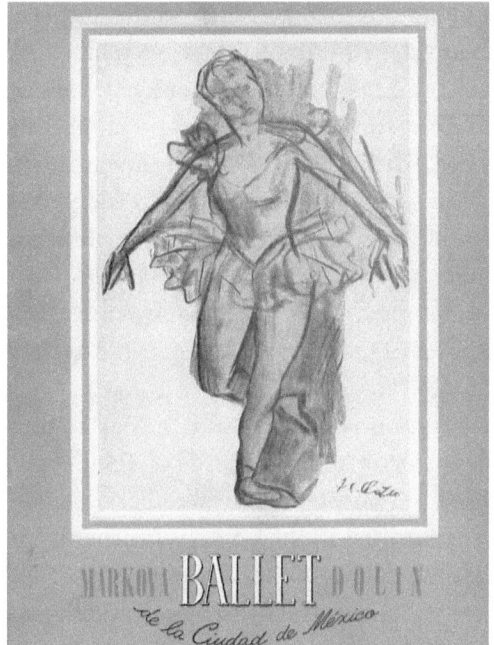

FIGURE 16. José Clemente Orozco. Program design for the Markova Dolin/Ballet de la Ciudad de México incorporating a drawing of Gloria Campobello. 1946. Archivo Vertical-CENIDI DANZA/INBA. Fondo documental Patricia Aulestia. © 2019 Artists Rights Society (ARS), New York/SOMAAP, Mexico City.

Mexican dancers refine their skills, which resulted in far better reviews in the press.[100]

The foreign-trained dancers received contrasting reviews for their performances in Nellie Campobello's Mexicanist works. Dolin danced the lead in her *Feria*, which told the story of a fair that drew dancers from throughout Mexico every year to compete for its trophy. The contest preparations, overseen by the mayor and the governor, led to a parade of dancers. The parade was interrupted by the arrival of the charro, a regional rogue. After demonstrating that he came in peace, he chose the most beautiful girl in the village as his winning partner in the dance competition.[101] Dolin's performance as the charro earned praise from *Tiempo* magazine for the "surprising realism" of his interpretation.[102]

By contrast, the pseudonymous "Junius," writing in the pages of *Excélsior*, thought Markova only received applause for her appearance in

Ixtepec because the audience was being polite in response to the surprise of seeing a foreigner recognize their dance heritage. Markova danced its lead, mourning her departed lover by the seaside. The young people of her community gathered nearby to pray to the god of love and attempted to hearten Markova with a sandunga. Their celebratory mood was interrupted by a remote melody that followed the joyless girl, who ceded her golden handkerchief to the dancers, bidding farewell to any hope of future happiness.[103] "Junius" thought Markova should stick with the classics. "We would say that we would have been happier to see the *Sandunga* and *Dios Nunca Muere* . . . with authentic natives of Oaxaca, with their typical dress and their characteristic musical groups."[104]

Ironically, it was the relative success of this joint venture in Mexico that provoked the Ballet de la Ciudad de México's undoing. Based on their experience with the Markova-Dolin Ballet, so many company members decided to pursue studies or performing opportunities in the US and elsewhere that the sisters were left without enough experienced dancers to mount any of their works. Although the Ballet de la Ciudad de México appeared again on stage—in 1949 at the Palacio de Bellas Artes and in 1951 in a tour of northern Mexico—it never again mounted a full season of works.[105]

The scenario for one final collaboration between Gloria and Orozco was printed in the 1947 programs for the Ballet de la Ciudad de México, though it seems not to have been produced.[106] It was for *Bailarina*, a storyline Orozco had written on his own. It shows him to be just as smitten with Gloria as he ever was and demonstrated a considerable lack of awareness of the needs for a serviceable ballet script. Save for its melodramatic denouement, its five scenes offered little to engage the interest of any member of the audience who did not share Orozco's obsession with Gloria.

The scenario opened with the Ballerina (always capitalized by Orozco in his scenario) applying her makeup while observing her passing companions through the mirror she used for that task. The second scene depicted the Ballerina taking her daily class at the barre, where the protagonist performs a "playful imitation of academic ballet, glacially perfect" for her classmates. In the ensuing section, the Ballerina is abandoned backstage by her studio companions and left to engage in painful self-reflection and doubt of her vocation, leading into the fourth scene where she weeps as she lets her hair down, having returned to the mirrors of the dressing room. The work closes with what Orozco called a

Fantastic scene. Forms and harmonies of color in continually changing movement. The Ballerina reacts and once again begins to smile
as she recognizes the reflection of the stage and its wonders in her
mirror. She prepares herself anew. She returns to the dance as impassioned as before, but softly, so much so that her body follows the
music with barely perceptible movements. The lights, in rapid or slow
succession, illuminate the Ballerina. She opens her arms and the set
opens as well, allowing her to view an endless countryside, without
mountains; then nothingness and the stars. The scenery changes: it
is now a small space, intimate and warm; then a dark space, in which
only the Ballerina is lit. A cold morning dawns, with a hurricane. All
is gray and the white of snow. A snow white boat disappears into the
dark. The fires of home. Peace returns, intimacy, warmth, quiet. One
can hardly hear the music. The Ballerina smiles and contemplates her
hand in the mirror. She arranges her hair. She relaxes at her vanity and
lets her imagination soar. Suddenly everything goes dark: a potent
light illuminates one sector of the stage and the Ballerina flees from
it every time it strikes her. At last, the Ballerina, exhausted, drops in
a faint. The light continues to move about and slowly diminishes in
intensity; but suddenly it intensifies to the maximum, and falls across
the Ballerina. She rises, for a few brief instants, and burns in the light.
It suddenly cuts out and the Ballerina falls, never to rise again.[107]

If this scenario had been realized, Orozco's Ballerina, burning under the
ballet's intense final spotlight, would have become the female counterpart
to the *hombre en llamas* (man in flames) he painted in the dome of Guadalajara's Hospicio Cabañas. Salvador Echavarría called this figure a spirit
that "enlightens the world," someone who "consumes himself to bring light.
He is the substance of this miraculous flame which is the ultimate end of
life: Conscience and Thought. If the world were deprived of it, the whole
creation would be meaningless and equivalent to Naught."[108]

According to Orozco's instructions, the five scenes of the ballet were
to be performed without a pause. The changes to the set he had in mind
for the work were to be carried out under normal stage lighting, in full
view of the audience—just as Seki Sano did in Waldeen's *La Coronela* in
1940. Other aspects of his scenario, such as the mirrors he specified for the
first and last scenes, as well as the "play of colors in continual movement,"

offered him the potential for exploring some potentially innovative and challenging formal opportunities. In his final ballet proposal for Gloria, he continued to experiment with the visual possibilities of stage effects that he had begun to use with *Umbral* and transformed her into the spiritual light that gave meaning to his world.

It is worth noting that none of the ballets that featured Orozco's collaboration with Gloria as the choreographer and star performer featured overtly Mexican themes. The music they selected for these works came from the acknowledged greats of the European canon—Beethoven for *Pausa* and Schubert for *Umbral* and *Bailarina*. When working with her, he was true to his more "universalist" approach to creating art. Orozco's sole incursion into the company's vein of nationalist ballet was his design work for Nellie's reworking of *30–30* as *Obertura Revolucionaria*.

The fact that several members of the Ballet de la Ciudad de México were recruited to the ranks of similarly young organizations in the US rebuts the harshest critics of the company. But Tibol's assessment of the company's efforts as "technically poor" was generally supported by the nonspecialist Mexican critical press. At a Christmas celebration in New York in 1947, Dolin told Segura, one of the many dancers who left Mexico to seek more remunerative employment elsewhere, that it was "a pity" that Gloria had not "developed her career in some other country; she would have been an international star."[109] Her personal efforts to excel as a dancer needed better coaching than she was able to receive in Mexico.[110]

The far better received scenic designs commissioned by the Ballet de la Ciudad de México proved to be almost as ephemeral as the dances for which they were created. Precious little remains to assess the works prepared for the Campobellos by Orozco and other leading artists of the era— a few bits of scenery, a small collection of black-and-white photographs, a handful of program covers featuring costume designs. Many of the studies were dispersed, and many of the sets themselves were destroyed in the events surrounding Nellie's death in July of 1986. Her younger sister Gloria, who according to Tapia may have been sent for treatment of alcoholism in 1948 but never gave up drinking, predeceased her in 1968.[111]

Nellie disappeared nearly completely from the public eye years before her death. The aides she appointed to assist her at the school, the husband-and-wife team of Claudio Niño and Cristina Belmont, insisted that Nellie didn't want to be bothered with visitors. One such group of visitors were curators of an exhibition commemorating the centennial of Orozco's birth who sought Nellie's loan of some of his scenic designs. Their request to meet with her was categorically denied by her assistants.[112] According to events pieced together by different investigators, Niño and Belmont sequestered Nellie. An attorney for the Instituto Nacional de Bellas Artes had the couple arrested for her kidnapping. They spent three months in jail before their attorney, Enrique Fuentes, produced Nellie at a hearing on April 10, 1985, the last time she was seen in public. Eventually Niño and Fuentes were arrested for Campobello's death. The state issued a warrant for Belmont as well, but she avoided arrest. Niño was sentenced, but the case against him was dismissed for "technical faults" in 2001.

During the time when Niño and Belmont where holding her incommunicado, public records show that Campobello supposedly made Belmont her sole heir—although Nellie's name is misspelled in the relevant documents and her nephew contested these wills—and assigned Belmont all the rights to the artworks in her possession. Shortly after Niño and Belmont were released from prison, Niño reported that the Campobellos's home was burglarized and all its artworks stolen. Niño then proceeded to "sell" the denuded home to Fuentes's wife. It was apparently left abandoned and eventually taken over by a group of some twenty families from the Mazahua tribe. When the newspaper *Excélsior*'s investigative reporter Juan Bautista entered the residence in February of 1999 he encountered what remained of the scenery tucked away in a disused second-story bathroom. The current inhabitants had been using the painted backdrops as fuel to heat their coffee.[113]

The paintings that were reported stolen consisted of twelve works by Orozco, including, it seems, the Madonna referred to by Tapia in his letter to Segura, and some forty works by Mérida, Montenegro, Castellanos, and Ruiz, then valued at sixty million dollars. González traced several of these works to different collections in Mexico. Some of Orozco's working designs for *Umbral* also appeared for sale in 1992 and 1993 at Mexico City's Galería 10/10. The same gallery provided additional studies for his ballet design projects to various auctions. All of these works were reportedly consigned to the gallery by Niño and Belmont's children.[114]

The vision of the Campobello sisters likely reached beyond their own capabilities as choreographers. Nonetheless, dance critic Alberto Dallal's summary of their careers, "with all their excesses," points to the sisters' successful efforts to incorporate folk dance instruction into the curriculum of Mexico's public schools, their preparation of a substantial number of trained dancers, and their incorporation of Mexican themes into the classical ballet.[115] As Tibol notes, it would, however, be up to the modern dancers to clear out the "shopworn" technique of the Campobello sisters and usher in the new style of Mexican dance.[116]

9

The Golden Age of Mexican Modern Dance

Miguel Covarrubias and the Academia de la Danza Mexicana

To help him shape the dance component of the new INBA, Carlos Chávez invited Waldeena Guillermina Bravo and Sokolova Ana Mérida, along with an array of painters, composers, and writers, to assist him. As part of the INBA's charge to create a universal culture attractive to international audiences, Chávez's team created a modern dance focused Academia de la Danza Mexicana (Academy of Mexican Dance). Chávez soon appointed polymath artist Miguel Covarrubias to lead INBA's dance department, ushering in a golden age for Mexican modern dance. INBA underwrote lavish productions by internationally recognized choreographer José Limón (1908–1972); it extended similar support to its novice choreographers who mounted productions with scenic designs by Mexico's leading artists and scores by its most noted composers.

The two opposing camps in the modern dance controversy reached a temporary truce toward the end of 1946 when Bravo and Mérida formed what they rather surprisingly called the Ballet Waldeen. Waldeen went to the US for health reasons, leaving no one to lead either of the antagonistic groups of dancers, giving the factions a short-lived opportunity to unite.[1]

As Bravo describes it, she and Mérida were "supposedly enemies in technique, but we had never met. When we discovered we had the same goal, to keep modern dance alive in our country, we decided to work together. That objective united us, despite our rivalry. In reality, we weren't enemies, it was our teachers who couldn't abide one another."[2]

With 150 pesos from the SEP, the help of Mérida's father, who provided scenic designs, and additional assistance from José Clemente Orozco, Diego Rivera, and Seki Sano, they arranged for a performance in the theater of the Hotel del Prado.[3] It consisted of established works by Waldeen and new works by Bravo and Mérida. According to the program, the Ballet Waldeen was intended to be "experimental; its objectives, to abandon both the technique and the ideology of classical ballet; to take fundamental indigenous and mestizo elements to create an art lifted from the heart and struggles of the people, to convert it into a direct and profound medium of expression that offers the people orientation, stimulus and culture; elevate the dance by giving it a worthy professional character, which places Mexico at the same level of other countries in this expression of art, striving to outdo them."[4]

It was the only performance by the independent Ballet Waldeen. Miguel Alemán assumed the Mexican presidency just days before its presentation and, as promised during his campaign, named Carlos Chávez to head his new INBA with "virtually absolute authority in the arts."[5] Chávez named himself to lead the institute's dance section and asked Bravo and Mérida to help him formulate a dance program "within a universal culture . . . attractive to international audiences."[6] As music historian Robert Parker noted, given his position, Chávez could "commission the production of any ballets he saw fit and finance them with what seemed almost an unlimited budget."[7]

Despite his consistent portrayal in the US as a musical nationalist, Chávez was a modernist at heart. Just as Alemán's administration was dedicated to the economic modernization of Mexico—as well as to the personal enrichment of the president and his numerous allies—Chávez was dedicated to the aesthetic modernization of his country.[8] His experience with classical ballet had been frustrating; modern dance represented the new wave of theatrical dance.

In addition to the successes of Sokolow and Waldeen in Mexico during the 1940s, it is worth noting that during World War II the US promoted its modern dance movement in Latin America as part of its ongoing propaganda efforts. In 1945 the Inter-American Office of the National Gallery of Art, a successor of the Office of the Coordinator of Inter-American Affairs run by Nelson Rockefeller, sponsored a traveling exhibition of photographs "illustrating the development of the Dance in this country through its leading exponents of the past decade."[9] Organized by the Museum of Modern Art under the title *Modern American Dance*, it featured more than forty black-and-white photographs by Barbara Morgan along with texts by the photographer and *New York Times* dance critic John Martin. Although she was uncomfortable being associated with propaganda efforts, Morgan asserted that American modern dance contained "the flux of joys and sorrows, the conflicts and certainties universally experienced by modern man—yet colored by the people and place, the atmosphere and living dynamics peculiar to the North."[10] Save for its passing reference to "the North," her text reads as if it could have been written by a Mexican promoter of the modern dance.

Martin's essay for the exhibition, which was translated into both Portuguese and Spanish, was even more pointed in its ascription of "universal principles" to what he claimed as a form original to his homeland. He specifically cited the Mexican origins of José Limón, then serving in the US Army, to underline his argument of universality:

> In the field of the dance the United States has made its most distinctive and original contribution to the fine arts. Like every other country it has, of course, developed its own folk forms, as well as its popular ballroom dances; but instead of acquiescing without question in the general acceptance of the academic ballet as the only possible art form for the dance in the Western World, it has also developed its own quite independent creative approach to the dance as a fine art. . . .
>
> The characteristic dance which it has evolved instead owes nothing whatever to tradition. It goes directly to life and individual emotional experience for its materials and its techniques, and deliberately avoids the setting up of any standardized vocabulary of movements or any arbitrary "school." The basic principle of the art is that the human body when acted upon from within by emotion, moves in its own creative way and by means of such movement conveys to the spectator the substance of the artist's intent, however subtle. Without resort to established symbols or literary connotations it translated inner experience directly through kinesthetic means.
>
> Isadora Duncan was the great prophet of the new art in the first years of the present century. Her dance was purely lyrical, the outpouring of her own deep feeling, with the music of the masters as her inspiration. . . .
>
> With Isadora Duncan the new dance went to Europe where it spread its influence widely. In Russia the reforms of Michel Fokine in the strict and tradition-bound Imperial Ballet were made possible by the success of Isadora's revolutionary appearances in St. Petersburg. All over Europe her ideas bore fruit, and in the days between the wars there developed a widespread movement which produced such great artists and teachers as the Austrian Wiesenthal Sisters, the Swedish Ronny Johansson, the Hungarian Rudolf von Laban, the German Mary Wigman.

If this art is sometimes known as the "American dance" because of its origin, it is in no wise nationalistic, but is based on a universal principle. Among its leading practitioners in the contemporary field in New York are the German-born Hanya Holm and the Mexican-born José Limon [*sic*] (now in the United States Army), who fall naturally into place beside such native-born leaders as Martha Graham, Doris Humphrey, Helen Tamiris, and Charles Weidman.[11]

Although this exhibition does not appear to have arrived in Mexico, it was but one manifestation of the emphasis on the new and the relationship between American modern dance and the "universal" that the United Sates was promoting at that time.[12] Combined with the modernizing impulse of the Alemán administration, Chávez's personal tastes, the influences of Sokolow and Waldeen, and the ongoing issues that the Campobello sisters created both within the SEP's bureaucracy and the parents of their students, modern dance became Mexico's state form. Ballet effectively became a backwater of Mexican theatrical dance in the coming decades.

Rather than have Bravo and Mérida continue with the Ballet Waldeen, Chávez engaged both the budding choreographers in the creation of the academy as part of his new institute, which initially was an arm of the SEP. According to Chávez, the objective of his new academy was to study Mexico's indigenous and mestizo folk dances as a means of putting dancers in contact with material to inspire new creations. The formal document establishing the academy within the SEP in February of 1947 asserted that the nation's folk dances could "reach a greater artistic level if they are assimilated and recreated by artists possessed of advanced professional and intellectual training."[13] The document went on to specify that these trained dancers were to be given the opportunities to develop their own styles "within the national style." Among its other directives was the establishment of a permanent professional dance company to present the works developed by its members.

While Chávez did not abolish the Escuela Nacional de Danza, the new academy effectively diluted the influence of the Campobello sisters. It became a hybrid institution, serving both as a teaching facility and as a professional modern dance company.

For Bravo, at least, "the initial period [of the academy] . . . was odious, we didn't have the least autonomy, we couldn't select our musicians, our painters."[14] Chávez seems to have maintained his view that dancers needed outside direction in order to avoid aesthetic differences. His other advisors were entirely male: painters Julio Castellanos, José Chávez Morado, Agustín Lazo, Carlos Mérida, Guillermo Meza, Julio Prieto (1912–1977), Diego Rivera, and Juan Soriano (1920–2006). He also engaged composers Blas Galindo, Carlos Jiménez Mabarak (1916–1994), José Pablo Moncayo, and Luis Sandi; and writers Celestino Gorostiza and Salvador Novo. It was this group of advisors that largely determined which works were to be developed by the academy's dancers.[15] When it came time to present the initial works of the academy to the Mexican public, Chávez tapped Rivera rather than one of his female choreographers to serve as its spokesman to the press. According to Mérida's biographer, her then husband Antonio Luna, "Diego availed himself of the opportunity to talk about imperialism, communism, the defects of banking organization, the need for a new commercial credit, the sociological utility of the anthropological . . . anything but dance. Finally, and before the anxious, mute request of the directors [Bravo and Mérida], he said four things about the beauty of the Mexican woman and two things about the program and sat down."[16]

Once the academy was established, and despite its specific charge to focus on the nation's folk dance as its source, it served as the arena for staging disagreements between the Waldeenas and Sokolovas. Miguel Covarrubias described the academy as consisting of "groups which had been maintained in continual and even overt competition, which was later accentuated when they broke into smaller entities, all rivaling each other."[17]

Tensions began to re-emerge in the spring of 1947 when all of the academy's members left for a research trip to the state of Oaxaca. Dancer Lin Duran, who was part of the expedition, recalled that Chávez believed that the academy's members could not create a Mexican form of theatrical dance "if we did not know our own dances, the roots, as he affirmed."[18] The trip to Zapotec indigenous communities, including San Pedro Cajonos and Yalalag in the mountains of Oaxaca, was rigorous for its participants, who were accustomed to urban amenities that were lacking in rural Mexico. Duran opined that Mérida "saw the difficulties and dangers that we were going to be exposed to and surely thought she was not going to return in time and in good condition to dance in Bellas Artes," where she was invited to perform as a guest with the company of Katherine Dunham (1909–2006); so she parted ways with her colleagues.[19]

Dunham was one of the favorite choreographers of Mérida's father, and dancing with her company influenced Ana's direction.[20] Dunham, who was educated as an anthropologist and wrote her doctoral thesis on Afro-Caribbean dance, created a technique based on dancing from the African diaspora in the Americas, classical ballet, and modern dance. Víctor Reyes, the music critic for *Hoy*, frowned on what he saw as Mérida's overly close imitation of Dunham's style in her 1947 *Balada del pájaro y las doncellas* (Ballad of the Bird and the Maidens).[21]

Dunham's appearance in Mexico was due to the success of her revue *Bal nègre* (1946), which she created to showcase her company of dancers, singers, and musicians. It included material drawn from Afro-Brazilian, Cuban, and Haitian cultures; the fighting dances of Martinique that Dunham had featured in her first full-length work *L'Ag'Ya* (1938); and African American jazz.[22] Dunham toured the *Bal nègre* across the US before landing on Broadway and then continuing on to Europe. Given the company's international success, tobacco heiress Doris Duke arranged for the group's 1947 visit to Mexico, where it premiered Dunham's *Rhumba Trio* at the Palacio de Bellas Artes.[23] Mérida performed there with Dunham's company in the choreographer's version of Maurice Ravel's *La Valse,* a work that theater critic Armando de María y Campos noted had "little or nothing to do with black folklore, but gives the Dunham dancers the opportunity to demonstrate that they are excellent dancers, not because they are black, but because they dominate the art of the dance."[24]

Covarrubias, who was fascinated by the cultural life in Harlem during his stay in the US in the 1920s and 1930s, thought Dunham's appearance in Mexico was important because of what her approach to staging ethnic dance represented. He declared her "a great choreographer with an ample culture and solid anthropological background, who has understood how to use the folklore of her race with excellent propriety, imagination and theatrical sense, relying, furthermore, on a numerous group of dancers with a great modern technique and an emotivity never seen in Mexico. One cannot say that the African-American dance of Katherine Dunham has left permanent traces in Mexican dance, although it did show our dancers and aspiring choreographers what can be done with folklore when it is managed with intelligence and artistic integrity, provided that one has good dancers with stage presence and high professional standards."[25]

If Dunham's appearance in Mexico left a mark on Mérida's work, the trip to Oaxaca was even more influential for Bravo. She claimed a foundational place for indigenous dance in the creation of her choreography:

My greatest teachers were, ahead of everyone, the Mexican Indians. I learned from them, I lived with them, I ate chili and tortillas, drank schnapps, slept on a *petate* [a palm-frond mat] and I rode mules, canoes and ox carts on my different travels.

I sought out my bread, my food, with the Indians. That year I saw a lot of dances and later I went on my own initiative. My desire to know the Indians has never been satiated.

My entire life has been impregnated with Mexican dancers. It is like a tattoo that one has.[26]

According to Margarita Tortajada, the academy's initial productions were split between dances with references to folk sources and "pure" dance without national elements.[27] Despite her training under Sokolow, Mérida's works, including the *Balada del pájaro,* all fell under the folk-influenced category. Bravo produced both "pure" and folk works; her *El zanate* was based on a Zapotec legend about an animal that stole household goods to build its nests that she encountered during the academy's research journey to Oaxaca.[28] Future folk promoter Amalia Hernández premiered an entirely "pure" work. Nonetheless, both aesthetic and political differences remained. The leftist Bravo was determined to produce dances with social content and the more conservative Mérida wished to ensure the dominance of a formal approach to dance creation.

These differences led to Bravo's departure from the academy in 1948 and the creation of her own company, which she dubbed the Ballet Nacional de México (National Ballet of Mexico). "Ideology separated us," Bravo told dance historian César Delgado. "Indeed, I did and do have political ideas. [Mérida] denounced me as a communist before Carlos Chávez and I had to leave the Academy. . . . She . . . had lived abstract art, the influence of her father Carlos Mérida and the intellectual world in which she was raised, we had to clash."[29] In her letter of resignation to Chávez, Bravo expressed hope that the new institution would not find itself in the "hands of mercenary people who use the funds you have so nobly provided for petty, and therefore unpatriotic, ends or for pure exhibitionism," which is perhaps a veiled reference to Mérida.[30] In another interview, Bravo also told critic Raquel Tibol that so long as "Maestro Chávez was not harassing us everything went well."[31] This suggests that Chávez's willingness to meddle in the dancer's affairs also influenced her decision to leave the academy.

Despite the differences between the two choreographers, Bravo believed their joint role in the establishment of the academy remained a critical step that ensured the survival of modern dance in Mexico: "Without the foundation of the Academy dance could not have sustained itself, because the Ballet Waldeen was a small group that had no school and nothing more than the desire to dance. The foundation of the Academy was what provided for dance instruction, not entirely complete, not entirely professional, without precise methods or techniques, but it was a seed, a way of keeping alive what had started with *La Coronela*, so that modern dance would not die."[32]

Bravo still relied on her instructor's salary from INBA and funds from other governmental agencies for her and her company's survival. Even though a group of dancers decamped en masse from the academy when she departed, divisions still remained within this combination school and company.[33] With Bravo gone, Mérida felt confident in asking Chávez to invite Sokolow to teach at the academy. While Sokolow turned down a full-time appointment, she did teach there while she was in Mexico City to mount choreography for the 1948 opera season.[34]

In fairly short order, Chávez realized that he could not simultaneously act as INBA's leader, artistic director of its Orquesta Sinfónica de México, and head of its dance program. Still adhering to his artist-in-charge proposition, in January of 1949 he named Stridentist sculptor Germán Cueto to a brief tenure as lead of INBA's dance program.[35] Shortly thereafter, Chávez moved the dance program under the direction of Novo in the new Department of Theater, Dance and Literature. In an attempt to broaden the academy's appeal in the spring of 1950, Chávez imported Adolph Bolm of Ballets Russes' fame to teach a brief course in classical ballet—a step that Mérida opposed as she thought the classical dancers should stay in the Campobellos's Escuela Nacional.[36]

The constant changes in focus and administration complicated preexisting divisions within the academy. Finally, in June of 1950 Chávez established dance as its own department within INBA under the lead of the multitalented Miguel Covarrubias, a position he held until the end of the Alemán presidency in 1952.[37] Covarrubias named another painter, Santos Balmori, to take charge of the academy.

Covarrubias and the New Department of Dance

When he assumed his new position, Covarrubias made indirect but pointed criticisms of the ideas of both Sokolow and Waldeen in an interview with *Revista Mexicana de Culture* (The Mexican Cultural Review):

Modern dance has fossilized within the routine or dogma surrounding the tendencies of 1935. It suffers from a limitation of gesture, of
expression; it bases itself in a dogmatic concept of ideas with grave
disregard for technique, as if that didn't matter to become a good
dancer, when in reality it is absolutely necessary, it is like exercise for
an athlete. An untrained body doesn't function. The lack of technique
and imagination screws many a dancer to the floor from which they
barely move. . . . They don't invent a single new step, they barely run,
they don't use their body, only their arms. On the other hand, some
believe that folklore, and nothing more, is Mexican dance and there
you get the steps from the jarabe, the maracas, the rebozos and the
huraches. All of these are Mexican elements of the dance, but they
are not the dance itself, particularly when they forget the Mexican
spirit.[38]

What he sought to achieve was "a school [of dance] that reaches the heights
of our pictorial school."

After he stepped down from his position with INBA, he defended his
choices to focus the efforts of the academy on modern dance and to model
its work on that of the Mexican school of painters. Acknowledging the lack
of a strong tradition of Mexican theatrical dance and echoing David Alfaro
Siqueiros's earlier declaration on the primacy of the Mexican school, Covarrubias proposed that:

We have important regional and indigenous ceremonial folk dances,
of great character and plasticity, but quite limited for transport to the
legitimate stage by the restrained use of the body one finds in it, given
that it is based almost exclusively in movements of the feet to mark
rhythms more or less complex, and ignoring the arms, the torso, the
neck and the face. Folkloric dance can and should provide important elements to the modern Mexican dance; but if one stylizes it for
the theater, it automatically becomes denatured and loses its greater
merit, its authentic flavor and character. It is as false to dance a jarabe
en pointe, or to mount a ballet with a Mexican theme using ballerinas
with their arms in arabesque and their feet in the fifth position, as
it is to pretend that one can make Mexican dance by adapting folkloric dances and sets or adding rebozos and maracas to a technique
of postures that is also applied to the music of Scarlatti, Stravinsky or
Blas Galindo. Mexican folkloric dance ought to be cultivated as an

essential part of the education of our dancers, not to "improve" it, but strictly as folkloric dance with veneration and respect.

Our schools of modern painting and music arose as should Mexican modern dance, from the new ideology of Mexican nationalism, revolutionary and essentially indigenist, of our modern artists, who understood how to interpret it through the universal language of modern painting and music. Thus, there is no other path to follow in creating Mexican dance than that which our painters and musicians have followed; the profound and sincere identification of our dancers and choreographers with Mexican artistic ideology and the intelligent use of our painting and music through the international modern dance of the post-war period, which will serve as the technical basis and as an instrument of movement, composition and theatrical expression. It is obvious that we reject the classical ballet to serve as a medium for this ideology, for its artificiality, its limitations and its psychology alien to our own and which represents its true antithesis.[39]

Covarrubias saw his first job as ridding the academy of its warring factions and bringing the dancers together in a single group free of "petty personal allegiances, rivalries and jealousies."[40] Unsurprisingly, not all of the dancers supported by INBA agreed with Covarrubias's attempts to do away with the multiple fiefdoms that permeated the academy. Just as different sectors of the SEP financed competing dance companies in the 1940s, Mérida received funding for her *Grupo Experimental* (Experimental Group) from museologist Fernando Gamboa (1909–1990), then the subdirector of INBA, within a month of Covarrubias's assumption of control.[41]

One of his first steps to accomplish this mission was hiring a qualified modern dance instructor with no direct ties to Sokolow or Waldeen. He chose African American dancer Xavier Francis (1928–2000), who was associated with the New Dance Group of New York. The New Dance Group was formed in 1932 by a group of left-wing women who wished to create socially engaged dance, much in the spirit of Sokolow, with whom they sometimes worked.[42] The group's classes cost ten cents per session and included instruction in technique, which expanded from modern dance to include folk dance and classical ballet, as well as discussions of Marxist philosophy. The group provided the first mainstream school to support African American students and choreographers. While Francis's left-leaning training was no longer congruent with the probusiness atmosphere of the

Alemán administration, his politics matched Covarrubias's personal stance as well as that of the majority of his colleagues in the academy. In a special issue of the vanguard magazine *Espacios* (Spaces) dedicated to dance in 1949, all of the major figures profiled, with the exception of Ana Mérida, declared themselves in favor of creating socially engaged dance for the nation.[43] A similar overview of leading dancers and choreographers by *Hoy* in 1951 showed no changes in attitude on the topic, although the Campobello sisters used this platform to continue their advocacy on behalf of classical ballet and attack "North American gymnastics, which in reality is what is being practiced by the girls who call themselves modern dancers."[44]

Francis happened on to his position at the academy by chance. While traveling in Mexico, he met a dancer he knew through the School of American Ballet who advised him to go to the academy and ask for a "Mr. Covarrubias," who was looking for dance instructors.[45] After Francis offered a sample class under Covarrubias's observation, he was immediately offered a job. Francis didn't report whether Covarrubias was accompanied by his wife, dancer Rosa Rolanda, during this audition, but she was frequently present at the academy in her husband's first months there and advised him on its students, teachers, and curriculum.[46]

Rosa initiated her formal dance studies with Marion Morgan (1881–1971) in Los Angeles, eventually rising to become a member of Morgan's company of interpretive, "barefoot dancers."[47] An English-language version of Charles Cuvillier's (1877–1955) operetta *The Lilac Domino* (1914) provided Rosa with her first solo engagement on Broadway. She soon began working in silent films as well, providing the choreography for several productions by French film director Maurice Tourneur (1876–1961) and for "The Ballet of Life" for Lois Weber's (1979–1939) melodrama *What Do Men Want?* (1921).

Multiple conflicting versions of Rosa's initial encounter with Miguel exist. In two of those narratives, Adolfo Best played a catalytic role. Covarrubias's biographer Adriana Williams proposes that Best brought Rosa to the apartment he shared with Miguel to paint her portrait, leading to their encounter.[48] Alternately, Juan Coronel notes that Rosa kept a newspaper photograph of Pavlova's *Fantasía Mexicana* in her files and suggests she sought out Best's assistance in the set designs for what became the *Garrick Gaities* production of "Rancho Mexicano," eventually leading to a contract with Covarrubias to create the set. "It is highly probable that Covarrubias, in order to conquer Rosa, offered her detailed explanations—such was his custom—of how the [Best] system of drawing worked and its infinite applications," Coronel writes.[49] It was with this performance, as Coronel also notes, that Rose became Rosa.

Based on materials from Rosa's scrapbooks, historian Mary Panzer believes that Covarrubias's friend, photographer Nickolas Muray (1892–1965), was responsible for introducing the pair.[50] Muray and Covarrubias cohosted regular parties in the photographer's Greenwich Village studio for the cultural vanguard of the time, with a guest list that featured such talents as guitarist Andrés Segovia (1893–1987), novelist Sinclair Lewis (1885–1951), and dramatist Jean Cocteau. These soirees also featured a house orchestra, whose members included Chávez and Rufino Tamayo, to provide impromptu renditions of popular music. Muray was a well-known dance photographer, having taken up the practice to satisfy the market Frank Crowninshield was establishing through *Vanity Fair*. Muray met Rosa, who became one of his favorite models, while shooting some publicity shots for a nationally touring performance of a revue centered around "The Rose Girl." He recalled Rosa's dancing style as "partly Spanish, partly African and partly Mexican."[51]

Whatever her dancing style, she had also earned a reputation for her domineering personality and sometimes violent temper.[52] Despite this, and taken by her beauty and talent, Covarrubias married Rosa in a small civil ceremony in rural New York in 1930. The pair then embarked on a honeymoon world tour to Japan, China, the Philippines, Indonesia, Singapore, Egypt, Italy, and France.[53] At their home in Mexico City, they hosted visitors including Martha Graham and her music director Louis Horst, who saw Miguel's latest works as inspired by his visit to Bali.[54] When Covarrubias was appointed head of INBA's dance department, Rosa joined him in his work with the dancers. She served as a kind of talent scout, bringing promising students, such as Guillermo Arriaga (1926–2014) and Rocío Sagaón (1933–2015), to his attention.[55] This was a practice she would come to regret.

THE RETURN OF JOSÉ LIMÓN

The second major step that Covarrubias took to improve the situation at the academy was to finalize the arrangements necessary for José Limón to return to Mexico and perform in the Palacio de Bellas Artes with his dance company. Actor Fernando Wagner (1905–1973), Covarrubias's predecessor as director of the dance division under Novo, began to explore the possibility of Limón's return to Mexico in 1949 following the successful premiere of his *The Moor's Pavane*.[56] Covarrubias, who met Limón in New York in the 1930s, ensured that Wagner's efforts were carried to fruition.

Like thousands of other Mexicans, the seven-year-old Limón left his homeland when the chaos of the revolution made it impossible for his father to support his family as director of the Academia de Música (Academy of Music) in Cananea.[57] He discovered his vocation for dance through a performance of Harald Kreutzberg and entered training at the school run by Doris Humphrey (1895–1958) and Charles Weidman (1901–1975). He began to explore what he understood of his Mexican roots in a pair of works produced before he returned to Mexico as a guest of its government. The first was *Danzas Mexicanas* (1939), which he created while he was still a member of the Humphrey/Weidman Dance Company. Limón classified the work, a collection of five solo dances, as representing "five symbolic figures from Mexican history—the Indio, Conquistador, Peón, Caballero and Revolucionario."[58] Limón specified that his conquistador was a vision of Córtez "as seen by José Clemente Orozco. An apocalyptic apparition, bringing doom and destruction, wielding the double-edged symbol of redemption and death." He returned to two of those figures, the mythic Indio, "half-man, half-pyramid," and the conquistador in a second work, *La Malinche* (1947), his interpretation of the story of the Indian woman who, as mistress to and translator for Córtez, aided in the conquest of what is now Mexico. Limón told photographer Morgan that he created *La Malinche* as an expression of his guilt over his male Spanish ancestor mating with a female Native American.[59] While Limón's Malinche is a peacemaker, she eventually sides with the Indian in the dance production to defeat the conquistador. Covarrubias described the work as "a kind of morality play based on the Conquest, seen though the naive eyes of a Mexican child from the other side of the Rio Grande, that is to say, through the hazy memories of José Limón."[60]

As the historian of literature José E. Limón affirms, the choreographer created his early Mexican works "on his own, dealing with the social and cultural contradictions of being a Mexican raised largely in the United States with whatever resources and symbolic solutions he could muster."[61] Orozco's murals in the US served as a point of reference for his efforts in this area. Limón himself had no background whatever in Mexican dance. *New York Times* critic Martin later pointed out that Limón "could not even do a jarabe" because his entire training as a dancer took place in the US where modern dance was "one of the most thoroughly indigenous art forms."[62]

According to Limón's *Memoir,* Miguel and Rosa arrived in his New York City studio to finalize the arrangements and view rehearsals of *La Malinche* and *The Moor's Pavane.* Limón recalled looking up from the floor at his audience of two at the completion of the *Pavane*: "Miguel was pale and speechless. Rose was weeping. It was moments before they could thank us."[63] When Covarrubias and his entourage of dancers met Limón and his company members at the Mexico City train station in September of 1950, it was Limón who was "close to tears."

Although Limón thought the Palacio de Bellas Artes was one of the ugliest buildings he had ever seen, he could not help but be impressed with the resources the facility placed at his disposal. Francis recalled that Limón and his compatriots in the field of modern dance were accustomed to renting a "professional theater in the theater district and dancing to recordings. With luck to a piano or piano and voice . . . maybe once a chamber group. But a symphony orchestra . . . never. José Limón was surprised by that here. In New York, José had danced, I believe, once with live music in City Center during a two week season."[64]

According to Novo, Covarrubias was worried that Limón would fail with the Bellas Artes audience accustomed to the touring ballet companies of the 1940s.[65] Rather like Stravinsky's fretting over the premiere of his *Firebird* in Paris, Covarrubias's concerns over Limón proved to be misplaced. Gabriel del Rio of *El Universal* praised Limón's "interest in Mexican visual art. His ideal has been to give life through dance to the masterful conceptions of José Clemente Orozco," which consecrated the choreographer as "the greatest dance artist that Mexico has produced."[66] Novo raised the same point in *Novedades,* citing the "living and dynamic paintings of Orozco" that Limón offered in *La Malinche.*[67] Art critic Jorge Juan Crespo de la Serna (1887–1978) declared that "Limón is more than a dancer and a choreographer: he is a true painter in the way that he conceives the least of the movements of himself and his group, at a scale and with a sense that are true concrete realizations of a perfect coloristic vision, filled with harmony; in which music provides the ideal binder for the background."[68]

Given the resounding success of his performance series, Limón was asked to return to Mexico in 1951 to teach at the academy and mount a new season of mostly Mexican dances at the Palacio de Bellas Artes with its members. The already generous resources he had at his disposal during his first visit became even more generous on his return. In December of 1950, as planned, the INBA became an independent government agency outside of the SEP's organizational structure. Chávez no longer answered to SEP

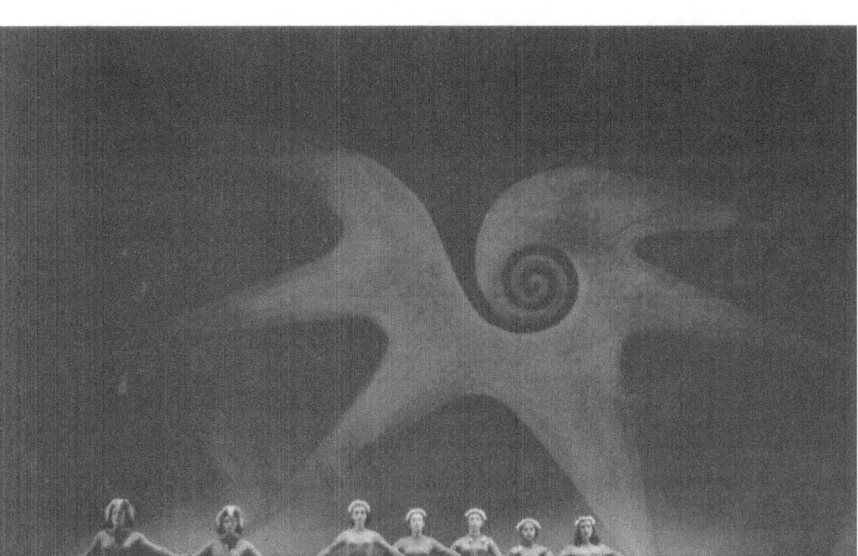

FIGURE 17. José Limón's *Los cuatro soles: Sol del aire* (The Four Suns: The Sun of Wind). 1951. Set and costume designs by Miguel Covarrubias (1904–1957). Dancers (*from left to right*): Ana Mérida, Martha Bracho, Diana Bordes, Rocío Sagaón, Martha Castro, Valentina Castro, and Raquel Gutiérrez. Photographer unknown. Acervo Miguel Covarrubias. Sala de Archivos y Colecciones Especiales, Dirección de Bibliotecas, Universidad de las Américas Puebla. © Maria Elena Rico Covarrubias.

leadership, and his control over the arts became nearly complete. He could finally muster the resources to secure the production of *Los cuatro soles* he envisioned decades earlier with Limón as his choreographer.

In his autobiography Limón offered few details about this work based on the Aztec mythology surrounding the creation of the world. Covarrubias, "with his passion for historical and artistic authenticity," served as Limón's guide to Mexico's preconquest past during their daily meetings on the project.[69] Limón himself danced the role of Quetzalcoatl, the feathered-serpent deity who served as the Aztec god of creativity. The event grew to epic proportions in what Limón dancer Ann Vachon described as its "attempt to mount a spectacle approaching the scale of an ancient ritual," incorporating even weight lifters and acrobats as part of its cast.[70] In the end, Covarrubias determined the work did not reach its full promise, being "undoubtedly premature, given that Limón had conceived it as a grand spectacle, ignoring the philosophical theme of the legend and failing to penetrate the essentially rhythmic spirit of pre-Hispanic dance and Chávez's music."[71] *Tiempo*, under the editorial direction the Campobello sisters' ally Martín Luis Guzmán, dismissed *Los cuatro soles* with little more than the single word *fracaso*—failure.[72]

Despite the work's failure, Chávez reportedly contacted Limón about the possibility of resetting *Los cuatro soles* in 1966, but the proposal never advanced beyond preliminary discussions.[73] It appears that Chávez found working with Limón to be easier than his prior interactions across gender lines with Graham and the Campobello sisters.

Tonantzintla, a more intimate Limón and Covarrubias collaboration set to Rodolfo Halffter's arrangements of keyboard sonatas by Father Antonio Soler (1729–1783), was the work that won audience approval. Named for the Chapel of Santa María de Tonantzintla (Saint Mary of Tonantzintla) whose exuberant, ultrabaroque decorations inspired it, Limón devoted a significant segment of his *Memoirs* to the events surrounding *Tonantzintla*'s creation as an example of the way Covarrubias worked:

> The chapel of Santa María Tonantzintla was all that we had seen in Puebla and Ecatepec rendered in the language and from the imagination and sensibility of the Indian. . . . In this chapel, in this isolated and forlorn village, the Spanish conquest and centuries of Spanish domination seemed nullified. . . . The Mother Goddess stood serene, holding her child. But she was surrounded by a joyous pandemonium. Every figure was playing some musical instrument, a viol, a trumpet, a guitar, cymbals, or drums. Heaven was a place for joy, for music, for celebration.
>
> "Miguel," I exclaimed, "the entire place is dancing! Heaven is a huge party."
>
> "I was hoping you would see that," he replied. "Perhaps you will make us a dance based on what you have seen today. We need it for our season."
>
> This was the Covarrubias method, manner, and style. Give people delight. And beauty. Take them to it. Let them see it, feel it, eat it, drink it. Instruct. Charm. Then, see what happens.[74]

Limón described the results of this encounter for the readers of *Dance* magazine when the work received its US premiere later that same year: "It was to be the birthday of the little siren, and an archangel and some angels, in all their fine array, were to enter in solemn cortege, bearing her aloft, and to her would present gifts and dance in solemn joy before her and with her. And the dances would be jotas and zarabandas, modified and transmuted from the Spanish, as were the baroque architecture and decor, by the Indian imagination."[75]

According to Covarrubias, *Tonantzintla* was the most resounding success of the season in Mexico.[76]

As part of his attempt to reunite the dancers who once belonged to the academy, Covarrubias also invited Bravo and her Ballet Nacional to present her ballet-cantata *Recuerdo a Zapata* (I Remember Zapata) as part of the same season, which he billed as *Ballet Mexicano*.[77] Bravo's work, based on the first formal historical study of the Zapatista movement in Mexico, Jesús Sotelo Inclán's (1913–1989) *Raíz y razón de Zapata* (1934), was performed in what dance historian Alberto Dallal designates as her nationalist, realist, socially relevant style.[78] The contrasts among Covarrubias's brilliantly decorated evocations of Mexico's preconquest and viceregal-period pasts for Limón's choreography and Bravo's spare elegy to one of the leading figures of its recent revolution were pronounced.

Her breakaway Ballet Nacional declared that "choreographic art does not constitute a simple abstract cultural expression but must fulfill the mission of contributing to the development and cultural, social and national integration of Mexico.... [The Ballet Nacional] strives to express the tragedy and vigor of Mexico, the problems and the anguish, hopes and yearnings of our genuine nation."[79]

Having departed Chávez's INBA, Bravo's group members lacked most of the resources that their former counterparts enjoyed. Bravo's company rehearsed wherever it could find space. Mostly under the sponsorship of government agencies other than INBA, the Ballet Nacional typically performed in ad hoc venues in rural communities, where, as Bravo later phrased it, "Spanish wasn't spoken" and the company "arrived by mule."[80] Despite these difficulties, Bravo found her work rewarding. "I had many satisfactions, such as the fact that the rural people watched us very attentively and showed their gratitude, to the degree that later they would offer us their own dances, and they gave us beans and tortillas."[81]

Looking back on the early years of her company, Bravo found that the lack of financial resources had other benefits as well. She could not rely on elaborate sets and costumes or the resources of a symphony orchestra to achieve her results; she was forced to master the dance itself: "I made my works with what I had and with what I had learned about the stage and through the choreography of our dancers. For example, how to distribute people through the *Danza de la pluma* [Dance of the Feather] or the *Danza de moros y cristianos* [Dance of the Moors and Christians], and, finding myself with the reality of an empty stage how to fill it, with what rhythm, with which dynamic, and with which bodies."[82]

For dancer and art critic Raúl Flores Guerrero writing in 1953, the "birth of [the Ballet Nacional] was not accidental. The initial impulse that gave it life and the trajectory that has followed, demonstrate that the Ballet Nacional was product of the same spirit of the post-revolutionary Mexico that first animated the painters. . . . The fact is that, for the first time in the history of art, a dance group has started to dance for the people, looking for them in their own environment. . . . Outdoor dance, the dance for the people that the National Ballet performs in Mexico, is not the culmination, but the beginning of a whole process."[83]

Bravo herself was unwilling to accept Flores's implied division between her dancers and their audience. She later told critic Raquel Tibol that she disliked being characterized as having decided to do "dance for the people; we are the people from among the people who dance."[84]

Although it was created for Bravo's rural audiences, *Recuerdo a Zapata* received its premiere on the stage of the Palacio de Bellas Artes alongside the works of Limón. Bravo divided the work into four segments, "El niño está . . ." (The Child Is), "Feria del pericón" (Fair of the Pericón [a psychoactive medicinal herb native to Mexico]), "La Revolución" (The Revolution), and "La espera." (The Hope). She later described it to dance historian César Delgado as

> a cantata about the federal troops who persecuted the peasants who planted corn. The military arrived and planted sugar cane because this [crop] offered more money for the landowner.
>
> There is a scene in *Recuerdo a Zapata* that now strikes me as extremely funny: some of the dancers would enter wearing sacks with headdresses that looked like sugar cane. They advanced over the fields of the peasants displacing the corn. It was something elemental, out of daily life, lacking in the language of dance. That was the problem with that time, I composed around the argument of the work. It is one thing to create an artistic language and other to create around a theme, political or not.
>
> I lacked a dance language. If there was a greeting, I had to include it, an embrace, I should create an embrace. There was no metaphor, the transposition from one language to another was nonexistent.[85]

While Bravo and her company were touring the Mexican countryside, Limón arranged for the dancers who performed with him in *Tonantzintla* to come to the US and present the work at the American Dance Festival at Connecticut College and at Jacob's Pillow. Covarrubias, who was identified by the US Department of State as harboring pro-Communist leanings, could not secure a visa to accompany his dancers north of the border.[86] Instead, Rosa chaperoned Rocío Sagaón, Martha Castro, Valentina Castro, and Beatriz Flores, along with Guillermo Keys, on their visit to the US.

John Martin of the *New York Times* praised Covarrubias's "gorgeous" costumes and sets as well as the "completely winning style" of its Mexican performers in *Tonantzintla*'s presentation in the "huge auditorium," which "was packed to the doors" during the American Dance Festival.[87] The dancers from Mexico not only performed and studied in Connecticut and at Jacob's Pillow; during their travels they were able to visit New York City and work in the studios of Martha Graham.[88] They also encountered Laban's system of dance notation, with which they were highly enthused, although the time allotted for their studies in this area was insufficient to allow them to apply what they learned on their return to Mexico.

Shortly after Rocío Sagaón settled back into her life in Mexico City, Miguel invited her to La Blanquita, one of the city's remaining vaudeville revue theaters, to "broaden her dance vocabulary."[89] The SEP and its employees did their upmost to maintain a clear division between the dance activities on the city's popular stages and the "artistic" dance that it sought to instill in its students and audiences. In 1938 Celestino Gorostiza reprimanded Nellie Campobello for allowing students from the National School of Dance to perform professionally during the motion picture intermissions at the Teatro Aldama because of the possibility that "artists of low degree" might appear on the same stage.[90] Campobello immediately requested a formal retraction. She asserted that she was unaware of this activity and would not have permitted it. To bolster her position, she pointed out that she had refused employment to the sister of one of her staff members because she appeared on the city's revue and cabaret stages and was thus an unfit example for the school's students.[91] It was during Covarrubias's visit to one of these theaters of "low degree" that he made the initial move that instigated a relationship with Sagaón, which continued until his death in 1957.

Sagaón was born Rocío López Bocanegra.[92] Her father was a sales representative for the Colgate-Palmolive company; due to his business activities the family moved about southeastern Mexico frequently during her formative years. Her childhood was somewhat atypical in other ways, as her father was also a noted bohemian who loved to host musicians such as Agustín Lara (1897–1970) and Pedro Vargas (1906–1989) and the nightclub dance duo Pepe Antinus and his "Balinese princess" Mimi Vegon at the Quinta Alicia, the family's home in Mérida. Watching them rehearse their routines in the patio is what persuaded Rocío to take up dancing as a career. Her older brother, photographer Nacho López (1923–1986), became one of Mexico's leading photojournalists and played a major role in documenting the dance productions mounted during the Covarrubias era.[93]

Rosa's discovery of her husband's ongoing affair with Rocío poisoned her attitudes about Miguel's participation in theatrical dance and led to a series of highly public scenes whenever she found Rocío together with her husband.[94] In one of these encounters, Rosa attacked Rocío with a knife.[95] In another, Rosa showed up at a performance at the Palacio de Bellas Artes armed with a pistol. These confrontations were understandably unnerving for Miguel and Rocío but they also had repercussions within the academy. In what appears to be a direct reference to the situation, Ana Mérida wrote the leaders of the incoming presidential administration specifically recommending that they "do away with . . . immorality" and "establish the rule that the employees of the Department of Dance have scant or no relation with the professional dancers and the choreographers, given that these vices determined the discredit of the activities of the dance."[96]

In the fall of 1951, Mérida received the backing of the governor of the state of Chiapas, General Francisco J. Grajales (1898–1985), to begin her own epic stage work based on Mexico's pre-Columbian past, *Bonampak*. Grajales commissioned the work to inaugurate his newly built, open-air Teatro del Pueblo (Theater of the People) in Tuxtla Gutiérrez.[97] Mérida's work was inspired in the then newly discovered murals of the Mayan ruins of Bonampak in the far south of Chiapas. Given her own Mayan heritage, this subject was particularly close to Mérida and to her father Carlos, who provided the scenic design for this project.[98]

Although *Bonampak* was also a well-funded epic work, it was created outside of the control of INBA—Mérida requested a three-month leave of absence to work on the piece.[99] Mérida employed nearly one hundred performers in *Bonampak*, most of whom were untrained dancers drawn from the schools, both secondary and advanced, of Tuxtla Gutiérrez. When the work premiered in November of 1951, the only experienced performers on stage were a group of "Conchero" dancers from Mexico City.[100] This was a curious choice given her father's insistence on authenticity and her own purported studies of the indigenous peoples of Chiapas.[101] As the program notes for the first public performance of the School of Dance under her father's direction indicated, the "Concheros" of Mexico City were mestizos who adopted an indigenous dance from the central state of Guanajuato as their own.[102] Nonetheless, Luna presented Ana Mérida's decision to incorporate them into her performance as an example of the "most pure, most ancient, most pregnant with historical quality. . . . Mérida understood that a dance like that which she had in mind could only be realized with this spirit of recollection, of simplicity, that the Indians presented."[103] *Bonampak* was successful enough that Mérida restaged it in a trio of performances in the Palacio de Bellas Artes in the spring of 1952, one of which was dedicated to the presidential candidacy of Adolfo Ruiz Cortines.[104] Luna situated the work as Mérida's response to Limón's failed *Los cuatro soles* and roundly criticized the waste of money that Covarrubias was overseeing in the Department of Dance. Mérida was equally displeased with Covarrubias's habit of underwriting similarly elaborate stagings of works by novice choreographers.[105]

Limón provided a contrasting view of Covarrubias's activities to the *New York Times*:

> Any one of these dancers, upon proving himself ready and able and accomplished, can submit an idea for a dance work, select his cast, chose any one of a fine group of composers to write his music, have Julio Prieto, the "jefe" in all matters pertaining to theatrical production, or another artist, design and execute the scenery. Further wonders: he can have ample rehearsals on the large beautiful stage, and he can have the entire and complete national symphony orchestra to play his ballet, with the composer himself conducting.
>
> And, as if all this delirious dream-come-true were not enough, the dancer can count on an intelligent, responsive and enthusiastic audience for his work. This I saw with my own astonished eyes.[106]

Rosa later complained to Limón that her husband had "put ballet in the hands of people who will never be able to do a choreography in a million years."[107] The fact that one of these untested choreographers was Sagaón, whose *Movimientos perpetuos* (Perpetual Motions) premiered with designs by Miguel in 1952, likely figured in Rosa's assessment of her husband's liberality.[108] Such critiques weren't limited to Rosa and Ana Mérida, who had direct personal interests in the operations of the academy. The pro-Campobello weekly, *Tiempo*, was just as critical of the funding going to modern dancers, Limón included.[109] But critics from *El Popular* and other writers who were once supportive also expressed similar doubts about artistic value.[110] Covarrubias defended himself publicly, affirming that "It is the point of view of the Department of Dance that it is preferable to experiment in every direction, offering complete liberty to the new choreographers, even at the risk of failure, rather than continue in the same routine or do nothing for fear of failure or criticism."[111]

Despite Covarrubias's claims of complete freedom for his choreographers, he placed some limits on the members of the academy. For a short time Amalia Hernández formed part of Bravo's breakaway Ballet Nacional. Carlos Chávez specifically recruited her to return to the academy because he thought she had the "capacities to be a choreographer."[112] But when Hernández approached Covarrubias with her idea of mounting *Sones antiguos de Michoacán* (Ancient Melodies from Michoacán) in 1951, a work that remains in the active repertory of her Ballet Folklórico today, he refused her "because everything had to be done with contemporary music."[113] This stance is consistent with Lavalle's memory of Covarrubias's artistic guidance: "Know the dance of Mexico. Dance it, practice it, and then, when you go to create, . . . forget it!"[114] It was this aesthetic position that led Hernández to begin operating independently of the academy, as Bravo had done before her. She formed her own Ballet Moderno de México, which rehearsed in her parent's home.[115] It was this company, initially under the artistic direction of Waldeen, that gave her *Sones antiguos* its first public performance.

The financial liberality that was true for Limón's seasons working with INBA was only partially true thereafter. The almost "unlimited" budget Parker described in his overview of Chávez's career at INBA did in fact have its limits. When INBA couldn't finance one of his productions, Covarrubias visited other government agencies in search of additional funds.[116] When that didn't work, he went to his home and, much to Rosa's distress, removed a work of art from its walls, took it to Alberto Misrachi's (1898–1963) gallery, then located across the street from the Palacio de Bellas Artes, and converted it into ready cash.[117] Promoting the creation of Mexican dance was not simply a job for Covarrubias; it was his passion in more ways than one.

Just before Ruiz Cortines ascended to Mexico's presidency in 1952, Covarrubias resigned from his position at INBA, which further angered Rosa. She believed that he could have continued in his political post, with all the benefits of a regular salary, despite the change in administration. Even more to her dismay, he continued to be actively involved in furthering the careers of the young artists to whom he was devoted.

Sadly, when it came time to rally support for an international tour of the dancers whose careers he supported, Covarrubias was no longer on hand to champion their efforts. Given the ongoing tensions created by his relationship with Rocío, he elected to move out of his home with Rosa in 1954, further inflaming her jealousy.[118] At the urging of his sister, who insisted that his civil marriage to Rosa was not recognized by the Catholic Church, Miguel married Rocío in a religious ceremony in 1955.[119] When he was subsequently hospitalized for a perforated ulcer complicated by the diabetes that he never seriously attempted to control, Rosa attempted to storm his hospital room in the company of Diego Rivera in order to force his hand on issues related to his estate. Miguel Covarrubias died on February 5, 1957, with Rocío, still dressed in the leotard from her daily dance class, holding his hand. His death did nothing to deter Rosa's histrionics. She threatened Sagaón's life with a pistol yet again during Covarrubias's funeral services.[120]

10

Dancing beyond the Cactus Curtain

Mexican Theatrical Dance Comes of Age

As the dance artists that the Mexican government created through its schools and companies matured, they carried its nation's dances across international borders. The tensions between nationalist aesthetics and more formal approaches to creating art were increasingly visible in both painting and in dance, yet Mexico's dancers established a unified front when it came to performing outside of Mexico. The resulting encounters with the official performing arts policies of the Soviet Union and China shifted their perspectives on issues of aesthetics and technique. Their government's concurrent discovery that the folk dances its modern dancers performed overseas provided positive press changed its perspective as well. Amalia Hernández and her Ballet Folklórico garnered direct support from Mexico's president; her success in providing potent stagings of national identity marked the moment when Mexico's dancers became the equals of its celebrated painters.

José Clemente Orozco was not the only Mexican artist who found his professional trajectory altered by the experience of watching Marc Chagall prepare his backdrops for *Aleko* on the stage of the Palacio de Bellas Artes. Guillermo Arriaga, one of the young dancer-choreographers Covarrubias was to champion, also discovered his desire to be a dancer through *Aleko*. Then a sixteen-year-old fledgling actor, Arriaga agreed to accompany a friend's mother to a 1942 performance of the American Ballet Theatre and found himself captivated by *Les Sylphides*. He began to skip classes so he could slip into the darkness of the theater's upper balcony and watch the company rehearse. He was particularly motivated by the opportunity to watch *Aleko* as it developed from a group of ideas into a full-fledged ballet.[1]

The experience of watching *Aleko* come together led him to the dance studio of Waldeen in 1949:

A combination of curiosity, fascination and terror shook me as I witnessed the class that the teacher was imparting. Everything was like an introduction to a magical universe; the phrases dictated by Waldeen to her young disciples were transformed into continuous movement, concentric circles in which the bodies were arrayed from nothingness into infinity and viceversa. . . .

During a short break, Waldeen approached us. She greeted [theater instructor José Ignacio] Retes familiarly and he, in turn, introduced me to the teacher. "Waldeen, let me introduce Guillermo Arriaga, who has worked with me in my theater group La Linterna Mágica [The Magic Lantern] as an actor, but his true vocation is the dance." Waldeen turned her gaze on my timid, unprotected self and immediately said "Guillermo, do you really want to be a dancer? Do you have any idea what that means?" To which I firmly replied, "Yes, Waldeen. I know very well what that might mean." "Well then," she said, "If you really want to dance, what are you waiting for? Take off your shoes right now and join the group." Trembling with that unexpected event, I rolled up my pant legs and without even saying goodbye or thanking Retes for his kindness, I took my first uncertain steps in what would be, with the passage of time, the destiny of my artistic life.[2]

Waldeen's question to Arriaga about the meaning of taking up dance as a career underlined the continued dominance of traditional gender roles in Mexico. While the ratios of women to men were slightly less radically skewed then they were when the SEP opened its first dance school with a 97 percent female population, dance was still not an acceptable career option for males. In part because there were so few male students, the staff of the National School of Dance petitioned the SEP to eliminate them from its student body in July of 1937. The SEP's leadership declined to do so as it understood they were necessary to the performing companies it wished to create.[3] Assumptions about the homosexuality of professional male dancers remained widespread. According to Carbajal, overt prejudice against males training to become professional dancers continued well into the 1970s.[4]

Despite having begun his dancing career in Waldeen's studios, Arriaga came to the public's attention in a work by the Sokolova Ana Mérida, the 1949 *La balada de la luna y el venado* (The Ballad of the Moon and the Deer). Mérida conceived the role of the deer for Ricardo Silva, one of the classical dancers who left the academy due to the dominance of modern dance in its programs; she tapped Arriaga to dance the role on Silva's departure.[5] In addition to days spent in rehearsal, Arriaga also spent hours in the city zoo in Chapultepec Park, studying the movements of the deer he was to dance. When it came time to present the work to Salvador Novo, who was then the chief of Bellas Artes's dance department, before its public performance there, Arriaga slipped, fell backward upon his entrance and slid across the stage on his backside. Arriaga's appearance before a paying audience was far more successful. Backed by music and libretto by Carlos Jiménez Mabarak and sets and costumes by Rufino Tamayo, both Arriaga and his dance partner/choreographer scored a major success.

Two years later, he was confident enough in what he had learned to approach Miguel Covarrubias about the possibilities of creating a work of his own, the 1951 *El sueño y la presencia* (The Dream and the Presence). Upon presenting his scenario, which traced the macabre fate of a vendor of the sugar candy skulls traditionally prepared as part of the commemoration of the Day of the Dead, Covarrubias had only one question of his fledgling choreographer: "Which musician and which scenic designer do you want?"[6] Covarrubias then went on to recommend Blas Galindo and José Chávez Morado for the respective positions. Arriaga "nearly fainted":

I was a kid of twenty-five and they were established figures; I didn't know them personally, but Blas was the director of the National Conservatory of Music and José a full-blown painter.

This was a characteristic of my generation. Teams of very young people with ultra-famous figures like Tamayo, Chávez Morado or Diego Rivera who collaborated with us as if they were kids.

To add to the gallery of notable figures who worked with Arriaga in his first choreographic essay, Doris Humphrey, then in México with José Limón's company, coached him in its creation.[7] Like his female counterpart, dancer/choreographer Rosa Reyna, Arriaga saw the opportunity of working with an older generation of creators to be a distinct advantage at the beginnings of his career.

Arriaga presented two additional works, *Antesala* (Waiting Room), about the misadventures of hapless citizens awaiting attention in Mexico's government agencies, and *La balada mágica* (The Magical Ballad), which contrasted love and war against the backdrop of the four seasons, in the spring of 1952.[8] As a result, he earned a scholarship from Josefina García, an instructor of kinesiology, to study under Ted Shawn at Jacob's Pillow in rural Massachusetts, as well as to perform there in a work García called *Mosaico Mexicano*.[9]

Her *Mosaico Mexicano* consisted of folk dances drawn from Chiapas, Mexico City, Michoacán, Oaxaca, Puebla, Sonora, Tlaxcala, Veracruz, and Yucatán, in a format similar to that which Amalia Hernández later used for her Ballet Folklórico.[10] García performed "La Zandunga" as a solo, while Ted Shawn served as her partner for a rendition of "La Bamba" from Veracruz. Arriaga appeared with Garcia and various members of the mostly non-Mexican cast in "Blanca rosa," a Yucatecan jarana; a "Jarabe Yalalteca" and the "Danza de la Pluma" from Oaxaca; and "Los Concheros," from Mexico City. He also performed solo in "El Venado y la Pascola," a version of the Yaqui deer dance that García extracted from Rosa Reyna's recently premiered *La Hija del Yori* (1952).[11]

Although Covarrubias stepped down from INBA at the end of 1952, he continued to provide financial support for Arriaga's work. Covarrubias underwrote the costs of a private studio space where Arriaga could continue to create, often alongside his preferred dance partner Rocío Sagaón.[12]

Arriaga first conceived the idea of mounting a homage to revolutionary leader Emiliano Zapata as a Sergei Eisenstein–style epic when Covarrubias was at the helm of INBA's dance department. "As we had everything, I thought about doing an immense *Zapata* . . . horses and rifles and shots and lots of sombreros and mustaches and to present it all on the stage of the Palacio de Bellas Artes. But all of that came to an end for us."[13] He rethought his approach, settling on presenting it as a duet for a male dancer, representing a rural agricultural worker, and a female dancer, representing the land. "It was to speak of the Birth-Life-Struggle-Death and Legacy of Zapata. That was all."[14]

When he shared his revised concept with his sponsor, Covarrubias advised him to abandon it. He thought attempting to represent the meaning that Zapata's life had come to assume for Mexico's people with only two dancers was ill considered. Nonetheless, Arriaga persisted, and with Sagaón as his partner, began to create *Zapata* (1953). The result was a work that came to define Covarrubias's era as a dance promoter.

Arriaga began *Zapata* without a score in mind, incorporating ideas and movement he had learned working alongside Humphrey and Limón. His wife, the Costa Rican dancer Graciela Moreno, heard José Pablo Moncayo's (1912–1958) 1949 *Tierra de temporal* (Land of Storm) on the SEP's weekly broadcast of *La Hora Nacional* and suggested Arriaga use it as his score.[15] With a few cuts to the original composition blessed by the composer, Arriaga had a work to present to Covarrubias. Admitting his error in advising the choreographer to abandon the project, Covarrubias agreed to prepare

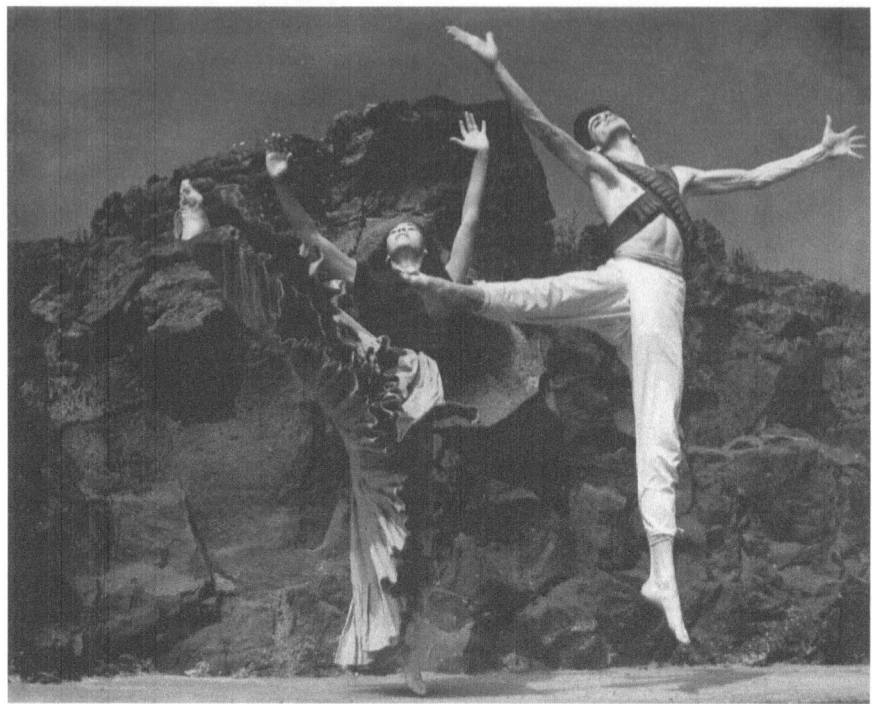

FIGURE 18. Guillermo Arriaga's (1926–2014) *Zapata* (1953) with Rocío Sagaón as Tierra (Earth) and Arriaga in the title role. Costume designs by Miguel Covarrubias. Both the choreography and the costuming were inspired by José Clemente Orozco's 1926 *La trinchera* (The Trench). Photography by Raúl Anaya Soto. Acervo Miguel Covarrubias. Sala de Archivos y Colecciones Especiales, Dirección de Bibliotecas, Universidad de las Américas Puebla. © Maria Elena Rico Covarrubias.

its designs—inspired, as Arriaga had been, by Orozco's 1926 mural *La trinchera* (The Trench).[16]

Arriaga also previewed the work for the family of socialist labor leader Vicente Lombardo Toledano (1894–1968), whose friendship he made during his days as an actor.[17] Impressed by what he saw, Lombardo arranged to premiere the work at the Fourth World Festival of Youth in Bucharest. Diego Rivera stepped in to provide assistance, writing letters to his patrons seeking funds to underwrite Arriaga's journey to present "Mexican dance in its highest form" in Romania.[18] When none of Rivera's clients stepped forward, Mariano Ramírez Vázquez (1903–1994), director of the Instituto de la Juventud (Institute of Youth), agreed to cover the entire cost of the trip for four dancers from Mexico, namely Arriaga and Sagaón along with Olga Cardona and Antonio de la Torre.

Zapata made its public premiere in Bucharest's National Stadium on August 10, 1953. According to Spanish-born painter Vicente Rojo (1932), who moved to Mexico at the fall of the Spanish Republic, the dramatic presentation by Arriaga and Sagaón received a warm reception from his fellow audience members in the stadium.[19] The four Mexicans also performed a selection of folk dances, following the performances of the "finest folklore ballet in the world, the Soviet group of Igor Moiseyev. . . . And there you had us, four monkeys in that enormous stadium dancing our jarabes. There we performed pure folklore. . . . And they liked it, but in front of the multitudes of the socialist countries, with those spectacular, beautiful costumes, we looked like four flies. Even then we did well."[20]

The Mexican dancers' return trip routed them through Cuba. Arriaga and his companions arrived in Havana shortly after Fidel Castro's September 22 attack on the army barracks at Santiago de Cuba. The Batista administration seized the Mexican dancers' passports and imprisoned them in a military jail because they arrived in Cuba from a socialist country, setting off a minor diplomatic confrontation with Mexico.[21] The contra temps caused Mexico's left-wing magazine *ABC* to chide the Batista administration for behaving as if "literature and music are atomic weapons."

Zapata saw its first Mexican performances at the Teatro Juárez in Guanajuato in October and in the Palacio de Bellas Artes in November. Even critics who expressed doubts about the quality of the works emanating from the Academia de la Danza Mexicana under Covarrubias's leadership were convinced that *Zapata* was a masterwork. Writing in *México en la Cultura*, Raúl Flores maintained: "The *Zapata* that Arriaga has presented in Bellas Artes is a work of art. The personality of Zapata has undergone a process of sublimation in the popular consciousness, and in its mythologizing of the revolutionary chief the people have created a new god. . . . Reflected through him, the public sees the drama and the joy of the earth and the joy of the man in whom they have always concentrated their hope of survival, of betterment and of transcendence. In the dance by Guillermo Arriaga, Zapata is finally and fully realized as a symbol, in such a way that the myth with all of its poetic force becomes an exciting, deeply felt artistic reality."[22]

The critical praise surrounding *Zapata*'s premiere in Mexico City was superseded in Arriaga's memory by a presentation of it for an audience of two. Rivera's wife Frida Kahlo was physically unable to attend any of the work's performances but wished to see it. Rivera asked Arriaga and Sagaón to dance the work for her, a request to which they readily assented. So, "among the magueys and cactus in the central patio of the Kahlo's blue house in Coyoacán," they presented the work to "Frida in her wheelchair, with Diego at her side. . . . At the end of the dance, a tear from Frida. Oh, that tear!"[23]

Zapata was not the only choreographic work that Covarrubias supported after he left the dance department of INBA, but without his leadership the various antagonistic factions resurfaced within the academy. Composer Ángel Salas (1930–1967) assumed the directorship of the department and named painter Gabriel Fernandez Ledesma as his deputy, while painter Santos Balmori continued as leader of the academy itself.[24] In late 1955 Salas, Fernandez, and Balmori lost their posts; the academy's students gained the opportunity to focus their professional training in either modern or folk dancing; and its professional company became an independent entity, although it was still known as the Ballet de Bellas Artes.[25] Waldeen assumed the direction of the new company, further complicating an already polarized situation.

Xavier Francis was one of several dancers who began to operate outside the academy following Covarrubias's departure. His new company, known as the Nuevo Teatro de Danza (New Dance Theater), lacked official government support and quickly found itself in financial difficulties.[26] To compound its problems, critics attacked its performances for being too abstract and too "North American." Nonetheless, Francis and the dancers who believed in what he was doing continued to work. In an effort to bolster morale, Francis invited David Alfaro Siqueiros to provide the company with his views on dance. Given that the dancers saw their art as springing from the same roots as the paintings of the muralists and that Siqueiros's daughter Adriana (1933–2012) was a modern dancer herself, a presentation by Siqueiros could provide a useful rallying cry for Francis's adherents. Siqueiros addressed the group on February 21, 1956, drawing attention to the divisions that existed among them and reinforcing their perception of the ties that united them to the muralists, whose hegemony in the arts of Mexico was already starting to wane as the artists of what became known as the *Ruptura* (Rupture) began to exhibit their creations.[27]

According to a summary Siqueiros provided to critic Raquel Tibol, he told the company members that by its nature theatrical dance could not flee into abstraction because the dancer's art was contained in the human body. Despite what he characterized as the "drama" that formal elements could contain, he challenged what he characterized as a habit among the dancers to enclose themselves in "simple cubes, ovals, parabolas, [and] angles."[28] Tibol countered with the observation that the painter might have given

Francis's dancers the impression that formal approaches to making art were harmful, to which Siqueiros replied:

> Quite the contrary! I consider the enrichment of forms in dance, and in any art, primordial, and I told them so; but I also think that formalism, that is to say the use of form as form itself, of language as language itself, impoverishes form because it operates in a necessarily limited field; its veins, being unilateral, or circumscribed, are lost in metaphysics. They learn—I said—to speak as dancers, reviewing all the techniques of dance, both classic and modern; but then they must speak and speak through the realistic logic of our time. It is not worth learning to speak if all you do is emit simple guttural sounds. Starting from the concept that the national in art is not a facade or a disguise, you will find that your man, your point of departure towards the universal man, is the one within you, the one closest to you, the one that has your same characteristics, your own language. You should not undervalue popular dance, for the same reason that it would be absurd for plastic artists to cover their eyes to the richness of the popular arts. Local sources have always been, everywhere, the seed of superior professional manifestations. On the other hand, it is the only way for you to offer your originality, or the originality of the land you inhabit, to the universal sum of originalities. Why should the painter be more of a citizen than the dancer? Do you not move within the same space, the same social-historical oxygen in which we painters move? My appreciations always arise from the concrete fact of painting; but who would dare to assert that the problem, in essence, is not the same? Dramatists, dancers, filmmakers and poets should analyze both the generalities and the specifics of our Mexican pictorial movement from the angle of their own problems. You would then see that the only thing that sets us apart is our vehicles of expression.
>
> But what is healthy in the current movement of dance in Mexico corresponds to the influence of contemporary Mexican painting with realistic, social intention.[29]

The tensions dividing the dance community continued to grow as non-nationalistic approaches to painting began to claim a place within Mexico's national consciousness. About the same time that Siqueiros was lecturing the Nuevo Teatro de Danza on humanism, José Luis Cuevas published his notorious "cortina de nopal" essay. Playing off the idea of the Iron Curtain separating the Communist world from the West, he decried the nationalist "cactus curtain" that separated Mexican artists from their counterparts in the rest of the world.

Cuevas's essay outlined the career of a visual artist, beginning with a visit to a "monastic official in the Palacio de Bellas Artes" who "ought to follow the dictates of the curia to which he belongs, acting as a secretary to one of the unions of intellectuals that proliferate in that dazzling palace whose shimmering curtain was executed by Tiffany," and culminating in a successful career repeating nothing more than the "customary cliches that make nationalism work."[30] The essay's highly satiric tone made it clear that this was a career path he rejected for himself and his colleagues. Cuevas emphasized, instead, his identification with "the Mexico of Silvestre Revueltas, of Antonio Caso, of Carlos Chávez, of Tamayo, of Octavio Paz, of Carlos Pellicer, of Carlos Fuentes, of Nacho López. It is a serious, studious Mexico presented outside of Mexico with great esteem, but generally attacked and vilified in its own land."[31]

The differences between the painters of the Mexican school and those of the Ruptura were echoed yet again in the final public standoff between Anna Sokolow and Waldeen later that same year. The members of the Ballet de Bellas Artes asked Waldeen to invite avant-garde choreographer Merce Cunningham (1919–2009) to present a five-week course, a request to which she acceded. By that time Cunningham was a leading figure of the dance vanguard in the US through the exploration of chance procedures in his choreography. Waldeen, not happily, provided the Spanish translations for Cunningham's lecture demonstrations.[32] It was, however, the insistence of her company members that she also invite Sokolow to mount one of her works that truly rankled Waldeen, although she also acceded to that request. The lectures Sokolow gave to the company just before her return to the US—this time with Spanish translations provided by Covarrubias—proved to be too much for Waldeen to abide, and she was not alone in her reaction.

According to Sokolow's biographer Larry Warren, Sokolow intended only to point out that "nationalistic or picturesque statements in art compromises the larger potential of that art," but her wording led many to believe she was attacking the nationalists themselves.[33] In what appears to be a truncated transcript of Sokolow's lecture on choreography in Warren's research materials, she noted that because Mexican dancers had decided to "wave the mexican [sic] flag," this action didn't make them "as strong as the mexican [sic] painters, because you are not. . . . I don't think that as a group that you have digested enough to be the instruments or to use what you feel is your culture. . . . If you took the title away and if you took the customs away, and if you took the music away, what would you have? That is why I present the problem, the hypothetical question, what is mexican [*sic*] dance?"[34]

Both Covarrubias and Siqueiros attempted to reframe Sokolow's comments for her by positing that she had only impugned "false" nationalism. According to Covarrubias, "what she meant to say was that the dance hasn't achieved the authentic nationalism that painting has, the authentic nationalism that music has, she said it in other words, but that's what she said."[35] Siqueiros affirmed that it was "indisputable that to carry out a work of universal value, you have to jump off the trampoline of nationality. Another thing is picturesqueness. . . . that is, false nationalism."[36] He concluded his remarks with a challenge to those assembled to carry on the discussion that Sokolow initiated: "The painters, as you will have realized, fought a lot, we argued a lot, we broke our throats screaming. You do the same in a certain way. By this I do not mean that you only talk, no. Work!"

Waldeen captured her response to Sokolow's message in an essay that appeared in the editorial pages of the daily newspaper *Excélsior*. Entitled "¿Dejaran morir la danza mexicana?" (Will They Let Mexican Dance Die?), it amplified her prior criticisms of Sokolow's approach to creating choreography:

During her lectures Anna Sokolow said:. . . . "Patriotism in art is something I do not understand. . . . First you have to be concerned about the movement in dance, not for the nationality that the movement might have."

Inexact. Movement in dance is the equivalent of language in literature. If neither movement nor language have root in the national consciousness one cannot create esthetically valid art. As for patriotism in art, if the lady does not understand it, allow me to suggest that she let herself be taught by the great American artists and patriots: Walt Whitman, Henry Thoreau, Sherwood Anderson, Theodore Dreiser, Arthur Miller, etc.

[Sokolow says:] "Thinking in terms of the Mexican is a limitation. . . . What I have seen of modern Mexican dance shows that it has not digested Mexican culture."

Another error. In the vast majority of cases in dance, it is not the Mexican that has not been digested, but the foreign influences that have not been uprooted. And, on the contrary, not thinking about the

Mexican is limiting, given that the richness of its culture, its tradition, its national art constitutes an inexhaustible field of experimentation for dancers and choreographers.

Anna says: "The Mexican school of dance seems disastrous to me. It has not introduced anything exciting." I ask: and Zapata by Guillermo Arriaga? If there is a ballet, not only in Mexico but in any other part of the world, capable of inspiring as deeply and validly as this masterpiece of Mexican dance, I would like to be told its name. . . .

Her views would be of no importance if they were only the personal expression of opinions by a guest teacher, but unfortunately there is a danger that the anti-nationalist and anti-patriotic tendencies proposed and supported by Missus Sokolow will disorient and uproot the modern dance movement in our country.

Faced with the anguished situation of an art that has already achieved a place in the artistic life of the country, what will be the attitude of Mexican artists and intellectuals, who with years of effort have struggled to give Mexico its own artistic expression, one which has been gaining its rightful place in universal culture? . . . Mexico's artists, intellectuals, critics and public have the floor.[37]

MEXICAN NATIONALISM FOR OLD WORLD AUDIENCES

Despite the furor caused by Sokolow's presentations, Waldeen's pronationalist arguments soon lost their relevance for Mexico's modern dance community. The rising generation of performers and choreographers was unwilling to let the "artists and intellectuals" continue to take the floor on its behalf. Like their counterparts among the younger painters, they wanted to make their own decisions on the future trajectory of their art form. Their resolve to determine their own future, to trespass the "cortina de nopal" surrounding Mexican dance, took concrete form as they prepared to cross the Iron Curtain—in opposition to the wishes of their government—and present their own works in a series of international engagements associated with the Sixth World Festival of Youth in Moscow.[38]

Both Guillermina Bravo's independent Ballet Nacional and the Ballet Contemporáneo, which arose within the academy to continue Covarrubias's legacy, received invitations to perform in Moscow through the Mexican Communist Party.[39] The dancers knew they had no hopes of securing support from INBA given the anti-Communist stance of President Adolfo Ruiz Cortines's administration.[40] INBA initially authorized the trip but declined to provide financing, then it withdrew its authorization to perform altogether and threatened those who left to perform with the loss of their positions within the academy. The stated reason for this reversal was that the absence of so many dance professionals for a prolonged period would damage the academy.

The process of working together to present their works in Moscow—and elsewhere in Europe and Asia as associated performance opportunities came into play—finally succeeded in uniting the battling cliques of dancers. As Tibol put it, "The daughters of Waldeen on one hand and of Sokolow on the other had militated for their specific tendencies with ardor, but by then they had evolved, they had moved forward and their prospects were broad and ambitious."[41]

Sagaón took Covarrubias's place in rallying support for the dancer's journey to Moscow from among Mexico's visual artists.[42] She was joined in this endeavor by Siqueiros's daughter Adriana, who entered the Ballet de Bellas Artes and the Ballet Contemporáneo in the spring of 1956.[43] Between them they secured works by Siqueiros and his associate Pedro Cervantes (b. 1933), Juan Soriano, and many of the friends of Covarrubias representing the established artists, along with a painting by Pedro Coronel (1922–1985), one of the artists of the Ruptura.[44] These they auctioned to raise funds to support their travel.

Both companies began to assemble programs to demonstrate the nationalist current of Mexican modern dance, though the differences between them were also visible in the works they selected to present.[45] However inadvertently, the selections of both companies also underlined a lesson that Mexico's visual artists had already learned—their vision of socially engaged art differed dramatically from that of the Soviets.

The Ballet Contemporáneo's selections stressed the Covarrubias legacy. It prepared Limón's *Tonantzintla*, along with the 1951 *Tierra* (Earth) and the 1954 *Tres juguetes mexicanos* (Three Mexican Toys) by Elena Noriega; the 1951 *La manda* (The Vow) by Rosa Reyna (1924–2006); the 1956 *Los gallos* (The Roosters) by Farnesio de Bernal (b. 1926); and a group of folk dances. Noriega's first work took the duality of the earth in pre-Columbian Mexico, which could bring life through the growth of corn or death through drought, as its theme; her second work presented a melodramatic love triangle that led to love between a mermaid doll and a toy bull.[46] Reyna's

La manda was based on a short story by author Juan Rulfo about the pilgrimage of a sick woman, accompanied by her husband and her friend, to a hilltop sanctuary known for its miraculous cures. The woman died in agony before reaching the sanctuary, while her husband engaged himself in seducing her friend.[47] Bernal's *Los gallos* used cockfighting as a metaphor for the Mexican cult of machismo, rendered visible in the conflict over a hen.[48]

Bravo's company rehearsed works that placed their engagement with Mexico's social issues on full display alongside a smaller representation of works rooted in popular culture. Her 1956 *El demagogo* (The Demagogue) told the story of a work stoppage brought to an unsuccessful end by the business owner's buying-off of its demagogic leader.[49] *Braceros* (1956) was a love story set against the economic conditions that produced continuous waves of migrant farm workers to the US and their unhappy conditions there.[50] Her work based on Mexico's indigenous roots was the 1953 *La nube estéril* (The Sterile Cloud). Based on her visit to the Otomi people in the Mezquital Valley of the state Hidalgo, which lacked a secure supply of water, it centered around the death of a child who was buried with a ceremonial broom so her spirit could sweep the clouds and produce rain, unfortunately to no effect.[51] On a lighter note, the company also prepared Josefina Lavalle's *Juan Calavera* (1956), which employed the animated skeletons popularized through the works of José Guadalupe Posada—in this case an angel, a demon, a pair of lovers, and the town drunk—who engaged in a satire of village life, and Waldeen's *En la boda* for the tour.

In June of 1957 a group of thirty-four dancers, directors, composers, and artists departed Mexico City for Moscow. Despite governmental concerns about the leftist orientation of the dancers, the Mexican contingent's encounter with Soviet-style communism did not encourage their personal politics. In a letter to her friend Carlos Sánchez Cárdenas, Bravo expressed dismay at what she discovered:

> Pardon me, but what is happening now cannot be. Socialism is for the happiness of the people and one can see that these people are not happy.
>
> Emilio Carballido and I had a great discussion with Galina Ulanova because I said "How is it possible that you continue mounting *Swan Lake* in a land of laborers? How can you dance in the wigs of princes?" She responded: "Ah, no; this is a tradition and we must preserve it. We

dance with a socialist stimulus." I laughed: "What socialist stimulus, there is none." It was a tremendous dispute.[52]

The Soviet critics deemed the Mexican modern dances they saw as "formalist," which they considered to be a stage of historical development that the Russian dance had already abandoned. Bravo circulated a Spanish translation of an article in *Soviet Culture* by P. Gusiev about their performances, which provided the official reaction to their performances:

> The group consists of a substantially limited number of artists and modest decorations, it is not a classical ballet, rather it represents a stage we have already passed through, the so-called "modern dance," which we rejected in a timely manner, considering that it would lead inevitably to the liquidation of the dance, which, in fact, was demonstrated to us by our guests from Mexico. . . .
>
> This is a complex discussion, not of tastes but of ideology. We could better examine how the Mexican choreographers present their programs. The free plastique, which recalls in part ancient Mexican sculpture and in part the works of Diego Rivera and western contemporary painting, is the foundation of the choreographic language of Mexican dance. The intelligent mounting of the plastic action on two or more planes, the audacious concordance of various themes in a single choreographic segment, and the intention of creating a plastic image, this is what we ought to learn from our guests. And it is a pity that these good intentions are lost in premeditated originality, in false importance, in the un-melodic constructions and the lack of logic in the movement, among which there were many that were anti-esthetic and sometimes simply disagreeable postures.[53]

Bravo later recalled approaching the tour with the belief that her dance was not well understood in Mexico but would be appreciated in the Soviet Union: "And just the opposite occurred, which was a tremendous blow to me. In *El demagogo*—one of the works that we took to Moscow—they thought that the capitalist with the top hat who was seated on the oil rig [in the production] was its manager. There [in Moscow] I learned that the Manichaeism of good and evil may be totally counterproductive. The interpretation depends upon the people who see the work."[54]

While some of Adriana Siqueiros's peers on the tour were disillusioned by their encounters with the results of the Soviet cultural bureaucracy, her still dogmatically Communist father and his peers were well aware of the problems the Soviet system posed for creators. The aesthetic concerns of the two nations diverged following their respective revolutions. Early Bolshevik declarations against easel painting and "individuality" bear a superficial resemblance to the muralists' assertions about the need to create large-scale public art and engage in collective creative labor.[55] But the April 23, 1932, edict of the Central Committee of the Communist Party, which defined modernism as foreign to Soviet peoples, underlined the profound differences between the artists of Mexico and the USSR. The leading Mexican muralists may have turned their work into politically engaged, leftist manifestos, but modernist ideas and experimental approaches remained central to their creations. Both Rivera and Siqueiros were critical of the official approach to creating art in the Soviet Union, albeit from different aesthetic and political standpoints. Rivera experienced a series of misadventures in attempting to use elements of Russian folk art in a mural in Moscow, while Siqueiros indicted what he saw as the academicism and formlessness of Soviet art.[56] The artists of the TGP also found their work rejected in Moscow in 1940 because its members—like the dancers with whom they associated—did not limit their print production to subjects that were "beautiful."[57]

The folkloric works that the Ballet Contemporáneo presented were, however, just as well received by the Soviet arts administrators and audiences as they were by the public of Bucharest years earlier. The Soviet system used the promotion of folk dance as an integral part of its international propaganda program given that it was an art form that it viewed as representative of "the people."[58]

It was under Stalin's administration that the Soviet state determined "the right kind of folklore could make the masses aware of their role in . . . history and could advance communism and foster patriotism among them."[59] The Communist Party began directing folklore studies in the Soviet Union in 1937, a time that coincided with Stalin's Great Purge, to ensure that its artists were producing the "right kind" of folklore. The party continued to supervise its study and presentation until after Stalin's death in 1953. According to ethnomusicologists Izaly Zemtsovsky and Alma Kunanbaeva, Stalin's intent in promoting this manufactured folklore was to replace the evidence of the pre-Communist society with new customs and traditions, to substitute the tractor for the ancient four-wheeled carts of Russia's rural past.[60] In the same interview in which he criticized the lack of experimentation in Soviet art, Siqueiros appeared to endorse Stalin's view when it came to technological modernization: "I say we have had enough of pretty pictures of grinning peons in traditional tehuana dress. I say to hell with ox carts—let's see more tractors and bulldozers."[61]

The rise and international triumph of the Moiseyev Dance Company and its balleticized folk dance corresponds almost precisely to this period. Igor Aleksandrovich Moiseyev was born in Kiev, Ukraine, and spent his early years in France.[62] He began studying ballet privately in Moscow and joined the Bolshoi Ballet School in 1921, performing as a member of its dance company from 1924 to 1939. According to dance historian Janice Ross, Moiseyev first came to Stalin's attention for his staging of an acrobatic parade on Red Square.[63] While still dancing with the Bolshoi, he was recruited by Prime Minister Vyacheslav Molotov (1890–1986) to organize the USSR's first festival of national dance in 1936. The following year he assembled a group of both amateur and professional dancers and began to teach them the dances he based on folk material. The first performance of his State Academic Folk Dance Ensemble of the Soviet Union, known as the Moiseyev Dance Company in the West, was received with great public acclaim. Although Moiseyev never joined the Communist Party, he was one of Stalin's favorites, and his company became the first Soviet dance group to perform outside of the USSR. The fact that two Mexican companies performed as part of the Moscow event in 1957 meant that a considerably larger contingent of its dancers were also exposed to the Moiseyev company's approach to staging folk dancing than the contingent who saw it in Bucharest.[64]

The Mexican dancers' performances as part of this tour were not restricted to the Soviet Union. The second part of their tour carried them to China, where both their folkloric dances and their modern dances were well received by the audiences. This led to productive discussions with their hosts about the best means of moving beyond the strictures associated with the traditional art forms in both countries.[65] Bravo was convinced that the organizational model presented by the Peking Opera was the most appropriate form for fully professionalizing theatrical dance in Mexico.[66] Curiously, the former Waldeena also decided shortly after that time to adopt the Graham technique for training her company—a decision that she promoted by seeing to it that the instructors she hired to train her dance company in the Graham technique also trained dancers studying at the academy.[67] Through her impetus, the argument over which technique was appropriate for Mexican dancers to use finally came to an end.

When the contingent of dancers who performed in Russia, China,

Romania, and Italy returned to Mexico after months of absence, INBA did not follow up on its threats. None of the dancers lost their positions within the academy. To the contrary, their critical success overseas was celebrated by INBA.[68]

For Bravo, the overseas tour was as important to her dancing career as her earlier studies in the indigenous communities of Oaxaca. The experiences it provided allowed her to move beyond the explicit nationalism that dominated her earlier work. She later told dance critic Alberto Dallal that as a result of the tour, "In the Ballet Nacional we no longer regard Mexico as a curiosity. We believe that Mexico now exists as part of the whole, that Mexico now exists as part of the world, that we don't need to force ourselves to encounter the Mexican. As we are Mexican, our creations must spring from what we are. . . . We began to rediscover the Mexican in Europe, in performing before other nationalities. The European critics classified us as abstract, but completely Mexican. That is, that the national does not need to be solely that which refers to reminiscences, to the past, to the roots, rather that we have today a national creation in Mexico. The European critics classified us as abstract. That is to say that the national does not have to refer to folklore."[69]

Bravo was not alone in recognizing her horizons had been too constrained. For example, following the tour, choreographer Rosa Reyna set her first work to a score of concrete music, a genre that lay outside of the nationalist compositions she used earlier in her career.[70] For dance, as had already occurred in painting and sculpture, the "cortina de nopal" was beginning to open.

THE TRIUMPH OF BALLETICIZED FOLKLORE

At the same time, Mexican cultural authorities began to pay increasing attention to the popular success of their own dancers when presenting folk dances overseas. The continuing personality-based struggles that plagued the academy since its beginnings did not help the position of Mexico's modern dancers within its arts bureaucracy. Furthermore, the works the dancers began to create following their extended tour outside of Mexico now lacked overtly nationalist references, which earned them a drubbing in its critical press.[71]

For Mexico's presentations at the Brussels World's Fair in 1958, the state tapped the newly formed Ballet Popular de México—yet another "independent" group within the academy, which emerged from the remains of

Ana Mérida's Ballet Mexicano—headed by Guillermo Arriaga. Among the works the company took with them to Europe were modern dances, such as Arriaga's *Zapata* and his codirector Josefina Lavalle's *Juan Calavera*. The nation's folk dances, however, were amply represented in their repertory.[72] Arriaga claimed he established the company to provide a conscious mix of both modern and folkloric dancing.[73] Its life was cut short when, following its successful presentation in Brussels, half the dancers decided to stay in Europe and continue performing under the direction of Lavalle, while the other half returned to Mexico.[74] This time INBA did not smile upon those who decided to tour Europe on their own initiative; all of them lost their posts.

Celestino Gorostiza took the reins of INBA in January of 1959. As dancer Lin Duran put it, his task was to address "the crisis produced by the discovery that social realism in the dance was nothing more than the Mexican curious with a message."[75] He announced yet another reorganization of the Ballet de Bellas Artes in April, naming Ana Mérida as its head. Mérida took this opportunity to settle scores with other dancers. She incorporated dancers from both the Ballet Contemporáneo and the Ballet Popular into her reorganized Ballet de Bellas Artes to such an extent that these two companies ceased to exist. She also lured dancers away from Bravo's Ballet Nacional. Mérida left the members of the Nuevo Teatro de Danza and other groups without financial support to wither away.

Even though Arriaga described Mérida's approach to Mexican modern dance as "following the path of her father, she told us that we had to learn from our things, to transform them, to make them sophisticated," many in the profolklore camp were unwilling to rally under her banner.[76] Arriaga's one-time codirector Lavalle wished aloud that Mexico had its own Moiseyev who could impose a clear technique on its folk material to create national dances.[77]

Amalia Hernández, was, by then, operating outside the academy and its modern dance focus to earn a name for herself by presenting folk dance on television. Because she separated herself from the academy before its dancers traveled to the Soviet Union, she does not appear to have seen the Moiseyev company firsthand at that point but she likely heard from her colleagues about its approach to folk dancing.[78] The Mexican dancers may not have been familiar with the sources he used as starting points for his work but they understood the choreographic and theatrical devices he used.

Covarrubias's teaching on Mexican anthropology and pre-Columbian art influenced Hernández's approach to choreography, but his aversion to staging folk dance led her to depart the academy in 1951. Hernández's separation was far easier and more immediately successful than any of the other groups that attempted to operate independently of the INBA. Having been raised in the household of a successful businessman and politician—her father Lamberto Hernández led Mexico City as the chief of the Departamento del Distrito Federal in 1930 and 1931—she understood better than any other dancer or choreographer of her time how Mexico's political system worked and how to effectively operate within it. After Covarrubias rejected Hernández's proposal to produce *Sones antiguos de Michoacán*, she went to Emilio Azcárraga Vidaurreta (1895–1972), the broadcasting magnate who was then laying the foundations for what became the media giant Televisa. She described their meeting: "'He probably won't even see me,' I thought. I announced myself as the daughter of my father. He said 'Yes, I've known you, since the days when you began to dance. What would you like?' 'Well, I'd like to create a dance company here.' 'Which studio would you like?' 'I'd like Studio A.' 'Alright, arrange your schedule and get to work.' Later he gave me studio C permanently so my company could dance there."[79]

It was expressly to create works for television that she organized the Ballet de México, with some of the same dancers who performed with her Ballet Moderno de México. The group was soon appearing on a regular basis for Azcárraga's television program *Función de Gala* (Gala Performance).[80] The exposure Hernández gained through this experience landed her additional support from the Dirección General de Turismo (General Directorate of Tourism), which provided funds for the company to undertake tours to Cuba, Canada, and California in 1958.

INBA had announced Mérida's Ballet de Bellas Artes as Mexico's representative to the cultural segment of the 1959 Pan-American Games in Chicago.[81] For reasons that aren't entirely clear, when it came time to travel to the US, it was Hernández and her company, grown from its initial eight to fifty members, along with its new artistic director Felipe Segura, who represented Mexico. The modern dancers of the Ballet de Bellas Artes believed they were replaced because they refused to present folk dance as part of their program.

Given her training under Waldeen, Hernández was at home with the task of incorporating modern dance idioms into her folk dance stylings. She confessed to happily borrowing from José Limon but made an only indirect nod to Martha Graham when she acknowledged that some of her work might incorporate contractions, though she worked throughout her career to counter what she viewed as Graham's hegemony in the areas of technique.[82] Nonetheless, Hernández was also interested in establishing a firm technical basis for her company in classical ballet. Mexican dance historian Margarita Tortajada identifies Hernández's 1959 collaboration with Segura and his Ballet Concierto as key to forming the Ballet Folklórico de México's repertory as we know it today.[83] Segura, she notes, served as the company's first artistic director, where he worked to "give unity to the works of the repertoire under the same concept and scenario."

Upon the company's successful return from its engagement at the Pan-American games, President Adolfo López Mateos (1908–1969) pledged to make it "the best ballet in the world."[84] Hernández converted her company into a nonprofit association, with any profits dedicated to the furthering of Mexican art.[85] With the support of the president, Hernández earned a weekly slot on the Palacio de Bellas Artes performance schedule every Sunday morning at 9:30, where her now official Ballet Foklórico de México made its first performance on October 11, 1959. While audiences were initially thin, within a few months the company's success was such that Gorostiza offered it a second fixed slot on Tuesday evenings. By 1960, the company was supporting itself on ticket sales alone and Hernández could assert that her style of theatricalized folk dance had "unseated" modern dance.[86] The following year, López Mateos saw to it that the Ballet Folklórico de México represented Mexico at the Festival of Nations in Paris. Ballet choreographer Agnes de Mille arrived in Mexico in April several months before the Paris performance to help the Hernández company prepare. Moiseyev's company also made its first visit to Mexico in the spring of that same year, as the Palacio de Bellas Artes increasingly began to schedule folk dance troupes from other nations.[87] Like the Moiseyev company did a few years before, Hernández's Ballet Folklórico took the festival's first prize, an event that finally conquered her father's resistance to her appearing on stage as a dancer.[88]

Shortly after Hernández' award-winning performance in Paris, critic Armando de Maria y Campos, who started his career as a theater critic in the 1920s and witnessed the dance performances mounted by José Vasconcelos, concluded that Hernández achieved the spectacle to which the educator aspired. Hernández, he wrote, "has managed to convert into reality the dream shared by a group of writers, composers and painters, who, more than 40 years ago under the economic direction of the Honorable José Vasconcelos, attempted to create a show composed of the dances and songs from the broad land of Mexico."[89]

Although her repertory encompassed a significant selection of dances that represented "the broad land of Mexico," elements of what folk dance scholar Anthony Shay calls "stereotypical" Mexico were and are to this day present in every performance.[90] Among the constants of the Ballet Folklórico's performances are segments dedicated to the jarabe tapitío of Jalisco, which echoes the pattern set during the Vasconcelos years. Another consistent element, however, the danza del venado of the Yaqui people, reflects the indigenism that blossomed post-Vasconcelos but from a standpoint that was Hernández's own. She premiered the work in Chicago during the Pan-American Games, transforming its teenaged performer Jorge Tyller into a celebrity and earning him a circle of admirers that grew to include Rudolf Nureyev.[91] Classical dancer Felipe Segura's appreciation of Hernández's staging places her version of the work squarely within the ballet tradition:

> In the areas most isolated from important population centers or inaccessible because of their geography, the customs of our aborigines are conserved for longer periods and they survive up to the present almost without alteration with the exception of some minimal details. From one of these recondite corners of the country a fascinating dance emerges, full of the movements and rhythms that strike us to the quick: *El venado*, which bewitches its public and leaves it breathless. It is the hunt of one of the most beautiful animals and the eternal tragedy of its death.
>
> For one very special dancer, this small piece provides the most important masculine solo of the entire dance repertory across all the centuries of theatrical dance. This dance is the equivalent of Anna Pavlova's *Dying Swan*. It is the great male solo.[92]

The spectacular leaps and aerial turns of Hernández's ballet-infused version of what Carlos Mérida classified as one of Mexico's handful of purely indigenous dances is one of the clearest demonstrations of how the ideals of dance performance evolved over the four decades since Vasconcelos became minister of education. He aimed to use folk elements in a leap toward the classical. With her balleticized version of the danza del venado, Hernández seems to have inverted Vasconcelos's ideas. Her version of the deer dance used the classical to popularize the indigenous, not the indigenous to attain the classical.

The company's success in Paris led to representation by impresario Sol Hurok (1888–1974) and the introduction of an extensive touring schedule in the US and Canada, including a command performance at the White House for President Kennedy in 1962.[93]

The reception of Hernández's group in the US by its Mexican American community proved to be little short of euphoric. As Shay notes: "The response . . . was so electrifying and politically transforming for that population's self-image that it spawned dozens of folkloric companies. Groups of Mexican-American activists lobbied for the formation of school programs—in grade schools through university level—to teach Mexican folk dance throughout California and the Southwest. These Chicano activists were not interested in an anthropological interpretation of folk dance. They wanted the dances that were created by Amalia Hernandez [sic] for the Ballet Folklorico and the spectacle and pride they represented."[94]

When the Ballet Folklórico visited the Soviet Union in 1965, the Mexican press reported that the dancers were praised for representing the long-standing Soviet folkloric ideal by "demonstrating with great force the magnificence of the art created by the people."[95] The company's success in the Soviet Union may cast some light on what appears to be one of the least likely matches in the long association of Mexican painters and dancers—the appearance of Amalia Hernández and her Ballet Folklórico de Mexico at the dedication of Siqueiros's 1971 mural for the Polyforum, *La marcha de la humanidad* (The March of Humanity).

Dance and the Polyforum

Once Siqueiros moved beyond his youthful painting of the dancers Anna Pavlova and Tórtola Valencia—a stage in his artistic development that, as has wife Angélica Arenal observed, he consigned to a "perhaps voluntary" forgetfulness—he was a dedicated opponent of folklore. He called it the "Mexican curious" in art.[96]

Beginning with his condemnation of Pavlova and Valencia's use of "typical Mexican costumes" as a manifestation of a "touristic orientation" that he authored with Jean Charlot under the pen name of Juan Hernández Araujo in 1923, he never let up on his criticism of painters who employed the colorful aspects of Mexican life.[97] In the following decade, Siqueiros called for discarding

folk art as a degraded manifestation, as a manifestation produced by popular masses and races economically reduced to slavery; as an aesthetic product of peoples who in different political moments created superior works of beauty and are capable of producing them in the future, in new forms of social life. Let us fight the descriptive, the picturesque, that pretend to provide the aesthetic essence of a region by the presentation of its simple, external aspects, of its superficial customs. Let us fight the trend in turning art into an aesthetic modality imposed by the palate of the capitalist classes that determines submission to the taste of the bourgeoisie, which has created and is creating all that puerile, intranscendental, mystified "art" that fills, until bursting, the modern museums of all the countries. We combat the demagogic art that serves the interests of the new bourgeoisie subjected to imperialism. All that deceitful and mediocre art that Rivera produces in painting and by almost intellectuals in other forms of expression.[98]

It is difficult, then, to envision Siqueiros approving of a performance by the Ballet Folklórico de Mexico as an integral element of the dedication of his final mural. Yet for this event, the plaza outside the Polyforum was filled with dancers costumed by US stage designer Dasha Topfer, who enlarged elements of traditional Mexican costumes to ensure they could be clearly seen from the last row of a large auditorium.[99] What is more, the interior of the Polyforum incorporated a dance space named for Hernández, which stood alongside a market for the best of Mexican folk art.[100] To further complicate the picture, Manuel Suárez, the Spanish-born developer who underwrote the Polyforum's creation and referred to it as the "Siqueiros chapel," outlined the express purpose of his investment at one of its multiple inaugural events: "Everything you contemplate in this complex is due to a directing idea and a team of professionals who have interpreted my desires to realize a landmark work for Mexico, to my desire to rouse tourism and to make it produce foreign exchange that is indispensable for an equilibrium in our balance of payments."[101] The fact that Suárez planned to charge admission to see the murals proved to be particularly controversial.[102]

With such emphasis on the touristic, it is little wonder that Siqueiros's colleagues viewed his participation in the Polyforum as a sell-out. Painter Mario Orozco Rivera (1930–1998), who was Siqueiros's principal assistant during the mural's creation, called it "the coffin for a kind of Muralism that today is only practiced on a bureaucratic level by a few painters."[103] Perhaps the most trenchant critique came from Siqueiros's champion Tibol. She turned Siqueiros's own words against him, calling the endeavor a "gigantic expression of the Mexican curious."[104] She went on to provide her own definition of the meaning of Siqueiros's phrase, calling it "the deformation of national art produced by tourist development, which Siqueiros combated for years with just argument and reasons." In an interview with journalist Jorge Saldaña (1931–2014) on his late night television talk show *Anatomías*, Tibol added that "Siqueiros wrote a tremendously polemic article he called 'The Counter-Revolutionary Road of Rivera.' If today, before the television camera you picked up that article, the only thing you would have to do is change the name to Siqueiros. . . . In his Message to a Young Mexican Painter, he said that you must work with the bourgeoisie and trick it; here I believe that the bourgeoisie tricked him."[105] As Tibol documented in her multiple studies on Siqueiros, among the sins for which he attacked Rivera in "The Counter-Revolutionary Road" were his use of folklore and painting works for tourists.

That was, of course, not the way Siqueiros saw his mural. For Siqueiros, *La marcha de la humanidad* was a dream years in the making. He called it the "greatest opportunity in my career as an artist."[106] Siqueiros developed more than three hundred drawings for the project while imprisoned for "public dissolution" in Lecumberri prison between 1960 and 1964.[107] He later told journalist Julio Scherer García (1926–2015) that though his stay at Lecumberri was productive, he perceived his imprisonment as a brutal punishment:

> There are those who think that artists enjoy sufficient time in jail to realize whatever works we want, that here we live a kind of painful, but fecund, retreat. I wish that were true in my case. But how could that be when my imaginative soul was given over to monumental work and I was held in a cell whose opposing walls I could almost touch by simply spreading out my arms? . . . I want to paint big facing a wall, to envision distant horizons, create multitudes, convert the most profound planes of spatial unity to my own, work with modern tools, with the best materials of contemporary chemistry, with electric projectors, surrounded by a large team of people who climb up and down scaffolding with mechanical precision, begin at the first light of day and end when the sun sets. But no. I have to settle for the poorest of handicrafts, painting little pictures.[108]

Manuel Suárez originally hired Siqueiros, newly released from prison, in 1964 to create a series of eighteen paintings on the theme of industry and the countryside for a planned convention center at his hotel, the Casino de la Selva (Jungle Casino) in Cuernavaca. *La marcha de la humanidad,* announced in 1965, grew out of this contract.[109] The industrialist claimed that he had developed a friendship with the painter when both were attending the Academy of San Carlos.[110] Suárez set aside his night-school studies at San Carlos and went on to invest in asbestos-cement operations that made him a successful contractor.[111] When he advised then President of Mexico Gustavo Díaz Ordaz (1911–1979) of his intention to create the largest mural in the world in Cuernavaca, the president suggested he move the project to Mexico City, where the great majority of tourists to Mexico could actually see it, rather than the more limited number who were likely to visit Cuernavaca.[112] Given that both the public and private sectors in Mexico, then preparing to host the 1968 Olympics, were increasingly focused on promoting tourism as an "industry without chimneys," Suárez determined to heed the president's recommendation.[113] Thus, his mural project was relocated to Mexico City, where it was to be part of a large hotel complex, a plan that was ultimately replaced by the city's World Trade Center.

As Siqueiros wrapped up his work on the Polyforum, Suárez began to plan a series of inaugural events. The first series was to take place outside of Mexico, in Paris and Madrid, in hopes of securing positive press in Europe—coverage that was intended to convince Mexicans that the Polyforum was an internationally important artistic achievement.[114] Among the featured participants for the promotional event in Paris in October of 1971, sponsored in part by Mexico's Consejo Nacional de Turismo (National Tourism Council), was Amalia Hernández, who triumphed there a decade earlier.[115]

Hernández and her entire company were on hand in Mexico a few weeks later when Mexican President Luis Echeverría Alvarez (b. 1922) dedicated the Polyforum on December 15. Most of the dance company performed for the crowds of guests gathered on the Plaza de las Naciones (Plaza of Nations) outside the Polyforum while the president formally inaugurated the facility for a more select group inside the building. Echeverría spoke of the Polyforum as representative of "a healthy nationalism which is being constructed . . . stimulating our poets to write with liberty, our painters to express themselves without hindrance, our intellectuals to speak without limits, and that there is criticism and dissent."[116] With little alteration, the same words could have been employed by his counterparts in the US who used the "freedom" represented by abstract expressionist art as a reply to Communist propaganda.

Siqueiros presented the *Marcha de la humanidad* as the crowning achievement of Mexican muralism, with himself as its maximum representative. At the same time, he claimed a role of hemispheric leadership for Mexico through the contributions of its muralists:

> It is possible that the only international prestige that our country enjoys in respect to art, and in a certain form, science, is Mexican Muralism. Why? Because it is doing something different, something that springs from the very entrails of its peoples; that isn't something nationalist but something continental. That is why you find murals being done everywhere: in the United States, in South America, and our work has transcended internationally. . . . The Mexican muralist movement arises from the Mexican Revolution; it is the work of the Mexican Revolution. That is why, in a sense, for having been its guardians, soldiers of the Revolution, we are today the guardians of its principles.[117]

After unveiling the dedicatory plaque, the president visited the folk art exhibition and witnessed a smaller contingent of Hernández's dancers performing one of her works for him in the Polyforum's theater, which, temporarily at least, bore her name.

Hernández directed a subsequent segment of the opening festivities, the Festival de Juventud, Danza y Folclor (Festival of Youth, Dance and Folklore) on December 20. During her remarks opening this event, she professed to have been surprised to discover the Polyforum's theater: "When I came in and discovered it was round, I began to have ideas about making a different kind of show than I have done. The first thing that occurred to me was that this circular stage would serve well as a cinema screen. A screen on which to project films that would serve as the scenery for theater or dance. There is a certain kind of dance that doesn't need a front, because from any angle it can be plastic and dynamic. . . . That is why I have planned distinct shows with different content: authentic folklore, popular, dance of various types, fundamentally autochthonous dance."[118]

Her pronouncement matches the rhetoric of authenticity surrounding state-sponsored folk ensembles everywhere in the world during that time. Yet her promise of innovation given a new theatrical space in which to perform was not fulfilled. The dances she presented that day, zapateados from Chiapas and Veracruz, were standards in her repertory and continue in performance today.

The inclusion of a folk art display and market in the Polyforum appears to have occurred directly as a result of Suárez's insistence.[119] The idea for incorporating a theater into the space was suggested by Juan Warner Paz during the design process and was immediately accepted by the project team.[120] While Amalia Hernández's work at the Polyforum was cut short, and her name removed from the theater following a dispute with Suárez, the individual responsible for giving her name to its theater and for including her as part of its inauguration is unclear.[121] It may have come from Siqueiros himself.

Unlike his early coauthor Jean Charlot, Siqueiros harbored no ideological animosity against theatrical dance. One of the panels on the exterior of his Polyforum mural was dedicated to it, though different sources provided different titles to the work, ranging from *La danza: Holocaust del indígena ante lo divino* (Dance: Indigenous Holocaust before the Divine) to *Danza autóctona: La victoria* (Autochthonous Dance: The Victory) and, somewhat more confusingly, *La danza* or *La huida* (The Flight).[122] One of the most recent publications of the Polyforum interprets *La huida* or *Sacrificio por la Liberación* (Sacrifice for Freedom) in a Marxist vein, asserting that the mural's dancing figure is fleeing an economic system, which leads to destruction, and inviting others to join her in her sacrifice.[123]

More to the point, Siqueiros was immensely proud of his dancer-daughter Adriana. Adriana began her dance studies under Lettie Carroll, the same instructor who prepared the Campobello sisters for their careers. Adriana's grandmother Electa determined that she would learn how to dance and to play the piano "as was the custom" and sought out the "best" instructor for her granddaughter.[124] Adriana continued studying at the Carroll studio until her father was exiled to Chile in the spring of 1941 for his role in one of the plots to assassinate Leon Trotsky (1879–1940). She recalled that one evening the family's Chilean host announced that his daughter danced, and a demonstration of her talents in pointe work quickly ensued. "After seeing her, my father said 'My daughter also dances,' and he asked me 'Isn't that true, Adriana? Choose whatever music you would like.' Embarrassed, I selected a bit of de Falla and began to dance, throwing myself to the floor, interpreting a different kind of dance, like Isadora Duncan. And those people were so surprised, 'What is this!' They didn't know it. My parents were happy watching me. All of this in consequence of my first classes with Miss Carroll."[125]

Adriana went on to study under the Campobello sisters, ballet instructor Nelsy Dambré (1903–1976), Waldeen, Sokolow, and Bravo in Mexico, and with Sophie Maslow in the US and Sigurd Leeder in London.[126] For a brief period in the early 1950s, Adriana was a member of Hernández's Ballet Moderno de México, one of the precursors to the Ballet Folklórico de

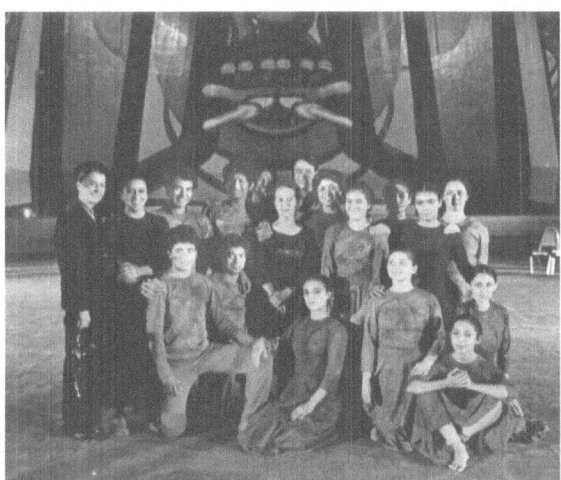

FIGURE 19. Adriana Siqueiros (*far left*) and Anna Sokolow (*center*) with the cast of Sokolow's *Homenaje a David Alfaro Siqueiros* in the theater of the Polyforum. 1984. Photographer unknown. Larry Warren Collection. Music Division. Library of Congress. © 2019 Artists Rights Society (ARS), New York/SOMAAP, Mexico City.

México. According to fellow company member Colombia Moya, Adriana danced "without pay, only for the love of dance and to collaborate with *Ami*."[127] Her father became acquainted with Hernández at that time. He subsequently created a program design for the Ballet Folklórico. It is possible that working with his daughter as a designer—he produced work for her choreography at least as early as 1958—expanded his views on dance.[128]

Adriana Siqueiros saw the Polyforum's theater as the ideal location for a modern dance tribute to her father and commissioned Anna Sokolow to create the 1984 *Homenaje a David Alfaro Siqueiros* (Homage to David Alfaro Siqueiros) in that space.[129] The resulting work took the building's mural as its subject. In an open letter to Sokolow printed in the program for the work's premiere, Siqueiros's wife Angélica wrote that the *Homenaje* provided "a resplendent sun, with your testimonies before the historical drama of our people, that is their small victories and their great periods of helplessness and misery, but a march that will one day arrive at the conquest of a more just society."[130] She was certain that Siqueiros himself viewed the choreography "with great emotion, wherever he is in the great cosmos, either on a star or in the Milky Way, or perhaps some other dazzling planet."

Apart from his family connection, it is also possible that Siqueiros, who, according to Rivera, believed it was impossible for a genuinely revolutionary artist to exist outside Stalinism, persuaded himself he was demonstrating his Communist bona fides by incorporating Moiseyev-style folk dance into his Polyforum.[131] Moiseyev presented his adoption of folk dance as an ethical decision that resonated with the muralists' stated goals of reaching a broad public through their paintings: "Folk art, whatever its form, is always on the side of good, always wholesome and optimistic. In folk-lore we find the vices denounced and held up to ridicule while praises are sung to man's better instincts. . . . Folk art, the art of the people, is a splendid means of educating the masses, for it can speak their own language, simple, colorful, and replete with wisdom."[132]

Shay argues that the Moiseyev model was "the most important and visible manifestation of the Soviet Union's interest in folk dance as a political tool."[133] Its intent was to "show the multicultural, multiethnic composition of the USSR . . . living in brotherly peace and friendly coexistence under the benign and careful eye of Mother Russia, whose dances would receive pride of place. This was an important message to send to governments and people in the undeveloped world whom the Soviet Union wished to influence." Shay's characterization of the ability of Moiseyev-style folk dancing to evoke "brotherly peace and friendly coexistence" could have described Siqueiros's own aspirations for one of the culminating scenes of his mural, which represented the ultimate victory of "the people."

In the 1950s the leadership of the Soviet Union exported the Moiseyev model throughout Eastern Europe by direct order from Moscow.[134] Other nations soon adopted the Moiseyev model on their own; Shay included Hernández's Ballet Folklórico in this group he designated as the "second tier." These countries "sought the political capital they observed with the success of the performances by Moiseyev and other Soviet bloc companies."[135]

Hernández's company was not a clone of the Soviet company. Among other differences, Shay notes, Hernández employed a sensuality in some of her works that is absent in Moiseyev's oeuvre—yet her public statements about her use of technique to adapt her original source material for the stage bear a striking similarity to those of Moiseyev.[136] From his vantage point as a classically trained choreographer, Moiseyev opined that to present folk dance "in its primitive form would be undramatic, dull, not suitable for stage. Our aim was not to act as literal copyist, nor to collect mechanically, but to enrich and develop the form while preserving the national character and original coloring. . . . We were compelled to discover our own ways and creative methods for the study and staging of a huge variety of national folk dances, so diversified in their character and style."[137] In describing her general approach to folk dance material, Hernández told dancer Rosa Reyna: "I realized that not only did I have to study all of this, I had to live it, make it mine, so that later, the results at the hour of creation weren't coldly intellectual, rather something full of life, as if the peoples of Mexico in their dance and in their folklore had wished to have technique and develop their strengths more and more, all of these traditions in terms of the dance, their necessity, their own tradition. I tried to be, first, like them, and later to use the technique that I have learned and which I knew to develop each one of the dances."[138]

Hernández went on to describe her adaptation of *los matachines*, one of the most widespread of the Mexican folk dances, for the stage, as representative of her approach to staging pre-existing dances: "It is necessary to analyze the dance because the richness of its steps is so extraordinary that the imagination of the best choreographer in the world could not invent more. There are dozens and dozens of steps: all I did was to select those that weren't similar one with the other and thus establish a contrast in the steps. Because, returning to the professional performance we realize that what the public wants is surprise, the new. That which is repeated, and repeated again, makes the public lose interest. One might say this Dance of the Matachines is merely a selection of autochthonous steps, but, in a sense, theatrically enriched in its choreographic drawing."[139]

According to her early collaborator Segura, what Hernández did was to reproduce the ambience of the folk dance within the theater. Sometimes she conserved elements of the dance she was staging but she also created freely.[140] He went on to explain that her dances "stand out for their spectacular presentation, the lavishness of their costuming and the dynamics that Amalia managed to give them in a theatrical duration, since some of them can last several hours in the villages."[141]

As Margarita Tortajada points out, the Hernández company set its basic repertory in 1960 and, although Hernández added new works to it on an annual basis during her lifetime, it has remained unchanged since that time.[142] The Moiseyev company and its direct descendants in Eastern Europe find themselves in similar situations.[143] More than half a century later, the repertory set by Hernández continues to purvey an image of México as a land of perpetual fiesta—albeit, as Carlos Monsiváis has noted, a revolutionary fiesta—through theatrical dance.[144] This is an image that continues to resonate as strongly within her own nation as it does outside of its boundaries.

Whether Siqueiros's acceptance of Hernández's central role in the dedication of his *Marcha de la humanidad* was due to the personal connections he enjoyed through his daughter, a shift in his aesthetic or political thinking, or some combination of all of these things, it marked a watershed in Mexican dance. Before this time, Mexican dancers depended on the nation's painters to legitimize their art; now it was a dancer who traveled to Europe to help legitimize the work of one of Mexico's best-known painters. Regardless of Siqueiros's motivation, he and his partners in the development of the Polyforum recognized Hernández as a peer among Mexico's internationally recognized leaders in the arts.

Epilogue

Mexican and Universal

Following the triumph of Amalia Hernández's folk dance company at the beginning of the 1960s, Mexico's modern dancers continued to interact with painters and musicians in creating their works for the public, just as they had done in the 1950s, but they no longer felt the impulse to develop explicitly nationalist works. Themes derived from indigenous music still populated the scores to which they danced, and ideas about movement and design that they gathered from folk sources maintained a place in their choreography, but the overt markers of Mexicanism that they once embraced largely disappeared. As choreographer Guillermina Bravo characterized her evolution as an artist, she finally understood "the dispute between Rufino Tamayo and Diego Rivera, when the prior spoke about the elements of painting in and of themselves (which I did not comprehend in that period) rather than the thematic on the other hand."[1]

As a young artist, Tamayo opposed what he characterized as his colleague's preoccupation with producing "art that was Mexican even though in appearance only," which he believed resulted in works that were "careless of the really plastic problems."[2] He was convinced that his nation's painting should, instead, "be Mexican in essence, but without omitting the technical side which was being neglected, [so] I reacted strongly against the established norms and together with other colleagues, initiated a movement tending to restore to our painting its pure qualities." He was treated harshly by his initially more famous colleagues for this formalist stance. Although he was no less committed to social causes than the "big three" muralists—José Clemente Orozco, Diego Rivera, and David Alfaro Siqueiros—he was unhappy when the Mexican government, in the context of the Cold War, grouped him with the members of the Mexican school of painting as the "fourth great" muralist.[3]

By contrast, as a young choreographer Bravo was a leader among the Waldeenas who rejected the "rigid techniques" of "foreign schools" and, as dance historian Margarita Tortajada notes, "emphasized . . . the expression of their bodies over technique."[4] Only after dancing in the Soviet Union and China did Bravo realize that she needed to master the formal aspects of her art. She became Mexico's leading promoter of Martha Graham's technique, which she once rejected.

Even as Bravo evolved as an artist, her engagement with social issues and her fascination with Mexico's indigenous cultures remained constants in her work. A collective approach to creation continued to reign at her Ballet Nacional. Although the choreographers who worked with the company could create whatever work they cared to perform, it was the company as a whole that decided whether the work merited a public performance.[5] Amalia Hernández and her Ballet Folklórico might have "unseated" modern dance from its dominant position as far as government support went; Bravo was regarded by most of the nation's dance community as its leading artist. As critic and historian Alberto Dallal put it, Bravo "completely filled the history of dance in Mexico."[6] In 1979, she was the first dancer to be awarded Mexico's Premio Nacional de las Artes (National Prize in the Arts), an honor granted annually since 1945.[7]

During the nationwide celebrations marking the seventieth anniversary of Tamayo's career as an artist, Bravo's Ballet Nacional was charged with providing the dance community's contribution to the celebration.[8] Like his contemporaries among the Mexican school, with whom he preferred to maintain a distance, dance was part of Tamayo's professional trajectory. Working in tandem with Agustín Lazo (1896–1971), Tamayo developed the sets for *Café negro*, a musical revue developed by the Contemporáneos in the 1920s.[9] He also appears to have played some part in Chávez's attempts to realize productions of *El fuego nuevo* and *Los cuatro soles* in New York later in the decade.[10] In the 1930s, he represented the visual arts in the SEP's commission that designed the program of what became the National School of Dance.[11] It was not until 1949, however, that he designed his first work specifically for theatrical dance, Ana Mérida's *La balada del luna y el venado*. In a review of Mexican artists active in stage design for the cultural supplement of the daily newspaper *Excélsior*, poet Xavier Villaurrutia wrote that when confronted with Tamayo's designs for Mérida's work, "one could but lament the infrequency of his interventions in stage design."[12] All of Tamayo's subsequent dance designs featured the cosmological elements that formed a central element of his work since World War II. The backdrop for his *Antigone,* with choreography by John Cranko (1927–1973), for the Royal Ballet in London in 1959, included a comet and a solar eclipse.[13] In its preview of the ballet, the *Times* of London found that Tamayo's designs recalled "the stark splendor of ancient Mexican art" but added a note of internationalism by observing that this choice was "curiously enough . . . extremely appropriate for this Greek tragedy."[14] In its subsequent review of the work, the *Times* opined that the "problem of modernizing a classical myth was successfully solved by the avoidance of realistic imitation. The décor by the Mexican artist, Rufino Tamayo, was geometrical in the modern, not the Hellenic, manner and against it Cranko set some groups that suggested sculptured friezes without looking like them; he had looked at vase paintings but not copied them."[15] As the review suggests, the approach to creating a "primitive" modernism that worked so successfully for the Ballets Russes' 1912 production of *L'Après-midi d'un Faune* was no longer an acceptable strategy for European audiences of the 1950s.

Tamayo returned to the dance stage in 1987 to work with the Ballet Nacional. By this time, heavily influenced by Bravo's insistence on forming dancers with strong technical backgrounds, most Mexican theatrical dance was no longer "modern," as Dallal points out.[16] It was adopting aspects of international contemporary dance.

According to Raquel Tibol, the lack of time to create a program in honor of Tamayo from the commissioning of the Ballet Nacional to the performance date allowed only two meetings between the artist and the company.[17] "In the first they spoke of everything and nothing, as if they were searching for points of connection. In the second, when the compositions were already quite advanced and time was at a premium, they asked Tamayo for his suggestions about backdrops." The company created three works for the evening-length program in Tamayo's honor. Rossana Filomarino (b. 1945) choreographed *Personajes* (Characters), based in part on Tamayo's many works depicting howling dogs, while Jaime Blanc (b. 1949) evoked the artist's frequent use of female figures in his *Mujer con Personaje* (Woman with Personage). For her part, Bravo created *Constelaciones y danzantes. Homenaje a Rufino Tamayo* (Constellations and Dancers. Homage to Rufino Tamayo). Bravo based her tribute on two different Tamayo paintings, a "man contemplating the universe," whose exact title was left unspecified, "and the other called *El danzante*" (The Dancer) from 1979.[18] Her intent was to create "a dance which attempts to unite the constellations with the communal life of Oaxaca." Tibol described it as a "grand ceremony" depicting the awe of man before the vastness of the universe,

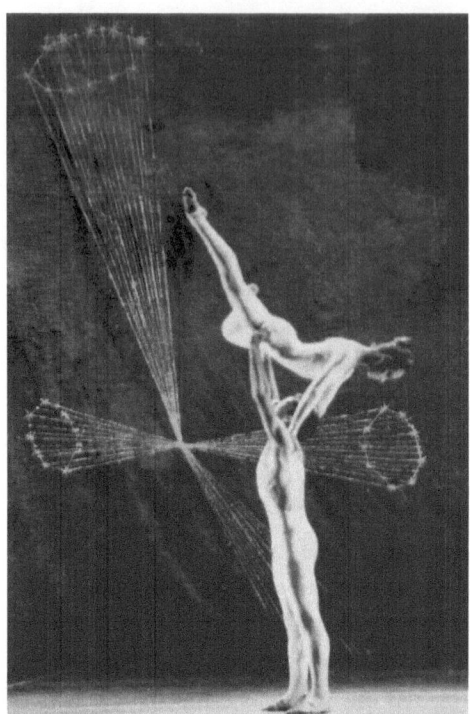

FIGURE 20. Rufino Tamayo (1899–1991). Detail from the set designs for Guillermina Bravo's *Constelaciones y Danzantes* with members of the Compañía Nacional de Danza. 1987. Photographer unknown. Collection of Patricia Aulestia, Mexico City. © 2019 Tamayo Heirs/Mexico/Licensed by VAGA at Artists Rights Society (ARS), New York.

tempered by his interactions with "his peers . . . in the terrestrial realms."[19] Tamayo designed the backdrop for Bravo's choreography, and the dancers from her company ended up executing the design while working under the painter's supervision.[20]

Bravo's *Constelaciones y danzantes* fits into a phase that dance writer César Delgado calls her return to her origins.[21] He points out that although her work changed in many ways, in *Constelaciones y danzantes* Bravo was still concerned with the central issues that motivated her at the beginning of her career, including indigenous dancing. In this stage of her work, Delgado identifies a "reencounter with the most ancient choreographic forms: the circle and lineal processions" as a resurgent component of her choreography. Segments of *Constelaciones y danzantes* are rich with references to the dance traditions Bravo encountered as a young choreographer in the highlands of Tamayo's home state of Oaxaca, which played a critical role in her artistic development. For philosopher Patricia Cardona, through *Constelaciones y danzantes* Bravo "introduced the essential rhythm of Mexican dance, stripped of its folkloristic mannerisms and everything was new and surprising, as is Tamayo in each of his paintings."[22]

Like the movement design for *Constelaciones y danzantes*, the work's score, created by composers Luis Rivero (1934–2005) and Rodolfo Sánchez Alvardo (b. 1937), also contained elements of indigenous Oaxacan culture. Part of it was recorded during Oaxaca's annual Guelaguetza festival, which evolved from a pre-Hispanic ceremony in honor of a corn deity into an event honoring Our Lady of Mount Carmel. Another segment came from a Oaxacan form of the jarabe. But the electronic score that sprang from the international trends of its time also incorporated Turkish and Portuguese songs along with bird calls, "all filtered and woven electronically to achieve," as Tibol described it, "not a sonic background but a vibratory space, an audible substance capable of sheltering and containing the dance."[23]

When Mexicanism was blossoming in the 1920s, Vasconcelos and his associates argued for building on the specifics of Mexico's popular mestizo arts to achieve the "universal classical." Tamayo was one of the few voices arguing for an art based on modernity itself as a route to achieving the "universal classical."[24] As his colleague Villaurrutia explained it, the efforts of the group of modernist artists who supported this position were met with an indifference bordering on hostility, but they, nonetheless, continued to produce works "that tend to spiritual unity with the rest of the world."[25] Bravo in the 1980s rendered homage to Tamayo through an expression that embraced both Mexico's local roots and its place in the broader world. She became, as Dallal concluded, "convinced that the universal technique of contemporary dance has yet to be determined and she does not cease in her efforts to study the various forms of world dance (antique, classical, primitive, current) to establish it."[26] This open embrace of potential sources was the approach Bravo took in creating her *Constelaciones y danzantes*. According to Delgado, in response to this work, the opening night audience "ignited . . . and in his place Rufino Tamayo's eyes glistened."[27]

NOTES

Introduction

1. The entire series of essays for the Mexico City newspaper *El Demócrata* is online at http://www.hawaii.edu/jcf/escritos/charlotescritos02.html (Accessed September 14, 2019). Unless otherwise noted, all translations from Spanish are my own.

2. Francisco Hernández Araujo, "El Movimiento Actual de la Pintura en México," *El Demócrata* (Ciudad de México), July 26, 1923.

3. Monsiváis, "Anita Brenner," xiii.

4. del Conde, "Mexico," 18.

5. Pineda, "Más allá," 156.

6. See Ortiz, "La ciudad de México durante el Porfiriato," 179–96.

7. Garelick, *Electric Salome*, 3.

8. de Olavarría y Ferrari, *Reseña histórica*, vol. 4, 370–75; Díaz de Léon, *El Renacimiento*, 29.

9. Gamboa, "Jose Guadalupe Posada," 17.

10. In all likelihood, the dancer Posada depicted was Jossie Lindsay, as he also illustrated programs and handbills for the Circo Teatro Orrin (see de los Reyes, ¡Tercera *llamada, tercera!*, 34–37).

11. Tablada quoted in Reyes de la Maza. *El teatro en México*, vol. 2, 344–45.

12. Ramos, *Danza teatral*, 48.

13. Duran quoted in Ramos, *Danza teatral*, 75.

14. Ramos, *Teatro musical*, 36–43.

15. Ramos, *Danza teatral*, 130.

16. Ramos, *Teatro musical*, 45.

17. Macias, "Women and the Mexican Revolution," 53–82.

18. Vaughn, "Pancho Villa," 23–24.

19. Rubenstein, "The War on Las Pelonas," 75.

20. Monsiváis, "Los que tenemos unas manos," 15–18; Rubenstein, "War on Las Pelonas," 57–80.

21. Carbajal, "El nacionalismo en transición," 38–39.

22. López, *Crafting Mexico*, 54–55.

23. Powell, "Eves of an Unknown Eden," 584.

24. Powell, "Eves of an Unknown Eden," 584–86.

25. Ramos-Smith, *Danza teatral*, 126; Monsiváis, "Anita Brenner," xv.

26. Kiddle, "*Cabaretistas* and *Indias Bonitas*," 264.

27. Bidault, *Nellie Campobello*, 19.

28. Anderson, *Imagined Communities*, 47–65.

29. Anderson, *Imagined Communities*, 62, 168.

30. Anderson, *Imagined Communities*, 156–59.

31. Clayton, "Modernism's Moving Bodies," 30.

32. Hobsbawm, *Nations and Nationalism*, 131–62.

33. Anderson, *Imagined Communities*, 4.

34. Rubín quoted in Aluestia, *Historias alucinantes*, 219.

35. The word sandunga appears as zandunga in multiple sources. The jarabe tapitío is also subject to a variety of capitalizations. My text will maintain these variations in individual citations.

36. Shay, *Choreographic Politics*, 40.

37. Ben Ali quoted in Aulestia, *Chicas bien*, 75.

38. See Vaughn, *Cultural Politics in Revolution*, 37.

39. Vasconcelos, *La creación*, 84.

40. Vaughn, *Cultural Politics in Revolution*, 25.

41. Alfonso Lorança, personal communication, July 9, 2019.

42. See Tortajada, *Amalia Hernández*, 29.

43. Muray quoted in Panzer, "The Essential Tact," 31.

44. Aulestia, "Miguel Covarrubias," 199.

45. Greeley, "Muralism and the State," 27.

46. In her *Making Art Panamerican*, Claire Fox credits the creation of the phrase to Cuban art critic José Gómez Sicre (1916–1991), who was then chief of the Fine Arts Unit of the anticommunist Organization of American States (152). Gómez Sicre was a major promoter of Cuevas's artwork as a counterpoint to the leftist Mexican school.

47. José Luis Cuevas. "La cortina de nopal." English translation in Fox, *Making Art Panamerican*, 159.

48. Tortajada, *Danza y poder*, vol. 1, 550.

49. Anna Kisselgoff, "Dance View: A Complex Artist of Simple Bearing," *New York Times*, March 29, 1998.

50. Tortajada, *Danza y poder*, vol. 1, 550.

51. Tortajada, *Danza y poder*, vol. 2, 565.

52. Dallal, *La danza en México*, 66.

Chapter 1. An Anthropologist Orders a Beer: The Development of Mexican Nationalism

1. Monsiváis, "La nación de unos cuantos," 184.

2. Krauze, *Redeemers*, 50–51.

3. Brenner, *Your Mexican Holiday*, 9.

4. López, *Crafting Mexico*, 31.

5. Fell, *Años del Águila*, 547.

6. Krauze, *Redeemers*, 51.

7. Florescano, "Semblanza de Francisco Javier Clavijero," *La Jornada Semanal* (Ciudad de México), March 31, 2002, 369.

8. Rueda, "A Battle for Anthropology," 37, 42.

9. de Moxó, *Cartas mejicanas*, 190.

10. Hobsbawm, *Nations and Nationalism*, 71–72.

11. Jiménez, "Death Is Nothing," 247; Florescano, "Los orígenes de la bandera mexicana." Presentation at the Mexican Cultural Institute, Washington, DC, September 10, 2011.

12. See Tenorio-Trillo, *Mexico at the World's Fairs*, 15–178 for discussion of the Diaz regime's use of Mexico's pre-Columbian cultures in international contexts.

13. Ortega y Medina, *Ensayos*, 37–86.

14. Laughlin, "The Emperor's New Clothes," 395.

15. Laughlin, "The Emperor's New Clothes," 398.

16. Laughlin, "The Emperor's New Clothes," 407–9; Velázquez and Vaughn, "*Mestizaje* and Musical Nationalism in Mexico," 96.

17. López, *Crafting Mexico*, 36.

18. Maximilian I quoted in Laughlin, "The Emperor's New Clothes," 409.

19. See Florescano, "Patria y nación," 163–67.

20. Gamio, *Forjando patria*, 18.

21. Gamio, *Forjando patria*, 19.

22. Gamio, *Forjando patria*, 20.

23. Cited in Hobsbawm, *Nations and Nationalism*, 14.

24. Gamio, *Forjando patria*, 67.

25. Gamio, *Forjando patria*, 93.

26. Gamio, *Forjando patria*, 205–6.

27. Monsiváis, "La nación de unos cuantos," 159–219.

28. Monsiváis, "La nación de unos cuantos," 186.

29. Vasconcelos, *La raza cósmica*, 39.

30. Vasconcelos, *La raza cósmica*, 23.

31. Stepan, *Hour of Eugenics*, 149.

32. Acevedo, "Las decoraciones," 185.

33. Claude Fell's *José Vasconcelos: Los años del águila, 1920–1925: Educación, cultura e iberoamericanismo en el México postrevolucionario* is the indispensable guide to Vasconcelos's tenure as minister of education. For the school construction budget, see page 106; library construction, pages 513–15; and the activities of the cultural missionaries, see pages 221–57.

34. Fell, *Años del* Águila, 489–90.

35. Lunacharsky, "Revolution and Art," English translation quoted in Bowlt, *Russian Art*, 192–93.

36. Vasconcelos quoted in Fell, *Años del* Águila, 550.

37. Vasconcelos, *De Robinson a Odiseo*, 210.

38. Fell, *Años del* Águila, 59.

39. Monsiváis, "Anita Brenner," xvi.

40. Greeley, "Muralism and the State," 26.

41. Acevedo, "Las decoraciones," 171–207.

42. Acevedo, "Las decoraciones," 199.

43. "Ramos Martínez y la Escuela de Coyoacán," *Revista de Revistas*, February 25, 1923. International Center for the Arts of the Americas at the Museum of Fine Arts Houston's Digital Archive and Publications Archive (hereinafter ICAA), ICAA Record ID: 760364.

44. Maples, English translation in Ades, *Art in Latin America*, 306–9.

45. Orozco quoted in Fernández, *Orozco*, 199.

46. Siqueiros, "Tres llamamientos," 1–2. Emphasis in the original.

47. Turino, "Nationalism and Latin American Music," 175–76.

48. Corn, *Great American Thing*, 12.

49. Montenegro, *Planos*, 87; "Entrevista con el pintor Diego Rivera," *El Universal* (Ciudad de México), July 21, 1921. ICAA Record ID: 746976.

50. Crowninshield quoted in Corn, *Great American Thing*, 81.

51. Hartley, "Red Man Ceremonials," 7–14.

52. Kendall, *Where She Danced*, 168.

53. Shawn, *The American Ballet*, 18, 20.

54. Graham, "Seeking an American Art," 254.

55. Shawn, *The American Ballet*, 16.

56. Wilson, "Indian Corn Dance," 361.

57. Wilson, "Indian Corn Dance," 365.

58. Charlot, "Esthetics," 4.

59. Charlot, "Esthetics," 5–6.

60. Mérida, "Pre-Hispanic Dance," 568.

61. Mérida, "Pre-Hispanic Dance," 563.

62. Mérida, "Pre-Hispanic Dance," 568.

63. Campobello and Campobello, *Ritmos indígenas*, 10.

64. Corn, *Great American Thing*, 50.

65. See Velasco "Nationalism" and Kolb "*Colorines*" for in-depth treatment of the US reception of Chávez and Revueltas, respectively.

66. Aaron Copland, "Mexican Composer," *New York Times*, May 9, 1935.

67. Saavedra, "Of Selves and Others," 160.

68. See, for example, the composer's program notes for the concert performance of an early segment of the ballet *H.P.*, quoted in Gibson, "Reception," 174–75.

69. See Snow, "Martha Graham," 1–16.

70. Ralph Barton, "It Is to Laugh," *New York Herald Tribune*, October 25, 1925.

71. Reilly, "Covarrubias," 28.

72. Sáenz quoted in López, *Crafting Mexico*, 128.

Chapter 2. Mexicanism Russian Style: Roberto Montenegro, Diego Rivera, and the Ballets Russes

1. See Ortíz Gaitán, "La ciudad de México," 179–96, for the place of Paris in Mexican culture during the dictatorship of Porfirio Díaz.

2. Tenorio-Trillo, *Mexico at the World's Fairs*, 119, note 87.

3. Fernández, *Arte moderno*, 63.

4. Charlot, *Mexican Art*, 142–44.

5. Montenegro, *Planos*, 10–13.

6. Montenegro, *Planos*, 13.

7. Tablada, *Diario*, 61.

8. Montenegro, *Planos*, 14; Ortíz, *Entre dos mundos*, 36.

9. Ortíz, *Entre dos mundos*, 38.

10. Ortíz, *Entre dos mundos*, 39.

11. Ortíz, *Entre dos mundos*, 38.

12. Ortíz, *Entre dos mundos*, 32.

13. Favela, *Diego Rivera*, 21–24.

14. Favela, *Diego Rivera*, 24–29.

15. Velázquez Guadarrama, "La exposición española," 7 and 18.

16. Lempérière, "Los dos centenarios," 329.

17. Lempérière, "Los dos centenarios," 331–32.

18. Ramírez, "Emblemas," 60.

19. Ramírez, "Hacia la gran exposición," 19.

20. Velázquez Guadarrama, "La exposición española," 14.

21. Atl had received the European scholarship in 1896 (see Espejo, *Dr. Atl*, 15). At the time of the centennial celebration he was curator of the academy's painting collection.

22. García de Germenos, "Exposición," 70.

23. Ramírez, "Hacia la gran exposición," 19.

24. Tablada quoted in García de Germenos, "Exposición," 74–75.

25. Ramírez, "Emblemas," 61.

26. García de Germenos, "Exposición," 84.

27. Ramírez, "Hacia la gran exposición," 19.

28. Morales Moreno, "Obras de arte y testimonios históricos," 74.

29. Charlot, *Mexican Mural Renaissance*, 58–59, 99.

30. Velázquez Guadarrama, "La exposición española," 16.

31. Fontbona, "Anglada-Camarasa," 73.

32. Fontbona, "Anglada-Camarasa," 16.

33. Ortíz, *Entre dos mundos*, 40.

34. Pizano y Saucedo, "Centenario del Teatro," 423; Balderas, *Roberto Montenegro: Ilustrador*, 17.

35. Maeztu quoted in Miralles and Sanjuán, *Anglada-Camarasa y Argentina*, 69–70.

36. Pellicer quoted in Ortíz, *Entre dos mundos*, 43.

37. Grover, "The World of Art Movement in Russia," 40.

38. Tablada quoted in Aulestia, *Historias alucinantes*, 32.

39. Montenegro, *Planos*, 35–36; Favela, *Diego Rivera*, 37.

40. Fontbona and Miralles, *Anglada Camarasa*, 80.

41. Gutiérrez, "Hermen Anglada Camarasa y Mallorca," 190.

42. Ortíz, *Entre dos mundos*, 25.

43. Torres, "Dibujos y grabados de Roberto Montenegro," 22.

44. Montenegro, *Planos*, 41.

45. Beaumont, *Bookseller at the Ballet*, 133.

46. Beaumont, "Note of Introduction," n.p.

47. Buckle, *Nijinsky*, 408.

48. Rutherford, "The Triumph of the Veiled Dance," 94.

49. At the insistence of Otto Kahn (1867–1934), chairman of the board of New York's Metropolitan Opera, which sponsored the Ballets Russes' tour of the United States, Nijinsky temporarily rejoined the company. Kahn also arranged for Nijinsky's release from house arrest in his wife's native Budapest, where he was being held as a foreign national of an enemy nation during World War I. Kahn believed that the presence of the superstar dancer was necessary to ensure a successful tour in the United States (See Garafola, *Diaghilev's Ballets Russes*, 203).

50. Lynn Garafola, personal communication, August 4, 2014.

51. Siqueiros, "Tres llamamientos," 2.

52. Siqueiros quoted in Acevedo, "Las decoraciones," 180.

53. Quoted in Garafola, *Diaghilev's Ballets Russes*, 374.

54. "La conferencia del pintor Diego Rivera," *Excélsior* (Ciudad de México), October 21, 1921.

55. Monsiváis, "Los que tenemos," 16.

56. Siqueiros, "Tres llamamientos," 2. Emphasis in the original.

57. Flores, *Mexico's Revolutionary Avant-gardes*, 39.

58. Ortíz, *Entre dos mundos*, 41.

59. Ramírez, *Crónica de las artes plásticas*, 117.

60. Saveliev, "Anglada–Camarasa en Rusia," 36–42.

61. Fontbona and Miralles, *Anglada Camarasa*, 110.

62. Fontbona, "Anglada Camarasa," 18.

63. S. Warren, "Crafting Nation," 758.

64. Salmond, *Arts and Crafts*, 5.

65. Salmond, *Arts and Crafts*, 1.

66. Loukowsky quoted in Salmond, *Arts and Crafts*, 13. After its revolution, Soviet Russia continued producing *kustar*-style objects despite initial concerns about their capitalist origins (see M. Miller, *Economic Development of Russia*, 230). Kustar arts, such as the famed *matrioshka* nesting doll, still serve as symbols of today's Russia. The doll was developed from Japanese prototypes in the last decade of the nineteenth century under the guidance of artist Sergei Malyutin (1859–1937) at Mamontov's Abramtsevo workshops (see Hilton, *Russian Folk Art*, 127).

67. Bowlt, *Moscow and St. Petersburg*, 168.

68. Garafola, *Diaghilev's Ballets Russes*, 154; Vasnetsov, English translation quoted in Shevelenko, "Empire and Nation," 4.

69. Vasconcelos, *La creación de la Secretaría de Educación Pública*, 74.

70. Shevelenko, "Empire and Nation," 22–23.

71. Bilibin, English translation quoted in Shevelenko, "Empire and Nation," 23–24.

72. Mérida quoted in Ramírez, *Crónica de las artes plásticas*, 155.

73. Salmond, *Arts and Crafts*, 105.

74. Bowlt, *Moscow and St. Petersburg*, 180.

75. Benois, English translation quoted in Shevelenko, "Empire and Nation," 22.

76. Orozco, English translation in *The Artist in New York*, 89–90.

77. Beaumont, *Michel Fokine*, 46–50.

78. Garafola, "The Travesty Dancer," 35–40.

79. Carbonneau, "Adolph Bolm," 222.

80. Jane Pritchard. "Creating Productions," 78.

81. Kennel, "Le Sacre du Printemps," 9.

82. Vasconcelos claimed to have attended the raucous premiere of *Le Sacre du Printemps* during his brief visit to Paris as an agent of Venustiano Carranza in 1913 (*La Tormenta*, 54). Since he also wrote that Nijinsky's notorious ballet was followed by *Schéhérazade*—whose sets and costumes, he believed, constituted the true "prodigy" of the evening—he did not attend the premiere. *Schéhérazade* formed part of the program for the few subsequent

performances the Nijinsky work received. Lynn Garafola, personal communication, August 4, 2014.

83. José Vasconcelos, *Estética*, 628–29.

84. Aulestia, *Historias alucinantes*, 260–75.

85. Marsh, "Serge Diaghilev," 25.

86. Diaghilev, English translation quoted in Homans, *Apollo's Angels*, 301.

87. Beaumont, *Michel Fokine & His Ballets*, 52.

88. Stravinsky and Craft, *Expositions and Developments*, 167.

89. *Le Figaro*, English translation quoted in Beaumont, *Michel Fokine*, 68.

90. Shevelenko, "Empire and Nation," 33.

91. Järvinen, "'The Russian Barnum,'" 18.

92. Sabaneev, English translation quoted in Järvinen, "'The Russian Barnum,'" 27.

93. "El movimiento actual," *El Demócrata* (Ciudad de México), August 2, 1923. Emphasis in the original.

94. Charlot, "Un Precursor," 25.

95. "Dos años," *Azulejos*, December 1923, 26, 41. ICAA Record ID: 734410. For a summary of the Picasso-Rivera rivalry see Oles, "Rivera's Trophy," 146–61.

96. Favela, *Diego Rivera*, 70.

97. Hilton, *Russian Folk Art*, 249.

98. Tugendhol'd, English translation quoted in Hilton, *Russian Folk Art*, 249.

99. Tugendhol'd, English translation quoted in Salmond, *Arts and Crafts*, 168–69. This "logical conclusion" to what the Ballets Russes began may have inspired Fokine's choreography for the company's 1913 production of *Le Coq d'Or*.

100. Favela, *Diego Rivera*, 70.

101. Mathieu, "Origin Points," 79.

102. Rivera, *My Art, My Life*, 65.

103. Oles, "Rivera's Trophy," 159–60.

104. Oles, "Rivera's Trophy," 151. As Oles demonstrates, the current title of the work did not appear in print until 1951 (157).

105. Guzmán, "Diego Rivera," 83.

106. See Montenegro, *Planos*, 35–37. Montenegro related a darkly comic episode in which an inebriated Gris appeared at his door at 3:00 a.m. pleading for money so he could flee Paris. Gris believed he had killed his girlfriend Lucia in a drunken rage. When Montenegro visited Gris's residence in the morning to see what occurred as a consequence of Gris's actions, Lucia responded to his knock at the door and told him that Gris had been too drunk to aim his revolver. She was in the process of packing her bags to permanently depart the premises (42–43).

107. Khvoshchinskia, the wife of a Russian diplomat, was a member of Diaghilev's circle (see the photograph of her with Stravinsky, Diaghilev, and Bakst in Switzerland reproduced in Bowlt, *Moscow and St. Petersburg*, 161 and the caption at page 162, which clarifies the transliteration of her name into English). Montenegro was initially drawn to Mallorca not by Anglada but by the presence of the Khvoshchinskia, whom he had hoped to capture in a portrait (see Miralles and Sanjuán, *Anglada-Camarasa y Argentina*, 106–8). Art historian Julieta Ortíz described her as "the only woman who Montenegro would always remember with special emotion" (*Entre dos mundos*, 49). During his stay in Mallorca, Montenegro was painted in a life-sized, full-length portrait by another prominent

Russian artist, Alexander Evgenievich Yakovlev (1887–1938), who was among the members of the "second phase" of the Mir iskusstva movement (see Kharitonova, *The World of Art Movement*, 295–98). The portrait is now in the collection of St. Petersburg's State Russian Museum.

108. Montenegro quoted in Ortíz, *Entre dos mundos*, 56.

109. Ortíz, *Entre dos mundos*, 87–88.

110. Balderas, *Robert Montenegro: La sensualidad renovada*, 32.

111. Gutiérrez, "Roberto Montenegro," 117.

112. Francés quoted in Gutiérrez, "Roberto Montenegro," 117.

113. Montenegro, *Planos*, 87.

Chapter 3. The Precursors of Mexicanism: Anna Pavlova and Tórtola Valencia

1. Hernández, "El movimiento actual," *El Demócrata* (Ciudad de México), August 2, 1923.

2. "Una Exposición sobre los bailes de Tórtola Valencia," *Excélsior* (Ciudad de México), January 17, 1918.

3. From an October 1918 issue of *Revista de Revistas* quoted in Rousset, *Siqueiros*, xiii.

4. de Mille, *Dance to the Piper*, 40.

5. P. Stein, *Siqueiros*, 29. Stein, Siqueiros's long-time studio assistant, also reported another early prize-winning work depicting the Argentine-born Spanish dancer La Argentinita, Antonia Mercé y Luque (1890–1936).

6. Moyssén, "Siqueiros antes de Siqueiros," 190.

7. Charlot, *Mexican Mural Renaissance*, 196.

8. Rousset, *Siqueiros*, xiii.

9. Siqueiros, *Me llamaban el coronelazo*, 52; Arenal, "Primera presentación critica," in Rousset, *Siqueiros*, vii.

10. Siqueiros, "Tres Llamamientos," 2–3. Emphasis in the original.

11. Charlot, "Estética," 6. This statement does not appear in Charlot's English version of the same article, which immediately precedes it.

12. Charlot, "Esthetics," 4.

13. Charlot quoted in John Charlot, "Jean Charlot's First Fresco: The Massacre in the Main Temple." The Jean Charlot Collection, University of Hawaii and Manoa Library. http://www.jeancharlot.org/onJC/writings/JohnCharlotOnJean/hs~johncharlot.html. (Accessed September 14, 2019).

14. Some of Charlot's animosity toward the Ballets Russes–infused approach of the "Mexicanists" likely stems from his family background. While his mother's family was of French and Mexican descent, his father was a Russian-born pro-Bolshevik living in exile in Paris. (See Thompson, "Jean Charlot: Artist and Scholar," 5, for Charlot's family background.) The earliest activities of Diaghilev in Paris were supported directly by the Romanovs, as was the Mariinsky Imperial Theatre, which supplied the early dancers of the Ballets Russes. This would automatically cast the company, its participants, and its supporters in the role of political enemies of the Charlot household regardless of any of the Ballet Russes' particular aesthetic merits or failings.

15. Clayton, "Modernism's Moving Bodies," 30.

16. Clayton, "Modernism's Moving Bodies," 31.

17. Ibarra, "Notas sobre la crítica de arte," 27. See Pérez, "Un nacionalismo sin nación

aparente," 184–85, for the dominant role of the China poblana. Although this "informal competition" between the China poblana and the Tehuana took place outside the official arena, it tends to confirm Anthony Shay's observations on the existence of primary and secondary national cultures as part of what he calls the "stereotypification" of the repertory of state-sponsored folk dance companies later in the twentieth century. (See Shay, *Choreographic Politics*, 39–40.)

18. Richardson, *Mexico through Russian Eyes*, 99.

19. Dallal, "Anna Pavlova," 166.

20. Svetloff, *Anna Pavlova*, 152.

21. Money, *Anna Pavlova*, 272.

22. Pavlova quoted in Richardson, *Mexico through Russian Eyes*, 100.

23. González Peña quoted in Lavalle, "Anna Pavlova," 639.

24. For Pavlova versus Diaghilev, see Garafola, *Diaghilev's Ballets Russes*, 215. For González's eventual acceptance of Pavlova, see Lavalle, "Anna Pavlova," 640.

25. "Pageant to be Staged Tonight," *Los Angeles Times*, October 3, 1925; Hall, *Dolores del Río*, 26.

26. Aulestia, "Nellie Campobello," 3.

27. González Peña, "Anna Pavlova y las danzas mexicanas," *El Universal*, March 19, 1919, reprinted in *La Danza en Mexico*, vol. 2, 327–29.

28. Garafola, *Diaghilev's Ballets Russes*, 88–93.

29. Kerensky, *Anna Pavlova*, 78.

30. Hurok, *Pavlowa*, 13.

31. Aulestia, *Historias alucinantes*, 87.

32. See Ramos and Cardona, *La Danza en Mexico*, vol. 2, 237–40.

33. Jáuregui, *El Mariachi*, 52, 237–40.

34. Orozco, *The Artist in New York*, 90; Corn, *Great American Thing*, 195.

35. Salazkina, *In Excess*, 172. It was likely Best, or his friend Montenegro, who arranged for Eisenstein's first homosexual experience (130).

36. Kendall, *Where She Danced*, 92.

37. Anna Pavlova, "El baile, una de las bellas artes," *Revista de Revistas*, November 2, 1913, reprinted in Ramos and Cardona, *La Danza en Mexico*, vol. 2, 318. Classical dancer Joseph C. Smith (1875–1932), the son of George Washington Smith (1820?–1899), the first known male professional classical dancer in the United States, claimed credit for the invention of the turkey trot (see Moore, "George Washington Smith," 187).

38. Poniatowska, *Miguel Covarrubias*, 74.

39. Lavalle, "Anna Pavlova," 643.

40. Saldivar, *El jarabe*, 8.

41. Lavalle, "Anna Pavlova," 646–47.

42. Kerensky, *Anna Pavlova*, 85.

43. González Peña quoted in Lavalle, "Anna Pavlova," 644. Ellipsis in the original.

44. Hurok, *Pavlowa*, 13. For the fictional nature of the China poblana and the details of the authentic costume, see Saldivar, *El jarabe*, 9–10.

45. Reynoso, "Choreographing Modern Mexico," 81.

46. Quoted in Lavalle, "Anna Pavlova," 648.

47. See Reynoso, "Choreographing Politics, Dancing Modernity," 86, for a reproduction

of an advertisement announcing the performance of *Fantasía Mexicana* in the bullring. This was not Pavlova's first performance in that space. See Reynoso, 118–19, 136.

48. López quoted in Lavalle, "Anna Pavlova," 635.

49. Fonteyn, *Pavlova*, 98.

50. Otilio Villaseñor, "Lo que dice Best Maugard del arte mexicano en Estados Unidos," *El Universal Ilustrado* (Ciudad de México), April 1925, reprinted in Instituto Nacional de Bellas Artes, *Adolfo Best Maugard*, 294.

51. Luis Lara Prado, "El arte nacionalista de Best Maugard," *Revista de Revistas*, December 12, 1920, 16–17, reprinted in Instituto Nacional de Bellas Artes, *Adolfo Best Maugard*, 303.

52. González Peña quoted in Lavalle, "Anna Pavlova," 645.

53. Favela, *Diego Rivera*, 37. Rivera captured Best while he was working on this project in *Retrato de Adolfo Best Maugard* (1913), which shows the nattily dressed Best on the balcony of Rivera's studio above the Montparnasse train station, with the gigantic Ferris wheel from the Paris Exposition of 1900 looming in the background. This invented scene, which combined multiple perspectives in a way that couldn't possibly have been seen from Rivera's balcony, was later dismissed by the all-purpose arts critic González Peña as a "practical joke played on Best Maugard by Rivera" (English translation quoted in Favela, *Diego Rivera*, 49).

54. Instituto Nacional de Bellas Artes, *Adolfo Best Maugard*, 354–55.

55. Acevedo and García, "Procesos de quiebre," 71.

56. Craven quoted in Delpar, *Enormous Vogue*, 132.

57. Rodríguez Ureña, "Arte Mexicano," 131–34.

58. Alfonso de Neuvillate, "Introducción," vi.

59. See Grimberg, "Un caballero educado," 43–49.

60. See Coronel, "Rosa Rolanda," 74–79.

61. Diego Rivera, "Children's Drawing in Present Day Mexico," *Mexican Folkways*, December–January 1926, 5–6.

62. Hernández, "El movimiento actual," *El Demócrata* (Ciudad de México), June 11, 1923.

63. Hernández, "El movimiento actual," *El Demócrata* (Ciudad de México), August 2, 1923.

64. Cordero, "The Best Maugard Drawing Method," 46.

65. Tibol quoted in Dallal, "Anna Pavlova," 168–69, note 13.

66. Charlot, *Mexican Mural Renaissance*, 62.

67. These postcards bear the name of Sabino Osuna's Casa Osuna. Osuna made the licensing agreement but did not take the photographs, which have been misattributed to German-born Mexican photographer Hugo Breme. See Arturo Guevara Escobar, "Hugo Breme y la pérdida de la fe," Protagonistas. Fotógrafos en México, March 14, 2011. http// fotografosdelarevolucion.blogspot.com/2011/03/hugo-brehme-y-la-perdida-de-la-fe. html. (Accessed September 14, 2019).

68. Álvarez, "La influencia de Best Maugard," 56.

69. English translation in Walsh, "'That Deadly Female Accuracy of Vision,'" 635.

70. Duberman, *The Worlds of Lincoln Kirstein*, 160. Duberman reports, incorrectly, that Porter's ballet scenario was performed by Pavlova in Mexico.

71. Porter, *Collected Stories and Other Writings*, 544–45.

72. For the US premiere see Lazzaroni, *Pavlova*, 167. The souvenir program was published by impresario Sol Hurok for her 1920–1921 tour of the United States.

73. Quoted in Lazzaroni, *Pavlova*, 167.

74. See Aulestia, *Historias alucinantes*, 113–18.

75. Lavalle, "Anna Pavlova," 649–50. Suggestions of a renewed popularity for the jarabe emerged even before Pavlova's visit. In a review of Azteca Films' production of the 1917 *La soñadora* (The Dreamer), the critic for *El Pueblo* complained about the work's poorly performed minuet and opined it would be far better to see the work's star Mimí Derba (1888–1953) "clad in the typical Mexican dress tracing out the steps of a daring and gay jarabe." English translation quoted in Mora, *Mexican Cinema*, 19.

76. Dallal, "El nacionalismo prolongado," 331.

77. Pérez, "Down Mexico Way," 19.

78. Vasconcelos quoted in Aulestia, *Historias alucinantes*, 93.

79. For the design of the SEP's early folk dance programs see Fell, *Años del Águila*, 547. For examples crediting Vasconcelos with declaring the jarabe as Mexico's national dance see Herrera-Sobek, *Celebrating Latino Folklore*, vol. 2, 91 and Greathouse, *Mariachi*, 22.

80. Frances Toor, "The Old and New Jarabe," *Mexican Folkways*, January–March, 1930, 26.

81. Toor, "Jarabe," 34–35.

82. Saldivar, *El Jarabe*, 9.

83. Saldivar, *El Jarabe*, 9.

84. Saldivar, *El Jarabe*, 14.

85. Saldivar, *El Jarabe*, 14.

86. Saldivar, *El Jarabe*, 9.

87. Saldivar, *El Jarabe*, 22.

88. Vaughn, *Cultural Politics*, 99.

89. Vaughn, *Cultural Politics*, 46.

90. See Flores, *Mexico's Revolutionary Avant Gardes*, 213–45 for a discussion of *Horizonte*. A reproduction of the González drawing appears on page 220. The pioneering stage designer and film director would go on to serve as director for the Mexican state's first attempt at a dancing school, the Escuela de Plástica Dinámica. His drawing originally appeared in the program for the 1924 production by the Teatro Mexicano del Murciélago (Mexican Theater of the Bat), a revue inspired by the Russian Nikita Balieff's (1877–1936) La Chauve-Souris (Bat) theater group, which had toured widely in Europe and the United States in the 1920s. (Luis Quintanilla, Teatro mexicano del murciélago, Mexico City: by the artist, 1924. ICAA Record ID: 799676.) González's drawing illustrated the scenario for "Aparador" (Shop Window), one of the production's four sketches treating contemporary Mexico. The scenario depicts the traditional rebozos and serapes shut off from the lively world beyond the shop window, gradually succumbing to a melancholic paralysis (7). Other illustrations by González in the program are inspired by the Best method. I thank Tatiana Flores for bringing this program to my attention.

91. Pérez, "Down Mexico Way," 32. For the popularity of theatricalized folk dances with United States citizens of Mexican descent, see Shay, *Choreographic Politics*, 87.

92. *Boletín de la Secretaría de Educación Pública* for 1923, quoted in Aulestia, *Historias alucinantes*, 98.

93. Clayton, "Touring History," 32.

94. Clayton, "Touring History" 31.

95. Quoted in Aulestia, *Historias alucinantes*, 78.

96. Quoted in Queralt, *Tórtola Valencia*, 16.

97. See Solrac, *Tortola Valencia*, 1; Garland, "Modernismo and the Dancer," n.p.; Clayton, "Touring History," 32.

98. Clayton, "Touring History," 32–33.

99. Garland, "Modernismo and the Dancer," n.p. If this were true, the likelihood is that it was almost meaningless. Because of the Christian "reconquest" of Spain, by the sixteenth century the majority of Castile's population had earned noble status. About 85 percent of the population of a district in Burgos, for example, could lay claim to nobility. See Vassberg, *Land and Society in Golden Age Castile*, 91–92.

100. Solrac, *Tortola Valencia*, 322.

101. Clayton, "Touring History," 31.

102. Garland, "Early Modern Dance in Spain," 4.

103. Clayton, "Touring History," 35.

104. Clayton, "Touring History," 35.

105. Garland, "Early Modern Dance in Spain," 8.

106. Garland, "Modernismo and the Dancer," n.p.

107. Garland, "Modernismo and the Dancer," n.p.

108. See Clayton, "Touring History" 30, 37.

109. Quoted in Aulestia, *Historias alucinantes*, 71.

110. Aulestia, *Historias alucinantes*, 67. Rouskaya, for example, showed up in Mexico City to premiere her own version of *Salome* just a few weeks after Valencia's presentation on April 25, 1918 (68).

111. For Rouskaya's Argentine citizenship see Gargurevich, *La prensa sensacionalista en el Perú*, 150; for the variations on her legal name see W. Stein, *Dance in the Cemetery*, 10.

112. See W. Stein, *Dance in the Cemetery*.

113. Aulestia, *Historias alucinantes*, 67.

114. Solrac, *Tortola Valencia*, 149.

115. See Aulestia, *Historias alucinantes*, 70–80 for the reviews of Valencia's *Salome*.

116. Aulestia, *Historias alucinantes*, 68.

117. El Abate de Mendoza quoted in Aulestia, *Historias alucinantes*, 68–69.

118. González quoted in Aulestia, *Despertar*, 65.

119. El Abate de Mendoza quoted in Aulestia, *Historias Alucinantes*, 69.

120. Diógenes Ferrand quoted in Aulestia, *Historias alucinantes*, 69.

121. I thank Michelle Clayton for identifying Solrac; personal communication, March 9, 2014.

122. Solrac, *Tortola Valencia*, 150.

123. Solrac, *Tortola Valencia*, 223.

124. Solrac, *Tortola Valencia*, 239.

125. Solrac, *Tortola Valencia*, 144.

126. de Hoyos y Vinent, English translation in Bargalló and Bargalló, "Collection or Inspiration?" 47–50.

127. Charlot, *Mexican Mural Renaissance*, 143.

128. Rivera quoted in Acevedo and García, "Procesos de quiebre," 32.

129. Charlot, *Mexican Mural Renaissance*, 143–44.

130. Charlot, *Mexican Mural Renaissance*, 266.

131. Hedrick, *Mestizo Modernism*, 167–68.

132. Bargalló and Bargalló, "Collection or Inspiration?" 37

133. Quoted in Aulestia, *Historias alucinantes*, 78.

134. Valencia quoted in Aulestia, *Historias alucinantes*, 65.

Chapter 4. The Philosopher as an Artist Writ Large: José Vasconcelos, Muralism, and Folk Art

1. Charlot, *Mexican Mural Renaissance*, 97–98.

2. Vasconcelos, *La creación*, 84.

3. Zurián, "Liquid Walls," 28. Very little information is available about Villaseñor and his workshop. In addition to realizing designs created by other artists, he did create his own designs, instructed a course in stained glass at the Academia de San Carlos, and wrote *El vitral* (Stained Glass), which was published in 1931 (see Zurián, "Liquid Walls," 26–28). Zurián attributes the "vibrant" colors of the widows to Villaseñor's influence, rather than Montenegro's "rather pallid watercolor sketches" that were used in its creation.

4. Vasconcelos, *La creación*, 75.

5. Torri quoted in Charlot, *Mexican Mural Renaissance*, 98.

6. Charlot, *Mexican Mural Renaissance*, 97.

7. Charlot, *Mexican Mural Renaissance*, 98.

8. Tiffany, Mosaic Curtain, n.p. Louis Comfort Tiffany (1848–1933) personally oversaw the construction and completion of the project. Although the promotional publication issued by Tiffany's studio did not provide the cost of this particular commission, it did report that the overall cost of the Palacio de Bellas Artes was more than US $8 million in gold. Charlot erroneously reported that Dr. Atl was responsible for the curtain's design in his *Mexican Mural Renaissance* (98).

9. Acevedo, "Las decoraciones," 171–207.

10. Vasconcelos, *Pitágoras*, 13.

11. Vasconcelos, *Pitágoras*, 106.

12. Ortiz, *Entre dos mundos*, 93.

13. López, "The Noche Mexicana," 24, 30.

14. López, *Crafting Mexico*, 78.

15. Atl, *Gentes profanos*, 59; López, "The Noche Mexicana," 24.

16. López, *Crafting Mexico*, 79.

17. Montenegro, *Planos*, 87.

18. Tugendhol'd, English translation quoted in Hilton, *Russian Folk Art*, 249.

19. Enciso, English translation quoted in López, *Crafting Mexico*, 80–81. This lack of awareness wasn't always the case. During the viceregal era, ceramics from Tonalá were popular in elite circles in Spain; in Diego Velázquez's (1599–1660) *Las Meninas* (1656), one of the maids of honor is handing one such cup to the Infanta Margarita Teresa (1651–1673). These ceramics were prized more for the "perfume" they reputedly emitted when they came into contact with water than for any other characteristic. Spanish women would even eat shards of these "exotic" ceramics as a kind of delicacy, ensuring a continued export market. (García Sáez, "Exotismo y belleza de una cerámica," 36–39.)

20. Many higher-class Mexican families held fine examples of lacquerware from

Olinalá that were popular with wealthy individuals on both sides of the Atlantic during the viceregal period. (See López, *Crafting Mexico*, 80, 206–11).

21. López, *Crafting Mexico*, 82.

22. Acevedo, "Las decoraciones," 177.

23. Atl, *Artes populares*, vol. 2, 91–95.

24. Rivera quoted in Atl, *Artes populares*, vol. 2, 94.

25. Hilton, *Russian Folk Art*, 110–13, 249.

26. English translation quoted in S. Warren, *Mikhail Larionov*, 76.

27. Scott, "La evolución de la teoría de la historia del arte," 75.

28. Barajas, *Posada: Mito y mitote*, 29.

29. Rangel quoted in *Artes populares*, vol. 2, 196.

30. Flores, *Mexico's Revolutionary Avant-Gardes*, 175.

31. Barajas, *Posada: Mito y mitote*, 29.

32. L. Suárez, "La exposición de Arte Popular," 569.

33. López, *Crafting Mexico*, 88.

34. Atl, *Artes populares*, vol. 1, 22.

35. Novo, *La estatua de sal*, 105.

36. Atl, *Artes populares*, vol. 2, 284.

37. See López, "The Noche Mexicana," 24–42, and Rodríguez, "La noche mexicana," 57–71, for the evening's activities.

38. Rodríguez, "La noche mexicana," 63.

39. Coignard, English translation quoted in Rodríguez, "La noche mexicana," 65–66.

40. Uncredited review quoted in Aulestia, *Historias alucinantes*, 107.

41. English translation of the program for the Noche Mexicana quoted in Pérez, "Nacionalismo y representación en el México posrevolucionario," 266.

42. Rodríguez, "La noche mexicana," 71.

43. Williams, *Covarrubias*, 13.

44. López, "The Noche Mexicana," 38–39.

45. Mérida quoted in Ramírez, *Crónica de las artes plásticas*, 155.

46. A. Root, "Destellos," *Excélsior* (Ciudad de México), October 8, 1921.

47. Hernandez, "El movimiento actual," *El Demócrata* (Ciudad de México), August 2, 1932.

48. Charlot, *Mexican Mural Renaissance*, 204.

49. Hernández, "El movimiento actual," *El Demócrata* (Ciudad de México), August 2, 1932.

50. Garafola, *Diaghilev's Ballets Russes*, 201–10.

51. Diego Rivera, "Dos años," *Azulejos*, December 1923, 26, 41. ICAA Record ID: 734410.

52. Vasconcelos, *Estética*, 628–29.

53. Cordero, "La invención del 'arte popular,'" 80.

54. Perhaps not coincidentally, the Tree of Life also appears in Diego Rivera's first mural commission, *Creation* (1922). It is possible that Vasconcelos suggested the same basic theme to both artists. While Vasconcelos did grant his painters a substantial amount of leeway in determining their subject maters, he was much more inclined to meddle in the musical aspects associated with his educational endeavors. See Saavedra, "Of Selves and Others," 127.

55. Vasconcelos, *La creación*, 85.

56. Fierro, *Templo del Colegio Máximo*, 114. The pseudo-Goethian theme was not the first solution to the problem of this introductory mural. According to architectural historian Rafael Fierro, the placard in a preliminary study for Montenegro's mural dated 1921 held a paraphrase attributed to Vasconcelos's beloved Homer—"The field of combat, where men achieve glory"—which was an even less apt companion to the scene Montenegro laid out in his study (121).

57. Although the decorative work that Montenegro produced for Vasconcelos appears to be bereft of the overt political agendas that would come to mark the Mexican school, it had a direct tie to the revolution. Montenegro's friend Dr. Atl persuaded him to sell one the few remaining copies of a limited-edition portfolio of his work, *Vingt Dessins* (1910), to support clandestine efforts to unseat the counterrevolutionary President Victoriano Huerta (1850–1916). Through Atl's contacts, Montenegro was able to sell this copy to a Guatemalan general, then visiting Paris as that nation's minister of foreign relations, for five hundred francs, which was multiple times its asking price. Montenegro never learned exactly how Atl used the funds from the sale of his portfolio; Atl thought it wisest to keep his basically apolitical friend in the dark as to his revolutionary activities to protect both of them. (See Montenegro, *Planos*, 50, 57–58). In his introduction to the portfolio, French Symbolist poet Henri de Régnier (1864–1936) identified *Vulerant omnes ultima necat* (All Wound, the Last Kills) (1908) as one of the publication's strongest drawings, a work that Montenegro may have selected to show in the 1910 Centennial Exhibition of the Society of Painters and Sculptors in Mexico. (See García de Germenos, "Exposición de los artistas mexicanos de 1910," 76.) This drawing, with its procession of provocatively clad femmes fatales in vaguely "oriental" costume surrounding Saint Sebastian in agony is the predecessor to the group of figures at the bottom on Montenegro's mural as it first appeared.

58. Ortiz, *Entre dos mundos*, 93.

59. Ortiz, *Entre dos mundos*, 96.

60. The *Boletín* de la Secretaría de Educación Pública for September 1922 contains photos of the still incomplete mural, labeled as "nationalist work" in the plates located between pages 314–15.

61. Fierro, *Templo del Colegio Máximo*, 121. This was not the last time the mural was altered. Photographs of the work's dedication show the knight's head still turned to one side, and his armor had the look of polished steel, not dark as it is today (See photographs reproduced on pages 122–23). Ortiz points out that an ill-conceived and improperly executed 1944 "restoration" of the work caused Montenegro to completely disown its authorship (*Entre dos mundos*, 92). Regardless of who instigated the alteration, the discomfort with the nude was not necessarily influenced by the figure's gender. Dr. Atl was also required to cover the female nudes of the murals he was painting in the same building's cloister in his supposedly permanent "atlcolors." Narciso Bassols (1897–1959), one of Vasconcelos's successors as minister of education, subsequently ordered that the Atl murals in the cloister be completely erased (see Espejo, *Dr. Atl*, 30).

62. Cartmel, "An Art Awakening," 403; Luna, *Panorama*, 65–66.

63. Fierro, *Templo del Colegio Máximo*, 123.

64. Fierro, *Templo del Colegio Máximo*, 118.

65. Charlot, *Mexican Mural Renaissance*, 97.

66. Efraín Pérez Mendoza, "Ramos Martínez y la Escuela de Coyoacán," *Revista de revistas*, February 25, 1923, 43. ICAA Record ID: 760364.

67. Charlot, *Mexican Mural Renaissance*, 65.

68. See Ortiz, "La ciudad de México durante el Porfiriato," 179–96. The general popularity of Poiret's fashion designs was also in decline by 1923. (See Harold Koda and Andrew Bolton, "Paul Poiret (1879–1944)," in *Heilbrunn Timeline of Art History* (New York: The Metropolitan Museum of Art, 2000). http://www.metmuseum.org/toah/hd/poir/hd_poir. htm. (Accessed September 17, 2019).

69. Rivera quoted in Charlot, *Mexican Mural Renaissance*, 100.

70. Hernández, "El movimiento actual," *El Demócrata* (Ciudad de México), August 2, 1923.

71. "Un Precursor del Movimiento de Arte Mexicano: El grabador Posadas," *Revista de Revistas*, August 30, 1925, 25.

72. Charlot, *Mexican Mural Renaissance*, 227.

73. David Alfaro Siqueiros, "Vasconcelos pasa del misticismo budista al catolicismo imperialista," *El Machete*, June 1927. ICAA Record ID: 764186.

74. Krauze, *Redeemers*, 67.

75. Fernández, *Montenegro*, 17.

Chapter 5. Dancing a Sandunga in English: Carlos Chávez and Diego Rivera in the United States

1. John Martin, "The Dance: A Handicap Event," *New York Times*, April 10, 1932.

2. Velasco, "Nationalism," 6.

3. Parker, "Carlos Chávez and the Ballet," 179. While Diaghilev did not pay his composers generous fees, the stream of subsequent commissions from other sources that flowed from a successful work for the Ballets Russes could prove quite lucrative (see Garafola, *Diaghilev's Ballets Russes*, 256–57 for a discussion of the economics associated with such commissions).

4. Chávez quoted in García Morillo, *Carlos Chávez*, 21.

5. Chavez's contact information is included in Bolm's address book from the 1920s. Adolph Bolm Collection, Music Division, Library of Congress (hereinafter ABC-LC), Box 3, Folder 4.

6. García Morillo, *Carlos Chávez*, 23. Bolm's passport for the period held in the Library of Congress indicates he crossed into Mexico on September 14, 1921, and returned to the US on October 6. ABC-LC, Box 3, Folder 12. Given the multiple days required to travel to Mexico City from Bolm's port of entry and return in El Paso, Texas, it is doubtful that he had time to carry out the activities García Morillo described.

7. The SEP was created by the decree of President Obregón on October 3, about the same time Bolm would have left the city. Vasconcelos was named minister on October 12.

8. According to the declaration Bolm completed before returning to the US from Mexico in 1921, he was invited to visit by the Centennial Committee. ABC-LC, Box 3, Folder 7. For Vasconcelos's opposition to the centennial celebration and his absence from the committee's membership see López, *Crafting Mexico*, 67 and 311, note 4. Unfortunately, Bolm recorded no information about this particular trip to Mexico in his incomplete memoirs, nor is the journey covered in the notes for an unpublished biography Bolm was working on with Hollywood writer Rosalind Shaffer. The page in the manuscript covering his experiences in 1921 bears nothing more than "? see notes," but no further references to the year appear in any of the associated materials. ABC-LC, Box 3, Folders 24, 27, 28.

9. Aulestia, *Despertar*, 106. The Bolm "photographic scrapbook, 1914–1962" in the New York Public Library's Performing Arts Division contains several pictures of Bolm dressed as a charro, one of which is dated Christmas 1919, which was before his trip to Mexico. It is possible that he was attired in a costume that Best created for the use of his friend Pavlova's company. The press release Bolm prepared announcing his return trip to Mexico in the spring of 1950 indicates a longstanding friendship with Best as well as with his fellow artists Miguel Covarrubias, Carlos Mérida, and Roberto Montenegro. ABC-LC Box 2, Folder 27.

10. Chávez quoted in García Morillo, *Carlos Chávez*, 21.

11. See García Morillo, *Carlos Chávez*, 19–20 and Parker, "Carlos Chávez and the Ballet," 180.

12. Saavedra, "Of Selves and Others," 161.

13. See Saavedra, "Of Selves and Others," 100–105.

14. Scheijen, Sjeng, "Diaghilev, a Russian Nationalist in the West," Presentation at Diaghilev Symposium: Worlds of Art: Diaghilev and the Ballets Russes, National Gallery of Art, Washington, DC, June 1, 2013. Recording available at http://www.nga.gov/content/ngaweb/global-site-search-page.html?searchterm=Scheijen&searchpath=%2Fcontent%2Fngaweb. (Accessed September 14, 2019).

15. Vasconcelos, *De Robinson a Odiseo*, 210.

16. Saavedra, "Of Selves and Others," 91–93.

17. Romero, "Historia," 769.

18. Uncredited employee of the SEP quoted in English translation in Saavedra, "Of Selves and Others," 93.

19. Saavedra, "Of Selves and Others," 126.

20. Saavedra, "Of Selves and Others," 162.

21. Sahagún, *Historia general*, book 7, chapters 10–13.

22. Chávez's scenario for *El Fuego Nuevo* from a program accompanying a November 4, 1930, performance of the Orquesta Sinfónica Mexicana at the Teatro Iris, reprinted in Aulestia, *Historias Alucinantes*, 145.

23. Garafola, *Diaghilev's Ballets Russes*, 52.

24. "Aztec Dance Coming, Says Famous Dancer," *Artcraft Advance*, November 12, 1917, 10. If DeMille filmed Kosloff performing an "Aztec" dance for *The Woman God Forgot*, the footage was not included in the surviving print of the motion picture. It appears that Kosloff premiered his *Aztec Spring* following the release of the film.

25. Shawn, *The American Ballet*, 19.

26. Velázquez and Vaughn, "Mestizaje and Musical Nationalism in Mexico," 101; Saavedra, "Of Selves and Others," 162. A few years before Chávez's first "Aztec" ballet, Italian-born Argentine composer Pascual de Rogatis (1880–1980) penned the music for his Aztec opera *Huemac* (1913–14), in the pentatonic mode (see Kuss, "Huemac," 68–87 and Kuss, "The 'Invention' of America," 194 for details on de Rogatis's compositional approach to this opera). De Rogatis hoped to find remnants of indigenous music in contemporary Mexican songs to provide sonic color to his composition but was disappointed with what he termed the "strange combination of Italian and Galician idioms" that he found. Instead, he turned to François Auguste Gevaert's (1828–1908) 1875 *Histoire et théorie de la musique de l'antiquité* (History and Theory of the Music of Antiquity) to represent a "prehistoric" American element. Ironically, the Italian singers who made up the original cast refused

to perform the work described by its composer as "Argentine music for America" in its original Spanish. All of its known performances were sung in Italian.

27. Parker, *Carlos Chávez*, 4.

28. Parker, *Carlos Chávez*, 123.

29. Parker, *Carlos Chávez*, 72.

30. García Morillo, *Carlos Chávez*, 11 and Halffter, *Carlos Chávez*, 19, 21.

31. Velázquez and Vaughn, "Mestizaje and Musical Nationalism," 104.

32. Letter from Octavio Barreda to Carlos Chávez dated 1925, quoted in Aluestia, *Despertar*, 111. Matisse designed the 1920 Ballets Russes production of *Le Chant du Rossignol* (The Song of the Nightingale). The libretto in question may not have been for a completed composition by Chávez. Barreda sent Chávez at least two librettos, the 1924 *La hija del boticario* (The Apothecary's Daughter) and the 1925 *El milagro de Nuestra Señora* (The Miracle of Our Lady) for his use as ballets. The poet José Gorostiza (1901–1973) also provided him with at least one proposed ballet libretto (see Aulestia, *Despertar*, 110–13).

33. Aulestia, *Despertar*, 107–8.

34. Letters from Augustín Lazo to Carlos Chávez dated 1925, quoted in Aulestia, *Despertar*, 107–8.

35. Garafola, *Diaghilev's Ballets Russes*, 218.

36. Letter from Miguel Covarrubias to Carlos Chávez dated July 20, 1927, quoted in Aulestia, *Despertar*, 115.

37. Gibson, Christina Taylor, "'Whirling around Mexico': Mabel Dodge Luhan and Carlos Chávez." Presentation at American Music Society Annual Meeting, November 5, 2016, Vancouver, Washington.

38. Rosenfeld, "Carlos Chavez," 157.

39. Parker, *A Guide to Research*, 41.

40. Parker, "Carlos Chávez and the Ballet," 194. The Vatican library contains several codices from both pre- and postconquest Mexico. The story Chávez chose to orchestrate was derived from Codex Vaticanus A, more popularly known as the Ríos Codex.

41. See Rodríguez Mortellaro, "Indigenous Antiquity," 256.

42. A digital version of the Ríos Códex is available at http://pueblosoriginarios.com/meso/valle/azteca/codices/rios/rios.html. (Accessed September 17, 2019). An English translation of a segment of the text is available through the Foundation for the Advancement of Mesoamerican Studies at http://www.famsi.org/research/pohl/jpcodices/rios/. (Accessed September 17, 2019).

43. Program notes for the Orquesta Sinfónica Mexicana, Teatro Iris, June 22, 1930, quoted in Aulestia, *Historias Alucinantes*, 147.

44. As Aztec scholar Miguel León-Portilla notes, the ten recorded versions of this creation myth that have come down to us offer some variations in the number and sequences of the various "suns." See León-Portilla, *Aztec Thought and Culture*, 37–45 for a transcribed "reading" from a preconquest codex of the *Leyenda de los soles* (Legend of the Suns) that was preserved in a text from 1558. This version corresponds to those represented in the Aztec "calendar stone." The first of the suns was that of earth, which Chávez chose to end his ballet score with as the "sun" of the Aztec state. The subsequent suns were wind, fire, water, and movement.

45. Saavedra, "Of Selves and Others," 169.

46. See Helen Delpar's *The Enormous Vogue of Things Mexican*, 123–64 for an overview of the influential promotional activities these women organized in the US at that time.

47. See Oettinger, *Folk Treasures of Mexico*, 16.

48. Delpar, *Enormous Vogue*, 84, 136–39. Apart from her Rockefeller connections and the communications with the various projects associated with the family and its patronage, very little information about Paine herself is available.

49. Dickerman, "Leftist Currents," 36.

50. Orozco, *Artist in New York*, 35.

51. Orozco, *Artist in New York*, 40.

52. Parker, "Carlos Chávez and the Ballet," 182–84.

53. Genauer, *Rufino Tamayo*, 38

54. Letter from Carlos Chávez to Pavley-Oukransky, May 24, 1928, quoted in Aulestia, *Despertar*, 108.

55. Undated typed document in the Chávez archives quoted in Aulestia, *Historias alucinantes*, 148–49.

56. Chávez quoted in García Morillo, *Carlos Chávez*, 21, in which the composer described the work as "adolescente" (adolescent).

57. Parker, "Carlos Chávez and the Ballet," 185.

58. Aulestia, *Historias alucinantes*, 147–48.

59. See Aulestia, *Historias aulcinantes*, 176–78.

60. Parker, "Carlos Chávez and the Ballet," 194–96.

61. Gibson, "Reception," 174.

62. Program notes for the International Composer's Guild, November 28, 1926, quoted in Gibson, "Reception," 174.

63. Velázquez and Vaughn, "Mestizaje and Musical Nationalism," 95–118.

64. Ballet impresario Lincoln Kirstein later claimed that he and Paine developed the scenario based on Rivera's sketches. See Gibson, "Reception," 173. Composer Rodolfo Hallfter's (1900–1987) catalogue of Chávez's work attributes its libretto to Chavez himself; see *Carlos Chávez*, 39.

65. Letter from Octavio Barreda in New York dated August 27, 1926, quoted in Aulestia, *Despertar*, 113.

66. June 10, 1927, letter from Augustín Lazo in the Chávez archives. Quoted in Aulestia, *Despertar*, 115.

67. Just as Lazo suspected, when *H.P.* was produced, John Martin of the *New York Times* found that "the subject itself is little more than 'pas d'acier' [*sic*] from another angle of vision. It perhaps seems less vital today than it did in 1926, when the composer first conceived it. From the choreographic point of view, machinery dances have been done to death" (John Martin, "Mexican Ballet in World Premiere," *New York Times*, April 1, 1932). Chávez's fellow composer Marc Blitzstein observed that machine music had become just as trite in the musical world (see Blitzstein, "Forecast and Review," 164–65). Years later Chávez acknowledged that his "machine music" followed a temporary fashion. "Although I was never one to follow trends, I liked the idea of the machine" (Chávez quoted in Daniel, *Stokowski*, 279). The idea to focus on machinery might have come from Rivera, who was fascinated by mechanical devices. The stock ticker that appeared in *H.P.* provided the only nourishment in his 1926 *Banquete de Wall Street* (Wall Street Banquet) for the walls of the SEP. Other works from the same cycle featured a sugar mill in *El trapiche* (1923) and a

generic manufacturing plant and oil derricks in the 1928 *El que quiera comer que trabaje* (He Who Would Eat Must Work). The inner workings of an electrical generator lie at the heart of his *The Making of a Fresco Showing the Building of a City* (1931) for the California School of Fine Arts (now the San Francisco Art Institute) and *Electric Power*, a portable mural created for his Museum of Modern Art solo show that he unveiled the following year. Rivera was set to begin painting his *Detroit Industry* (1932–1933) mural cycle, whose protagonist is arguably the Ford Motor Company's River Rouge manufacturing plant, shortly after the premiere of *H.P.*

68. Unidentified newspaper clipping in the archives of the Philadelphia Orchestra, December 16, 1930, quoted in Daniel, *Stokowski*, 277.

69. Christina Taylor Gibson, "'Whirling around Mexico': Mabel Dodge Luhan and Carlos Chávez." Presentation at American Music Society Annual Meeting, November 5, 2016, Vancouver, Washington.

70. Parker, "Carlos Chávez and the Ballet," 187; Daniel, *Stokowski*, 278–79.

71. In February of 1931, Stokowski seemed to describe Lazo's scenic design for *El fuego nuevo* when he told the Philadelphia *Public Ledger* that he wanted "to produce an Aztec music drama that I have found during my recent trip to Mexico. This would call for a temple on top of a pyramid. The drama has not yet been presented because the stage requirements are inadequate" (*Philadelphia Public Ledger*, February 19, 1931, quoted in Daniel, *Stokowski*, 281–82).

72. Letter from Frances Flynn Paine to Carlos Chávez, May 1, 1931, quoted in Gibson, "Reception," 173.

73. Parker, "Carlos Chávez and the Ballet," 187. For Chávez's interactions with Graham see Shirley, *Ballet for Martha*, 13–57.

74. See Gibson, "Reception," 175.

75. Parker, "Carlos Chávez and the Ballet," 187.

76. Gibson, "Reception," 175.

77. In publicizing his prior ballet presentation, the first full mounting of Igor Stravinsky's *The Rite of Spring* in the US in 1930, Stokowski attempted to provide the "primitive" modernist work with a Native American frame. Stokowski told the musical press that "many tribes of Indians in this country have similar ritualistic ceremonies every spring. . . . For this reason we are not making this particular production of any particular country or period" ("Stokowski Discusses 'Le Sacre,'" *Musical Leader*, March 20, 1930). The production, however, basically recycled Nicholas Roerich's (1874–1947) costumes and sets for Diaghilev's 1913 production inspired by the Russian past. If the audience knew of Stokowski's claims, Roerich's evocation of prehistoric Russia must have stuck them as equally applicable to the pre-Columbian Americas. *Time* magazine even opened its review of what it characterized as "the musical event of the year" by noting that the Stravinsky work was presented at the same time that Yaqui Indians—a people common to both Mexico and the US—were "performing their vernal rites in desert Arizona" ("Spring Rite," *Time*, April 28, 1930, 57).

78. Daniel, *Stokowski*, 282–83.

79. See Instituto Nacional para el Federalismo y el Desarrollo Municipal, "Santo Domingo Tehuantepec. Estado de Oaxaca," *Enciclopedia de los Municipios y Delegaciones de México*. http://www.inafed.gob.mx/work/enciclopedia/EMM20oaxaca/. (Accessed September 14, 2019).

80. "Salió para Michoacán el maestro Stokowski," *Excélsior* (Mexico City), February 17, 1932.

81. "Chokopul's Travels," *Time*, April 11, 1932, 28. "Chokopul" does not appear to be a word belonging to the Purépecha of the Trascan people or the Nahuatl people still in use by some descendants of the Aztecs.

82. Harry L. Hewes, "The Mexican Ballet-Symphony 'H.P.,'" 421.

83. Quoted in Gibson, "Reception," 168.

84. Gibson, "Reception," 168.

85. According to García Morillo's biography of the composer, his father's family was of entirely Spanish descent. His maternal grandfather did have some Indian ancestry (*Carlos Chávez*, 11).

86. See Gibson, "Reception," 168.

87. Quoted in Garafola, "*H.P.*," 226.

88. Gibson, "Reception," 182.

89. "En lo futuro no sera el arte cosa de lujo sino necesidad vital," *Excélsior* (Mexico City), April 19, 1932.

90. Garafola, "*H.P.*," 226.

91. Program notes reprinted in Hewes, "The Mexican Ballet-Symphony 'H.P.,'" 421–22.

92. Program notes reprinted in Hewes, "The Mexican Ballet-Symphony 'H.P.,'" 424.

93. Program notes reprinted in Hewes, "The Mexican Ballet-Symphony 'H.P.,'" 423–24.

94. See Belnap, "Diego Rivera's Greater America," 61–98.

95. Martin quoted in Parker, "Carlos Chávez and the Ballet," 192.

96. Garafola, "*H.P.*," 227.

97. Belnap, "Diego Rivera's Greater America," 85–86.

98. "En lo futuro no sera el arte cosa de lujo sino necesidad vital," *Excélsior* (Mexico City), April 19, 1932.

99. For Dolinoff's dancing career see Garafola, "*H.P.*," 246, note 41.

100. Martin, "Mexican Ballet," 16.

101. Mary F. Watkins, "Chavez's Ballet, 'H.P.,' Has Debut in Philadelphia," *New York Herald Tribune*, April 1, 1932.

102. Mary F. Watkins, "Current Events in Dance World," *New York Herald Tribune*, April 10, 1932.

103. Martin, "Mexican Ballet," 16.

104. Carlos Mérida claimed to have seen *Parade* during his Paris sojourn (Mendoza, "Su contribución a la danza," 58). Mérida shared Rivera's social circle while the two were working and studying in Paris and subsequently worked with Rivera in Mexico in painting the 1922 *Creación* (Creation), which was Rivera's first mural (Monsiváis, "Perdurabilidad," 21). He could have discussed the work with him.

105. Watkins, "Chavez's Ballet."

106. Martin, "Mexican Ballet."

107. Martin, "The Dance: A Handicap Event."

108. Blitzstein, "Forecast and Review," 166. Rivera's "The Cocoanut" and "On the Boat," for *H.P.* appeared in the March–April 1932 issue of *Modern Music* on pages 98 and 114, respectively.

109. Kahlo, quoted in H. Herrera, *Frida*, 132.

110. Portell Vila quoted in Aulestia, *Despertar,* 119.

111. Blitzstein, "Forecast and Review," 164.

112. Paul Rosenfeld, "American Premières," *New Republic*, April 20, 1932, 273–74.

113. Bltizstein, "Music and Theatre," 165.

114. "Chokopul's Travels," *Time*, April 11, 1932.

115. Reiss quoted in Gibson, "Reception," 158.

116. Edward Allen Jewell, "Mural Artists a TipToe," *New York Times*, April 10, 1932.

Chapter 6. A Question of Technique: Carlos Mérida and a Mexican School of Dance

1. Pedroza, "José Vasconcelos," 137.

2. Krauze, *Mexico*, 430.

3. Buchenau, "Plutarco Elías Calles," 239.

4. English translation quoted in Buchenau, "Plutarco Elías Calles," 235.

5. Vaughn, *Cultural Politics in Revolution*, 5.

6. See Buchenau, "Plutarco Elías Calles," 229–53 for a discussion of the Maximato and Calles's role in the era's politics.

7. Ortíz quoted in Aulestia, *Despertar*, 258.

8. Aulestia, *Despertar*, 259.

9. Aulestia, *Historias alucinantes*, 207–9.

10. Carbajal, "El nacionalismo," 69, 71.

11. Aulestia, *Historias alucinantes*, 205.

12. Garduño, "Diego Rivera," 14.

13. Vasconcelos quoted in Tovar, "Presentación," 7.

14. Santiago, *Las Misiones Culturales*, 18.

15. Morales Mora, "Utopía," 104.

16. Santiago, *Las Misiones Culturales*, 26.

17. Mendoza reprinted one of these efforts documenting the danza de los viejitos (dance of the little old men) from Michoacán in *Escritos de Carlos Mérida sobre la danza*, 78–85.

18. Carbajal, "El nacionalismo," 80.

19. Vaughn, *Cultural Politics*, 25.

20. Vaughn, *Cultural Politics*, 12, 45–46.

21. *La educación pública en México, 1934–40*, quoted in Santiago, *Misiones Culturales*, 48.

22. Letter from Alfonso Pruneda to Hipólito Zybin, February 6, 1931, quoted in Aulestia, *Despertar*, 261.

23. For Chávez's participation in this discussion see Tortajada, *Danza y poder*, vol. 1, 87.

24. Carbajal, "El nacionalismo," 76.

25. Carbajal, "El nacionalismo," 71.

26. Aulestia, *Despertar*, 51–52, 262.

27. Carbajal, "El nacionalismo," 75.

28. Carbajal, "El nacionalismo," 90.

29. Carbajal, "El nacionalismo," 171.

30. Carbajal, "El nacionalismo," 73.

31. See Ramos, *La danza en México durante la* época *colonial*, 29–30.

32. Aulestia, *Las "chicas bien,"* 39.

33. Zybin quoted in Tortajada, *Danza y poder*, vol. 1, 85.

34. Festival program, Teatro de la SEP, October 23, 1931, reprinted in Aulestia, *Despertar*, 262.

35. Oficina Cultural Radiotelefónica, English translation quoted in Hayes, "National Imaginings on the Air: Radio in Mexico, 1920–1950," 249.

36. Carbajal, "El nacionalismo," 84.

37. Aulestia, *Despertar*, 263. Gómezanda's entire Aztec ballet, sometimes known as *Xiuthtzquilo*, received a performance in Berlin's Nollendorfplatz Theater in 1928 (Aulestia, *Las "chicas bien,"* 8). Its production under Erwin Piscator featured choreography by Ruth Allerhand, who was subsequently active in Workers Dance League productions in the US.

38. "Grandes fiestas para celebrar la fecha de la Revolución mañana," *Excélsior* (Ciudad de México), November 19, 1931.

39. See Aulestia, *Despertar*, 280–83.

40. "Hermoso festival habido en la Secretaría de Educación para celebrar nuestra Revolución," *Excélsior* (Ciudad de México), November 23, 1931.

41. Aulestia, "Nellie Campobello," 15.

42. Carbajal, "El nacionalismo," 80.

43. Zybin quoted in Aluestia, *Despertar*, 263–64.

44. See Flores, *Mexico's Revolutionary Avant Gardes*, 72–80 for a discussion of the political implications associated with this festival and Fernando Leal's *The Feast of the Lord of Chalma* (1922–1923), one of Vasconcelos's early mural commissions.

45. Tortajada, *Danza y poder*, vol. 1, 88.

46. Aluestia, *Despertar*, 264.

47. Tortajada, *Danza y poder*, vol. 1, 89. Tortajada did not indicate at whose behest the Mexican Secretaría de Gobernación issued its expulsion order.

48. Mendoza, Introducción, 17.

49. Aulestia, *Despertar*, 258.

50. Aulestia, *Despertar*, 265.

51. See Aulestia, *Despertar*, 312–16.

52. Tamayo quoted in Madrigal, "Tamayo y los Contemporáneos," 162.

53. Diego Rivera, "Arte puro, puros maricones," *Choque, Órgano de la Alianza de Trabajadores de las Artes Plásticas* (Mexico City), March 27, 1934. ICAA Record ID: 822465.

54. See Madrigal, "Tamayo," 165–67.

55. See Monsiváis, "Los que tenemos," 18–21.

56. de los Reyes, "Tres documentos," 250.

57. "Documento del Consejo de Bellas Artes," reprinted in de los Reyes, "Tres documentos," 256.

58. "Documento del Consejo de Bellas Artes," reprinted in de los Reyes, "Tres documentos," 256–57.

59. Undated letter from Carlos Chávez to Narciso Bassols, reprinted in de los Reyes, "Tres documentos," 253.

60. "Documento del Consejo de Bellas Artes," reprinted in de los Reyes, "Tres documentos," 257.

61. "Documento del Consejo de Bellas Artes," reprinted in de los Reyes, "Tres documentos," 254.

62. For Tamayo's use of Best's *Metodo* see M. Velázquez, "The Best Maugard Drawing

Method," 291–95; "Documento del Consejo de Bellas Artes," reprinted in de los Reyes, "Tres documentos," 254–55.

63. "Documento del Consejo de Bellas Artes," reprinted in de los Reyes, "Tres documentos," 255.

64. See "La Escuela de Danza de la Secretaría de Educación Pública," March 15, 1932, reprinted in Mérida, *Escritos*, 279–83.

65. de los Reyes, "Tres documentos," 251.

66. Mérida, "Autorretrato," quoted in Mendoza, Introducción, 31.

67. See Mendoza, Introducción, 28–29. Critic Raquel Tibol also attributed Merida's interest in establishing a Mexican dance culture to his years in Paris but claimed it was his friendships with Picasso and Kees Van Dongen (1877–1968) that provoked this interest. Both Rivera and Siqueiros, whose work Tibol supported, derided Anglada's work and his influence on Latin American painters (Tibol quoted in Tortajada, *Danza y Poder*, vol. 1, 93.)

68. See Mendoza, "Contribución," 162.

69. Mérida quoted in Ramírez, *Crónica de las artes plásticas*, 115.

70. Mérida, *Modern Mexican Artists*, 106.

71. See Espinoza, "Notas," 47.

72. Torres Michúa, "Geometría," 53.

73. See Mendoza, Introducción, 33.

74. See Saavedra, "Of Selves and Others," 234–37.

75. Mérida, "Pre-Hispanic Dance," 564.

76. Mérida, "Pre-Hispanic Dance," 568.

77. Carbajal, "El nacionalismo," 106.

78. Mérida, "Pre-Hispanic Dance," 564.

79. "Programa del Festival de Danzas Mexicanas," November 10, 11, and 13, 1934, in Mérida, *Escritos*, 96.

80. Mérida, "Pre-Hispanic Dance," 567.

81. I have been unable to locate a published version of the legend on which this dance was purportedly based.

82. See Luna, *Ana Mérida*, 84–85, which reprints the work's program notes.

83. Delpar, *Enormous Vogue*, 75.

84. Carbajal, "El nacionalismo," 123; Aulestia, *Despertar*, 352–53.

85. See Aulestia, *Historias alucinantes*, 263–73.

86. Aulestia, *Historias alucinantes*, 260.

87. Arturo Zepeda, "El plastodonte blanco o Palacio de Bellas Artes," *Frente a frente* 1, November 1934, 15. ICAA Record ID: 774376.

88. "Tres bellas obras de ballet para el deleite de la clase trabajadora de esta capital," *Excélsior* (Ciudad de México), October 8, 1934.

89. Aluestia, *Historias alucinantes*, 270.

90. "Programa del Festival de Danzas Mexicanas," November 10, 11, and 13, 1934, in Mérida, *Escritos*, 91.

91. Letter to the minister of education dated August 1, 1934, quoted in Carbajal, "El nacionalismo," 124.

92. See "En el Palacio de Bellas Artes fue inaugurado ayer el nuevo Museo de Arte Popular nuestro," *Excélsior* (Mexico City), October 2, 1934, for the announcement of the

new museum. Montenegro directed the Museum of Popular Arts that was installed in the building's galleries between 1940 and 1947 (Fernandez, *Roberto Montenegro*, 19).

93. John Simon Guggenheim Foundation, "Martha Graham. Report." http://www.gf.org/fellows/all-fellows/martha-graham/. (Accessed September 14, 2019). For an overview of Graham's activities during her 1932 trip to Mexico see Snow, "Martha Graham."

94. Stark Young, "Town Melange," *New Republic*, December 23, 1931, 163.

95. McDonagh, *Martha Graham*, 85. If this interview was ever printed, it was not included in Graham's extensive scrapbooks of clippings now housed in the Library of Congress.

96. Soares, *Louis Horst*, 94.

97. McDonagh, *Martha Graham*, 85.

98. For Mérida, see Mendoza, "Contribución," 168; for Campobello see Tortajada, *Danza y Poder*, vol. 1, 97.

99. Louis Horst's unpublished "Professional Chronology," held in the Performing Arts Division of the New York Public Library, offers the only detailed information about Graham's visit to Mexico. These dates are derived from that document. See Snow, "Martha Graham," 9.

100. Freida Balk, "An Interview with a Great Danseuse," *Scope* (Newark, NJ), March 30, 1933; Dallal, "Martha Graham," 141–63.

101. Letter from Carlos Chávez to Martha Graham, August 29, 1931. Robert L. Parker Collection, Latin American Center for Graduate Studies in Music, Catholic University of America.

102. Herrera Carrillo, *Pablo Herrera Carrillo*, 239.

103. Cornejo quoted in Cartmel, "An Art Awakening," 402.

104. Villalba, *Mexican Calendar Girls*, 131.

105. J. Ortiz, "Desaparecerá el Rancho del Artista?" *Jueves del Excélsior* (Ciudad de México), February 27, 1958; "El Rancho del Artista ha entrado en agonía," *Impacto*, January 29, 1958: 38–41.

106. Tortajada, *Danza y poder*, vol. 1, 120.

107. For Mérida's exhibition opportunities in the US as compared to Mexico, see Monsiváis, "Perdurabilidad," 24.

108. Mérida, "La danza y el teatro," *Escritos*, 143.

109. Mérida, "Pre-Hispanic Dance and Theatre," 568.

110. Graham, "Seeking an American Art," 252.

Chapter 7. Competing Modernisms: Anna Sokolow and Waldeen

1. Carbajal, "El nacionalismo," 179–92.

2. Cárdenas quoted in Tortajada, "La Coronela," 54.

3. Tortajada, *Danza y poder*, vol. 1, 149–51; Carbajal, "El nacionalismo," 145–52. Gorostiza led a campaign to have Nellie removed from her position and nearly succeeded, though the decision was apparently overturned by someone at a higher level of command within the Mexican government (Tortajada, *Danza y poder*, vol. 1, 151, note 72).

4. Tortajada, *Danza y poder*, vol. 1, 245.

5. M. Covarrubias, "Florecimiento," 413.

6. Bravo quoted in Delgado, *Guillermina Bravo*, 27.

7. Barros Sierra, quoted in Tortajada, *Danza y poder*, vol. 1, 227.

8. Mérida, "Notas autobiográficas," quoted in Mendoza, Introducción, 32–33.

9. Carbajal, "El nacionalismo," 127–31.

10. "Síntesis de los principios declarativos de la LEAR," *Frente a Frente,* November 1934, 3. ICAA Record ID: 774370.

11. Mérida, *Escritos,* 144.

12. See Homans, *Apollo's Angels,* 341–95 for a succinct trajectory of classical ballet in the Soviet Union. In a document that Mérida scholar Cristina Mendoza believes contained the preliminary notes for his remarks before the congress, the artist included a brief analysis of *The Red Poppy* (1927) as a typical example of Soviet ballet (Mérida, *Escritos,* 140–41).

13. Mérida, *Escritos,* 146.

14. Mérida, *Escritos,* 146–48.

15. "El socialismo en la danza y en la música," *Excélsior* (Mexico City), January 24, 1937, 10.

16. "Resumen del Congreso Nacional de Escritores y Artistas convocado por la LEAR," Frente a Frente 8, March 1937, 24. ICAA Record ID: 779402.

17. For a review of Sokolow's central place in the socially conscious dance of the twentieth century see Kosstrin, "Inevitable Designs," 4–24.

18. Sokolow quoted in Lynton, "Anna Sokolow," 12. Warren relates a similar story in *Anna Sokolow,* 63.

19. Mérida, *Escritos,* 147.

20. See Jones, "American Modernism," 51–69.

21. Kosstrin, "Inevitable Designs," 7.

22. See Kosstrin, "Inevitable Designs," 5–23.

23. Lynton, "Sokolow," 9.

24. Sokolow quoted in L. Warren, *Anna Sokolow,* 45.

25. Sokolow quoted in Kosstrin, "Inevitable Designs," 8.

26. L. Warren, *Anna Sokolow,* 63.

27. L. Warren, *Anna Sokolow,* 64; Kosstrin, "Inevitable Designs," 6.

28. Kramer quoted in L. Warren, *Anna Sokolow,* 66.

29. Rodríguez quoted in Musacchio, *Taller,* 25.

30. Musacchio, *Taller,* 27.

31. Sokolow quoted in Lynton, "Anna Sokolow," 13.

32. Perucho, "El surgimiento," 45.

33. Uncredited article quoted in English translation in L. Warren, *Anna Sokolow,* 68.

34. Carbajal, "El nacionalismo," 194.

35. Reyna quoted in Lynton, "Anna Sokolow," 16.

36. L. Warren, *Anna Sokolow,* 70.

37. Carredano, "Hasta los verdes maizales," 70.

38. Carredano, "Hasta los verdes maizales," 74.

39. See L. Warren, *Anna Sokolow,* 71.

40. Perucho, "Surgimiento," 45; Lynton, "Anna Sokolow," 14.

41. Carredano, "Hasta los verdes maizales," 87.

42. Bal y Gay quoted in Carredano, "Hasta los verdes maizales," 87–88.

43. Uncredited newspaper review quoted in Perucho, "Surgimiento," 45.

44. Bellas Artes Program, March 1940, quoted in Lynton, "Anna Sokolow," 15.

45. Flores, quoted in Lynton, "Anna Sokolow," 15.

46. Nabor Hurtado González, "Notas del Arte: 'El Renacuajo Paseador' Obra Póstuma del Gran Silvestre Revueltas," *El Nacional*, October 7, 1940.

47. Kolb, *Silvestre Revueltas*, n.p.

48. Tortajada, *Danza y poder*, vol. 1, 202.

49. Revueltas quoted in Kolb, "Colorines," 211.

50. Kolb, "Colorines," 196, 212.

51. Margarita Tortajada reconstructs the battle through selections from a series of newspaper and magazine articles in *Danza y poder*, vol. 1, 213–18.

52. See Tortajada, *Danza y poder*, vol. 1, 211.

53. Tortajada, *Danza y poder*, vol. 1, 210.

54. Barros Sierra quoted in Tortajada, *Danza y poder*, vol. 1, 204.

55. See, for example, Moya quoted in Tortajada, *Danza y poder*, vol. 1, 229.

56. "Martha Graham Reflects on Her Art and a Life in Dance," *New York Times*, March 31, 1985.

57. L. Warren, *Anna Sokolow*, 74.

58. L. Warren, *Anna Sokolow*, 85.

59. Sokolow quoted by Angelina B. Camargo, "La mayoría de bailarines jóvenes copia a los grandes de la danza, sin buscar nuevos lenguajes: Anna Sokolow," *Excélsior* (Mexico City), May 18, 1980.

60. Horst quoted in L. Warren, *Anna Sokolow*, 114.

61. Lynton, "Anna Sokolow," 29.

62. Reyna quoted in Lynton, "Anna Sokolow," 15–16.

63. Cohen, "Waldeen," 226.

64. Lavalle, *En busca*, 119.

65. Cohen, "Waldeen," 226.

66. Pierre, "A Dancer Emerges," 9.

67. Cohen, "Waldeen," 227–28; Pierre, "A Dancer Emerges," 9.

68. Pierre, "A Dancer Emerges," 9.

69. Lavalle, *En busca*, 120. For Wigman's tours see Wigman, *Liebe Hanya*, 11–20 and Jennifer Dunning, "Hanya Holm Is Dead at 99—Influential Choreographer," *New York Times*, November 4, 1992. Wigman completed a third US tour in 1932–1933, after Waldeen joined Ito's company. See Wigman, *Liebe Hanya*, 35.

70. Lavalle, *En busca*, 121.

71. Quoted in Aulestia, *Historias alucinantes*, 254.

72. Quoted in Aluestia, *Despertar*, 336.

73. Dancer, composer, and mask-maker "Josef," born José Cordelio Cárdenas and also known as Joseph Broun, remained along with her (Aulestia, *Despertar*, 371). He went on to adopt a new stage name, the pseudo-Mayan "Dzul" and present imagined recreations of pre-Columbian dance from 1935 to 1937 in both Mexico and the US (Aluestia, *Historias alucinantes*, 277–85).

74. Waldeen quoted in Cohen, "Waldeen and the Americas," 229.

75. Núñez y Domínguez, quoted in Aulestia *Despertar*, 343.

76. Pierre, "A Dancer Emerges," 9, 39.

77. Lavalle, *En busca*, 128.

78. John Martin, "The Dance: Organization. New Federation on West Coast Has Broad Scope," *New York Times*, February 20, 1938.

79. Cohen, "Waldeen," 227.

80. John Martin, "The Dance. New York Debut of Waldeen," *New York Times*, February 14, 1938, 21.

81. Jerome D. Bohm, "Walden Seen 1st Time Here in Dance Program," *New York Herald Tribune*, February 14, 1938.

82. Tortajada, *Danza y poder*, vol. 1, 219.

83. Tortajada, "La Coronela," 55.

84. Boletín no. 1 of the Teatro de las Artes, May 22, 1940, quoted in Lavalle, *En busca*, 135–36.

85. Mérida, *Modern Mexican Artists*, 65.

86. Lavalle, *En busca*, 150.

87. Lavalle, *En busca*, 137.

88. Tortajada, *Danza y poder*, vol. 1, 225–26.

89. Lavalle, *En busca*, 142.

90. Waldeen quoted in Lavalle, *En busca*, 143

91. Lavalle quoted in Tortajada, *Danza y poder*, vol. 1, 225. According to Tortajada, multiple individuals reported Nellie Campobello as having threatened them with a gun. Personal communication, January 9, 2017.

92. Bravo quoted in Delgado, *Guillermina Bravo*, 21.

93. Delgado, *Guillermina Bravo*, 21; Tortajada, *Amalia Hernández*, 20.

94. Lavalle, *En busca*, 174.

95. Lavalle, *En busca*, 146–48.

96. Moya quoted in Tortajada, *Danza y poder*, vol. 1, 229.

97. L. Warren, *Anna Sokolow*, 75.

98. Waldeen quoted in Tortajada, "La Coronela," 55.

99. Program, Palacio de Bellas Artes, November 23, 1940, quoted in Tortajada, *Danza y poder*, vol. 1, 231.

100. Waldeen quoted in Cohen, "Waldeen," 234.

101. Revueltas was at work on the score for *La Coronela* when he died, having completed only short piano sketches for the first three segments of the dance, with minimal indications as to orchestration. See Kolb, "Silvestre Revueltas," 29–30. Blas Galindo composed the remainder of the score.

102. Perucho, "Surgimiento," 50.

103. Perucho, "Surgimiento," 52.

104. Program, Ballet de Bellas Artes, Palacio de Bellas Artes, November 1940, quoted in Lavalle, *En busca*, 160.

105. Lavalle, *En busca*, 161.

106. Musacchio, *Taller*, 21, 28.

107. Barajas's *Posada: Mito y mitote* provides a highly detailed account of the muralist's adoption, and sometimes misrepresentation, of Posada's work.

108. Barajas, *Posada*, 22. Barajas went on in his study to deconstruct Posada's imputed prorevolutionary sympathies.

109. Lavalle, *En busca*, 170–71.

110. Tortajada, "La Coronela," 59.

111. Corn, *Great American Thing*, 103–4, 346.

112. Lavalle, *En busca*, 157.

113. Orozco quoted in González, *Orozco, escenógrafo*, 46.

114. Tortajada, *Danza y poder*, vol. 1, 490.

115. Lavalle, *En busca*, 162.

116. Charlot, *Mexican Mural Renaissance*, 154.

117. Moya quoted in Tortajada, *Danza y poder,* vol. 1, 235.

118. Lavalle, *En busca*, 162.

119. Lavalle, *En busca*, 105.

120. Covarrubias, "Florecimiento," 412.

121. Tortajada, "La Coronela," 58.

122. Tortajada, "La Coronela," 59.

123. Delgado, *Guillermina Bravo*, 23.

124. Tortajada, *Danza y poder,* vol. 1, 323, note 136.

125. Tortajada, *Danza y poder,* vol. 1, 325.

126. Delgado, *Guillermina Bravo*, 24.

127. Tortajada, *Danza y poder*, vol. 1, 325.

128. Cohen, "Waldeen," 235.

129. "Premiere of Tudor Work by Ballet Theatre," *New York Times*, April 11, 1948. Because the title of the work is the only piece of information provided by the *Times*, it is impossible to know if this work was a direct precursor to her 1949 performance of Neruda's *Let the Rail Splitter Awake* at the American Continental Congress for World Peace in Mexico City. Like *La Coronela*, the work included a mix of music and spoken text, part of which was provided by actress Rosaura Revueltas, composer Silvestre's younger sister, as well as by Bolivian painter Roberto Berdecio and Neruda himself. Music for the work was penned by Hershey Kay based on North American folk songs (Cohen, "Neruda in English," 58).

Chapter 8. Ballets without Ballerinas? José Clemente Orozco and the Ballet de la Ciudad de México

1. In her study of Nellie Campobello, dance historian Sophie Bidault proposes that the Campobellos's decision to re-embrace classical ballet was largely shaped by their contact with Martín Luis Guzmán (Bidault, *Nellie Campobello*, 136–73).

2. Tortajada, *Danza y poder*, vol. 1, 273–74. Although Massine severed his partnership with de Basil and, following a legal battle, won the right to call his new company the Ballets Russes de Monte Carlo, he lost the rights to the choreography he created over much of the 1930s. Thus, his symphonic ballets such *Les Présages* (1933) and *Choreartium* (1933) remained in the de Basil repertory. The company's programs in Mexico City weren't entirely composed of older works. George Balanchine's (1904–1983) *Cotillion* (1932) was new to the Mexican audience, as was David Lichine's (1910–1972) *Graduation Ball* (1940).

3. Quoted in Tortajada, *Danza y poder*, vol. 1, 275.

4. Salazar quoted in Tortajada, *Danza y poder*, vol. 1, 283.

5. Campobello quoted in Tortajada, *Danza y poder*, vol. 1, 285.

6. Sutton, *The Making of Markova*, 432–33.

7. Massine, *My Life*, 224.

8. Norris, *Leonide Massine*, 268.

9. Massine, *My Life*, 225. Just as the Russian dancer and choreographer identified the Yaqui work with the rustic peasant rather than the indigenous primitive, he also responded

to the city differently from his colleagues in the US, who almost uniformly found Mexico inherently primitive. He thought Mexico City a "cosmopolitan town which seemed neither American nor European" (223).

10. Norris, *Leonide Massine*, 268.

11. Souchy quoted in Tortajada, *Danza y poder*, vol. 1, 284–85.

12. Salazar quoted in Tortajada, *Danza y poder*, vol. 1, 283–84.

13. Robbins quoted in Jowett, *Jerome Robbins*, 62.

14. Norris, *Leonide Massine*, 353, note 1098.

15. Robert Lawrence, "Mexican Problem," *New York Herald Tribune*, October 10, 1942.

16. Bowles, "Films and Theater," *Modern Music*, November–December 1942, reprinted in *Paul Bowles on Music*, 55. Currently available recordings of the "score" for *La Coronela* are based on a "recreation" of the work in the 1950s by José Limantour (1919–1976), which ignored Revueltas's original intent. See Kolb, "Silvestre Revueltas," 29–30.

17. John Martin, "Mexican Ballet Given by Theatre," *New York Times*, October 10, 1942.

18. Aulestia, "Nellie Campobello," 15–16.

19. Vargas y Garcia quoted in Bidault, *Nellie Campobello*, 95–96, 105. Klahn, "Nellie Campobello," 60 provides one English-language version of Nellie Campobello's origin story.

20. Campobello, quoted in Aluestia, "Nellie Campobello," 2.

21. Campobello, "Yo," reprinted in Aulestia, "Nellie Campobello," 2.

22. Bidault, *Nellie Campobello*, 115, note 32.

23. Rosas, "Nahui, Antonieta y Nellie," 5.

24. Bidault, *Nellie Campobello*, 105.

25. Aulestia, "Nellie Campobello," 3.

26. Quoted in Aulestia, *Las "chicas bien,"* 74.

27. Aluestia, *Historias alucinantes*, 203; Klahn, "Nellie Campobello," 60.

28. Carbajal, "El nacionalismo," 64.

29. Toor, "Jarabe," 34.

30. Reynoso, "Choreographing Politics," 188–89.

31. Bidault, *Nellie Campobello*, 48.

32. Quoted in Tortajada, *Danza y poder*, vol. ,1 162.

33. Quoted in Tortajada, *Danza y poder*, vol. 1, 163.

34. Bidault, *Nellie Campobello*, 129

35. Mérida, *Escritos*, 142.

36. Barros Sierra, quoted in Tortajada, *Danza y poder*, vol. 1, 169.

37. Dromundo quoted in Tortajada, *Danza y poder*, vol. 1, 172.

38. Barros Sierra quoted in Tortajada, *Danza y poder*, vol. 1, 168–69.

39. See Aulestia, *Historias alucinantes*, 267–68 for the lengthy critical drubbing of *Union Pacific* by "Elizondo," likely the dramatist José Elizando, the critic for *Excélsior*.

40. Barros Sierra quoted in Tortajada, *Danza y poder*, vol. 1, 168–69.

41. Dromundo, "El teatro," quoted in Tortajada, *Danza y poder*, vol. 1, 171.

42. Diego Rivera, *Retrato de Martín Guzmán* (1915), Colección Fundación Televisa. Like Rivera's monumental *Paisaje Zapatista* (Zapatista Landscape) from the same year, the portrait of Guzmán incorporates a serape as a symbol of Mexican identity.

43. Quoted in Tortajada, *Danza y poder*, vol. 1, 271–72.

44. Guzmán, "España," 275.

45. Tortajada, *Danza y poder,* vol. 1, 272.

46. Nellie's subsequent presentation of *Spectre* featured a female dancer in the role. See Tortajada, *Danza y poder*, vol. 1, 287.

47. Tortajada, *Danza y poder,* vol. 1, 272–73.

48. Orozco quoted in González, *Orozco, escenógrafo*, 46.

49. Segura, *Gloria Campobello*, 8.

50. Orozco, *Artist in New York*, 90.

51. Tibol, *Orozco*, 172.

52. Tibol, *Orozco*, 174.

53. Orozco quoted in Segura, *Gloria Campobello*, 58. Nellie Campobello's claim that she owned more than two thousand would have required an almost daily correspondence between them from the time they met until Gloria broke off their relationship early in 1946 (55).

54. Segura, *Gloria Campobello*, 59.

55. Segura, *Gloria Campobello*, 59–62.

56. Reed, *Orozco*, 282. For Reed's possible nonbusiness relationship with Orozco see Anreus, *Gringoland*, 2, 30–31, 40, and 153,note 60. Reed's memory of Orozco's relationship with the Campobello sisters and the dance is subject to some question. She also reported that the composer José Pablo Moncayo told her that Orozco's designs for *Alameda 1900*, which were the work of Julio Castellanos, "were a great work of art" (*Orozco*, 282–83).

57. Brenner, *Mexican Holiday*, 261.

58. González, *Orozco, escenógrafo*, 12, 14.

59. González, *Orozco, escenógrafo*, 20.

60. Orozco quoted in González, *Orozco, escenógrafo*, 22.

61. For Montenegro's participation in *Aleko* see Balderas, *Sensualidad renovada*, 111.

62. Orozco, quoted in Tortajada, *Danza y poder,* vol. 1, 289.

63. Tibol, *Orozco*, 173.

64. González, *Orozco, escenógrafo*, 48–50.

65. Orozco, *Orozco Explains*, 6–7. Emphasis in the original.

66. González, *Orozco, escenógrafo*, 23.

67. Orozco quoted in González, *Orozco, escenógrafo*, 53.

68. Luna quoted in Tortajada, *Danza y poder*, vol. 1, 289.

69. Tortajada, *Danza y poder*, vol. 1, 289.

70. Tortajada provides extensive citations from the reviews of various critics who attended the premiere in *Danza y poder*, vol. 1, 289–93.

71. See Aulestia, "Nellie Campobello," 22.

72. "Bella función de ballet hubo en el Palacio de B. Artes," *Excélsior* (Ciudad de México), June 29, 1943.

73. González, *Orozco, escenógrafo*, 62.

74. González, *Orozco, escenógrafo*, 61.

75. *Tiempo* quoted in Tortajada, *Danza y poder*, vol. 1, 293.

76. See Tortajada, *Danza y poder,* vol. 1, 294–96 for a discussion of the company's working conditions.

77. Reyes quoted in Tortajada, *Danza y poder*, vol. 1, 302.

78. Mora, quoted in Tortajada, *Danza y poder*, vol. 1, 299.

79. Tibón quoted in Tortajada, *Danza y poder*, vol. 1, 303.

80. *El Redondel* quoted in Tortajada, *Danza y poder*, vol. 1, 305.

81. S. H. quoted in Tortajada, *Danza y poder*, vol. 1, 304.

82. José Clemente Orozco, "No es una Improvisación el Ballet Organizado Aquí. Lo Estuvieron Preparando 10 Años y es una 'Realidad Indestructible,'" *Excélsior* (Ciudad de México), March 21, 1945.

83. John Martin, "Ballet Theatre Opens Its Season," *New York Times*, October 7, 1942.

84. John Martin, "Decor by Chagall Dominates Ballet," *New York Times*, October 25, 1945.

85. Velasco, "Nationalism," 14–18.

86. Segura, *Gloria Campobello*, 49.

87. Carlos Chávez, quoted in translation in Velasco, "Nationalism," 15.

88. Carbajal, "El nacionalismo," 201, note 261.

89. Presidential decree quoted in Aulestia, "Nellie Campobello," 13.

90. Segura, *Gloria Campobello*, 47.

91. Anreus, *Gringolandia*, 135–41.

92. Tortajada, *Danza y poder*, vol. 1, 431.

93. Tapia quoted in Segura, *Gloria Campobello*, 60.

94. Segura, *Gloria Campobello*, 59.

95. Tapia quoted in Segura, *Gloria Campobello*, 61.

96. Tapia quoted in Segura, *Gloria Campobello*, 62.

97. Reed, *Orozco*, 273–74.

98. Quoted in Tortajada, *Danza y poder*, vol. 1, 431.

99. Segura, *Gloria Campobello*, 47.

100. Sutton, *The Making of Marakova*, 491.

101. See Aulestia, "Nellie Campobello," 23.

102. Quoted in Tortajada, *Danza y poder*, vol. 1, 314.

103. See Aulestia, "Nellie Campobello," 22–23.

104. Junius, "Chopiniana-Ixtepec-Divertissement no. 2," *Excélsior* (Ciudad de México), September 7, 1947.

105. For the final performances of the company, see Tortajada, *Danza y poder*, vol. 1, 431.

106. Program quoted in González, *Orozco, escenógrafo*, 72.

107. Souvenir program, Ballet de la Ciudad de México, 1947, quoted in González, *Orozco escenógrafo*, 81–82.

108. Echavarría, *Orozco*, 58.

109. Segura, *Gloria Campobello*, 55.

110. Gloria's principal teacher Lettie Carroll claimed that she learned classical ballet through studies under Martha Graham and, somewhat more credibly, Alexander Kotchetovsky (1889–1952). (See Aulestia and Snow, *Victoria Ellis*, 13–33). It is possible that Carroll participated in one of the Denishawn School's evening classes for working women that Graham taught. While these classes included some classical technique, they were focused on Denishawn's particular form of early modern dance. Carroll's studies under Kotchetovsky appear to have been limited to an intensive course offered at the 1928 Normal School of the Dancing Masters of America, about a year after the Campobello sisters began to study with her. From whom Miss Carroll actually learned the "classical ballet" she taught in Mexico City beginning in 1923 is unclear.

111. Tapia quoted in Segura, *Gloria Campobello*, 61.

112. "Investigación del Museo Carillo Gil," *Proceso*, May 8, 1995. http://www.proceso.com.mx/168978/investigacion-del-museo-carrillo-gil. (Accessed March 22, 2019).

113. This story was laid out in detail by Juan Bautista in "La herencia de Campobello ¿Donde Esta?" *Excélsior* (Ciudad de México), November 7, 2002, for which he received the National Prize for General Reporting, presented by Mexico's José Pagés Llergo Foundation.

114. Dora Luz Haw, "Los Bienes de Campobello," *Reforma* (Mexico City), December 5, 1999. http://www.terra.com.mx/noticias/articulo/16128/Donde+esta+Nellie+Campobello.htm&paginaid=2. (Accessed June 19, 2015).

115. Dallal, *La danza en México*, 61.

116. Tibol, *Orozco*, 176.

Chapter 9. The Golden Age of Mexican Modern Dance: Miguel Covarrubias and the Academia de la Danza Mexicana

1. Tortajada, *Danza y poder*, vol. 1, 349.

2. Bravo quoted in Delgado, *Guillermina Bravo*, 27.

3. Delgado, *Guillermina Bravo*, 27; Mendoza, Introducción, 15.

4. Program, Ballet Waldeen, December 3, 1946, quoted in Luna, *Ana Mérida*, 36.

5. Parker, "Chávez and the Ballet," 196.

6. Chávez quoted in English translation in Velasco, "Nationalism," 15; Parker, "Chávez and the Ballet," 197.

7. Parker, "Chávez and the Ballet," 197.

8. For a brief overview of the rampant corruption that accompanied Alemán's modernization of Mexico, see Krauze, *Mexico*, 526–600.

9. Garrett, *Report*, 4. The exhibition reportedly originated with a request from the government of Brazil for information on the topic. The office's publication only specified venues in Rio de Janeiro and Havana, although it indicated that the tour was ongoing. Art historian Brett Knappe has documented positive press coverage of the exhibition in Buenos Aires, Argentina ("Barbara Morgan," 103). Mexico was, however, a principal audience for the office, whose largest project was an exhibition of North American Indian art at the National Museum in Mexico City under the curation of Miguel Covarrubias and René d'Harnoncourt (Garrett, *Report*, 2–3). The office also worked in partnership with the SEP's Dirección de Educación Extra-Escolar y Estética on other efforts (Garrett, *Report*, 8).

10. Morgan quoted in Museum of Modern Art, "Exhibition of Dance Photographs to be Circulated in South America," undated press release numbered 45323–13, https://www.moma.org/momaorg/shared/pdfs/docs/press_archives/982/releases/MOMA_1945_0016_1945-03-23_45323-13.pdf?2010. (Accessed September 14, 2019). For Morgan's discomfort with an earlier propaganda project see Knappe, "Barbara Morgan," 103–5.

11. Martin quoted in Museum of Modern Art, "Exhibition of Dance Photographs to be Circulated in South America," n.p.

12. Naima Prevots documents the more formal continuation of this policy during the early years of the Cold War under US President Dwight D. Eisenhower (1890–1969) in *Dance for Export: Cultural Diplomacy and the Cold War*. The first dance-related effort of Eisenhower's initiative was to send José Limón's dance company to Latin America in 1954 (8, 23–28). As Prevots also notes, during World War II, Rockefeller, in his position of coordinator of Inter-American Affairs, arranged a twenty-eight-week tour by the American

Ballet Caravan under the direction of Lincoln Kirstein and George Balanchine (1904–1983) throughout South America (19). A subsequent iteration of Eisenhower's cultural propaganda program sent US folk dancers to Mexico and its neighbors in 1961 (119).

13. Accord 4644 of the SEP, February 1, 1947, quoted in Luna, *Ana Mérida*, 114.

14. Tibol, *Pasos*, 108–9.

15. Tortajada, *Danza y poder*, vol. 1, 353–62.

16. Luna, *Ana Mérida*, 41.

17. M. Covarrubias, "Florecimiento," 412.

18. Duran quoted in Delgado, *Guillermina Bravo*, 29.

19. Duran quoted in Delgado, *Guillermina Bravo*, 30.

20. Mérida, *Escritos*, 32.

21. Reyes quoted in Tortajada, *Danza y poder*, vol. 1, 355–56.

22. Library of Congress, "Notes on Bal nègre," Performing Arts Encyclopedia. http://memory.loc.gov/diglib/ihas/html/dunham/dunham-notes-balnegre.html. (Accessed September 14, 2019).

23. Library of Congress, "Timeline: The Katherine Dunham Collection at the Library of Congress," Performing Arts Encyclopedia. http://memory.loc.gov/diglib/ihas/html/dunham/dunham-timeline.html. (Accessed September 14, 2019).

24. Armando de Maria y Campos, "Los ballets de Dunham y de Montecarlo. Las comedias de la Conesa. La zarzuela en el Arbeu. Las revistas del Tívoli," *Novedades*, May 27, 1947. http://criticateatral2021.org/html/resultado_bd.php?ID=592. (Accessed September 14, 2019).

25. M. Covarrubias, "Florescimento," 413.

26. Bravo quoted in Delgado, *Guillermina Bravo*, 31.

27. Tortajada, *Danza y poder*, vol. 1, 354–55.

28. Delgado, *Guillermina Bravo*, 31, 75.

29. Bravo quoted in Delgado, *Guillermina Bravo*, 30.

30. Letter of renunciation from Guillermina Bravo to Carlos Chávez, January 16, 1948, quoted in Tortajada, *Amalia Hernández*, 24.

31. Bravo quoted in Tibol, *Pasos*, 116.

32. Bravo quoted in Delgado, *Guillermina Bravo*, 31.

33. Delgado, *Guillermina Bravo*, 32–33.

34. Tortajada, *Danza y poder*, vol. 1, 362.

35. Tortajada, *Danza y poder*, vol. 1, 365.

36. Tortajada, *Danza y poder*, vol. 1, 369–70.

37. Aulestia, "Covarrubias," 199.

38. Covarrubias quoted in Aulestia, "Covarrubias," 219–22.

39. M. Covarrubias, "Florescimento," 418.

40. M. Covarrubias, "Florecimiento," 414.

41. Tortajada, *Danza y poder*, vol. 1, 362.

42. Victoria Phillips, "New Dance Group (1932–2009)," Dance Heritage Coalition, 2012. https://dhctreasures.omeka.net/new_dance_group2. (Accessed September 16, 2019).

43. Tortajada, *Danza y poder*, vol. 1, 413–17.

44. Nellie and Gloria Campobello quoted in Tortajada, *Danza y poder*, vol. 1, 416.

45. Francis quoted in Aulestia, "Covarrubias," 208.

46. Williams, *Covarrubias*, 181.

47. Williams, "Rosa Covarrubias," 27–29.

48. Williams, *Covarrubias*, 22. Williams described the homosexual Best as a "ladies man."

49. Coronel, "Rosa Rolanda," 77.

50. Panzer, "Essential Tact," 25–33.

51. Muray quoted in Panzer, "Essential Tact," 33.

52. Williams, *Covarrubias*, 23–24, 29, 97, 154–55, 178–79.

53. Aulestia, "Covarrubias," 201.

54. Horst, "Chronology of Professional Career, 1901–1962," entry for July 5, 1932, Louis Horst Collection, New York Public Library, Performing Arts Division.

55. Williams, *Covarrubias*, 182.

56. Tortajada, *Danza y poder*, vol. 1, 386.

57. Limón, *Memoir*, 3. Limón's vivid description of witnessing the death of his maternal uncle, shot through the head by a stray bullet during the battle of Cananea, must be taken as a repetition of an often-repeated family story. This violent cross-border labor incident, often portrayed as a precursor to the Mexican Revolution, took place in 1906, before Limón was born. See Bacon, *The Children of NAFTA*, 241.

58. Limón, *Memoir*, 90.

59. Vachon, "Limón in Mexico," 77.

60. M. Covarrubias, "Florecimiento," 415.

61. Limón, "Greater Mexico," 92.

62. John Martin, "The Dance: Diplomacy," *New York Times*, January 23, 1955. Martin went on to question whether the arts were good ambassadors and whether "political utility was a legitimate demand to make of art" but granted that the tour turned the Limón company into a "national institution."

63. Limón, *Memoir*, 126.

64. Francis quoted in Aulestia, "Covarrubias," 208–9.

65. Aulestia, "Covarrubias," 209.

66. del Río quoted in Tortajada, *Danza y poder*, vol. 1, 389.

67. Novo quoted in Tortajada, *Danza y poder*, vol. 1, 392.

68. Jorge J. Crespo de la Serna, "Artes plásticas. El arte de José Limón," *Excélsior*, September 30, 1950.

69. Limón, *Memoir*, 128.

70. Vachon, "Limón in Mexico," 78–79.

71. M. Covarrubias, "Florecimiento," 415.

72. Guzmán quoted in Tortajada, *Danza y poder*, vol. 1, 411.

73. See Parker, "Chávez and the Ballet," 197.

74. Limón, *Memoir*, 131.

75. Limón, "Tonanzintla," 12.

76. M. Covarrubias, "Florecimiento," 416.

77. M. Covarrubias, "Florecimiento," 415.

78. Dallal, "Guillermina Bravo," 9.

79. Bravo quoted in Tibol, *Pasos*, 116.

80. Bravo quoted in Tibol, *Pasos*, 117. Bravo's sponsors in 1951 included the Comisión de Tepalcatepec (an agricultural community development project in the lowlands of the State of Michoacán), Sindicato Mexicano de Electricistas (Mexican Electrician's Union),

Secretaría de Recursos Hidráulicos (Secretariat of Water Resources), Comisión Nacional del Maíz (National Corn Commission), Dirección General de Alfabetización (General Direction of Literacy), and former President Lázaro Cárdenas (Tortajada, D*anza y poder*, vol. 1, 424).

81. Bravo quoted in Delgado, *Guillermina Bravo*, 36.

82. Bravo quoted in Delgado, *Guillermina Bravo*, 38.

83. Flores Guerrero quoted in Tortajada, *Danza y poder*, vol. 1, 377.

84. Bravo, quoted in Tibol, *Pasos*, 118.

85. Delgado, *Guillermina Bravo*, 76.

86. Williams, *Covarrubias*, 188.

87. John Martin, "Mexican Dances Featured at Fete," *New York Times*, August 18, 1951. Sagaón recalled performing the piece without the sets and costumes in the US, but the Martin review singles these elements of the performance out for particular praise. (See Lynton, "Rocío Sagaón," 300.)

88. R. Covarrubias, "A Letter," 102–03.

89. Williams, *Covarrubias*, 194.

90. Gorostiza, quoted in Carbajal, "El nacionalismo," 147.

91. Carbajal, "El nacionalismo," 148.

92. López Binnqüist, "En Tiempos de la Quinta Alicia," 6–21.

93. Uretta, "Danzas y remembranzas," 313–325.

94. Williams, *Covarrubias*, 204.

95. Williams, *Covarrubias*, 208.

96. Mérida quoted in Luna, *Ana Mérida*, 143.

97. Luna, *Ana Mérida*, 50–51.

98. Luna, *Ana Mérida*, 56. Carlos Mérida described the project as the "most ambitious" of his career (*Escritos*, 35).

99. Luna, *Ana Mérida*, 51. Luna's assertion that the absence was granted by the secretary of education when INBA was independent of that organization does raise questions. Luna's interpretation of *Bonampak*, which he called "the most distinguished choreographic creation that has been achieved in our country" (50), and the situation surrounding its creation and its relationship with *Los cuatro soles* is highly colored by his personal relationship with Mérida, who was his wife when he wrote the book.

100. For Carlos Mérida's ethnological work see Espinoza, "Notas," 47.

101. For Ana Mérida's studies in Chiapas, see Luna, *Ana Mérida*, 56.

102. "Programa del Festival de Danzas Mexicanas," in Mérida, *Escritos*, 92.

103. Luna, *Ana Mérida*, 57.

104. Tortajada, *Danza y poder*, vol. 1, 422.

105. Luna, *Ana Mérida*, 40.

106. José Limón, "The Dance: A Visitor in Mexico," *New York Times*, July 22, 1951.

107. Rosa Covarrubias quoted in Williams, *Covarrubias*, 198.

108. Lynton, "Rocío Sagaón," 306.

109. Tortajada, *Danza y poder*, vol. 1, 410–12.

110. Tortajada, *Danza y poder*, vol. 1, 479.

111. M. Covarrubias, "Florecimiento," 421.

112. Chávez quoted in Tortajada, *Amalia Hernández*, 20, 26.

113. Hernández quoted in Tortajada, *Amalia Hernández*, 29.

114. Lavalle quoted in Malvido, *Zapata*, 143.

115. Tortajada, *Amalia Hernández*, 32.

116. Tortajada, *Danza y poder*, vol. 1, 405.

117. Williams, *Covarrubias*, 197.

118. Williams, *Covarrubias*, 208.

119. Williams, *Covarrubias*, 215–16.

120. Williams, *Covarrubias*, 224–27.

Chapter 10. Dancing beyond the Cactus Curtain: Mexican Theatrical Dance Comes of Age

1. Arriaga, *La* época, 69.

2. Arriaga, *La* época, 47–48.

3. Carbajal, "El nacionalismo," 167–68.

4. Carbajal, "El nacionalismo," 172.

5. Malvido, *Zapata*, 59–64.

6. Arriaga quoted in Malvido, *Zapata*, 77.

7. Malvido, *Zapata*, 75.

8. M. Covarrubias, "Florecimiento," 423.

9. Tortajada, "Guillermo Arriaga," 44–46.

10. Program, Jacob's Pillow, August 22–23, 1952. Jacob's Pillow Archives. http://archives.jacobspillow.org/index.php/Detail/objects/4798. (Accessed September 14, 2019).

11. Arriaga's solo performance is preserved in the film archives of Jacob's Pillow as Moving Image 0.353.

12. Malvido, *Zapata*, 80.

13. Arriaga quoted in Malvido, *Zapata*, 88–89.

14. Arriaga quoted in Malvido, *Zapata*, 89.

15. Hayes, "National Imaginings on the Air," 253 discusses the role the *Hora Nacional* played in promoting musical nationalism.

16. Lester Horton (1906–1953) created his *Dedications in Our Time—to José Clemente Orozco* (1954) the following year. It too made clear use of Orozco's *La Trinchera* as a source. See Owen, *A Certain Place*, 25 for a photograph of Carmen de Lavallade (b. 1931) and Alvin Ailey (1931–1989) in a performance of the work at Jacob's Pillow.

17. Tortajada, "Guillermo Arriaga," 34.

18. Rivera quoted in Malvido, *Zapata*, 94.

19. Rojo quoted in Malvido, *Zapata*, 95.

20. Arriaga quoted in Malvido, *Zapata*, 95–96.

21. Malvido, *Zapata*, 97–102.

22. Flores Guerrero quoted in Tortajada, "Guillermo Arriaga," 55.

23. Arriaga, *La* época, 102–3.

24. Tortajada, *Danza y poder*, vol. 1, 470.

25. Tortajada, *Danza y poder*, vol. 1, 491–92.

26. Tortajada, *Danza y poder*, vol. 1, 484–88.

27. Tibol, *Pasos*, 63.

28. Siqueiros quoted in Tibol, *Pasos*, 64.

29. Siqueiros quoted in Tibol, *Pasos*, 64–65.

30. Cuevas, "La cortina de nopal," 87–89.

31. Cuevas, "La cortina de nopal," 91.

32. Tortajada, *Danza y poder*, vol. 1, 497.

33. L. Warren, *Anna Sokolow*, 122.

34. "Second conference," 13–15. Larry Warren Collection, Subject files "The Infamous Conference," Music Division, Library of Congress.

35. "Second Conference," 19.

36. "Second Conference," 23–24.

37. Waldeen. "¿Dejaran morir la danza mexicana?" *Excélsior*, July 20, 1956.

38. Tibol, *Pasos*, 124.

39. For the emergence of the Ballet Contemporáneo see Tortajada, *Danza y poder*, vol. 1, 526.

40. Tortajada, *Danza y poder*, vol. 1, 544–45.

41. Tibol, *Pasos*, 122.

42. Tortajada, *Danza y poder*, vol. 1, 545.

43. Tortajada, *Danza y poder*, vol. 1, 497.

44. Tortajada, *Danza y poder*, vol. 1, 545.

45. Tortajada, *Danza y poder*, vol. 1, 550.

46. Covarrubias, M., "Florecimiento," 422; Colombia Moya, "Andanzas: *Tierra*, de Elena Noriega" *La Jornada* (Ciudad de México), May 4, 2009. https://www.jornada.com.mx/2009/05/04/opinion/a1801esp (Accessed September 14, 2019).

47. Covarrubias, M., "Florecimiento," 416.

48. Tortajada, *Danza y poder*, vol. 1, 530.

49. Delgado, *Guillermina Bravo*, 83.

50. Delgado, *Guillermina Bravo*, 86.

51. Delgado, *Guillermina Bravo*, 78.

52. Bravo letter to Sánchez quoted in Delgado, *Guillermina Bravo*, 40.

53. From a Spanish translation of an article by P. Gusiev in *Soviet Culture* provided by Bravo to Tibol, quoted in Tortajada, *Danza y poder*, vol. 1, 551–52.

54. Bravo quoted in Delgado, *Guillermina Bravo*, 41.

55. See Bowlt, *Russian Art of the Avant Garde*, xxxvii–xxxviii on the Institute for Artistic Culture's November 24, 1921, condemnation of easel painting and of "individualistic" art that ran counter to the needs of a collective society.

56. Apel, "Diego Rivera and the Left," 63–65; "Mexican Muralist Deplores Art He Saw on Recent Trip to Soviet," *New York Times*, December 11, 1955.

57. Mussachio, *Taller*, 27.

58. Shay, *Choreographic Politics*, 144.

59. F. Miller, *Folklore*, 9.

60. Zemtsovsky and Kunanbaeva, "Communism and Folklore," 8.

61. "Mexican Muralist Deplores Art He Saw on Recent Trip to Soviet," *New York Times*, December 11, 1955.

62. Jack Anderson, "Igor Moiseyev, 101, Choreographer, Dies," *New York Times*, November 3, 2007.

63. Ross, *Like A Bomb Going Off*, 133.

64. Tortajada, *Danza y poder*, vol. 1, 562.

65. Tortajada, *Danza y poder*, vol. 1, 563. These discussions took place nearly a decade before Mao's Cultural Revolution.

66. Dallal, "Guillermina Bravo," 8.

67. Tibol, *Pasos*, 143.

68. Tortajada, *Danza y poder*, vol. 1, 562.

69. Bravo quoted in Dallal, *La danza en México*, 92–93.

70. Tortajada, *Danza y poder*, vol. 1, 574.

71. See Tortajada, *Danza y poder*, vol. 1, 576–81.

72. Tortajada, *Danza y poder*, vol. 1, 583.

73. Arriaga quoted in Malvido, *Zapata*, 141.

74. Tortajada, *Danza y poder*, vol. 1, 584–87.

75. Durán, quoted in Tortajada, *Danza y poder*, vol. 1, 786.

76. Arriaga quoted in Malvido, *Zapata*, 143.

77. Tortajada, *Danza y poder*, vol. 1, 654.

78. Adriana Siqueiros did travel to the Soviet Union and worked with Hernández in a precursor group to her Ballet Folklórico. See Colombia Moya, "Andanzas: Recuerdos de Adriana Siqueiros," *La Jornada* (Ciudad de México), January 10, 2012. https://www.jornada.com.mx/2012/01/10/opinion/a1001esp (Accessed September 14, 2019).

79. Hernández quoted in Tortajada, *Amalia Hernández*, 36.

80. Aguirre, "El ballet y su creadora," 36.

81. Tortajada, *Danza y poder*, vol. 1, 654–55.

82. See Tortajada, *Amalia Hernández*, 34. Shay argues the Hernández's "pre-Columbian" works are indebted to Martha Graham (*Choreographic Politics*, 36, 96). Through her sponsorship of instructors such as Alwin Nikolais, Hernández actively resisted what Tortajada calls Bravo's "hegonomic" imposition of the Graham technique (*Amalia Hernández*, 60).

83. Tortajada, *Amalia Hernández*, 39.

84. López Mateos quoted in Aguirre, "El ballet y su creadora," 40.

85. Tortajada, *Amalia Hernández*, 42.

86. Tortajada, *Danza y poder*, vol. 1, 738; Hernández, quoted in Tortajada, *Amalia Hernández*, 52.

87. Tortajada, *Danza y poder*, vol. 2, 56.

88. Tortajada, *Amalia Hernández*, 46.

89. de Maria y Campos quoted in Tortajada, *Amalia Hernández*, 46.

90. See Shay, *Choreographic Politics*, 40–41, 102.

91. Tortajada, *Amalia Hernández*, 39, 48

92. Segura, "La obra," 138.

93. Aguirre, "El ballet y su creadora," 52. According to Guillermo Arriaga, his Ballet Popular initially substituted for the Ballet Folklórico de México in its Bellas Artes performances during its absences for international tours. He alleges that Hernández's personal friendship with Mexico's then First Lady Eva Sámano de López was behind the presidential support for the Ballet Folklórico de México and that Sámano worked to minimize support for other Mexican dance companies that included folk dance in their repertories, including his own Ballet Popular (Malvido, *Zapata*, 156). Other choreographers reported more supportive measures taken by Hernández to assist them with launching their own nonfolkloric dance companies. Balanchine-trained neoclassical choreographer Gloria Contreras, for example, recalled receiving a large box full of ballet shoes from Hernández for her newly created Taller Coreográfico at a time when it was nearly impossible to find them in Mexico (Snow, *Movimiento*, 164–65).

94. Shay, *Choreographic Politics*, 4–5.

95. *Tiempo*, November 1, 1965, quoted in Aguirre, "El ballet y su creadora," 62.

96. Arenal, "Primera presentación critica," vii.

97. Hernández, "El movimiento actual," *El Demócrata* (Ciudad de México), August 2, 1923.

98. Siqueiros, David. "El arte al servicio del proletariado." *Llamada, periódico de pared* (Mexico City), October 1931. ICAA Record ID: 822471.

99. Segura, "La obra," 164–70.

100. For the "Capilla Siqueiros" see Fernández Márquez, "Inauguración," 13. For the theater's original name see García Cortés, *Siqueiros*, 218, note 1.

101. Suarez's opening remarks at the Primera Confrontación Turística, January 10, 1972, quoted in García Cortés, *Siqueiros*, 221.

102. See García Cortés, *Siqueiros*, 13.

103. Mario Orozco Rivera, "Carencia de unidad: Féretro del muralismo." *Excélsior* (Ciudad de México), supplement *Revista Dominical*, December 12, 1971.

104. Raquel Tibol, "Curiosidad mexicana," *Excélsior* (Ciudad de México), supplement *Revista Dominical*, December 12, 1971.

105. Tibol interview with Jorge Saldaña, transcript in García Cortés, *Siqueiros*, 239.

106. Siqueiros, English translation quoted in *Poliforum*, 14.

107. Juárez, "Polyforum," 42.

108. Siqueiros interview with Julio Scherer García quoted in Juárez, "Polyforum," 42–43.

109. Juárez, "Polyforum," 42.

110. García Cortés, *Siqueiros*, 67.

111. García Cortés, *Siqueiros*, 52–57.

112. García Cortés, *Siqueiros*, 7.

113. *Poliforum*, 4.

114. García Cortés, *Siqueiros*, 200.

115. Tortajada, Danza y poder, vol. 2, 565.

116. Echeverría quoted in García Cortés, *Siqueiros*, 211–12.

117. Siqueiros quoted in García Cortés, *Siqueiros*, 210–11. Ironically, given the anticlerical impulses ascribed to the revolution that Siqueiros claimed to represent, the Polyforum's dedication ceremony also included the reading of a telegram from Cardinal Villot conveying a blessing from His Holiness Paul V for its message of "Peace, Justice, Hope, [and] Fraternity" (Telegram from Cardinal Villot on behalf of Paul V quoted in García Cortés, *Siqueiros*, 214).

118. Hernández quoted in García Cortés, *Siqueiros*, 218.

119. See the comments of Manuel Suárez's son Ernesto on the topic in Suárez, "Unas palabras," xv.

120. García Cortés, *Siqueiros*, 121.

121. Garcia Cortés, *Siqueiros*, 218, note 1. Despite the dispute, folk dance continued to play a role in the Polyforum. The Ballet México Folklórico of Artemisa Barrios provided Sunday performances in that space between 1974 and 1976 (Tortajada, *Danza y poder*, vol. 2, 842, 1350).

122. See Fernández Márquez, "Inauguración," 13; Juárez, "Polyforum," 45 and Guadarrama, *Ruta*, 179, respectively.

123. *Polyforum Siqueiros*, 95.

124. Aulestia, *Chicas bien*, 49

125. Adriana Siqueiros quoted in Aulestia, *Chicas bien*, 50.

126. Aulestia, *Lettie H. Carroll*, 24.

127. Columbia Moya, "Andanzas: Recuerdos de Adriana Siqueiros." *La Jornada* (Ciudad de México), January 10, 2012.

128. Tortajada, *Danza y poder*, vol. 1, 574.

129. L. Warren, *Anna Sokolow*, 302.

130. Program, Palacio de Bellas Artes, September 25, 1984.

131. Rivera, "Raíces políticas," 112.

132. Moiseyev quoted in Shay, *Choreographic Politics*, 74.

133. Shay, *Choreographic Politics*, 64.

134. Shay, *Choreographic Politics*, 28.

135. Dance historian Naima Prevots documents the unsuccessful effort of the US to identify a folk dance troupe that could serve to counterbalance the potent presence of Moiseyev's company on the international stage in *Dance for Export*.

136. Shay, *Choreographic Politics*, 24.

137. Moiseyev, 1968 souvenir program quoted in Shay, *Choreographic Politics*, 72.

138. Hernández interview with Rosa Reyna quoted in Segura, "La obra," 134.

139. Hernández interview with Rosa Reyna quoted in Segura, "La obra," 140–42.

140. Segura, "La obra," 134.

141. Segura, "La obra, "142.

142. Tortajada, *Amalia Hernández*, 70.

143. Tortajada, *Amalia Hernández*, 70. For the contemporary state of professional folk dance troupes in Eastern Europe see Petkovski, "Professional Folk Dance Ensembles," 173–78.

144. Monsiváis quoted in Tortajada, *Amalia Hernández*, 40.

Epilogue: Mexican and Universal

1. Bravo quoted in Delgado, *Guillermina Bravo*, 38.

2. Tamayo quoted in Mérida, *Modern Mexican Artists*, 191.

3. Fabiola Martínez Rodríguez. "Between Figuration and Abstraction: The Cultural Cold War and Tamayo's Art in the 1950s." Presentation at "'A Line That Birds Cannot See': Mexican/US Art and Artists Crossing Borders in the 20th Century," Smithsonian American Art Museum, Washington, DC, November 3, 2017.

4. Tortajada, *Amalia Hernández*, 29.

5. Raquel Tibol, "Gran salto estetico de Ballet Nacional," *Proceso*, December 19, 1987.

6. Dallal, *La Danza en México*, 88.

7. Amalia Hernández received the prize in 1992. The other dancer-choreographers to receive the award are Guillermo Arriaga in 1999, Gloria Contreras in 2005, and Pilar Rioja in 2017.

8. Tibol, "Gran salto estetico de Ballet Nacional," *Proceso*, December 19, 1987.

9. Tamayo, *Textos*, 129.

10. Parker, "Carlos Chávez and the Ballet," 184.

11. See Mendoza, Introducción, 17.

12. Xavier Villaurrutia, "Los pintores mexicanos y el teatro," *Excélsior*, October 22, 1950.

13. Pereda, "Tamayo's Gouaches," 4.

14. Quoted in Museo Tamayo Arte Contemporáneo, *Antígona*, 4.

15. Quoted in Museo Tamayo Arte Contemporáneo, *Antígona*, 5.

16. See Dallal, *La danza en México*, 86–93.

17. Tibol, "Gran salto estetico de Ballet Nacional," *Proceso*, December 19, 1987.

18. Bravo quoted in Delgado, *Guillermina Bravo*, 110.

19. Tibol, "Gran salto estetico de Ballet Nacional," Proceso, December 19, 1987.

20. Héctor Garay, personal communication, December 1, 2017.

21. Delgado, *Guillermina Bravo*, 108.

22. Cardona quoted in Delgado, *Guillermina Bravo*, 112.

23. Tibol, "Gran salto estetico de Ballet Nacional," *Proceso*, December 19, 1987.

24. Madrigal, "Tamayo y los Contemporáneos," 155–99.

25. Villaurrutia quoted in Madrigal, "Tamayo y los Contemporáneos," 163.

26. Dallal, *La danza en México*, 93.

27. Delgado, *Guillermina Bravo*, 112.

BIBLIOGRAPHY

Acevedo, Esther. "Las decoraciones que pasaron a ser revolucionarias." In *El nacionalismo y el arte mexicano. IX Coloquio de Historia del Arte*, 171–207. México: Instituto de Investigaciones Estéticas, 1986.

Acevedo, Esther, and Pilar García. "Procesos de quiebre en la política visual del México posrevolucionario." In *México y la invención del arte latinoamericano, 1910–1950*, edited by Esther Acevedo and Pilar García, 25–96. México: Secretaría de Relaciones Exteriores, 2011.

Ades, Dawn. *Art in Latin America*. New Haven, CT: Yale University Press, 1989.

Aguirre Cristiani, Gabriela. "El ballet y su creadora." In *El ballet Folklórico de México de Amalia Hernández*, edited by Gabriela Aguirre Cristiani and Felipe Segura Escalona, 15–120. México: Fomento Cultural Banamex, 1994.

Álvarez, Ruth M. "La influencia de Best Maugard en el arte y la estética de Katherine Anne Porter." In *Adolfo Best Maugard. La espiral del arte*, edited by Miguel Fernández Félix and José Valtierra, 55–78. México: Instituto Nacional de Bellas Artes, 2016.

Anderson, Benedict. *Imagined Communities: Reflections on the Origins and Spread of Nationalism*. Rev. ed. London: Verso, 2006.

Anreus, Alejandro. *Orozco in Gringoland. The Years in New York*. Albuquerque: University of New Mexico Press, 2001.

Apel, Dora. "Diego Rivera and the Left: The Destruction and Recreation of the Rockefeller Center Mural." *Left History* 6, no. 1 (1999): 57–75.

Arenal de Siqueiros, Angelica. "Primera presentación critica." In *Siqueiros: Primeras obras: Neoimpresionismo y art nouveau*, edited by Guillermo Rousset, vii–ix. Ciudad Juárez, México: Universidad Autónoma de Ciudad Juárez, 1996.

Arriaga, Guillermo. *La época de oro de la danza moderna mexicana*. México: Consejo Nacional para la Cultura y las Artes, 2008.

Atl, Dr. [Gerardo Murillo]. *Las artes populares en México*. México: Editorial Cultura, 1922.

———. *Gentes profanas en el convento*. 1950. Reprint. México: Senado de la República, 20003.

Aulestia, Patricia. "Nellie Campobello." *Cuadernos del CID Danza*. 15, 1987.

———. "Miguel Covarrubias: Su lección." In *Miguel Covarrubias: Homenaje*, 199–284. México: Centro Cultural/Arte Contemporáneo, 1987.

———. *Lettie H. Carroll pionera de la enseñanza de la danza 1923–1964*. Culiacán: Colegio de Bachilleres del Estado de Sinaloa, 2002.

———. *Las "chicas bien" de Miss Carroll: Estudio y Ballet Carroll (1923–1964)*. México: Instituto Nacional de Bellas Artes, 2003.

———. *Despertar de la república dancística mexicana*. México: Ríos de Tinta, 2012.

———. *Historias alucinantes de un mundo ecléctico. La danza en México, 1910–1939*. México: Impresos Chávez, 2013.

Aulestia, Patricia, and K. Mitchell Snow. *Victoria Ellis—Cosmic Ballerina: A Story of Dance, Identity and Race in Post-Revolutionary Mexico*. México: Impresos Chávez, 2018.

Bacon, David. *The Children of NAFTA: Labor Wars on the U.S./Mexico Border*. Berkeley: University of California Press, 2004.

Balderas, Esperanza. *Roberto Montenegro: Ilustrador (1900–1930)*. México: Circulo de Arte, 2000.

———. *Robert Montenegro: La sensualidad renovada*. México: Fondo Editorial de la Plástica Mexicana, 2001.

Barajas Duran, Rafael. *Posada: Mito y mitote. La caricatura política de José Guadalupe Posada y Manuel Alfonso Manilla*. México: Fondo de Cultura Económica, 2009.

Bargalló Sánchez, Isabel, and Montserrat Bargalló Sánchez. "Collection or Inspiration? Carmen Tórtola Valencia's Latin American Textiles." *Datatèxtil* 22: 30–54.

Beaumont, Cyril W. Introduction to *Vaslav Nijinsky: An Artistic Interpretation of His Work in Black, White and Gold*, n.p. London: C. W. Beaumont, circa 1913.

———. *Michel Fokine & His Ballets*. London: C. W. Beaumont, 1935.

———. *Bookseller at the Ballet. Memoirs 1891–1929*. London: C. W. Beaumont, 1975.

Belnap, Jeffrey. "Diego Rivera's Greater America: Pan-American Patronage, Indigenism, and H. P." *Cultural Critique* 63 (Spring 2006): 61–98.

Bidault de la Calle, Sophie. *Nellie Campobello: Una escritura salida del cuerpo*. 2nd ed. México: Instituto Nacional de Bellas Artes, 2003.

Blitzstein, Marc. "Forecast and Review." *Modern Music* 9, no. 4 (May–June 1932): 164–68.

Bowles, Paul. *Paul Bowles on Music*. Edited by Timothy Mangan and Irene Herrman. Berkeley: University of California Press, 2003.

Bowlt, John E. *Moscow and St. Petersburg 1900–1920: Art, Life and Culture of the Russian Silver Age*. New York: Vendome Press, 2008.

Bowlt, John E., ed. and trans. *Russian Art of the Avant Garde: Theory and Criticism 1902–1934*. New York: Viking Press, 1976.

Brenner, Anita. *Your Mexican Holiday*. New York: G. P. Putnam's Sons, 1932.

Buchenau, Jürgen. "Plutarco Elías Calles and the Maximato in Revolutionary Mexico: A Reinterpretation." *Jahrbuch für Geschichte Lateinamerikas* 43 (2006): 229–53.

Buckle, Richard. *Nijinsky*. Harmondsworth: Penguin Books, 1975.

Campobello, Nellie, and Gloria Campobello. *Ritmos indígenas de México*. México: Editorial Popular, 1940.

Carbajal, Claudia. "El nacionalismo en transición. La institucionalización de la danza de concierto en México. Debates ideológicos, artísticos y vínculos políticos." Masters thesis, Universidad Nacional Autónoma de México, 2015.

Carbonneau, Suzanne. "Adolph Bolm in America." In *The Ballets Russes and Its World*, edited by Lynn Garafola and Nancy Van Norman Baer, 219–44. New Haven, CT: Yale University Press, 1999.

Carredano, Consuelo. "Hasta los verdes maizales de México: Rodolfo Halffter y *Don Lindo de Almería*." *Anales del Instituto de Investigaciones Estéticas* 93 (2008): 69–101.

Cartmel, D. "An Art Awakening." *School Arts Magazine* 20, no. 7 (1921): 401–8.

Charlot, Jean. "Un Precursor del Movimiento de Arte Mexicano: El grabador Posadas." *Revista de Revistas*, August 30, 1925, 25.

———. "Esthetics of Indian Dances." *Mexican Folkways*, August–September, 1925: 4–8.

———. *Mexican Art and the Academy of San Carlos, 1785–1915*. Austin: University of Texas Press, 1962.

———. *The Mexican Mural Renaissance, 1920–1925*. New Haven, CT: Yale University Press, 1963.

———. *El renacimiento del muralismo mexicano, 1920–1925*. México: Editorial Domés, SA, 1985.

Clayton, Michelle. "Touring History: Tórtola Valencia between Europe and the Americas." *Dance Research Journal* 44, no. 1 (Summer 2012): 28–49.

———. "Modernism's Moving Bodies." *Modernist Cultures* 9, no. 1 (2014): 27–45.

Cohen, Jonathan. "Waldeen and the Americas: The Dance Has Many Faces." In *A Woman's Gaze: Latin American Women Artists*, edited by Marjorie Agosín, 224–42. Fredonia, NY: White Pine Press, 1998.

———. "Neruda in English: Waldeen's 'Lost' Translations from *Canto General*," *Translation Review* 88 (2014): 56–74.

Cordero Reiman, Karen. "La invención del 'arte popular': Una estrategia para la construcción del arte mexicana moderno." In *Facturas y manufacturas de la identidad: Las artes populares en la modernidad mexicana*, edited by Mieredia Velázquez, 73–95. México: Museo de Arte Moderno, 2010.

———. "The Best Maugard Drawing Method: A Common Ground for Modern Mexicanist Aesthetics." *Journal of Decorative and Propaganda Arts* 26 (2010): 44–79.

Corn, Wanda. *The Great American Thing: Modern Art and National Identity, 1915–1935*. Berkeley: University of California Press, 1999.

Coronel Rivera, Juan. "Rosa Rolanda: Yo me llamo como quiero." In *Rosa Rolanda (1898–1970): Una orquídea tatuada y la danza en las manos*, edited by M. Monserrat Sánchez Soler, 73–141. México: Museo Casa Estudio Diego Rivera y Frida Kahlo, 2011.

Covarrubias, Miguel. "Florecimiento de la danza." 1952. Reprinted in *Danza en México: Visiones de cinco siglos*. Vol. 2, *Antología: Cinco siglos de crónicas, critica y documentos (1521–2002)*, edited by Maya Ramos Smith and Patricia Cardona Lang, 409–24. México: Centro Nacional de Investigación, Documentación e Información de la Danza "José☒ Limón," 2002.

Covarrubias, Rose. "A Letter to Miguel Covarrubias from Rose Covarrubias." *Dance Observer* (August–September 1951): 102–3.

Cuevas, José Luis. "La cortina de nopal." 1951. Reprinted in *Ruptura*, 84–91. México, DF: Museo Carrillo Gil, 1988. ICAA Record ID: 788032.

Dallal, Alberto. "El nacionalismo prolongado: El movimiento mexicana de danza moderna 1940–1955." In *El nacionalismo y el arte mexicano. IX Coloquio de Historia de Arte*, 297–350. México: Instituto de Investigaciones Estéticas, 1986.

———. "Martha Graham." *Anales del Instituto de Investigaciones Estéticas* 14, no. 56 (1986): 141–63.

———. "Anna Pavlova en México." *Anales del Instituto de Investigaciones Estéticas* 15, no. 60 (1989): 163–78.

———. *La danza en México en el siglo XX*. México: Consejo Nacional para la Cultura y las Artes, 1994.

———. "Guillermina Bravo: La danza total." *Interdanza* 4 (December 2013): 4–11.

Daniel, Oliver. *Stokowski: A Counterpoint of View*. New York: Dodd, Mead & Company, 1982.

del Conde, Teresa. "Mexico." In *Latin American Art in the Twentieth Century*, edited by Edward Sullivan, 18–49. London: Phaidon, 1996.

Delgado Martínez, César. *Guillermina Bravo: Historia Oral*. México: INBA, 1994.

de los Reyes, Aurelio. "Tres Documentos sobre la fundación de la Escuela de Danza." *Anales del Instituto de Investigaciones Estéticas* 15, no. 60 (1989): 249–61.

———. *¡Tercera llamada, tercera! Programas de espectáculos ilustrados por José Guadalupe Posada*. Aguascalientes: Instituto Cultural de Aguascalientes, 2005.

Delpar, Helen. *The Enormous Vogue of Things Mexican: Cultural Relations between the United States and Mexico, 1920–1935*. Tuscaloosa: University of Alabama Press, 1992.

de Mille, Agnes. *Dance to the Piper*. Boston: Little, Brown and Company, 1952.

———. *The Life and Work of Martha Graham*. New York: Random House, 1991.

de Moxó, Benito María. *Cartas mejicanas*. Geneva: Tipografía Pellas, 1837.

de Neuvillate, Alfonso. Introducción to *Método del Dibujo*, v–vii. 2nd ed. México: Editorial Viñeta, 1964.

de Olavarría y Ferrari, Enrique. *Reseña histórica del teatro en México, Tomo 4*. 2nd ed. México: La Europea, 1895.

Dickerman, Leah. "Leftist Currents." In *Diego Rivera: Murals for the Museum of Modern Art*, edited by Leah Dickerman, 10–47. New York: Museum of Modern Art, 2011.

Duberman, Martin. *The Worlds of Lincoln Kirstein*. New York: Alfred A. Knopf, 2007.

Echavarría, Salvador. *Orozco. Hospicio Cabañas*. México: México en el Arte, 1968.

Espejo, Beatriz. *Dr. Atl: El paisaje como pasión*. México: Fondo Editorial de la Plástica Mexicana, 1994.

Espinoza Campos, Eduardo. "Notas sobre la relación de Carlos Mérida con la música y la danza." In *Entre acordes y pinceladas. La música en imágenes pictóricas*, edited by Beatriz Zamorano Navarro, 46–64. México: Instituto Nacional de Bellas Artes, 2006.

Favela, Ramón. *Diego Rivera: The Cubist Years*. Phoenix: Phoenix Art Museum, 1984.

Fell, Claude. *José Vasconcelos: Los años del águila, 1920–1925: Educación, cultura e iberoamericanismo en el México postrevolucionario*. México: Universidad Nacional Autónoma de México, 1989.

Fernández, Justino. *Orozco. Forma e idea*. 2nd ed. México: Editorial Porrúa, 1956.

———. *Roberto Montenegro*. México: Universidad Nacional Autónoma de México, 1962.

———. *Arte moderno y contemporáneo de México*. México: Universidad Nacional Autónoma de México, 1993.

Fernández Márquez, Pablo. "Inauguración del Polyforum Cultural Siqueiros." Originally published in *El Nacional*, November 26, 1971. Reprinted in *Reencuentro con la obra mural de Siqueiros: Proceso creativo del Polyforum*, 12–13. México: Instituto Nacional de Bellas Artes, 1999.

Fierro Gossman, Rafael R. *Templo del Colegio Máximo de San Pedro y San Pablo: Museo de la Luz: 400 años de historia*. México: Universidad Nacional Autónoma de México, 2003.

Flores, Tatiana. *Mexico's Revolutionary Avant Gardes. From Estridentismo to ¡30–30!* New Haven, CT: Yale University Press, 2013.

Florescano, Enrique. "Patria y nación en la época de Porfirio Díaz." *Signos Históricos* 13 (January–June, 2005): 153–87.

Fontbona, Francesc. "Anglada Camarasa y su mundo." In *El món d'Anglada-Camarasa*, edited by Francesc Fontbona. Barcelona: Fundació "La Caixa," 2006.

Fontbona, Francesc, and Francesc Miralles. *Anglada Camarasa*. Barcelona: Ediciones Polígrafa, SA, 1981.

Fonteyn, Margot. *Pavlova: Portrait of a Dancer*. New York: Viking, 1984.

Fox, Claire F. *Making Art Panamerican: Cultural Policy and the Cold War*. Minneapolis: University of Minnesota Press, 2013.

Gamboa, Fernando. "Jose Guadalupe Posada: The Man, His Art, His Times." In *Posada: Printmaker to the Mexican People*, 9–24. Chicago: Art Institute of Chicago, 1944.

Gamio, Manuel. *Forjando patria (pro nacionalismo)*. México: Porrúa Hermanos, 1916.

Garafola, Lynn. "The Travesty Dancer in Nineteenth-Century Ballet." *Dance Research Journal* 17, no. 2 and 18, no. 1 (1985–1986): 35–40.

———. *Diaghilev's Ballets Russes*. New York: Da Capo Press, 1998.

———. "*H.P.*: A Lost Dance of the Americas." In *Dance: American Art, 1830–1960*, edited by Jane Dini, 220–47. New Haven, CT: Detroit Institute of Arts/Yale University Press, 2016.

García Cortés, Adrián. *Siqueiros, Suárez y el Polyforum: Vidas paralelas, sin paralelos*. México: Polyforum Siqueiros, 2000.

García de Germenos, Pilar. "Exposición de los artistas mexicanos de 1910." In *1910: El arte en un año decisivo. La exposición de artistas mexicanos*, 65–84. México: Museo Nacional de Arte, 1991.

García Morillo, Roberto. *Carlos Chávez vida y obra*. México: Fondo de Cultura Económica, 1960.

García Sáez, María Concepción, and Maria Angeles Albert. "Exotismo y belleza de una ceramica." *Artes de Mexico* 14: 35–49.

Garduño Palido, Blanca. "Diego Rivera y las Misiones Culturales." In *Misiones Culturales: Los años utópicos 1920–1938*, 11–26. México: Museo Casa Estudio Diego Rivera y Frida Kahlo, 1999.

Garelick, Rhonda. *Electric Salome*. Princeton, NJ: Princeton University Press, 2007.

Gargurevich, Juan. *La prensa sensacionalista en el Perú*. Lima: Fondo Editorial de la Pontificia Universidad Católica del Perú, 2000.

Garland, Iris. "Early Modern Dance in Spain: Tórtola Valencia, Dancer of the Historical Intuition." *Dance Research Journal* 29, no. 2 (Autumn 1997): 1–22.

———. "Modernismo and the Dancer, Tórtola Valencia." *Corner, Women Artists and Writers and the Avant Garde* 2 (Spring 1999). http://www.cornermag.net/corner02/page08.htm.

Garrett, Margaret D. *Report of the Inter-American Office: National Gallery of Art. January 1944–May 1946*. Washington, DC: US Government Printing Office, 1946.

Genauer, Emily. *Rufino Tamayo*. New York: Harry N. Abrams, 1974.

Gibson, Christina Taylor. "The Reception of Carlos Chávez's *Horsepower*: A Pan-American Communication Failure." *American Music* 30, no. 2 (Summer 2012): 157–93.

González Matute, Laura. *J. C. Orozco, escenógrafo*. Guadalajara, México: Instituto Cultural Cabañas, 2000.

Graham, Martha. "Seeking an American Art of Dance." In *Revolt in the Arts: A Survey of the Creation, Distribution and Appreciation of Art in* America, edited by Oliver M. Sayler, 249–55. New York: Brentanos, 1930.

Greathouse, Patricia. *Mariachi*. Layton, UT: Gibbs Smith, 2009.

Greeley, Robin Adèle. "Muralism and the State in Post-Revolutionary Mexico, 1920–1970." In *Mexican Muralism: A Critical History*, edited by Alejandro Anreus, Leonard Folgarait, and Robin Adèle Greeley, 13–36. Berkeley: University of California Press, 2012.

Grimberg, Salomon. "Un caballero educado." In *Adolfo Best Maugard. La espiral del arte*, edited by Miguel Fernández Félix and José Valtierra, 19–52. México: Instituto Nacional de Bellas Artes, 2016.

Grover, Stuart. "The World of Art Movement in Russia." *Russian Review* 32, no. 1 (January 1973): 28–42.

Guadarrama Peña, Guillermina. *La ruta de Siqueiros. Etapas en su obra mural*. México: Instituto Nacional de Bellas Artes y Literatura, 2010.

Gutiérrez Viñuales, Rodrigo. "Hermen Anglada Camarasa y Mallorca: Su significación para el arte iberoamericano." In *El arte español del siglo XX: Su perspectiva al final del milenio*, edited by Miguel Cabañas Bravo, 189–203. Madrid: Editorial CSIC-CSIC Press, 2001.

———. "Roberto Montenegro y los artistas americanos en Mallorca (1914–1919)." *Anales del Instituto de Investigaciones Estéticas* 25, no. 82 (2003): 93–121.

Guzmán, Martín Luis. "Diego Rivera y la filosofía del cubismo." In *Obras completas de Martín Luis Guzmán I*, 83–86. México: Compañía General de Ediciones, SA, 1961.

———. "España y el Ballet Ruso." In *Obras completas de Martín Luis Guzmán I*, 274–75. México: Compañía General de Ediciones, SA, 1961.

Halffter, Rodolfo. *Carlos Chávez: Catálogo completo de sus obras*. México: Sociedad de Autores y Compositores de Música, S. de A., 1971.

Hall, Linda. *Dolores del Río: Beauty in Light and Shade*. Stanford, CA: Stanford University Press, 2013.

Hartley, Marsden. "Red Man Ceremonials." *Art and Archaeology* 9, no. 1 (January 1920): 7–14.

Hayes, Joy Elizabeth. "National Imaginings on the Air: Radio in Mexico, 1920–1950." In *The Eagle and the Virgin: Nation and Cultural Revolution in Mexico, 1920–1940*, edited by Mary Kay Vaughn and Stephen E. Lewis, 243–58. Durham, NC: Duke University Press, 2006.

Hedrick, Tace. *Mestizo Modernism: Race, Nation and Identity in Latin America*. New Brunswick, NJ: Rutgers University Press, 2003.

Herrera, Haydn. *Frida: A Biography of Frida Kahlo*. New York: Harper and Row, 1983.

Herrera Carrillo, Pablo. *Pablo Herrera Carrillo: Sus combates por la historia*, edited by Aidé Grijalva, Max Calvillo, and Leticia Landín. Mexicali, México: Universidad Autónoma de Baja California, 2005.

Herrera-Sobek, Maria, ed. *Celebrating Latino Folklore: An Encyclopedia of Cultural Traditions*. Santa Barbara, California: ABC-CLIO, 2012.

Hewes, Harry L. "The Mexican Ballet-Symphony *H.P.*" *Bulletin of the Pan American Union* 66, no. 6 (June 1932): 421–24.

Hilton, Alison. *Russian Folk Art*. Bloomington: Indiana University Press, 1995.

Hobsbawm, Eric J. *Nations and Nationalism since 1780: Programme, Myth, Reality*. 2nd ed. Cambridge: Cambridge University Press, 2012.

Homans, Jennifer. *Apollo's Angels: A History of Ballet*. New York: Random House, 2010.

[Hurok, Sol]. *Pavlowa*. New York: Wander Press, 1921.

Ibarra Chávez, Fernando. "Notas sobre la crítica de arte en el México revolucionario." *Discurso Visual* 35 (January–June 2015): 24–33.

[Instituto Nacional de Bellas Artes]. *Adolfo Best Maugard. La espiral del arte*. Edited by Fernández Félix and José Valtierra. México: Instituto Nacional de Bellas Artes, 2016.

Järvinen, Hanna. "'The Russian Barnum': Russian Opinions on Diaghilev's Ballets Russes, 1909–1914." *Dance Research Journal* 26, no. 1 (Summer 2008): 18–41.

Jáuregui, Jesús. *El Mariachi: Símbolo Musical de México*. México: Instituto Nacional de Antropología e Historia, 2007.

Jiménez Codinach, Guadalupe. "Death Is Nothing When One Dies for the Nation." In *Forging patrias: Iberoamérica 1810–1824, Some Reflections*, edited by Guadalupe Jiménez Codinach, 233–85. México: Fomento Cultural Banamex, 2010.

Jones, Kim. "American Modernism: Reimagining Martha Graham's Lost Imperial Gesture (1935)." *Dance Research Journal* 47, no. 3 (December 2015): 51–69.

Jowett, Deborah. *Jerome Robbins: His Life, His Theater, His Dance*. New York: Simon & Schuster, 2004.

Juárez Reyes, América, "Polyforum Cultural Siqueiros: La trayectoria de una magna obra." In *Reencuentro con la obra mural de Siqueiros: Proceso creativo del Polyforum*, 42–46. México: Consejo Nacional para la Cultura y las Artes, Instituto Nacional de Bellas Artes, 1999.

Kendall, Elizabeth. *Where She Danced: The Birth of American Art-Dance*. Berkeley: University of California Press, 1979.

Kennel, Sarah. "Le Sacre du Printemps: Primitivism, Popular Dance, and the Parisian Avant-Garde." *Nottingham French Studies* 44, no. 3 (2005): 4–23.

Kerensky, Oleg. *Anna Pavlova*. London: Hamish Hamilton, 1973.

Kharitonova, Irina, ed. *The World of Art Movement in Early 20th-Century Russia*. Leningrad: Aurora Art Publishers, 1991.

Kiddle, Amelia M. "*Cabaretistas* and *Indias Bonitas*: Gender and Representations of Mexico in the Americas during the Cárdenas Era." *Journal of Latin American Studies* 42 (2010): 263–91.

Klahn, Norma. "Nellie Campobello." In *Concise Encyclopedia of Mexico*, edited by Michael S. Werner, 60–61. Chicago: Fitzroy Dearborn Publishers, 2001.

Knappe, Brett. "Barbara Morgan's Photographic Interpretation of American Culture, 1935–1980." PhD diss., Res Foundation Department of the History of Art, University of Kansas, 2008.

Kolb-Neuhaus, Roberto. *Silvestre Revueltas (1899–1940). Catálogo de sus obras*. México: Universidad Nacional Autónoma de México, Escuela de Música, 1998.

———. "Silvestre Revueltas's *Colorines* vis-à-vis US Musical Modernisms: A Dialogue of the Deaf?" *Latin American Music Review* 36, no. 2 (Fall/Winter 2015): 194–230.

Kosstrin, Hannah. "Inevitable Designs: Embodied Ideology in Anna Sokolow's Proletarian Dances." *Dance Research Journal* 45, no. 2 (August 2013): 5–23.

Krauze, Enrique. *Mexico: Biography of Power*. Translated by Hank Heifetz. New York: Harper Perennial, 1998.

———. *Redeemers: Ideas and Power in Latin America*. Translated by Hank Heifetz and Natasha Wimmer. New York: Harper Perennial, 2012.

Kuss, Malena. "*Huemac*, by Pascual de Rogatis: Native Identity in the Argentine Lyric Theatre." *Anuario Interamericano de Investigacion Musical* 10 (1974): 68–87.

———. "The 'Invention' of America: Encounter Settings on the Latin American Lyric Stage." *Revista de Musicología* 16, no. 1 (1993): 185–204.

Laughlin, Eleanor A. "The Emperor's New Clothes: Maximilian von Habsburg and the Visual Culture of Dress during Mexico's Second Empire." *Hispanic Research Journal* 18, no. 5 (2017): 391–410.

Lavalle, Josefina. "Anna Pavlova y el jarabe tapatío." In *Danza en México: Visiones de cinco siglos*. Vol. 1. *Ensayos históricos y analíticos*, edited by Maya Ramos Smith and Patricia Cardona Lang, 635–50. México: Centro Nacional de Investigación, Documentación e Información de la Danza "José Limón," 2002.

———. *En busca de la danza moderna mexicana: Dos ensayos*. México: INBA, 2002

Lazzaroni, John, and Rebecca Lazzaroni. *Pavlova: Repertoire of a Legend*. New York: Schirmer Books, 1980.

Lempérière, Annick. "Los dos centenarios de la independencia mexicana (1910–1921): De la historia patria a la antropología cultural." *Historia Mexicana* 45, no. 2: 317–52.

León-Portilla, Miguel. *Aztec Thought and Culture*. Translated by Jack Emory Davis. Norman: University of Oklahoma Press, 1963.

Limón, José. "The Making of Tonantzintla." *Dance Magazine*, August 1951: 12–15.

———. *José Limón: An Unfinished Memoir*. Edited by Lynn Garafola. Middletown, CT: Wesleyan University Press, 2001.

Limón, José E. "Greater Mexico, Modernism, and New York: Miguel Covarrubias and José Limón." In *The Covarrubias Circle*, edited by Kurt Heinszelman, 83–100. Austin: University of Texas Press, 2004.

López, Rick A. "The Noche Mexicana and the Exhibition of Popular Arts: Two Ways of Exalting Indianness." In *The Eagle and the Virgin: National and Cultural Revolution in Mexico, 1920–1940*, edited by Mary Kay Vaughn and Stephen E. Lewis, 24–42. Durham, NC: Duke University Press, 2006.

———. *Crafting Mexico: Intellectuals, Artisans, and the State after the Revolution*. Durham, NC: Duke University Press, 2010.

López Binnqüist, Citlalli. "En Tiempos de la Quinta Alicia." *Luna Córnea* 31: 6–21.

Luna Arroyo, Antonio. *Ana Mérida en la historia de la danza mexicana moderna*. México: Publicaciones de danza moderna, 1959.

———. *Panorama de la escultura mexicana Contemporánea: Estudio precedido de un ensayo histórico-estético sobre la escultura prehispánica, colonial y del México*. México: Instituto Nacional de Bellas Artes, 1964.

Lynton, Anadel. "Anna Sokolow." *Cuadernos del CID Danza* 20, 1988.

———. "Rocío Sagaón: El gozo de vivir al fondo la danza, el arte, la vida." In *Lazos y ecos de la obra de Miguel Covarrubias. Arriaga, Castro, Sagaón*, 273–357. México: Instituto Nacional de Bellas Artes y Literatura, 2013.

Macias, Anna. "Women and the Mexican Revolution, 1910–1920." *Americas* 37, no. 1 (July 1980): 53–82.

Madrigal, Érika. "Tamayo y los Contemporáneos. El discurso de lo clásico y lo universal." *Anales del Institute de Investigaciones Estéticas* 92 (Spring 2008): 155–89.

Malvido, Adriana. *Zapata sin bigote*. México: Plaza Janés, 2003.

Marsh, Geoffrey. "Serge Diaghilev and the Strange Birth of the Ballets Russes." In *Diaghilev and the Golden Age of the Ballets Russes 1909–1929*, edited by Jane Pritchard, 15–26. London: Victoria and Albert Museum, 2010.

Massine, Léonide. *My Life in Ballet*. New York: MacMillan, 1968.

Mathieu, Camille. "Origin Points, Archaeology, and the Search for Authenticity." In *Picasso and Rivera: Conversations across Time*, edited by Diana Magaloni and Michael Govan, 72–95. New York: Delmonico Books, 2016.

McDonagh, Don. *Martha Graham: A Biography*. New York: Praeger Publishers, 1973.

Mendoza, Cristina. Introduction to *Escritos de Carlos Mérida sobre el arte: La danza*, edited by Cristina Mendoza, 13–37. México: INBA/Centro Nacional de Investigación y Documentación de Artes Plásticas, 1990.

———. "Su contribución a la danza." In *Homenaje nacional a Carlos Mérida. Americanismo y abstracción*, edited by Mario de la Torre, 161–88. Monterrey, México: Museo de Monterrey, 1993.

Mérida, Carlos. *Modern Mexican Artists*. México: Frances Toor Studios, 1937.

———. "Pre-Hispanic Dance and Theatre." *Theatre Arts Monthly*, August 1938: 561–69.

———. *Escritos de Carlos Mérida sobre el arte: La danza*, edited by Cristina Mendoza. México: Centro Nacional de Investigación y Documentación de Artes Plásticas, 1990.

Miller, Frank J. *Folklore for Stalin: Russian Folklore and Pseudofolklore of the Stalin Era*. New York: M. E. Sharp, 1990.

Miller, Margaret Stevenson. *The Economic Development of Russia: 1905–1914*. London: Frank Cass and Company, 1967.

Miralles, Francesc, and Charo Sanjuán. *Anglada-Camarasa y Argentina*. Barcelona: Ausa, 2003.

Money, Keith. *Anna Pavlova: Her Life and Art*. New York: Alfred A. Knopf, 1982.

Monsiváis, Carlos. "La nación de unos cuantos y las esperanzas románticas: Notas sobre la historia del término 'Cultura Nacional' en México." In *En torno a la cultura nacional*, edited by Héctor Aguilar Camín, 159–221. México: Instituto Nacional Indigenista, 1989.

———. "La perdurabilidad de los orígenes (crónica de un artista latinoamericano)." In *Homenaje nacional a Carlos Mérida. Americanismo y abstracción*, edited by Mario de la Torre, 16–29. Monterrey: Museo de Monterrey, 1993.

———. "'Los que tenemos unas manos que no nos pertenecen' (A propósito de lo 'Queer' y lo 'Rarito')." *Debate Feminista* 16 (October 1997): 11–33.

———. "Anita Brenner: The (Multiple) Story of Origins." In *Avant-Garde Art and Artists in Mexico: Anita Brenner's Journals of the Roaring Twenties*, edited by Susannah Joel Glusker, xi–xxiv. Austin: University of Texas Press, 2010.

Montenegro, Roberto. *Planos en el tiempo*. México: Imprenta Arana, 1962.

Moore, Lillian. "George Washington Smith." In *Chronicles of the American Dance from the Shakers to Martha Graham*, edited by Paul Magriel, 139–88. New York: Da Capo Press, 1978.

Mora, Carl J. *Mexican Cinema: Reflections of a Society*. Rev. ed. Berkeley: University of California Press, 1989.

Morales Mora, Mario. "Y la utopía se hizo luz." In *Misiones Culturales: Los años utópicos 1920–1938*, 69–131. México: Museo Casa Estudio Diego Rivera y Frida Kahlo, 1999.

Morales Moreno, Jorge. "Obras de arte y testimonios históricos: una aproximación al objeto artístico como representación cultural de la época." *Sociológica* 24, no. 71 (September–December 2009): 47–87.

Moyssén, Xavier. "Siqueiros antes de Siqueiros." *Anales del Instituto de Investigaciones Estéticas* 13, no. 45 (1976): 177–93.

Musacchio, Humberto. *El Taller de Gráfica Popular*. México: Fondo de Cultura Económica, 2007.

[Museo Tamayo Arte Contemporáneo]. *Antígona*. México: Museo Tamayo Arte Contemporáneo, 2014.

Norris, Leslie. *Leonide Massine and the 20th Century Ballet*. Jefferson, NC: McFarland and Company, 2004.

Novo, Salvador. *La estatua de sal*. México, DF: Consejo Nacional para la Cultura y las Artes, 2002.

Oettinger Jr., Marion. *Folk Treasures of Mexico: The Nelson A. Rockefeller Collection*. Houston: Arte Público Press, 2010.

Oles, James. "Rivera's Trophy." In *Picasso and Rivera: Conversations across Time*, edited by Diana Magaloni and Michael Govan, 146–61. New York: Delmonico Books, 2016.

Orozco, José Clemente. *Orozco "Explains."* New York: Museum of Modern Art, 1940.

———. *Artist in New York: Letters to Jean Charlot and Unpublished Writings, 1925–1929*, edited by Jean Charlot, translated by Ruth L. C. Simms. Austin: University of Texas Press, 1974.

Ortega y Medina, Juan. *Ensayos, tareas, y estudios históricos*. Xalapa, México: Universidad Veracruzana, 1962.

Ortíz Gaitán, Julieta. *Entre dos mundos: Los murales de Roberto Montenegro*. México: Instituto de Investigaciones Estéticas, 1994.

———. "La ciudad de México durante el Porfiriato: 'El París de América.'" In *México Francia. Memoria de una sensibilidad común; siglos XIX–XX*, edited by Javier Perez-Siller and Chantai Cramaussel, 179–96. Puebla: Centro Francés de Estudios Mexicanos y Centroamericanos, 2004.

Owen, Norton. *A Certain Place: The Jacob's Pillow Story*. 3rd ed. Becket, MA: Jacob's Pillow Dance Festival, 2017.

Panzer, Mary. "The Essential Tact of Nickolas Muray." In *The Covarrubias Circle*, edited by Kurt Heinzelman, 21–45. Austin: University of Texas Press, 2004.

Parker, Robert L. *Carlos Chávez: Mexico's Modern-Day Orpheus*. Boston: Twayne Publishers, 1983.

———. "Carlos Chávez and the Ballet: A Study in Persistence." *Dance Chronicle* 8, no. 3–4 (1985): 179–210.

———. *Carlos Chávez, A Guide to Research*. New York: Garland Publishing, 1998.

Pedroza, José Luis. "José Vasconcelos Calderón 1882–1959." In *Misiones Culturales: Los años utópicos 1920–1938*, 133–39. México: Museo Casa Estudio Diego Rivera y Frida Kahlo, 1999.

Pereda, Juan Carlos. "Los gouaches de Tamayo/Tamayo's Gouaches." In *Antígona*, 2–3. México: Museo Tamayo Arte Contemporáneo, 2014.

Pérez Montfort, Ricardo. "Un nacionalismo sin nación aparente. (La fabricación de lo 'típico' mexicano 1920–1950)." *Política y Cultura* 12 (1999): 177–93.

———. "Down México way. Estereotipos y turismo norteamericano en el México de 1922." *Cuadernos del Patrimonio Cultural y Turismo* 14 (2006): 13–32.

———. "Nacionalismo y representación en el México posrevolucionario: Una síntesis sobre la construcción de estereotipos nacionales." In *Facturas y manufacturas de la iden-*

tidad: Las artes populares en la modernidad mexicana, edited by Mieredia Velázquez, 97–123. México: Museo de Arte Moderno, 2010.

Perucho, Arturo. "El surgimiento de la danza moderna en México." *Artes de México* 8–9 (March–August 1955): 45–60, 70–122. Reprint of an article originally appearing in *Nuestra Música* 8 (October 1947).

Petkovski, Filip. "Professional Folk Dance Ensembles in Eastern Europe and the Presentation of Folk Dance on Stage." In *Music and Dance in Southeastern Europe: New Scopes of Research and Action*, 173–78. Belgrade, Serbia: ICTM Study Group on Music and Dance in Southeastern Europe, 2016.

Pierre, Dorathi Bock. "A Dancer Emerges." *American Dancer*, November 1936: 9, 39.

Pineda Franco, Adela. "Más allá del interior modernista: El rostro porfiriano de la *Revista Moderna* (1903–1911). *Revista Iberoamericana* 72, no. 214 (January–March 2006): 155–69.

Pizano y Saucedo, Carlos. "Centenario del Teatro 'Degollado' de Guadalajara." *Historia Mexicana* 16, no. 3 (January–March 1967): 419–26.

[Poliforum Siqueiros]. *Poliforum Siqueiros: Siqueiros, 1896–1996*. México: Poliforum Siqueiros, 1996.

[Polyforum Siqueiros]. *Polyforum Siqueiros: El legado de dos visionarios*. México, DF: Polyforum Siqueiros, 2012.

Poniatowska, Elena. *Miguel Covarrubias. Vida y mundos*. México: Ediciones Era, 2004.

Porter, Katherine Anne. *Katherine Anne Porter: Collected Stories and Other Writings*. New York: Library of America, 2008.

Powell, E. Alexander. "Eves of an Unknown Eden." *Everybody's Magazine* 23, no. 5 (November 1910): 579–92.

Prevots, Naima. *Dance for Export: Cultural Diplomacy and the Cold War*. Middletown, CT: Wesleyan University Press, 1998.

Pritchard, Jane. "Creating Productions." In *Diaghilev and the Golden Age of the Ballets Russes 1909–1929*, edited by Jane Pritchard, 71–88. London: Victoria and Albert Museum, 2010.

Queralt, María Pilar. *Tórtola Valencia. Una mujer entre sombras*. Barcelona: Lumen, 2005.

Ramírez, Fausto. *Crónica de las artes plásticas en los años de López Velarde, 1914–1921*. México: Instituto de Investigaciones Estéticas, 1990.

———. "Hacia la gran exposición del Centenario de 1910: El arte mexicana en el cambio del siglo." In *1910: El arte en un año decisivo*, 19–63. México: Museo Nacional de Arte, 1991.

———. "Emblemas y relatos del mundo prehispánico en el arte mexicano del siglo XIX." *Arqueología Mexicana*, November–December 2009: 54–61.

Ramos Smith, Maya. *La danza en México durante la época colonial*. México: Alianza Editorial Mexicana, 1990.

———. *Teatro musical y danza en el México de la belle epoque (1867–1910)*. México, Grupo Editorial Gaceta, 1995.

———. *Danza teatral en Mexico durante el virreinato (1521–1821)*. México: Escenologia, 2013.

Ramos Smith, Maya, and Patricia Cardona Lang, eds. *La Danza en México: Visiones de cinco siglos*. Vol. 1, *Ensayos históricos y analíticos*. Vol. 2, *Antología: cinco siglos de cróni-*

cas, crítica y documentos (1521–2002). México: Centro Nacional de Investigación, Documentación e Información de la Danza "José Limón," 2002.

Reed, Alma. *Orozco*. New York: Oxford University Press, 1956.

Reilly, Bernard F., Jr. "Miguel Covarrubias: An Introduction to the Caricatures." In *Miguel Covarrubias Caricatures*, edited by Beverly J. Cox, 23–38. Washington, DC: Smithsonian Institution Press, 1985.

Reyes de la Maza, Luis. *El teatro en México durante el Porfirismo. 1888–1899*. México: Instituto de Investigaciones Estéticas, 1965.

Reynoso, José L. "Choreographing Politics, Dancing Modernity: Ballet and Modern Dance in the Construction of Modern México (1919–1940)." PhD diss., University of California Los Angeles, 2012.

———. "Choreographing Modern Mexico." *Modernist Cultures* 9, no. 1 (2014): 80–98.

Richardson, William Harrison. *Mexico through Russian Eyes, 1806–1940*. Pittsburgh: University of Pittsburgh Press, 1988.

Rivera, Diego. *My Art, My Life*. With Gladys March. New York: Dover Publications, 1991.

———. "Raíces políticas y motivos personales de la controversia Siqueiros-Rivera. Stalinismo vs. Bolchevismo leninista." 1936. Reprinted in *Arte y política*, edited by Raquel Tibol, 111–25. Mexico City: Grijalbo, 1979. ICAA Record ID: 792906.

Rodríguez, María de las Nieves. "La 'noche mexicana' como parte de los festejos de celebración de la independencia de 1921." *Estudios* 105, no. 11 (Summer 2013): 57–71.

Rodríguez Mortellaro, Itzel A. "Indigenous Antiquity in the Work of Diego Rivera." In *Picasso and Rivera: Conversations across Time*, edited by Diana Magaloni and Michael Govan, 250–65. New York: Delmonico Books, 2016.

Rodríguez Ureña, Pedro. "Arte Mexicano." Epilogue to *Método del Dibujo*. 2nd ed., 130–134. México: Editorial Viñeta, 1964.

Romero, Jesús C. "Historia de la música." With Daniel Ayala Pérez and Fernando Burgos Samada. In *Enciclopedia Yucatanense*. 2nd ed. 4:669–767. México: Gobierno de Yucatán, 1977–1981.

Rosas Lopátegui, Patricia. "Nahui, Antonieta y Nellie: Transgresoras del siglo XX." *Casa del Tiempo* III, IV, no. 28 (February 2010): 2–6.

Rosenfeld, Paul. "American Composers, VIII: Carlos Chavez." *Modern Music* 9, no. 4 (May–June 1932): 153–59.

Ross, Janice. *Like a Bomb Going Off: Leonid Yakobson and Ballet as Resistance in Soviet Russia*. New Haven, CT: Yale University Press, 2015.

Rousset Banda, Guillermo, ed. *Siqueiros: Primeras obras: Neoimpresionismo y art nouveau*. Ciudad Juárez, México: Universidad Autónoma de Ciudad Juárez, 1996.

Rubenstein, Anne. "The War on Las Pelonas: Modern Women and Their Enemies, Mexico City, 1924." In *Sex in Revolution: Gender, Politics and Power in Modern Mexico*, edited by Jocelyn Olcott, Mary Kay Vaughn, and Gabriela Cano, 57–80. Durham, NC: Duke University Press, 2006.

Rueda, Salvador. "A Battle for Anthropology: The Legacy of Alfonso Caso." In *National Museum of Anthropology: 50th Anniversary*, edited by Antonio Saborit and Carla Zarebska, 30–50. México: Cooperativa La Joplin, 2014.

Rutherford, Annabel. "The Triumph of the Veiled Dance: The Influence of Oscar Wilde and Aubrey Beardsley on Serge Diaghilev's Creation of the Ballets Russes." *Dance Research* 27, no. 1 (Summer 2009): 93–107.

Saavedra, Leonora. "Of Selves and Others: Historiography, Ideology, and the Politics of Modern Mexican Music." PhD diss., University of Pittsburgh, 2001.

Sahagún, Bernardino de. *Historia general de las cosas de Nueva España*. Edited by Ángel María Garibay. 4th ed. México, DF: Editorial Porrua, SA, 1981.

Salazkina, Masha. *In Excess: Sergei Eisenstein's México*. Chicago: University of Chicago Press, 2009.

Saldivar, Gabriel. *El jarabe: Baile popular mexicano*. México: Talleres Gráficos de la Nación, 1937.

Salmond, Wendy R. *Arts and Crafts in Late Imperial Russia: Reviving the Kustar Art Industries, 1870–1917*. Cambridge: Cambridge University Press, 1996.

Santiago Sierra, Augusto. *Las Misiones Culturales (1923–1973)*. México: Secretaria de la Educación Pública, 1973.

Saveliev, Yuri R. "Anglada-Camarasa en Rusia a traves de la revista Mir Iskusstva (El Mundo del Arte)." In *El món d'Anglada-Camarasa*, edited by Francesc Fontbona, 36–42. Barcelona: Fundació "La Caixa," 2006.

Scott, John F. "La evolución de la teoría de la historia del arte por escritores del siglo XX sobre el arte mexicano del siglo XIX." *Anales del Instituto de Investigaciones Estéticas* 10, no. 37 (1968): 71–104.

[Secretaría de Educación Pública]. *Boletin de la Secretaría de Educación Pública* 1, no. 2 (September 1922).

Segura, Felipe. "La obra de Amalia Hernández." In *El ballet Folklórico de México de Amalia Hernández*, edited by Gabriela Aguirre Cristiani and Felipe Segura Escalona, 125–74. México: Fomento Cultural Banamex, 1994.

Shawn, Ted. *The American Ballet*. New York: Henry Holt, 1926.

Shay, Anthony. *Choreographic Politics: State Folk Dance Companies, Representation and Power*. Middletown, CT: Wesleyan University Press, 2002.

Shevelenko, Irina. "Empire and Nation in the Imagination of Russian Modernism." *Ab Imperio* 3 (2009): 171–206. English translation at https://sites.google.com/site/idshevelenko/.

Shirley, Wayne D. *Ballet for Martha: The Commissioning of Appalachian Spring and Ballets for Martha: The Creation of* Appalachian Spring, Jeux de Printemps *and* Hérodidae. Washington, DC: Library of Congress, 1997.

Siqueiros, David Alfaro. "Tres llamamientos de orientación actual a los pintores y escultores de la nueva generación americana." *Vida Americana* 1, no. 1 (May 1921): 2–3. ICAA Record ID: 801659.

———. *Me llamaban el coronelazo: Memorias*. México: Grijalbo, 1977.

Snow, K. Mitchell. *Movimiento, ritmo, música. Una biografía de Gloria Contreras*. México: Fondo de Cultura Económica, 2008.

———. "Martha Graham, Mexico and the American Gesture." *Dance Chronicle* 40, no. 1 (2017): 1–24.

Soares, Janet Mansfield. *Louis Horst: Musician in a Dancer's World*. Durham, NC: Duke University Press, 1992.

Solrac, Odelot. *Tortola Valencia and Her Times*. New York: Vantage Press, 1982.

Stein, Philip. *Siqueiros: His Life and Works*. New York: International Publishers, 1994.

Stein, William W. *Dance in the Cemetery: José Carlos Mariátegui and the Lima Scandal of 1917*. Lanham, MD: University Press of America, 1997.

Stepan, Nancy Leys. *"The Hour of Eugenics." Race, Gender and Nation in Latin America.* Ithaca, NY: Cornell University Press, 1991.

Stravinsky, Igor. *Expositions and Developments.* With Robert Craft. Garden City, New York: Doubleday, 1962.

Suárez Longoria, S. "La exposición de Arte Popular." *Azulejos,* October 1921. Reprinted in *La critica de arte en México: Estudios y documentos (1914–1921),* edited by Xavier Moyssén Echeverría and Julieta Ortíz Gaitán, 567–69. México: Instituto de Investigaciones Estéticas, 1999.

Suárez Ruiz, Ernesto. "Unas palabras." Introduction to *Siqueiros, Suárez y el Polyforum: Vidas paralelas, sin paralelos,* by Adrián García Cortés, xiii–xv. México: Polyforum Siqueiros, 2000.

Sutton, Tina. *The Making of Markova: Diaghilev's Baby Ballerina to Groundbreaking Icon.* New York: Pegasus Books, 2013.

Svetloff, Valerian. *Anna Pavlova.* Translated by A. Gray. New York: Dover Publications, 1974.

Tablada, José Juan. *Diario: 1900–1944.* México: Universidad Nacional Autónoma de México, 1992.

Tamayo, Rufino. *Textos de Rufino Tamayo.* Edited by Raquel Tibol. México: Universidad Nacional Autónoma de México, 1987.

Tenorio-Trillo, Mauricio. *Mexico at the World's Fairs: Crafting a Modern Nation.* Berkeley: University of California Press, 1996. http://ark.cdlib.org/ark:/13030/ft2k4004k4/.

Thompson, Karen. "Jean Charlot: Artist and Scholar." In *Jean Charlot: A Retrospective,* edited by Tom Kolbe. Honolulu: University of Hawai'i Art Gallery, 1990. https://jeancharlot.org/books-on-jc/1990_thomas-klobe_retrospective.pdf.

Tibol, Raquel. *Pasos en la danza mexicana.* México: Universidad Nacional Autónoma de México, 1982.

———. *José Clemente Orozco: Una vida para el arte. Breve historia documental.* México: Secretaria de Educación Pública, 1984.

Tiffany Studios. *Mosaic Curtain for the National Theatre of Mexico.* New York: Tiffany and Company, 1911.

Torres, Ana María. "Dibujos y grabados de Roberto Montenegro." In *Roberto Montenegro: Donación doctores John y Marie Plakos,* 20–24. México: Universidad Nacional Autónoma de México, 2011.

Torres Michúa, Armando. "Una geometría de resonancias mitológicas." In *Homenaje nacional a Carlos Mérida. Americanismo y abstracción,* edited by Mario de la Torre, 30–61. Monterrey, México: Museo de Monterrey, 1993.

Tortajada Quiroz, Margarita. *Danza y Poder.* 2 vols. México: Conaculta-INBA-Cenart, Biblioteca Digital Cenidi Danza, 2006. http://cenididanza.inba.gob.mx/PublacionesBD/MTortajada/index.html.

———. "La Coronela de Waldeen: Una danza revolucionaria." *Casa del Tiempo* I, V, no. 8 (June 2008): 54–60.

———. "Guillermo Arriaga, aferrado a su tierra y a su danza." In *Lazos y ecos de la obra de Miguel Covarrubias. Arriaga, Castro, Sagaón,* 27–113. México: Instituto Nacional de Bellas Artes y Literatura, 2013.

———. *Amalia Hernández. Artista universal y profeta en su tierra.* Ciudad de México: Ballet Folklórico de México, Secretaría de Cultura, INBA, Fomento Cultural Banamex, Fundación Roberto Hernández Ramírez, 2017.

Tovar, Rafael. "Presentación." Introduction to *Misiones Culturales: Los años utópicos 1920–1938*, 7–8. México: Museo Casa Estudio Diego Rivera y Frida Kahlo, 1999.

Turino, Thomas. "Nationalism and Latin American Music: Selected Case Studies and Theoretical Considerations." *Latin American Music Review* 24, no. 2 (Autumn/Winter 2003): 169–209.

Vachon, Ann. "Limón in Mexico; Mexico in Limon." In *José Limón: The Artist Re-Reviewed*, edited by Jane Dunbar, 71–84. New York: Routledge, 2000.

Vasconcelos, José. *Pitágoras: Una teoría del ritmo*. México: Cultura, 1921.

———. *La raza cósmica, misión de la raza iberoamericana*. Paris: Agencia mundial de librería, 1924.

———. *De Robinson a Odiseo. Pedagogía estructurativa*. 1935. Reprint. Monterrey, México: Senado de la República, 2002.

———. *La tormenta*. México: Ediciones Botas, 1936.

———. *Estética*. México: Ediciones Botas, 1936.

———. *La creación de la Secretaría de Educación Pública*, edited by Carlos Betancourt Cid. México: Instituto Nacional de Estudios Históricos de las Revoluciones de México, 2011.

Vassberg, David E. *Land and Society in Golden Age Castile*. New York: Cambridge University Press, 1984.

Vaughn, Mary Kay. *Cultural Politics in Revolution: Teachers, Peasants and Schools in Mexico 1930–1940*. Tucson: University of Arizona Press, 1997.

———. "Pancho Villa, the Daughters of Mary, and the Modern Woman: Gender in the Long Mexican Revolution." In *Sex in Revolution: Gender, Politics and Power in Modern Mexico*, edited by Jocelyn Olcott, Mary Kay Vaughn, and Gabriela Cano, 21–32. Durham, NC: Duke University Press, 2006.

Velasco Pufleau, Luis. "Nationalism, Authoritarianism and Cultural Construction: Carlos Chávez and Mexican Music (1921–1952)." Translated by Silvio J. dos Santos. *Music & Politics* 6, no. 2 (Summer 2012): 1–19.

Velázquez, Marco, and Mary Kay Vaughn. "Mestizaje and Musical Nationalism in Mexico." In *The Eagle and the Virgin: Nation and Cultural Revolution in Mexico, 1920–1940*, edited by Mary Kay Vaughn and Stephen E. Lewis, 95–118. Durham, NC: Duke University Press, 2006.

Velázquez, Mereida. "The Best Maugard Drawing Method and a New Generation of Artists." In *Paint the Revolution: Mexican Modernism, 1910–1950*, edited by Matthew Affron, Mark A. Castro, Dafne Cruz Porchini, and Renato González Mello, 291–99. Philadelphia: Philadelphia Museum of Art, 2016.

Velázquez Guadarrama, Angélica. "La exposición española de arte e industrias decorativas de 1910." In *1910: El arte en un año decisivo: Exposición española—exposición japonesa*, 7–30. México: Museo Nacional de Arte, 1991.

Villalba, Angela. *Mexican Calendar Girls. Golden Age of Calendar Art: 1930–1960*. San Francisco: Chronicle Books, 2006.

Walsh, Thomas. "'That Deadly Female Accuracy of Vision': Katherine Anne Porter and 'El Heraldo de Mexico.'" *Journal of Modern Literature* 16, no. 4 (Spring 1990): 635–43.

Warren, Larry. *Anna Sokolow: The Rebellious Spirit*. Amsterdam: Harwood Academic Publishing, 1998.

Warren, Sarah. "Crafting Nation: The Challenge to Russian Folk Art in 1913." *Modernism/ Modernity* 16, no. 4 (November 2009): 743–65.

———. *Mikhail Larionov and the Cultural Politics of Late Imperial Russia*. Burlington: Ashgate, 2013.

Wigman, Mary. *Liebe Hanya: Mary Wigman's Letters to Hanya Holm*. Edited by Claudia Gitelman. Translated by Marianne Forster and Catherine T. Klinger. Madison: University of Wisconsin Press, 2003.

Williams, Adriana. *Covarrubias*. Austin: University of Texas Press, 1994.

———. "Una breve mirada a Rosa Covarrubias." In *Rosa Covarrubias una americana que amó México*: 27–39. Puebla, México: Universidad de las Américas Puebla/Lunwerg Editores, 2007.

Wilson, Edmund. "Indian Corn Dance." Originally published in *The New Republic*, October 7, 1931. Reprinted in *American Earthquake: A Document of the Twenties and Thirties*, 361–65. New York: Farrar, Straus & Giroux, 1979.

Zemtsovsky, Izaly, and Alma Kunanbaeva. "Communism and Folklore." In *Folklore and Traditional Music in the Former Soviet Union and Eastern Europe*, edited by James Porter, 3–23. Los Angeles: UCLA, Department of Ethnomusicology, 1997.

Zurián de la Fuente, Carla. "Liquid Walls: Stained Glass in Mexican Art, 1900–1935." *Journal of Decorative and Propaganda Arts* 26 (2010): 12–43.

INDEX

Abbot Mendoza (pseudonym), 73
aborigines, 26, 131, 133, 242
Academia de la Danza Mexicana, 157–58, 199, 227, 231
Academy of San Carlos, 36–38, 54, 246, 271n3 (chap. 4)
Acevedo, Esther, 22
Adamchevsky, Carol, 121, 177
Aeschylus, 23
aesthetics, 10, 21, 28, 41, 48, 56, 87, 105, 162, 200, 222; contemporary Indian, 69; development, 25, 48; modernist, 27, 36, 69; values, 111
Aguilar, Fernando Ramirez de, 147
Aguirre, Ignacio, 151, 157
Ailey, Alvin, 295n16 (chap. 10)
Alemán, Miguel, 172, 190, 200, 202, 206, 209, 291n8 (chap. 9)
Allen, Maud, 71
Allerhand, Ruth, 281n37 (chap. 6)
Altamirano, Ignacio M., 123
American Ballet Theatre, 171–73, 175–76, 189, 192, 222, 287n129 (chap. 7)
Amero, Emilio, 148
Anaya Soto, Raúl, 226
Anderson, Benedict, 8–9, 17
Anderson, Sherwood, 231
Anglada Camarasa, Hermen, 40–42, 45–46, 53, 70, 131, 265–66n107 (chap. 2), 282n67 (chap. 6)
anthropology, 13, 20, 203–4, 243
Antinus, Pepe, 218

architecture, 75, 88, 162, 179; baroque, 215; colonial, 53; postconquest, 90
Arenal, Angélica, 243
Argentina, 89, 131, 291n9 (chap. 9)
Arriaga, Guillermo, 210, 222–27, 232, 239, 297n93 (chap. 10); Zapata, 225–28, 239
art: aboriginal, 47, 81, 86–87, 131; decorative, 34, 64, 129; folk, 2, 9, 36, 46, 51, 54, 64–65, 67, 83–84, 87, 89–90, 102, 138, 243, 250; high, 62, 83, 174; indigenous, 21, 131; Mexican, 14, 39, 61–62, 66, 102, 139, 241, 255; national, 16, 21, 25–26, 51, 116, 232, 245; nationalist, 17, 21–22, 27, 31, 47, 87, 88, 89, 131, 148; preconquest, 28, 63; visual, 9, 28, 166, 212, 254
art forms, 8, 57, 120, 145, 183, 201, 232, 236; new, 152; indigenous, 59; traditional, 237
art history, 37, 61, 216
artists, Mexican, 28, 34, 79, 89, 114, 158, 160, 222, 232, 254–55
Atl, Dr. See Dr. Atl
Aulestia, Patricia, 126, 176
authenticity, 27, 213 218, 247
Ávila Camacho, Manuel, 169, 172, 186, 189
Azcárraga Vidaurreta, Emilio, 240
Aztecs, 18, 39–40, 75, 95, 97–99, 101, 108, 176, 276n44 (chap. 5); calendar, 97; creation story, 101, 276n44 (chap. 5); dances, 73–74, 118, 125, 275n24 (chap. 5); mythology, 97, 213; Sunstone, 17, 101; warriors, 65, 90; world, 97, 100

Bach, Johann Sebastian, 165

Bakst, Léon, 30, 41, 50–51, 56, 58, 89, 92, 265–66n107 (chap. 2)

Balanchine, George, 287n2 (chap. 8), 291–92n12 (chap. 9), 297n93 (chap. 10)

Balderas, Esperanza, 53

ballet: Aztec, 29, 100, 122, 275n26 (chap. 5), 281n37 (chap. 6); classical, 9, 13–14, 120–21, 125, 126, 130, 138, 146, 173, 188, 198, 200, 204, 206, 208–9, 235, 241, 284n12 (chap. 7), 287n1 (chap. 8); Mexican, 53, 95, 124, 172–74, 179–80

Ballet de Bellas Artes, 143, 154, 163, 228, 233, 239–40

Ballet Folklórico (Hernández), 15, 220, 222, 225, 241–44, 248–50, 254, 297n78 (chap. 10)

Ballet Moderno de México (Hernández), 220, 240, 248

Ballet Nacional (Bravo), 205, 215–16, 220, 232, 238, 239, 254–55

Ballet Popular (Arriaga), 238–39, 297n93 (chap. 10)

Ballet Waldeen (Bravo and Mérida), 199–200, 202, 206

Ballets Russes, 8, 12, 31–32, 41–44, 47–52, 55, 70, 74, 81, 89, 92, 94–95, 99–100, 117, 131, 159, 171, 179, 181–82, 206, 255, 263n49 (chap. 2), 265n99 (chap. 2), 266n14 (chap. 3), 274n3 (chap. 5). See also Diaghilev, Serge

Ballets Russes de Monte Carlo, 49, 136–38, 287n2 (chap. 8). See also de Basil, Wassily

Balmori, Santos, 147, 206, 228

Bal y Gay, Jesús, 153

Barajas Duran, Rafael, 83, 167

Barbier, George, 43

Barili, Aldo, 121

Barreda, Octavio, 100, 106, 276n32 (chap. 5)

Barricada (Campobello sisters), 178–80

Barros Sierra, José, 144, 156–57, 179–80

Barton, Ralph, 34

Bassols, Narciso, 138, 273n61 (chap. 4)

Baudelaire, Charles, 42

Bautista, Juan, 197, 291n113 (chap. 8)

Beardsley, Aubrey, 42–43, 45

Beaumont, Cyril, 42–43

Beethoven, Ludwig van, 67, 71, 106, 196

Belmont, Cristina, 196–97

Belnap, Jeffrey, 110–11

Beloff, Angelina, 45

Ben Ali (pseudonym), 10–11

Benois, Alexandre, 47–49, 50

Berdecio, Roberto, 287n129 (chap. 7)

Bergamín, José, 152–54, 158

Berlin, 60, 70, 281n37 (chap. 6)

Bernal, Farnesio de, 233–34

Best, Emma, 41

Best Maugard, Adolfo, 55, 61, 65 85, 87, 92, 95, 209, 268n52 (chap. 3); designs, 63, 65; method, 63–64, 269n90 (chap. 3); Metodo de Dibujo, 129; Noche Mexicana, 85–87

Bidault, Sophie, 8, 177–78, 287n1 (chap. 8)

Bilibin, Ivan, 47

Bismarck, Otto von, 159

Blake, William, 159

Blanc, Jaime, 255

Blitzstein, Marc, 113

Boas, Franz, 20, 63

body, human, 103, 146, 201, 228

Bohm, Jerome D., 161

Bolio, Mediz, 74

Bolm, Adolph, 49, 65, 95, 145, 206, 274–75n8 (chap. 5)

Bolshoi Ballet, 14, 237

Bordes, Diana, 213

Bowles, Paul, 175, 288n16 (chap. 8)

Bracho, Martha, 157, 213

Braque, Georges, 34

Bravo, Guillermina, 14, 143, 163, 169, 199–200, 202–6, 215–17, 220, 232, 234–35, 237–38, 248, 253–56, 293–94n80 (chap. 9), 297n82 (chap. 10); Constelaciones y danzantes, 255–57; as leftist, 205; as young choreographer, 254. See also Ballet Nacional; Ballet Waldeen

Breme Hugo, 268n67 (chap. 3)

Brenner, Anita, 2 16, 102, 183
Broadway, 9, 66, 204, 209
Broun, Joseph. *See* Cordelio Cárdenas, José
Bucharest, 226–27, 236–37
Buenos Aires, 41, 59, 291n9 (chap. 9)

Cabildo, Raziel, 55–56
Calles, Plutarco Elías, 116–17, 121–22, 124, 138, 190
Campobello, Gloria, 12–13, 32–33, 58, 67, 121, 171, 177, 178, 181–86, 188, 190–94, 196, 290n110 (chap. 8); *Alameda 1900*, 186, 192; *Pausa*, 187, 196; works, 187. See also *Barricada*; Campobello, Nellie; Orozco, José Clemente
Campobello, Nellie (María Francesca Moya Luna), 12–13, 24, 32–33, 59, 67, 121–23, 127, 130, 139–40, 143–44, 152, 163, 167, 171–79, 181–83, 189–90, 192, 196, 197, 283n3 (chap. 7), 287n1 (chap. 8); *30-30*, 122–24, 127, 143, 178, 186–87, 196; conflict with others, 143, 283n3 (chap. 7); *Obertura Mexicana*, 186–87; sister's correspondence with Orozco, 289n53 (chap. 8); novels of, 12, 178; violence, 286n91 (chap. 7). See also *Barricada*; Campobello, Gloria; Escuela Nacional de Danza; Mérida, Carlos; SEP
Campos, Lourdes, 169
Carbajal, Claudia, 120, 121, 122, 223
Carballido, Emilio, 234
Cárdenas, Lázaro, 140, 142–43, 152, 169, 171
Cárdenas Samada, Cornelio, 96
Cardona, Olga, 226
Cardona, Patricia, 257
Carranza, Venustiano, 16, 58, 117, 151, 264–65n82 (chap. 2)
Carredano, Consuelo, 153
Carroll, Lettie, 10–11, 121, 177, 248, 290n110 (chap. 8)
Caso, Antonio, 230
Castellanos, Julio, 166, 172, 175–76, 186–87, 197, 203, 289n56 (chap. 8)
Castillo, Jesús, 132

Castro, Fidel, 227
Castro, Martha, 213, 217
Castro, Valentina, 213, 217
Castro Leal, Antonio, 137
Castro Padilla, Manuel, 60, 68, 95
catalogues: 1913 Russian folk art exhibit, 81, 82; Dr. Atl and, 81, 82, 83, 84–85; Posada and, 82, 83; Tugendhol'd and, 52
Celli, Vincenzo, 190, 192
Centurión, Manuel, 90, 140
Cervantes, Pedro, 233
Chagall, Marc, 172, 184–85, 189, 222
Charlot, Jean, 2, 10, 31–32, 38–39, 50–51, 55–57, 59, 64–65, 76–79, 83, 88–89, 91–92, 168, 243, 248, 266n11 (chap. 3), 271n8 (chap. 4); family background, 266n14 (chap. 3); *Mexican Mural Renaissance*, 2, 40, 56, 65, 88, 271n8 (chap. 4)
Chávez, Carlos, 12–13, 33, 94–111, 113–14, 116, 120, 127–30, 132, 134, 139, 140, 153, 154, 157, 158, 186, 188, 190, 199, 200, 202–3, 205–6, 212, 214, 254, 275n22 (chap. 5), 275n26 (chap. 5), 276n32 (chap. 5), 276n40 (chap. 5), 276n44 (chap. 5), 277n64 (chap. 5), 277–78n67 (chap. 5); and Diego Rivera, 109–11, 113, 115, 203, 205, 206, 210, 212–14, 220, 230, 276n32 (chap. 5); and Aztec culture, 97, 101, 275n26 (chap. 5); *Los cuatro soles*, 100–101, 104, 254; *H.P.*, 94, 106–8, 109–13, 139, 277n67 (chap. 5); ethnicity, 101, 105–6, 109; indigenous influences, 34, 94, 99; *Llamadas: Sinfonía proletariat*, 137; *Toxiumolpia: El fuego nuevo*, 95–99, 100, 101, 102–3, 104, 107, 254. *See also* Littlefield, Catherine; Flynn Paine, Frances; Stokowski, Leopold
Chavez Morado, José, 150, 170, 180, 203, 224
Chiapas, 20, 49, 218–19, 225, 247
Chicago, 3, 145, 159, 240, 242
Chichén Itzá (Mayan ruins), 74, 97, 101, 106
China, 15, 210, 222, 237, 254

China poblana, 6–7, 10, 19, 57, 60–63, 65–67, 69, 72, 79, 86, 182, 266–67n17 (chap. 3)

choreographers, 9, 13–14, 94, 102–3, 113, 119, 135, 142–44, 154, 159, 162, 168, 187–88, 196–97, 205, 208–9, 211–13, 218, 220, 225, 232, 240, 254, 297n93 (chap. 10)

choreography, 5, 32, 49, 103, 106, 112–13, 115, 139, 141, 154–55, 174, 179–80, 182, 187, 189, 204, 209, 215, 219, 226, 230–31, 239, 249, 253, 255–56; modern, 50, 89; popular Mexican, 146

Christians, Christianity, 101, 125, 135–36, 216, 270n99 (chap. 3)

churches, 47, 53, 79, 82, 135, 151, 186; colonial, 79; deconsecrated, 79

Ciocca, Giovanna, 59

Cirici Pellicer, Alexandre, 41

Clavijero, Francisco Javier, 17

Clayton, Michelle, 8, 57, 71

Cocteau, Jean, 100, 210

codexes, codices, 73, 99, 101, 103, 104, 276n40 (chap. 5), 276n44 (chap. 5)

Cold War, 253, 291–92n12 (chap. 9)

collaboration, 122, 130, 132, 154, 158, 165, 185, 194, 196, 241

communism, 162, 203, 234, 236–37, 250

Communist Party, 170, 236–37

concheros, 135, 218–19, 225

Contemporáneos (artists' group), 126–27, 254

Copland, Aaron, 31, 33

Coquet, Benito, 181

Cordelio Cárdenas, José (pseud. Josef; Joseph Broun), 285n73 (chap. 7)

Cordero Reiman, Karen, 65

Corn, Wanda, 28

Cornejo, Francisco, 29, 90, 139–40

Coronel, Juan, 209–10

Coronel, Pedro, 233

Cortéz, Hernan, 39, 121, 211

Costa, Adela, 120–21, 177

Costa, Linda, 121, 177

costume, costuming, 61, 65, 100, 104, 111, 133, 153, 155, 168, 172, 185, 196, 213, 226, 251

Covarrubias, Miguel, 13, 34, 64, 87, 100, 104, 162, 168, 199, 203, 204, 206–14, 215, 217–21, 224–25, 226, 228, 230–31, 233, 240, 291n9 (chap. 9); caricatures, 13; legacy, 232; method, 214; teachings, 239

crafts, 46, 52, 112. See also kustar

Cranko, John, 255

Craven, Thomas, 64

Creoles, 17, 96

Crespo de la Serna, Jorge Juan, 212

Crowninshield, Frank, 13, 28, 210

Cuauhtémoc, 18

Cuba, 58, 178, 204, 227, 240

cubism, 34, 51–53

Cuevas, José Luis, 14, 229–30, 260n46 (Intro.)

culture, 11, 16, 22, 28, 32, 34–35, 66, 69, 96, 118, 120, 143, 145, 162, 200, 204, 206, 231–32; and bureaucracy, 8, 94, 105, 235; folk, 23, 27, 117, 119; Mexican, 25, 29, 107, 109, 231; universal, 96, 190, 199–200, 232

Cunningham, Merce, 230

customs, 54, 75, 231, 242, 244; new, 236; regional, 55

Cuvillier, Charles, 209

Dallal, Alberto, 15, 139, 215, 238, 254–55, 257

Dambré, Nelsy, 158, 248

dance: Afro-Caribbean, 203; African-American, 5, 204; American, 30, 200, 202, 217; classical, 24, 96, 126, 146, 164; community, 145, 229, 254; groups, 133, 148, 164, 216, 237; Indian, 30, 34, 173; performances, 67, 86, 133, 137, 179, 241–42; programs, 13–14, 117–19, 147, 200, 206, 269n79 (chap. 3). See also theatrical dance

dancers: classical, 59, 146, 182, 206, 223; female, 5, 98, 225, 289n46 (chap. 8); Mexican, 8, 14, 66, 119, 141, 157, 169, 193, 205, 227, 230, 237, 239, 252;

modern, 15, 164, 198, 209, 222, 228, 238, 240, 253; professional, 7–8, 12, 129–30, 164, 218, 223, 237; trained, 9, 129, 198, 202, 237

dances: autochthonous, 247–48; folk, 9, 12, 15, 62, 67–68, 70, 208, 222, 225, 227, 233, 236, 239, 243, 250–51, 298n121 (chap. 10); Mexican folk, 7, 13, 57, 85, 97, 121, 165, 172–73, 251; Mexican theatrical, 8–9, 32, 143, 149, 165, 177, 202, 207, 255; national, 11, 67–68, 95, 132, 144, 222, 237, 239, 269n79 (chap. 3); regional, 9, 129–30, 133; ritual, 9, 125, 133; symbolic, 71, 108; traditional, 76, 103; Yaqui deer, 10, 33, 69, 97, 111, 118, 173, 225, 242. See also under indigenous

Daniel, Oliver, 108

Darío, Rubén, 37–38

de Basil, Wassily, 104, 136, 172, 182, 287n2 (chap. 8). See also Ballets Russes de Monte Carlo

de Bernal, Farnesio, 233

Debussy, Claude, 46

de Falla, Manuel, 152, 248

Delgado, César, 205, 216, 256–57

Delibes, Leo, 71

de los Reyes, Aurelio, 130

Delpar, Helen, 277n26 (chap. 5)

del Rio, Dolores, 58, 140

del Rio, Gabriel, 212

de Mille, Agnes, 56, 145, 241

DeMille, Cecil B., 75, 99, 275n24 (chap. 5)

Denishawn School of Dance, 290n110 (chap. 8)

Derba, Mimi, 269n75 (chap. 3)

designers, 9, 14, 89, 104, 188, 249

d'Harnoncourt, René, 291n9 (chap. 9)

Diaghilev, Serge, 36, 43, 46–50, 58, 89, 94, 96, 98–100, 136, 138, 146, 152, 274n3 (chap. 5); circle, 53, 265–66n107 (chap. 2); focus on folklore, 49; production style, 46, 58–59. See also Ballets Russes

Díaz, Porfirio, 18–19, 27, 37–40, 59, 136, 261n12 (chap. 1)

Díaz Ordaz, Gustavo, 246

Disney, Walt, 105

Dolin, Anton (Sydney Francis Patrick Chippendall Healey-Kay), 145, 192–93, 196

Dolinoff, Alexis, 112

Domingo, Francisco, 76

Domínguez, Francisco, 122, 132, 135–36, 160

Don Lindo de Almería (Sokolow), 152–54

Doráti, Antal, 173

Dr. Atl (Gerardo Murillo), 10, 39, 41, 80, 82, 84–85, 87, 177, 263n21 (chap. 2), 271n8 (chap. 4), 273n57 (chap. 4). See also under catalogues

Dreiser, Theodore, 231

Dromundo, Baltasar, 179–80

Duncan, Isadora, 7, 69, 86, 104, 159, 164, 201, 248

Dunham, Katherine, 145, 203–4

Duran, Diego, 5

Duran, Lin, 203, 239

Echavarría, Salvador, 195

Echeverría Alvarez, Luis, 246

Eisenhower, Dwight D., 291–92n12 (chap. 9)

Eisenstein, Sergei, 60, 180, 225

El Greco, 159, 164

Elizando, José, 288n39 (chap. 8)

Enciso, Jorge, 10, 39–41, 53, 55, 76, 79–81, 91

Escuela de Plástica Dinámica (part of SEP), 117, 120, 122–23, 126, 169, 179, 269n90 (chap. 3). See also Escuela Nacional de Danza; SEP

Escuela Nacional de Danza (part of SEP), 12–13, 129, 144, 152, 179, 190, 202, 217, 223, 254. See also SEP

Espert, Rosa, 59

Estrada, Enrique, 78

European: art, 21, 28, 83; classicism, 11, 22; cultures, 11, 96

Excélsior (newspaper), 55, 88, 111, 122, 147, 186–87, 193, 197, 231, 254

Fabrés, Antonio, 37
Fantasía Mexicana (Pavlova), 61–63, 65,
 85–86, 95, 118, 122, 172, 209
Favela, Ramon, 52
femininity, 6–7, 19, 156
Fernández, Justino, 36, 93, 166
Fernández Ledesma, Gabriel, 158, 90, 158,
 162, 165, 228
Ferrand, Diógenes, 74
festivals, 23, 56, 66, 68, 108, 119–20, 134,
 241, 247; Guelaguetza, 257; religious, 75;
 traditional, 162
Fierro, Rafael, 273n56 (chap. 4)
Flaccheba, Alberto, 73
Flores, Beatriz, 217
Florescano, Enrique, 17
Flores Guerrero, Raúl, 154, 216, 227
Flynn Paine, Frances, 101
Fokina, Vera, 29
Fokine, Mikhail, 29, 49, 50, 74, 172, 118,
 189, 201
folklore, 32, 45–46, 49, 52, 162, 165, 204,
 207, 236, 238, 243, 245, 247, 251; black,
 204; Caribbean, 145; national, 117, 131
Follet, Stella, 3
Fontbona, Francesc, 40, 46
Fonteyn, Margot, 62
Formoso, Adela, 156
Fox, Claire, 260n46 (Intro.)
France, 2, 49, 92, 210, 237
France, Anatole, 21
Francesco, Delia. *See* Rouskaya, Norka
Francis, José, 53
Francis, Xavier, 208–9, 212, 228–29
Franciscus, Delia. *See* Rouskaya, Norka
Franco, Rodolfo, 41
Fuentes, Carlos, 230
Fuentes, Enrique, 197
Fuller, Loïe (Marie Louise), 3–5, 6, 71

Galé, Carme, 177
Galindo, Blas, 153–54, 158, 165–66, 203, 207,
 286n101 (chap. 7)
Galletti, Armella, 59
Gamio, Manuel, 19–22, 25, 46, 81, 132

Garafola, Lynn, 110
García, Pilar, 63–64
García, Josefina, 224–25
García Morrillo, Roberto, 95, 96, 274n6
 (chap. 5), 279n85 (chap. 5)
Garfias, Alba Estela, 155
gender, 7, 121, 223
Gevaert, François Auguste, 275n26 (chap.
 5)
Glazunov, Alexander, 58
Goethe, Johann Wolfgang von, 23, 89–90
Golovin, Alexander, 50
Gómezanda, Antonio, 122, 281n37 (chap.
 6)
Gómez Sicre, José, 260n46 (Intro.)
Goncharova, Natalia, 63, 83
González, Carlos E., 120, 122
González Camarena, Jorge, 140
González Matute, Laura, 183, 185, 197
González Peña, Carlos, 58, 61, 63, 69, 73,
 76, 267n24 (chap. 3)
Gorky, Maxim, 23
Gorostiza, Celestino, 143–44, 149, 151,
 158, 162, 163, 203, 217, 239, 241, 283n3
 (chap. 7)
Gorostiza, José, 125, 276n32 (chap. 5)
Gounod, Charles, 58
Goya, Francisco, 154
Graham, Martha, 13, 29, 34, 94, 99, 107,
 136, 138, 142, 154, 157, 164–65, 202, 210,
 217, 240, 283n93 (chap. 6), 290n119
 (chap. 8); technique, 144–49, 237, 254,
 297n82 (chap. 10)
Grajales, Francisco J., 218
Greece, Greek, 36, 146; classics, 78; dance,
 130; figures, 86, 255
Greeley, Robin, 14, 25
Gris, Juan, 53, 265n106 (chap. 2)
Guadalupe Posada, José, 3–4, 51, 82, 166,
 234
Gutiérrez, Raquel, 213
Gutiérrez, Rodrigo, 41
Guzmán, Martín Luis, 52, 95, 147, 180,
 186, 214, 287n1 (chap. 8), 288n42
 (chap. 8)

Halffter, Rodolfo, 152–54, 158, 162, 214
Hartley, Marsden, 28
Henríquez, Pedro, 95
Hernández, Amalia, 164, 205, 220, 222, 225, 239–43, 246–252, 253, 254, 297n78 (chap. 10), 297n93 (chap. 10). See also Ballet Folklórico; Ballet Moderno de México
Hernández, Lamberto, 240
Hernández Araujo, Juan (pseud. of Jean Charlot and David Alfaro Siqueiros), 1, 64, 76, 88–89, 92; and dance, 1, 10, 50–51, 55; and Mexicanism, 1, 50, 55, 64, 76, 77, 88; See also Charlot, Jean; Siqueiros, David Alfaro
Hernández Moncada, Eduardo, 165
Hewes, Harry, 108
Hobsbawm, Eric, 9, 18
Hollywood, 30, 58, 75, 140, 160–61
Holm, Hanya, 202
homosexuality, 6, 45, 126–27, 223
Horst, Louis, 139, 149, 154, 157, 210, 283n99 (chap. 6)
Horton, Lester, 295n16 (chap. 10)
Hoy (newsmagazine), 172, 182, 184, 187, 192, 204, 209
Hoyos y Vinet, Antonio de, 75, 187, 226
Huerta, Efrain, 165
Huerta, Victoriano, 273n57 (chap. 4)
Hughes, Langston, 178
Huichol (people), 20, 112
Huízar, Candelario, 165
Humphrey, Doris, 202, 211, 224
Hurok, Sol, 242

Ibarra, Fernando, 57
imagination, 42, 167, 187, 204, 214, 251
imperialism, 145, 203, 244
INBA (Instituto Nacional de Bellas Artes), 13, 105, 147, 190, 199–200, 206–8, 212, 215, 218, 220, 225, 228, 233, 238–40, 294n99 (chap. 9); dance department, 206, 199, 210, 225. See also SEP
Inca, Incan, 74–76

Indians, 18, 26–32, 39, 62, 81, 102, 105, 108–9, 113, 131, 173, 205, 211, 214, 219; tribes, 128, 278n77 (chap. 5); tunes, 105, 114. See also under dance
indigenism, 25, 27, 242
indigenous: communities, 12, 118, 238; cultures, 11, 21, 96, 254; dances, 31–32, 56–57, 120, 133, 173, 204, 219, 242; music, 96, 99, 132, 253, 275–76n26 (chap. 5); past, 26, 28, 36, 130
intellectuals, 16, 46, 57, 145, 167, 230, 232, 244, 246
intelligentsia, 36, 70
Iron Curtain, 229, 232
Italian, Italy, 15, 48, 59, 210, 238, 275–76n26 (chap. 5)
Ito, Michio, 144, 159, 160, 285n69 (chap. 7)

Jacob, Max, 100
Japan, 159, 161, 162, 210, 264n66 (chap. 2)
jarabe (dance), 57, 59–61, 65–69, 79, 207, 227, 257, 269n75 (chap. 3); balleticized, 59, 87
jarabe tapatío (dance), 9–11, 51, 57, 59, 62, 66–67, 69, 79, 86, 95, 133, 136, 178, 182, 242, 260n35 (Intro.)
Järvinen, Hanna, 50
Jewell, Edward Allen, 114
Jiménez, Herminio, 91
Jiménez Mabarak, Carlos, 203, 224
Johansson, Ronny, 201
Josef. See Cordelio Cárdenas, José
Juárez, Benito, 90
Junius (pseudonym), 193–94

Kahlo, Frida, 64, 76, 113, 227–28
Kahn, Otto, 263n49 (chap. 2)
Kandinsky, Wassily, 40
Kay, Hershey, 287n129 (chap. 7)
Kendall, Elizabeth, 29
Kennedy, John Fitzgerald, 243
Kerensky, Oleg, 61
Keys, Guillermo, 217
Khvoshchinskia, Ruzhena, 53, 265n107 (chap. 2)

Kirstein, Lincoln, 104, 277n64 (chap. 5), 291–92n12 (chap. 9)
Kisselgoff, Anna, 14
Klimt, Gustave, 51
Knappe, Brett, 291n9 (chap. 9)
Kolb, Roberto, 156
Kosloff, Theodore, 29, 99, 159, 275n24 (chap. 5)
Kostakovsky, Iàkov (Jacobo), 179
Kotchetovsky, Alexander, 290n110 (chap. 8)
Kramer, Rebecca, 150
Krauze, Enrique, 6, 17
Kreutzberg, Harald, 159, 211
Kunanbaeva, Alma, 236
kustar, 46–47, 52, 264n66 (chap. 2)

Laban, Rudolph von, 119, 201, 217
Lagos Nocetti, Alberto, 41
language, 63, 81, 86, 124, 143, 169, 214, 216, 229, 231, 250; artistic, 216; choreographic, 235; universal, 208
Lara, Agustín, 218
Larionov, Mikhail, 51, 83
Latin America, Latin American, 27, 38, 41, 43, 69, 70, 71, 200, 282n67 (chap. 6), 291–92n12 (chap. 9)
Lavallade, Carmen de, 295n16 (chap. 10)
Lavalle, Josefina, 66, 162, 164, 166–68, 220, 239
Lawrence, Robert, 175
Lazo, Agustin, 100, 106, 203, 254, 277n67 (chap. 5); designs, 103, 278n71 (chap. 5)
League of Revolutionary Artists and Writers. See LEAR
Leal, Fernando, 83, 281n44 (chap. 6)
LEAR (Liga de Escritores y Artistas Revolucionarios), 137, 145, 148–51
Leeder, Sigurd, 248
Leidy, Philip, 109
León-Portilla, Miguel, 276n44 (chap. 5)
Lepri, Amalia, 121
Lerdo de Tejada, Miguel, 67, 85, 178
Lewis, Sinclair, 210

libraries, 23, 48, 84, 99; private, 99; public, 23
Lichine, David, 287n2 (chap. 8)
Limón, José, 13, 199, 201, 210–14, 216–17, 219–20, 224–25, 240, 291–92n12 (chap. 9); autobiography, 213, 293n57 (chap. 9)
Limón, José E., 211
Lindsay, Jossie, 3–4, 259n10 (Intro.)
List Arzubide, Germán, 147–48
Littlefield, Catherine, 94, 109, 112–13, 115
Littlefield, Dorothie, 112
Lombardo Toledano, Vicente, 226
London, 66, 248, 255
López, Amadao, 169
López, Nacho, 218, 230
Lopez, Rafael, 62
López, Rick, 7, 17, 19, 81, 87
López Mateos, Adolfo, 241
López Naguil, Gregorio, 41
Los Angeles, 139, 159, 161, 209
Luhan, Mabel Dodge, 30–31
Lukowsky, Georges, 47
Luna, Antonio, 203, 219, 294n99 (chap. 9)
Luna, Jaime, 185
Lunacharsky, Anatoli, 23

Madero, Francisco, 40, 63, 90, 117
La Malinche (Limón), 211–12
Mamontov, Slava, 47, 264n66 (chap. 2)
Mancisador, José, 147
Maples, Manuel, 26, 125
María y Campos, Armando de, 77, 204, 241
Markova, Alicia, (Lilian Alice Marks) 172, 192–94
Markova-Dolin Ballet, 192–94
Marks, Lilian Alice. See Markova, Alicia
Marsh, Geoffrey, 49
Martin, John, 94, 112–13, 161, 176, 189, 200–201, 211, 217, 277n67 (chap. 5), 293n62 (chap. 9), 294n87 (chap. 9)
Martin, Linton, 110
Martínez del Río y Viñent, Jaime, 59–61, 66
Marxism, 110, 208, 248

Maslova, Vlasta, 121

Maslow, Sophie, 248

Massine, Léonide, 102, 104, 145, 171–75, 180, 189, 287n2 (chap. 8); *Aleko*, 172, 176, 185, 189, 222; *Don Domingo de Don Blas*, 171, 172, 175

Matisse, Henri, 100, 276n32 (chap. 5)

Maximilian I, 18–19

Mayan, Mayas, 19 32, 74, 97, 106; architecture, 18; communities, 20; heritage, 218; ruins, 18, 74, 218

Maya-Quiché (people), 131–32

Mazahua (people), 100, 197

McDonagh, Don, 139

Mediz Bolio, Antonio, 73

Méndez, Leopoldo, 64, 137, 150

Mendoza, Cristina, 280n17 (chap. 6), 282n67 (chap. 6), 284n12 (chap. 7)

Mercé y Luque, Antonia (La Argentinita), 266n5 (chap. 3)

Mérida, Ana, 12, 134, 135, 148, 157, 199–200, 202, 206, 209, 213, 218, 223–24, 239, 240, 254, 294n99 (chap. 9); *Bonampak*, 218–19; and Guillermina Bravo, 205; influence of Katherine Dunham, 203–4; *Grupo Experimental*, 208. *See also* Ballet de Bellas Artes; Ballet Waldeen

Mérida, Carlos, 7, 9, 41, 87, 130, 135, 145, 158, 162, 179, 187, 197, 203; as artist, 140–41, 187; and Best method, 64; and dance technique, 145–47, 282n67 (chap. 6); designs, 155, 188, 199, 275n9 (chap. 5); and Escuela Nacional de Danza, 12, 136, 137; and Martha Graham, 139–40, 142; and indigeneity, 32, 130–36; and nationalist art, 47; and Diego Rivera, 279n104 (chap. 5); and Anna Sokolow, 145, 148–149

mestizos, 7, 16, 18, 20, 116, 128, 131, 219

Mexicanism, Mexicanists, 15, 27, 50–51, 55–57, 64, 69, 76–77, 96, 102, 126, 253, 257, 266n14 (chap. 3). *See also under* Hernández Araujo, Juan

Mexican Mural Renaissance. See under Charlot, Jean

Mexican Revolution, 2, 6, 11, 12, 16–17, 19, 22, 25, 27, 32, 35, 38, 40, 52, 58, 72, 79, 82, 89, 94, 117, 122, 166, 167, 178, 211, 273n57 (chap. 4), 293n57 (chap. 9); and art, 169, 247; and modernism, 2; and women, 6, 19, 165. *See also* Díaz, Porfirio; Villa, Francisco ("Pancho"); Zapata, Emiliano

Mexican school of painting, 25, 38, 45, 65, 93, 167, 207, 230, 253–54

Mexico, conquest of, 18, 25, 39, 99, 125, 211, 214

Meyerhold, Vsevolod Emilyevich, 46

Miller, Arthur, 231

Miramontes, Arnulfo, 72

Mir iskusstva group, 46–47

Misrachi, Alberto, 220

missionaries, cultural, 23, 118–19, 129, 132, 136, 261n33 (chap. 1)

Mistral, Gabriela, 123

Moctezuma, 29, 39, 75

modernism, modernists, 2, 13, 27–28, 45, 60, 69, 107, 127, 200, 236; European, 25; international, 34; Mexican, 2, 27, 34

modernity, 25–26, 62, 111, 180, 186, 257

Moiseyev, Igor Aleksandrovich, 15, 227, 237, 239, 250

Moiseyev Dance Company, 237, 239, 241, 251, 299n135 (chap. 10)

Molotov, Vyacheslav, 237

Moncayo, José Pablo, 203, 225, 289n56 (chap. 8)

Monferrer, Ulises, 184

Monsiváis, Carlos, 6–7, 16, 22, 25, 45, 251

Montenegro, Roberto, 1, 9, 10, 28, 36–38, 39, 42, 53–54, 56, 79–80, 81, 84, 89, 92, 93, 138, 184, 187, 197, 265n106 (chap. 2), 271n3 (chap. 4), 273n56 (chap. 4), 273n57 (chap. 4), 273n9 (chap. 5), 282–83n92 (chap. 6); aesthetics, 45; and Hermen Anglada, 40–42; approach to art, 87, 138; *Arbol de la Vida*, 1, 89–92, 273n61 (chap. 4); and Rubén Darío, 37–38; drawings, 42–44; homosexuality, 45, 92, 126, 267n35 (chap. 3); set design, 172, 184, 186, 187

Mora, Víctor, 187
Morales, Estrella, 163
Mordkin, Mikhail, 60
Moreno, Graciela, 225
Morgan, Barbara, 200, 211, 291n10 (chap. 9)
Morgan, Marion, 209
Morinigo, Higinio, 186
Morley, Sylvanus G., 74
Moscow, 14, 41, 150, 232–37, 250
Moxó y Francoli, Benito María, 18
Moya, Colombia, 249
Moya, Mauro Rafael, 33
Moya, Víctor, 164, 168
Moyssén, Xavier, 56
Muñoz Cota, José, 140
muralism, muralists, 2, 11–12, 14, 57, 78, 83, 92–93, 95, 114, 162, 167–68, 185, 228, 236, 244, 247, 250, 253
murals, 11, 25, 40, 76, 80, 88–93, 102, 110, 124, 138–39, 150–51, 182, 184–85, 192, 218, 226, 236, 243–48, 250, 273n56 (chap. 4)
Muray, Nickolas, 210
Murillo, Gerardo. See Dr. Atl
Musacchio, Humberto, 150
music, 19, 33, 68, 72, 99–100, 106, 108, 109, 155, 165, 200, 212; American Indian, 106; choral, 119; concrete, 238; early, 154; machine, 277–78n67 (chap. 5); nationalist, 27; native, 108; popular, 210
musicians, 8–9, 30, 35, 79, 85, 94–96, 130, 134, 140, 181, 202, 204, 208, 224, 253; mariachi, 6, 10
Mussorgsky, Modest, 58
myth, mythology, 2, 32, 38, 61, 74, 101, 135, 211, 213, 227, 276n44 (chap. 5); classical, 255; nationalist, 6

Nahuatl (people), 69, 74, 279n81 (chap. 5)
National Institute of Fine Arts (Mexico). See INBA
nationalism: nationalists, 3, 8–9, 14–15, 17, 20–21, 48, 51, 64, 73, 87, 126, 140, 215, 229–31, 233, 238, 246–47; extreme, 84; false, 231; Mexican, 16–17, 51, 97, 208, 232

National School of Dance (Mexico). See Escuela Nacional de Danza
Neighborhood Playhouse (New York), 101, 149, 161
Neruda, Pablo, 170, 287n129 (chap. 7)
Nervo, Amado, 37
New York City, 65, 139, 149, 157, 161, 170, 212, 217
New York Herald Tribune, 112, 161, 175
New York Times, 33, 94, 114, 157, 161–62, 176, 189, 200, 211, 217, 219
Nieves Rodríguez, María de las, 85
Nijinsky, Vaslav, 42–44, 46, 49, 74, 89, 263n49 (chap. 2), 264–65n82 (chap. 2)
Nikolais, Alwin, 297n82 (chap. 10)
Niño, Claudio, 196–97
Noriega, Elena, 233
Norris, Leslie, 173
North, Alex, 149
Novarro, Ramon, 140
Novo, Salvador, 84, 203, 224
Nuevo Teatro de Danza, 228–29, 239
Núñez, Roberto, 160
Nureyev, Rudolf, 242

Oaxaca, 7, 10, 49, 76, 84–85, 103, 116, 135, 194, 203–5, 225, 238, 255–57
Obregón, Adela, 154
Obregón, Álvaro, 80, 81, 90, 117, 122, 274n7
Obregón, José, 36
Obregón, Luis Felipe, 169
Obregón Santacilia, Carlos, 154, 156
Oles, James, 52
Ordoñez Ochoa, Salvador, 125
Orozco, Margarita, 191
Orozco, José Clemente, 9, 13, 26, 28, 38, 39, 48, 59, 93, 102, 138–39, 150, 167, 191, 199, 211–12, 222, 226, 253, 289n53 (chap. 8), 289n56 (chap. 8), 295n16 (chap. 10); and ballet, 171–98. See also Umbral
Orozco Rivera, Mario, 244
Orozco Romero, Carlos, 135
orquestas típicas, 19, 85, 106
Ortega y Medina, Juan, 18

Ortiz Gaitán, Julieta, 53, 90, 265–66n107, 273n61
Ortiz Rubio, Pascual, 116, 117, 125–26
Osuna, Sabino, 268n67 (chap. 3)
Otomi (people), 135, 234

painters, Mexican, 12, 128, 243, 245
Palacio, Antonio, 153
Paloma Azul, 154, 156
Pani, Alberto, 81
Panzer, Mary, 210
Papagos (people), 32
Paris, 2–3, 9, 18, 28, 36–38, 40–42, 49–53, 60, 66, 70, 73, 81, 89, 92, 100, 112, 117, 131, 138, 152, 181, 212, 241–42, 246
Parker, Robert, 96, 101, 104, 200
Partido Revolucionario Institucional. *See* PRI
Pas d'Acier, Le (Ballets Russes), 100, 106, 277n67 (chap. 5)
patriotism, 20, 231, 236
Paul V (pope), 298n117 (chap. 10)
Pavlova, Anna, 1, 6, 7, 8, 12, 55, 56, 57, 71, 112, 118, 121, 137, 177, 242, 243, 267n24 (chap. 3); death of, 122; and the jarabe tapatío, 57–69, 85–86, 95, 269n75 (chap. 3). See also *Fantasía Mexicana*
Paz, Octavio, 230
Pellicer, Carlos, 230
Pereda, Armando, 86
Pereda, María Cristina, 86
Peredo, Melchor, 191–92
Pérez, Eva, 7–8, 61, 66, 69, 118
Pérez Mendoza, Efrain, 25–26
Pérez Montfort, Ricardo, 66
Perucho, Arturo, 151, 153, 159, 166
Petrouchka, 42, 74, 101, 137, 175
Philadelphia, 106–10, 113–14, 188
Pianowski, Mieczyslaw, 60–61
Picasso, Pablo, 34, 51, 112, 137, 152, 153, 282n67 (chap. 6)
Pierre, Dorathi, 159–60
Piscator, Erwin, 281n37 (chap. 6)
PNR (Partido Nacional Revolucionario), 116–17, 124

Poe, Edgar Allan, 42
poets, 3, 37, 50, 71, 100, 118, 126, 170, 178, 186, 229, 246
Poiret, Paul, 92, 274n68 (chap. 4)
Poliakova, Elena, 117
Polovtsian Dances, 49, 118, 137
Polyforum, 243–44, 246–50, 252, 298n117 (chap. 10); mural, 248; theater, 247, 249
Pombo, Rafael, 154
Porfirian era, Porfiriato, 46, 79, 166
Porfirian-Sierra, Justo, 90
Portell Villa, Herminio, 113
Porter, Katherine Anne, 65
Posada, José Guadalupe, 3, 51, 83–84, 166–67, 259n10 (Intro.)
positivism, 20, 46
Potapovich, Mol, 12, 177
Powell, Alexander, 7
Prescott, William H., 99
Prevots, Naima, 291–92n12 (chap. 9), 299n135 (chap. 10)
PRI (Partido Revolucionario Institucional), 116
Prieto Posadas, Julio, 170
Prokofiev, Sergei, 106
propaganda, 110, 121, 143, 172, 200 246
Pruneda, Francisco, 120
Puebla, 7, 10, 133, 214, 225
pulque, 36, 48, 63, 66, 69

Quetzalcoatl, 73, 213

races, 19, 22, 26, 48, 57, 73, 87, 131, 133, 204, 243; barbarian, 32; mixed, 16; white, 30
Ramaugé, Roberto, 41
Rambova, Natacha (Winifred Kimball Shaughnessy), 75
Ramírez, Fausto, 39–40, 45
Ramirez de Aguilar, Fernando (pseud. Jacobo Dalevuelta), 147
Ramírez Vázquez, Mariano, 226
Ramos-Smith, Maya, 5
Rangel, Nicolás, 83
Ravel, Maurice, 204
rebozo, 72, 168, 207, 269n90 (chap. 3)

Reed, Alma, 2, 102, 183, 192, 289n56
(chap. 8)
Régnier, Henri de, 273n57 (chap. 4)
Reilly, Bernard, 34
Reiss, Robert, 114
repertories, 49, 57, 60, 65, 70, 90, 118,
136, 171, 176, 220, 239, 242, 247, 251,
266–67n17 (chap. 3), 297n93 (chap. 10)
representation, 4, 6, 10, 27, 31, 34, 46, 52,
56, 87–88, 135, 234, 242
Retes, José Ignacio, 223
Revista de Revistas, 25, 60, 73, 83, 92
Revista Moderna, 2, 42
Revueltas, Consuelo, 155
Revueltas, Fermín, 155
Revueltas, José, 155
Revueltas, Rosaura, 155, 287n129 (chap. 7)
Revueltas, Silvestre, 33–34, 153, 154–56,
158, 162, 165, 172–76, 230, 286n101
Reyes, Victor, 187, 204
Reyna, Rosa, 152, 157–58, 224–25, 233, 234,
238, 251
Reynoso, José, 62, 178
rhetoric, 117, 146, 166, 247; macho, 45,
102; populist, 143
Rico Covarrubias, Maria Elena, 213, 226
Rimsky-Korsakov, Nikolai, 58
Rios, José, 122
Riva Palacio, Vicente, 19
Rivera, Diego, 2, 9, 28, 36–40, 45, 51,
53, 63, 64, 82, 88, 89, 92, 93, 102, 109,
117, 124, 138–39, 167, 188, 199, 203,
221, 224, 226–27, 235, 244, 245, 253,
268n53 (chap. 3), 277–78n67 (chap.
5), 279n104 (chap. 5), 282n67 (chap.
6); 1931 MoMA show, 102, 107; and
the Contemporáneos, 126–27; and
design, 104, 105; and *H.P.,* 109–15;
leftism, 110, 117, 236; librettos, 106; and
Roberto Montenegro, 36–37; and Salon
d'Automne, 51–52; reaction to cubism,
51, 52, 180–81; and Tehuanas, 76. *See
also* SEP; *under* Zapatistas
Rivero, Luis, 257
Robbins, Jerome, 174

Rockefeller, Abby Aldrich, 102, 111
Rodríguez, Luis, 62
Rodríguez Lozano, Manuel, 64, 154
Roerich, Nicholas, 49, 278n77 (chap. 5)
Rogatis, Pascual de, 275–76n26 (chap. 5)
Rojo, Vicente, 227
Rolanda, Rosa (Rosemonde Della Cowan
Ruelas), 64, 209–10, 212, 217–21
Romero Rubio, Carmelita, 38
Rosado Vega, Luis, 183
Rosas, Patricia, 177
Rosenfeld, Paul, 100
Ross, Janice, 237
Rothafel, Samuel Lyon, 102, 103
Rouskaya, Norka (pseud. of Delia Fran-
cesco, Delia Franciscus), 71–74, 76, 97,
270n110 (chap. 3)
Rousset Banda, Guillermo, 56
Rubín, Pedro, 9, 66
Rubinstein, Ida, 112
Ruiz, Antonio ("El Corzo"), 153, 158, 187
Ruiz Cortines, Adolfo, 219, 233

Saavedra, Leonora, 96, 97, 99
Sáenz, Moisés, 35
Sagán, Rocío (Rocío López Bocanegra),
210, 213, 217–19, 221, 225–26, 228, 233,
294n87 (chap. 9)
Salas, Ángel, 228
Salazar, Adolfo, 172, 174
Salazkina, Masha, 60
Saldaña, Jorge, 245
Saldivar, Gabriel, 68
Salmond, Wendy, 46
Salome (Wilde), 45, 71, 270n110 (chap. 3)
Salon d'Automne (Paris), 51, 81–82
Salvador, Rueda, 17
Sámano, Eva, 297n93 (chap. 10)
Sánchez Cárdenas, Carlos, 234
Sandi, Luis, 147, 203
sandunga (dance), 10, 57, 69, 76–77,
85–86, 95, 108–9, 113, 136, 188, 194,
260n35 (Intro.)
Sano, Seki, 162, 167, 195, 199
Scarlatti, Domenico, 207

scenographers, scenography, 130, 180, 184–85

Schaffenburg, Fernando, 190

Schéhérazade, 42–44, 49, 264–65n82 (chap. 2)

Scheijen, Sjeng, 96

Scherer García, Julio, 245

School of Dynamic Plastique (Mexico). *See* Escuela de Plástica Dinámica

Schubert, Franz, 185, 196

Scott, John, 83

sculptors, 14, 148, 165

sculptures, 17, 39, 75, 90, 103, 235, 238

Secretaría de Educación Pública. *See* SEP

Segovia, Andrés, 210

Segura, Felipe, 182–83, 190–92, 196–97, 240–42, 251

SEP (Mexican Ministry of Education), 1, 6, 10, 12, 23, 95, 120, 122, 123, 124, 125, 127, 132, 138, 140, 199, 202, 223, 225, 254, 274n7 (chap. 5); arts in, 12, 25, 180, 181; and Campobello sisters, 13, 124, 129, 142, 177–78, 202; dance in, 66, 67–69, 97, 116–18, 120–22, 130–40, 217; and INBA, 212–13; publications, 64, 119 162; Rivera's murals in, 76, 88, 92, 93, 111, 117; scope, 11, 23, 68, 119. *See also* Campobello, Nellie; Escuela Nacional de Danza; Escuela de Plástica Dinámica; Graham, Martha; INBA; Sokolow, Anna; Vasconcelos, José; Waldeen

serapes, 52, 69, 72, 84, 269n90 (chap. 3), 288n42 (chap. 8)

Shaffer, Rosalind, 274n8 (chap. 5)

Shawn, Ted, 29–30, 73, 99, 224–25

Shay, Anthony, 10, 243, 250, 266–67n17 (chap. 3), 297n82 (chap. 10)

Shevelenko, Irina, 50

Sierra, Justo, 39–40, 90

Silva, Ricardo, 223

Singerman, Berta, 93

Siqueiros, Adriana, 228, 233, 235, 248–49, 297n78 (chap. 10)

Siqueiros, David Alfaro, 1, 7, 14, 93, 167, 207, 228–29, 231, 233, 236–37, 243–44, 246–50, 252, 253, 282n67 (chap. 6), 298n117 (chap. 10); manifesto in *Vida Americana,* 27–28, 43–45, 165; paintings, 15, 55–56, 150, 243, 244–46; *See also* Hernández Araujo, Juan

Smith, George Washington, 267n37 (chap. 3)

Smith, Joseph C., 267n37 (chap. 3)

Sokolovas, 143, 152 157–58, 203

Sokolow, Anna, 13, 142, 148–57, 159, 162–66, 169, 171, 205–6, 208, 230–32, 233, 248–49; politics, 143–44, 149; technique, 142, 144, 145, 151; and Waldeen, 142–43, 164, 200, 202, 206; works, 148. See also *Don Lindo de Almería;* Graham, Martha; LEAR; Mérida, Carlos

Soler, Antonio, 154, 214

songs, 3, 16, 23, 62, 67, 120, 241, 275–76n26 (chap. 5), 287n129 (chap. 7); popular, 48, 63, 183

Soriano, Juan, 203, 233

Sotelo Inclán, Jesús, 215

Souchy, Agustin, 174

South America, 42, 247, 291–92n12 (chap. 9)

Soviet Union, 14–15, 145, 149–50, 235–37, 239, 243, 250, 284n12 (chap. 7), 297n78 (chap. 10); arts, 236; and China, 222, 254

Spain, 2, 16, 18, 36, 38, 59, 65, 69–70, 75, 78, 152, 154, 181, 270n99 (chap. 3), 271n19 (chap. 4)

Spaniards, 25, 39, 46, 131

Stalin, Joseph, 162, 165, 206

Stalinism, 250

St. Denis, Ruth, 7, 71

Stokowski, Leopold, 105–9, 113, 139, 278n77 (chap. 5)

Stoner, Harry, 79

St. Petersburg, 49, 117, 201

Strauss, Johann II, 190

Stravinsky, Igor, 50, 94, 136, 139, 207, 212, 278n77 (chap. 5); ballet, 139, 175; primitivism, 100

Suárez, Manuel, 244–48

Sutton, Tina, 172

Svetloff, Valerian, 58
Swan Lake, 118, 172
Sylphides, Les, 42, 137, 181, 192, 222
symbols, 7, 17–19, 34, 69, 192, 201, 211, 227, 264n66 (chap. 2), 288n42 (chap. 8); national, 17, 19, 85

Tablada, José Juan, 5, 37, 39, 41
Tagore, Rabindranath, 23, 93
Tamayo, Rufino, 101, 103, 125–26, 129, 150, 224, 230, 253–57
Tamiris, Helen, 202
Tapia, Mariano, 191–92, 196–97
Tarahumara (people), 32, 69
Taylor Gibson, Christina, 109
Tchaikovsky, Pyotr Ilyich, 58, 71
Tehuana, 7, 10, 19, 32, 57, 65, 76, 85–86, 266–67n17 (chap. 3)
Tenisheva, Maria, 47
Teotihuacán, 93, 120, 132
TGP (Taller de Gráfica Popular, People's Graphic Workshop), 150–52, 154, 162, 166, 169, 236
theaters: professional, 5, 212; puppet, 155; urban, 68; vaudeville, 29, 217; working-class, 59–60
Theatre Arts Monthly, 32, 135
theatrical dance, 5–6, 8–9, 15, 24, 25, 28, 56–57, 71, 73–74, 94, 104, 114, 120, 146–47, 163, 168, 200, 203, 218, 242, 248, 251, 254; modern, 130; national, 179; nationalist, 94, 117; professionalizing of, 237; state-sponsored, 94; universal, 12
Thierry, Celestina, 59
Thoreau, Henry David, 159, 231
Tiempo (magazine), 181, 184, 186, 193, 214, 219
Tiffany, Louis Comfort (man and work), 79, 230, 271n8 (chap. 4)
Toledo, Carlos (pseud. Odelot Solrac), 74–75
Tolstoy, Leo, 23
Toor, Frances, 67–68, 102, 132, 178
Topfer, Dasha, 244

Toro, Oliver, 182
Torregrosa, Dina, 169
Torres, Armando, 132
Torres, Ana María, 42
Torres Bodet, Jaime Mario, 169
Torri, Julio, 79
Tortajada, Margarita, 8, 140, 143, 167–69, 186, 205, 241, 281n47 (chap. 6), 285n51 (chap. 7), 286n91 (chap. 7), 297n82 (chap. 10)
Tórtola Ferrer, Llorenc, 70
tourism, tourists, 51, 55, 69, 183, 240, 243–46
Tourneur, Maurice, 209
tragedy, 23, 143, 168, 178, 215, 242
Tree of Life. See *Arbol de la Vida* under Montenegro, Roberto
Trejo y Lerdo de Tejada, Carlos, 67, 85, 178
Trotsky, Leon, 248
Tugendhol'd, Iakov, 52
Turino, Thomas, 27

Ulanova, Galina, 14, 234
Umbral (Orozco), 185–86, 196–97
El Universal (newspaper), 10, 45, 56, 58, 62, 73, 74, 86, 131, 147, 153, 172, 179, 212

Vachon, Anne, 213
Valencia, Tórtola, 8, 55–57, 60, 69–72, 74–77, 243
Valencia Valenzuela, Georgina, 70
Van Dongen, Kees, 282n67 (chap. 6)
Vanegas Arroyo, Antonio, 3, 21, 82–83
Varèse, Edgard, 105
Vargas, Pedro, 218
Vasconcelos, José, 1, 10–11, 15, 47, 66–67, 79–80, 84, 89, 95–96, 116, 118, 119, 261n33 (chap. 1), 273n57 (chap. 4), 274n7 (chap. 5), 274n8 (chap. 5); and dance, 96, 136, 241, 242, 264–65n82 (chap. 2), 269n79 (chap. 3); European classicism, 22–25; and folklore, 49, 69; and indigeneity, 25; and Mexicanism, 257; and muralism, 11–12, 76, 78–79, 89–92, 93, 120, 272n54

(chap. 4), 281n44 (chap. 6); and music, 95–96; and painting, 36; politics, 93, 116. *See also* missionaries, cultural

Vasnetsov, Viktor, 47

Vasquez Vela, Gonzalo, 143, 151

Vaughn, Mary Kay, 6, 68, 100

Vegon, Mimi, 218

Vela Quintero, Enrique, 187

Velázquez, Diego, 21, 271n19 (chap. 4)

Velázquez, Marco, 100

Velez, Lupe, 140

Veracruz, 19, 37–38, 58, 69, 108, 181, 225, 247

Villa, Francisco "Pancho," 12, 16, 58, 117, 177

Villalpando, Fernando, 122

Villaseñor, Enrique, 79–80, 271n3 (chap. 4)

Villaseñor, Otilio, 62

Villaurrutia, Xavier, 125, 254, 257

Villot, Jean-Marie, 298n117 (chap. 10)

Wagner, Fernando, 210–11

Waldeen (Waldeen Falkenstein), 13, 142–44, 151, 158–65, 167–71, 173, 195, 199–200, 202, 206, 208, 220, 222–23, 228, 230–31, 232, 233–34, 240, 248, 285n69 (chap. 7); approach to dance, 164–65; *La Coronela*, 165–69, 173, 176, 195, 206, 286n101 (chap. 7), 287n129 (chap. 7), 288n16 (chap. 8)

Waldeenas, 143, 170, 203, 237, 254

Wallace, Lew, 99

Warner Paz, Juan, 247

Warren, Larry, 149–52, 230

Watkins, Mary, 112

Weidman, Charles, 145, 202, 211

Westrup, Franklin, 118

Whitman, Walt, 231

Wiesenthal Sisters, 201

Wigman, Mary, 159, 168, 201, 285n69 (chap. 7)

Williams, Adriana, 209

Wilson, Edmund, 30–31

World War I, 27, 28, 32, 53, 86, 89, 152, 263n49 (chap. 2)

World War II, 13, 200, 254, 291–92n12 (chap. 9)

Xochitl, 29, 36, 73–74, 99, 139

Yakovlev, Alexander Evgenievich, 265–66n107 (chap. 2)

Young, Stark, 138, 157

Yucatan, 19–20, 74, 85, 97, 106, 138, 225

Zalce, Alfredo, 150

Zamora, Francisco (pseud. Jerónimo Coignard), 86

Zandunga. *See* sandunga

Zapata, Emiliano, 6, 16, 62, 117, 215–16, 225–28, 232

Zapata, Enrique, 121

Zapatistas, 38, 82, 147, 215; *Zapatista Landscape* (Rivera) 52–53

Zapotec (people), 76, 203, 205

Zayas, Marquis de, 53

Zemtsovsky, Izaly, 236

Ziegfeld, Florenz, 9

Zuñiga, Francisco, 140

Zurián de la Fuente, Carla, 271n3 (chap. 4)

Zybin, Hypolite, 117–18, 120–22, 124–26, 130, 138, 158, 163

K. Mitchell Snow is the author of *Movimiento, ritmo y música*, a biography of Mexican choreographer Gloria Contreras. He has written about Latin American art and culture for publications such as *Américas, Art Nexus, Dance Chronicle, Dance Research Journal, History of Photography, Review: Literature and Arts of the Americas,* and *Interdanza.*

www.ingramcontent.com/pod-product-compliance
Lightning Source LLC
Chambersburg PA
CBHW020853180526
45163CB00007B/2494